Wilderness Lost

The Religious Origins
of the American Mind

David R. Williams

Selinsgrove: Susquehanna University Press
London and Toronto: Associated University Presses

© 1987 by Associated University Presses, Inc.

Associated University Presses
440 Forsgate Drive
Cranbury, NJ 08512

Associated University Presses
25 Sicilian Avenue
London WC1A 2QH, England

Associated University Presses
2133 Royal Windsor Drive
Unit 1
Mississauga, Ontario
Canada L5J 1K5

Library of Congress Cataloging-in-Publication Data

Williams, David R. (David Ross), 1949–
Wilderness lost.

Bibliography: p.
Includes index.
1. United States—Intellectual life—18th century.
2. United States—Intellectual life—1783–1865.
3. American literature—19th century—History and
criticism. 4. United States—History—Revolution,
1775–1783—Religious aspects. 5. United States—
Religion—To 1800. 6. United States—Religion—
19th century. 7. Calvinism—United States—History.
I. Title.
E162.W75 1987   973   85-43475
ISBN 0-941664-21-X (alk. paper)

Printed in the United States of America

To
Carolyn Taylor,
my wife, who baked
our bread and endured
the wilderness of Providence, R.I.,
while I labored on this book;

and

To
Nathan and Sam,
my sons, that they might
better understand when they
are older what a complex
fate it is to have been
born Americans.

And I will bring you into the wilderness of the people, and there I will plead with you face to face.
Like as I pleaded with your fathers in the wilderness of the land of Egypt, So I will plead with you saith the Lord God.
And I will cause you to pass under the rod, and I will bring you into the bond of the covenant.

Ezekiel 20.35–37

Stand fast therefore in the liberty wherewith Christ hath made us free, and be not entangled again in the yoke of bondage.

Gal. 5.1

"I mean, man, whither goest thou? Whither goest thou, America, in thy shiny car in the night?"

Jack Kerouac,
On The Road

Contents

Acknowledgments

Parts of this book have previously appeared in print.

Much of Chapter 4, "Revival and Revolution," was published as part of the introduction to *Revolutionary War Sermons*, David R. Williams, ed., Delmar, New York: Scholars' Facsimiles and Reprints, 1984.

A larger version of Chapter 4, parts IV, V, and VI, appeared as "Horses, Pigeons, and the Therapy of Conversion: A Psychological Reading of Jonathan Edwards' Theology," in *Harvard Theological Review*, 74, October, 1981. Copyright 1981 by the President and Fellows of Harvard College. Reprinted by permission.

Chapter 5, parts I, II, and III, appeared as "The Wilderness Rapture of Mary Moody Emerson: One Calvinist Origin of Transcendentalism," in *Studies in the American Renaissance 1986*, Charlottesville: University Press of Virginia, 1986, and is reprinted here by permission of the editor, Joel Myerson.

Chapter 6, part III, appeared as " 'This Consciousness that is Aware': Emily Dickinson in the wilderness of the mind," in *Soundings: An Interdisciplinary Journal*, LXVI, Fall, 1983.

The letters and journals of Mary Moody Emerson are quoted by permission of the Houghton Library;
The letters of Emily Dickinson and the Journals of Ralph Waldo Emerson are quoted by permission of Harvard University Press;
Emily Dickinson's poetry is reprinted by permission of the publishers and the Trustees of Amherst College from *The Poems of Emily Dickinson*, Thomas H. Johnson, ed., Cambridge, Mass.: Harvard University Press, Copyright 1951, © 1955, 1979, 1983 by the President and Fellows of Harvard College; Permission is also granted for *The Complete Poems of Emily Dickinson* edited by Thomas H. Johnson, Copyright 1914, 1929, 1935, 1942 by Martha Dickinson Bianchi; copyright © renewed 1957,

1963 by Mary L. Hampson, by Little, Brown, and Company; "Desert Places," from *The Poetry of Robert Frost* edited by Edward Connery Lathem, Copyright 1936 by Robert Frost, Copyright © 1969 by Holt, Rinehart, and Winston. Reprinted by permission of Holt, Rinehart, and Winston Publishers;

Jones Very's letters are quoted by permission of the Massachusetts Historical Society.

The photographs on the jacket were taken by Larry Higgins of Hamilton, Va.

Introduction

At the very beginning of American culture, freedom was valued because it was the means of salvation, and the means of freedom was an experience of terror called the Fear of God. To pass from the tyranny of structure to the liberation of spirit required a purifying journey through the terrifying, chaotic wilderness of self-consciousness. Before freedom could be attained, the layers of conditioning that control human behavior and protect humans from themselves had to be abandoned. The old, the comfortable, the secure first had to be burned away in what once was called the terror of divine wrath. Only after this experience of descent into the hell in consciousness could even the hope of salvation be expected.

To step back that first degree and to see oneself as a behaving mechanism tossed in the streams and eddies of the onrushing flood of human history was what it meant to the New England Puritans to take the first step into the wilderness. To "see" the meaning of the doctrines of determinism, predestination, unconditional election, and irresistable grace opened the curtain on the drama of salvation. At first, the soul recoiled in horror, resisting the suggestion that it might not be in control, that it might not really know what it was doing or where it was or why. The acceptance of this judgment, if it came, came as a gift that either arrived in a flash or dawned with anxious incredulity. But as it came, it separated the self, if only for a moment, and the soul saw itself caught haplessly in the turbulence of cause and effect, reacting only to its lusts and hidden instincts, unable to affirm anything but its own immense helplessness, sinfulness, and fear. The terror of this revelation was the NO that the universe thundered against man's feeble yes. This experience was considered ultimate. This was the sound of the voice of God. Any human attempt to affirm it, as Karl Barth later wrote, would itself have been convicted for "its utter perversion and nullity." Religion in America began not with the conviction of certainty but with the

11

conviction of unbelief and uncertainty to the point of terror. Even theology had to always be "a theological warning against theology."[1]

To experience such uncertainty was to experience terror. Not to be able to make a move without the realization of hypocrisy, to have all thoughts condemned the instant they arose, for perception itself to be called into question was the pit of confusion, the wilderness of despair and doubt. Yet this madness was the wilderness that had to be crossed before there could be any hope of reaching the promised land. This madness was the "liberty" that led to salvation. Only out of this destruction of the old dependencies, so the Puritans believed, could there arise the possibility of a better way of being. Another world could be revealed only after the old one had crumbled. The "fabrication" of a new regenerate identity required the destruction of the old identity before the community of redeemed sinners could create the new world.[2]

Once conversion had been accomplished, a new consciousness, with new perception, was believed to replace the old, but the new vision could not come before the old one had collapsed and the soul had experienced its moment in hell. Israel in the wilderness, Jonah in the whale, and Christ upon the cross all were symbols of this process. They were the types of which the third person of the trinity, the Holy Spirit, was believed the continuing reality. Their suffering pointed the way to liberation. Assuming there was a truth, and rest could be found there, the Puritans insisted that this wilderness had to be crossed before sinners could enter the promised land freed from all that had ensnared them. Liberation was the goal, the violence of regeneration the only means. Despite their boastful optimism, Protestant Americans, heirs of the dominant Calvinist strain of American culture, have harbored the fear that there might be no other way. Although we prefer to celebrate the positive, there is in the American psyche still a distant memory that whispers, "He who flees at the sound of the terror shall fall into the pit, and he who climbs out of the pit shall be caught in the snare. For the windows of heaven are opened, and the foundations of the earth tremble" (Isaiah 24.18).

ii

American culture needs to be seen from the perspective of colonial America's foremost Calvinist preacher, Jonathan Edwards. When the categories used to interpret literature are drawn from disciplines or worldviews alien to that culture, the results can be misleading. As Richard Slotkin has said, "In the attempt to recover the world of primary myth and universal archetypes, the consumnatory myth-maker must draw upon the vocabulary of myth-images and structures that is his cultural heritage."[3] All who would place a structure of interpretation on culture are myth-makers and should heed this advice. One result of not doing so can be a forced and unsympathetic reading that discourages further study. In America, despite the efforts of a very few, the Calvinist heritage has been subject to this fate.

"[P]reaching in a known tongue," wrote Edwards, "conveys something to the understanding which preaching in an unknown tongue doth not."[4] An inability to enter into the theological language of early American culture is largely responsible for the painful tedium of much that is written about the New England Puritans. Not until they reach the eighteenth century and the secular writings of Jefferson and Tom Paine do most students begin to pay attention to their nation's literature. Only when they come to Whitman or Melville in the nineteenth century do these students begin to respond sympathetically to what they are reading. Because these authors speak in a modern tongue, and are therefore easily accessible, they seem to speak to the modern condition. It is not easy to understand what Hooker or Edwards meant. Emerson, on the other hand, seems much more comprehensible.

But those who dig no deeper than the sandy topsoil of Concord need to see these deeper, stronger roots upon which the Transcendental growth was but a human graft. Many Americans, alienated from their own traditions, persuaded that the West is material and the East is spiritual, have felt it necessary to travel to exotic lands in search of spiritual sustenance. This need not be. Under all of the flag waving and commercialism, American culture rests on a foundation worthy of understanding, if not respect. The literature in which our ancestors defined their struggle with existence contains an understanding of man's relationship to consciousness as profound as anything the East has yet to offer. Emily Dickinson and Herman Melville cannot be understood, much less appreciated, without a prior understanding of the tradition of Calvinist mysticism in which they were nurtured and out of which they wrote. This book explores a new approach to the study of early American literature and culture in order to clear a path by which modern students can enter into the beginnings of their own culture.

The identity created in the colonial forge and hammered into shape by the Revolution and the Civil War remains the foundation of American consciousness today. No one brought up in the United States can entirely avoid it. In each individual American's consciousness, and in the culture's collective consciousness, exist attitudes and feelings, the products of unconscious beliefs, that shape the American character. Both our politics and our literature are influenced by forces from the "invisible world" of our history, and the language in which those beliefs were first articulated was religious. Understanding the wilderness tradition of Puritanism is thus an important step toward understanding ourselves and our occasional desire to break out of structure, to transcend our often stale and boring lives, and to plunge into a wilderness in the hope of being transformed and brought into the promised land of freedom.

The distinction between "wilderness" and "Canaan" was that used by the New England Calvinists to articulate their own experience. Using it, we enter into the language and imagery used in Puritan New England. By using the words of their myth-making we can be more sensitive to the later reverberations of their language. The wilderness for the Puritans was more than a physical locality, more than a Biblical myth. It was the symbol of an unstructured state of mind that today would be labelled madness. The use of this tradition assumed a model of human consciousness in which that state of mind, the wilderness, undermined the foundations of sanity, and it was used to preach madness as the only path to God. It called on all human beings not to shun the wilderness but to surrender their security to madness. Canaan, on the other side of the river, was the land of promise, Zion, the final goal of the odyssey of consciousness.

My central argument is that there is a consistent tradition of wilderness imagery in American literature that embodies implicit assumptions about human consciousness and the means of reconciling that depraved consciousness with the Universal Consciousness called God. With this in mind it is possible to identify a pattern running through American culture, political and literary, which speaks directly to the alienated twentieth century from the heart of seventeenth-century piety. Because the language of psychology is the language with which modern Americans speak about the mind, a psychological reading of theology is here applied to an analysis of American culture, not in just one or another example but on a grand scale. The sustaining assumption is that patterns uncovered here were important determinants of American consciousness and that as such they are with us yet, deeply buried but still influential among the guiding myths of the collective American subconscious. At least in the beginning, the Christian language of the founders of America had significant meaning; as the words became robbed of their original content, that content, subtly transformed, passed into secular literature and popular consciousness. Our culture today is still under the influence of ideas first articulated at the dawn of American history.

In "The Return of the Jedi," the second film of George Lucas's *Star Wars* trilogy, Luke Skywalker, at the climax of his training to become a Jedi Knight, must leave his weapons behind and descend alone into a jungle swamp. He there encounters a personification of evil, which he defeats in battle, and after he removes his opponent's mask, he discovers the face to be his own. This descent into the wilderness to wrestle with one's own evil before returning to the world a hero has deep roots in American culture. Luke Skywalker's battle in the wilderness is but the latest expression of an archetypal theme that must be traced back to the founding of our culture.

iii

The original settlers of New England brought with them a desire to suffer in the wilderness in order to be ravished by the love of God. They came to the literal wilderness, so they repeatedly said, for the express purpose of entering the mental wilderness and being converted in the fires of conversion from ego-centered stupidity to the regenerate perception of infinite self-less love. Those first settlers understood that the experience was spiritual and that their sojourn in the literal wilderness was but a symbol of a spiritual state. They knew that they had to lose themselves to terror before they could hope to enter Canaan. They intended to create a spiritual community in which divine vision could be sought without the restraints and temptations of worldly pursuits. Their goal was a spiritual freedom toward which political freedom was only a means.

Their descendants, however, forgot the difference between symbol and substance, between type and anti-type. Mistaking the literal wilderness for the spiritual, the "howling wilderness" of America for the "howling wilderness" of the soul, they assumed themselves already in Canaan in a state of grace. They were not, of course, and the desperate attempt to justify their presumption led them to oppression. Believing they had crossed the river, they imagined New England to be heaven on Earth and tried to freeze their Israel into permanence, forgetting in the process that higher heaven beyond New England that should have been their goal.

In 1741, in the Great Awakening, Jonathan Edwards tried to reassert the primacy of symbolic consciousness. He reminded New Englanders that the wilderness was a state of mind and that their pride had to be crucified in this hell in madness before they could claim salvation. However, his efforts were only immediately effective. In a short time, his followers repeated the mistake of their ancestors and mistook literal signs for evidence of true conversion. They came to believe, once again, that they had crossed through the wilderness and entered into Canaan. Defending their holy Israel from Egypt, they plunged into the literal wilderness of war in order to build the New Jerusalem, the United States.

But as from the beginning, a few remembered that the kingdom of the devil and the kingdom of God are not literal kingdoms but states of mind, "within you." These upheld the wilderness strain of Calvinism against those who would destroy it. Emerson's Calvinist aunt, Mary Moody Emerson, urged her nephew to lose himself in the spiritual wilderness that he might be converted from a consciousness built on ego to one that was built on God. Because she failed, Emerson's contribution to American culture was another instance of a literal misreading of what was originally a spiritual metaphor. He went into the woods and sat on a log and wondered why the promised vision never came. Having heard the mystic promise but not wanting to lose himself to terror, he proclaimed the ability of "natural" men to enter the promised land without having to face the wilderness. Thoreau's quest for wildness, Hawthorne's use of wilderness imagery, Melville's odyssey on the "watery wilderness," and Dickinson's sojourn in the wilderness of mind all need to be seen from the perspective of this wilderness tradition. The insistence that human beings surrender their rational egos to a subconscious sea of terror in order to achieve true freedom is a recurring theme that runs from the very beginning down to the twentieth century.

Moreover, this theme speaks to us today. For not only does it continue to sound through the caverns of collective consciousness in the "mystic chords of memory" that bind us together as a people, but the message itself is one that modern man, using a different language, is just beginning to rediscover. The alienation and despair so characteristic of the twentieth century had its counterpart in earlier eras under different guises. But without a sympathetic understanding of the theological language in which those concerns were articulated, it is impossible for modern readers to comprehend the extent to which their own heritage has something to communicate to them.

The theology of Calvinist New England began in an experiential knowledge of the extreme subjectivity of human knowledge and human perception. These theologians realized that all of their best knowledge was mere speculation spun out by the brain to try to fill the void. No human knowing, they maintained, could be justified; it all collapsed ultimately into a pit of unknowing, a sea of madness, the wilderness of the subconscious soul. After two centuries of scientific certainty, American intellectuals are beginning to rediscover this view of human consciousness. Yet even the best minds remain ignorant of the past. Consider, for example, this statement by Lewis Thomas in a recent essay in *The Atlantic Monthly:*

In the eighteenth century there were no huge puzzles; human reason was all you needed in order to figure out the universe. And for most of the earlier centuries, the Church provided both the questions and the answers, neatly packaged. Now, *for the first time in human history* [emphasis mine], we are catching glimpses of our incomprehension.[5]

The credit for this discovery, of course, is given to science. One purpose of this book is to try to some extent to bridge the gap between the seventeenth century and our own, to show to those who have never looked that orthodox religion in America has not always meant fundamentalism and that even Calvinism had a purpose beyond social control.

Last, rather than adhere to a formal methodology, I have simply made the best argument I could for my point of view. I have assumed, as did Perry Miller, "that the mind of man is the basic factor in human history."[6] However much they have added to our knowledge of Puritan New England, none of the demographic studies published since Miller's death have contradicted his thesis that the Puritan settlers of New England were motivated primarily by belief. Even historians who recognize the "ideological" basis of much of history often write as if material and social factors are the only hidden shapers of belief and behavior. But the subconscious, if it exists at all, is a realm of belief, of thought, of ideas with great influence on conscious thought and hence behavior. Indeed, as I try to show in more detail in Chapter 3, I maintain with Edwards against Skinner that no thorough behaviorism can exist without some theory of mind interceding between stimulus and response. In all cases, the mind judges before reacting to stimuli; it is not "stimulus-bound." Material considerations may override "ideological" objections, but they must be judged by them nonetheless. However a certain set of beliefs, such as Puritanism, first arises, once in place it takes on a life of its own until overwhelming material considerations force it to change. And even after that, such ideas, if deeply rooted, as the new intellectual history has tried to show, are never completely eradicated but influence even those who imagine their wills to be thoroughly objective and value free:

. . . if even scientists are firmly tethered to their deepest-lying assumptions, as Kuhn suggests, then so is everyone else. It follows that historians ought to assign a high priority indeed to the exploration of these controlling presuppositions that shape thought, and thus behavior, in every sphere of life.[7]

Indeed, ideas, both at the conscious and the subconscious level, are a central requirement of human security, and the defense of belief is as much a part of self-interest as the defense of property. Hence, ideas are very much a primary causal factor in human motivation.

On the question of style, I have followed the suggestion of James Bryce: "An author who finds himself obliged to choose between repetition and obscurity ought not to doubt as to his choice." When cowed into humility by the erudition of better-read scholars, I have been encouraged by Emerson: "To believe your own thought, to believe that what is true for you in your private heart is true for all men, that is genius. Speak your latent conviction, and it shall be the universal sense." And I have tried to live up to George Bancroft's advice to his fellow historian Jared Sparks: "Do not allow any job-work into your series. Let it be a series of works, written each in a fine fit of enthusiasm."[8]

Wilderness Lost

PART I
The Biblical Errand

1
The Wilderness

If we consider the *letter* alone, the departure of the children of Israel from Egypt in the time of Moses is signified; if the *allegory,* our redemption accomplished by Christ is signified; if the *moral* meaning, the conversion of the soul from the sorrow and misery of sin to a state of grace is signified; if the *anagogical,* the departure of the sanctified soul from the slavery of this corruption to the liberty of everlasting glory.

                                                            Dante

i

The howling wilderness into which the New England saints were called was a wilderness of fact, of type, of the world, and of the mind. It was a dense and dangerous forest; it was a parallel type of the wilderness through which God's Israel of old had to pass before entering Canaan; it was the world itself in which the faith of God's people constantly had to be tried; and, by no means least, it was the wilderness of human consciousness, the howling chaos in the depths of the mind into which every sinner was called to be crucified before there could be any hope of salvation.

It would be misleading to suggest that every Puritan in seventeenth-century New England when thinking about the wilderness always kept all four of these versions in mind. The many overlapping meanings of cultural symbols are rarely seen together, but they are there nonetheless as part of culture.

It could even be said that such symbols are the culture, for together the many ways in which people make sense of existence, the ways in which they view reality, become imbedded in their language and behavior. In return, the symbolic meanings of their words reflect their shared beliefs, memories, and values. Together, these constitute a people's cultural identity. Just as individuals, cultures, if they are truly cohesive, require some consistent self-image, some identity or "myth," by which they define themselves, justify themselves, and locate themselves in the universe. Such an identity need not be wholly conscious. In time, attitudes and symbols becomes the only visible outcroppings of identity. But even in the unconscious, identity continues to provide a common sense of purpose that makes of an otherwise heterogeneous community a culture.

Because language exists within such a cultural context, certain words often carry with them meanings of which we are only dimly aware. Words like "freedom" and "liberty" command respect and reverence though few can clearly explain why. The explanation requires an understanding of the relationship between cultural and universal psychology. Northrop Frye has explained:

> Man lives, not directly or nakedly in nature like the animals, but within a mythological universe, a body of assumptions and beliefs developed from his existential concerns. Most of this is held unconsciously, which means that our imaginations may recognize elements of it, when presented in art or literature, without consciously understanding what it is that we recognize. Practically all that we can see of this body of concern is socially conditioned and culturally inherited. Below the cultural inheritance, there must be a common psychological inheritance; otherwise forms of culture and imagination outside our own traditions would not be intelligible to us. But I doubt if we can reach this common inheritance directly, by-passing the distinctive qualities in our specific culture. One of the practical functions of criticism, by which I mean the conscious organizing of a cultural tradition, is, I think, to make us more aware of our mythological conditioning.[1]

Thus, within a given culture, certain words become symbols of larger hidden psychological and existential concerns. In uncovering the symbolic "meaning" of our language, we uncover the layers of mythological conditioning in which our very thoughts and beliefs are clothed.

The symbolic word, "wilderness," is one of the most powerful in the Judeo-Christian tradition and particularly in the American strain of that tradition. The most ancient and revered of those "mystic chords of memory that bind the nation together," to use Lincoln's phrase, have to do with wilderness. Even today, our every use of the word echoes with unconscious meaning. At the heart of American culture, in what Jung called the collective unconscious, a deep memory insistently calls the self to lose itself in the wilderness.

A symbol so powerful, as Frye said, requires a more than literary or political significance to become so deeply imbedded in the collective consciousness. It must reflect something of universal psychological significance that then becomes fused with and indistinguishable from the cultural. Such a symbol, according to Rollo May, "brings together the various unconscious urges and desires, of both a personal depth on the one hand and an archaic archetypal depth on the other; and it unites these with conscious [cultural] elements."[2]

For the first settlers of New England, the wilderness was such a symbol. It brought together realities of what has come to be called depth psychology with a clear cultural tradition of wilderness imagery, and it was in their understanding of their role in the drama of salvation, in the experience of conversion, that the symbols burned in their souls and minds. These first settlers believed that it was only by losing themselves in the wilderness of self that they might ever achieve salvation. But in time, these first pioneers forgot the spiritual meaning of the metaphor. Confusing the literal woods with the spiritual wilderness, they plunged violently into the forests expecting somehow that they would then be led out of the wilderness into the promised land.

ii

To appreciate the full significance of "wilderness" in early American culture, it is necessary, briefly, to look back to scripture, to the significance attributed to the wilderness there, and then to the early Christian church to follow the development of wilderness imagery through the Christian tradition.

Cruden's *Comprehensive Concordance to Holy Scripture* lists over two hundred fifty references to the wilderness in both the Old and the New Testament. It is not possible to read the Bible without being impressed by the importance of the experience of God's people in the wilderness to the writers of scripture. There, at the dawn of Western culture, when the oral tales of the nomadic tribes were first written down, the wilderness already was a powerful symbol firmly embedded in the culture's growing consciousness.

Of all the references to the wilderness in the Old Testament, the experience of the children of Israel during their forty year sojourn in the Sinai desert is the most important. It is the model and the original of all subsequent wilderness imagery. All of the elements that would later go into the development of the image can be found there. The flight from Egypt was only the beginning of the return of the children of Israel to God. Even the crossing of the Red Sea was a sign only of God's presence and support. It was the forty years in the wilderness that brought God's people to the promised land of Canaan. The wilderness was a sanctuary from Pharoah's army, but it was also a place of trial and

temptation. It was the place where the Jews were taught the law amidst
thunder and lightning. It was the place of their murmurings and their
rebellions, their trials, their punishments, their tribulations. It was in the
wilderness that God sent manna and caused water to gush from the rock.
And it was from the wilderness that the children of the original wanderers finally crossed the Jordan and entered into Canaan.

The significance of the wilderness both in the Hebrew and the Christian traditons has been examined in Ulrich Mauser's *Christ in the Wilderness* and George Williams' influential *Wilderness and Paradise in Christian
Thought.* A brief survey of the ground already covered by these scholars
should provide the foundation needed to appreciate the use to which
this imagery was put later in the English and American traditions.[3]

According to Ulrich Mauser, in the Old Testament the wilderness is
not "primarily a locality," but "a theme full of theological implications."
The two Hebrew words most commonly used to designate the wilderness
"combine the notion of confusion and destruction with the image of the
barren land."[4] The return to the wilderness was a basic symbol of
repentance, a rejection of the sinful ways acquired during the Egyptian,
and later the Babylonian, captivity. By going defenseless into the desert,
the Jews expressed their willingness to abandon contrived and sacrilegious notions and to wait, empty-handed, upon the mercy of Yahweh.
Being in the wilderness was a sign of their complete dependence.

There were always these two elements combined in the imagery, the
destruction of the old dependencies and the expectation of grace. The
wilderness "threatens the very existence of Yahweh's chosen people, but
it is also the stage that brightly illumines God's power."[5] The Old Testament speaks more in communal than in personal terms, but according to
the way in which Protestant Christians would come to interpret the Old
Testament, this two-part imagery of desolation and grace became tied to
the idea of personal conversion, of the self's need to abandon its idolatries and to enter into its own desert wastes to await the revelation of
truth. The accustomed beliefs and values that seem to give meaning to
life were those idols; the meaninglessness that takes over when these
have been abandoned was the desert wilderness.

As such the image of the wilderness has had a more than historical or
literary importance. It became a symbol of emptiness at the core of
human consciousness, of the profound loneliness that seemed to open
like a bottomless pit underneath the vanity of each of humankind. It
became the symbol of a place located in the mind, a black hole of
unknowing around which orbit all the temporary illusions of human
self-confidence. It became a universal symbol of a widely acknowledged
feeling, and as such it can be found in all traditions. It has been used by

almost every person who ever wrote about the soul from Augustine to C. G. Jung, who confessed:

> When a man is in the wilderness, the darkness brings the dreams . . . that guide him. It has always been so. I have not been led by any kind of wisdom; I have been led by dreams, like any primitive. I am ashamed to say so, but I am as primitive as any nigger, because I do not know![6]

George Williams, in his book, emphasizes the "incantational potency" of the word "wilderness." He ties the power of the word to its use as a symbol for human psychology:

> [T]he wilderness motif might be said to exceed in significance the frontier as a category in interpretation not only of American history but of church history in general; for, like the frontier, the wilderness is not only geographical but psychological.[7]

The idea reified by the Old Testament's wilderness imagery was that of a realm of chaos that completely surrounded and undermined the vanities of human consciousness. Not only did eternity bracket human life, it also undermined rational consciousness during life. The pit that preceded and followed life could also be found in the depths of the subconscious, a region of terror beyond reason and control, a wasteland inhabited by demons and flying serpents. Death and the desert were seen by the Jews as two representations of this hell. There was a third region used to depict demonic chaos, the oceans, which they believed not only surrounded but also raged underneath the land. They depicted the earth as a floating shell on a sea of chaos. This image of the earth was itself a projection of their conception of consciousness as well as matter. Thus, the Jews' image of the ocean was "a still awesome reminder of the primordial chaos . . . which lies lurking under the world of man and which like the desert is the haunt of serpents and dragons." All three regions of desert, death, and sea were, as Williams says, "wilderness," to the ancient Hebrew "a symbol of the uncreated order and a surrogate in the poetry of the prophet and psalmist for the primordial abyss at the beginning of creation and for death at the end."[8] It was a symbol of the pit of God's wrath that seemed to undermine all of human existence.

This wilderness, however, was also the place of revelation. One had to descend into the desert wastes before one could hope to discover God. But the experience of God that could occur there more than justified the ordeal. To symbolize this, the scriptures abound with imagery of gardens growing in the desert and of water flowing in the barren land. Thus, according to Mauser, "the wilderness becomes the image of a spiritual condition and the miraculous watering of the parched land a figure of the spirit which restores life in man."[9] The Exodus chronicle, indeed the whole Old Testament, is saturated with this image of water in the desert, an image explicitly brought into the New Testament to symbolize Christ's mercy to those in despair. The Apostle Paul says of the children of Israel that "they did all drink the same spiritual drink; for they did drink of that spiritual rock that followed them: and that rock was Christ" (1 Cor. 10.4). The water that Moses had brought forth from the rock, explained Paul, was none other than Christ or a type of Christ.

Another image used to symbolize the coming of grace to the needy was that of marriage in the wilderness: "Who is this that cometh up from the wilderness leaning upon her beloved? . . . Set me as a seal upon thine heart, as a seal upon thine arm: for love is strong as death" (Cant. 8.5–6). Here the image has been interpreted by Christians to be that of the church coming out of the wilderness leaning upon Christ's grace. God and Israel were said to have been covenanted together in the wilderness in marriage. It was an image that the prophets refused to let Israel forget. Thus Jeremiah 2.2, with the prophet speaking for Yahweh: "I remember the devotion of your youth, your love as a bride, how you followed me in the wilderness, in a land not sown." And Hosea (2.14) speaking as Yahweh looking forward to His renewal of marriage to a fallen Israel, said, "Therefore, behold, I will allure her, and bring her into the wilderness and speak tenderly to her. . . . And there she shall answer as in the days of her youth, as at the time when she came out of the land of Egypt."

Implicit in the Exodus narrative is one other use of wilderness imagery. The desert wilderness, while a place of purgation and restoration, also served as a place of refuge. It is only superficially a contradiction that the desert was seen as a place both of refuge and of terror, of death and of deliverance. For it is the experience that occurs in the wilderness, first of crucifixion and then of resurrection, that allows these seemingly contradictory images to be tied to the same symbol. Thus, as Williams has shown, the return to the wilderness came to symbolize both punishment and a return to Godliness. The return to the wilderness came to be viewed as "therapeutic punishment"[10] for a degenerate people who had forgotten what it meant to fear God. Yahweh's call to repentance, spoken through the prophets, was a call to return to the wilderness. This is the traditional interpretation of Hosea's words (17.9), "I am the Lord your God from the land of Egypt; I will again make you dwell in tents. . . ."

This association of the wilderness with repentance continued to have a symbolic as well as a literal significance. The Essene community at the time of Christ was established in the wilderness to symbolize this need to return to purity to await the expected coming. Repelled by the corruptions into which Israel had fallen, the Essenes intentionally "imitated the ancient sojourn in the wilderness of Sinai, hoping to prepare a way in the wilderness for the coming of the Messiah."[11]

Thus was the symbol of the wilderness carried into the New Testament where it had a powerful influence on the Christian religion. Of the many uses of wilderness in scripture, three stood out as of particular importance for this new religion: the forty-year sojourn in the Sinai wilderness, John the Baptist's ministry in the wilderness, and the temptation of Christ in the wilderness. There are other instances of wilderness imagery that are of importance in Christianity: for instance, the woman who fled into the wilderness on the "wings of a great eagle" (Rev. 12.14). Such minor uses however are of less importance than these first three to which they often refer. And even these first three are not distinct, for in all of them the wilderness bears the same symbolic significance. It is the location of refuge, trial, temptation, and ultimate victory over Satan. And in all of them, as George Williams has stated, it is "a state of mind as well as a state of nature,"[12] the place where the soul dies unto itself and is reborn unto God.

When John the Baptist came "crying in the wilderness prepare ye the way of the Lord" (Mat. 3.3), he was preaching in a set tradition that already associated the journey into the wilderness with repentance. And when the people went out from Jerusalem to hear him preach in the wilderness of the Jordan, they too were participating in a highly symbolic act. "The Baptist's call to repentance and his call to come to him in the wilderness to be baptized are but two aspects of the same thing," explains Mauser. "A renewal of the Exodus into the desert was necessary for the restoration of Israel's status as Son of God. . . . The march into the wilderness *is* the repentance. . . ."[13]

It was then after his baptism by John that Christ was "led of the spirit into the wilderness to be tempted of the devil" (Matt. 4.1). The parallel to the forty years of trial in the Sinai is made explicit by Christ's fasting in the wilderness "forty days and forty nights." It was not until after the devil had been defeated and angels had come "and ministered unto him," that Christ went up out of the wilderness and began his ministry.

In the Gospel of John, the significance of the Exodus sojourn for the Christian community is made explicit: "And as Moses lifted up the serpent in the wilderness, so must the Son of Man be lifted up" (John 3.14). The children of Israel, stung by poisonous serpents in the wilderness, had been instructed to "look upon" a serpent of brass set upon a pole, "and it came to pass that if a serpent had bitten any man, when he beheld the serpent of brass he lived" (Num. 21.9). This brazen serpent is interpreted by John to have been a prefiguration of Christ, who although hung upon a pole also had the power to save those who looked upon him. This correlation of the crucifixion with the wilderness sojourn became a major feature of wilderness symbolism in the Christian tradition. Paul made further use of the wilderness sojourn when he reminded the Corinthians (1 Cor. 10.1–5) that "although our fathers all were baptized unto Moses in the cloud and in the sea, . . . with many of them God was not well pleased, for they were overthrown in the wilderness." It is in this same passage that Paul identifies the water sent from God out of the rock as "the same spiritual meat" and the "same spiritual drink" as Christ. Clearly the Apostles knew the significance of the wilderness and consciously made full use of it in their ministry.

iii

In the early Christian church, the theme of wilderness was carried on, not as the total symbol it had been for the early Jews or even for Paul, but as it fit particular needs. The monastic movement, particularly, picked up the theme of wilderness as a place of refuge from the world and as the location of the divine encounter. Withdrawal from the world was justified in terms of the call to return to the simplicity of the wilderness. The monasteries were seen as places of refuge from the world. A separate use made of wilderness imagery was to identify the wilderness with the world, comparing the sojourn of the Jews to the sojourn of good Christians through the temporal world, as if Sinai and not Egypt had been meant to symbolize the world's corruption. This use of wilderness imagery became more important during later Protestant reaction against Catholic monasticism.

However, the association of the wilderness sojourn with the experience of conversion more often caught the imagination of the mystical fringes of the church. It was in the long mystical tradition of medieval Catholicism that the wilderness of the soul was celebrated as the location of mystical insight. According to Williams, "the most distinctive medieval development" of the wilderness theme was "the mystical interiorization of the wilderness as state of mind through which the mystic passes to the consummation of the divine nuptials."[14]

For example, fourteenth-century Rhenish mysticism perceived the state of soul, the *via negativa,* that led to the divine vision as a way prepared in the wilderness for the coming of Christ. They saw a need to break away not just from the world but from the self with all of its attachments to the external world of sense, to descend into the abyss that underlies all conscious sense perception. They strove to stand outside all worldly frames of reference and somehow wait, in utter emptiness, upon their Lord. Hence Meister Eckhart: "The genuine word of eternity is spoken only in the spirit of that man who is himself a wilderness alienated from self and all multiplicity."[15]

In the sixteenth century, the Carmelite tradition exemplifed by St. John of the Cross carried forward this mystic understanding of wilderness. Death, desert, and darkness all became symbols of that mystic state of consciousness in which the soul was prepared for marriage to Christ. This was the wilderness in which

> the soul sees itself distinctly as far away from, and abandoned by, all created things; it looks upon itself as one that is placed in a wild and vast solitude whither no human being can come, as in an immense wilderness without limitations; a wilderness, the more delicious, sweet, and lovely, the more it is wide, vast, and lonely, where the soul is the more hidden, the more it is raised up above all created things.[16]

The Protestant Reformation, at least in its magisterial center, as Williams has explained, concerned itself primarily with the state of the church in the world. The first reformers were hardheaded men in rebellion against the mysticism of monks living unproductive lives in isolated monasteries. Their crusade against the otherworldliness of much of Catholic tradition made them suspicious of all wilderness imagery. They wanted to call pious men back to the world, and they therefore used the wilderness theme primarily when castigating monks for hiding in their monasteries from the true arena of the battle between Christ and Satan, the wilderness of the world.

The early reformers nevertheless recognized the validity of the wilderness as psychic chaos for explaining the conversion experience. They still expected sinners to experience the trials of the wilderness in order to suffer conversion. They simply were not to remain in that wilderness of self with their backs turned to the world. A true convert, once having experienced the wilderness within the soul, then returned to the wilderness of the world in order to wage the fight against Satan and in the process glorify God. It was thus in the more pietistic Radical Reformation and not in the Magisterial Reformation that the mystic interpretation of the wilderness entered into Protestantism with the greatest power.

Given the correlation of the wilderness sojourn with the experience of conversion, it is to be expected that those who emphasized the radical conversion experience would be those who made the most of the mystical interpretation of wilderness. And such Anabaptists as Melchor Hoffman did use the word "wilderness" to mean "utter emptiness of soul." According to these radical separatists,

Before believers give themselves individually or corporately to the
Bridegroom, they have already been sought out by him in the wilderness in the double sense of being in flight from the established church
and of being utterly open to Christ in mystical *Gelassenheit* ("yielded-
ness").[17]

And as the full weight of the establishment came down upon these
radicals, they also made use of the theme of wilderness as a place of
refuge, just as the Waldensians literally had fled into the wilderness in
order to escape persecution.

Nevertheless, despite these other uses, the most important use of
wilderness imagery continued to be as a symbol in the process of conversion. There was always the wilderness of the world and the wilderness
as a place of refuge, but "there was also an inner wilderness through
which the baptized elect has to pass even after being saved from the
wilderness of the world."[18] When in the sixteenth century the Reformation finally crossed the channel and invaded England, it was inevitable
that the image of the wilderness would have a part in the struggle.

iv

The English Reformation that eventually washed over the Atlantic and
onto the shores of New England began in earnest in the sixteenth
century when the Marian exiles returned to England with the Geneva
Bible under their arms and the arguments of Calvin's *Institutes* on their
lips. These English reformers and their immediate successors were content with the new religion as it had been taught to them. The few
changes that they did make were more of style than of substance. Even
of the early seventeenth century it could still be said, as Perry Miller did,
"that New Englanders took most of their beliefs from the reformers, and
that their sermons were substantially restatements of positions already
defined in Geneva."[19]

What was true of doctrine was also true of imagery. In the Geneva
Bible of 1650 the story of the crossing of the Red Sea is illustrated with a
print depicting the Jews before the crossing into the wilderness. The
marginal notes make explicit one symbolic meaning of the image:

In this figure, foure chief points are to be considered. First, that the
church of God is ever subject in this world to the cross and to be
afflicted after one sort or another. . .[20]

There was no escaping the comparison of the crossing into the wilderness to the crucifixion of Christ. The reference to the wilderness of the

world was obvious. But even the most literal reader was forced to realize that this was more than an historical narrative, that it was also a symbolic depiction of conversion from the bondage of sin to the freedom of the spirit.

Calvin himself was not much given to the use of symbolic imagery. It was a part of his labor to pierce the veil of symbolism under which he believed Catholicism had obscured the true meaning of the Gospel. Symbols all too easily become mere idols when the original meaning of the symbol has been forgotten. Calvin believed of the Papists that "while they superstitiously cling to the joining together of syllables, they disregard the meaning that binds these words together."[21] It has become an academic cliché that Protestantism strove to return to the literal word of scripture. Yet in his Biblical commentaries Calvin did acknowledge that the word "wilderness" might be used to describe a spiritual state as well as a literal location: "Jerusalem was in this sense a wilderness, for all had been reduced to wild and frightful confusion."[22] For Calvin, such a statement was an unusual acknowledgement of the typological use of scripture. It was not that he rejected the validity of the symbolic or allegorical interpretation of scripture. Rather, it must be remembered that he was on the attack against the otherworldly asceticism of the Papist monasteries as well as the rich and overwhelming idolatry into which the Catholic use of symbolism had degenerated. Wilderness imagery, used to symbolize both a place of refuge and the state of souls in betrothal to God, had been used to justify both of these Catholic traditions. Calvin the polemicist was as careful as he could be not to use words that could be turned against him by his enemies.

Yet if we look in Calvin not for specific references to the wilderness but for references to that which the wilderness had come to symbolize, we can appreciate his contribution to the development of the image of the wilderness of the mind.

The very first words of Calvin's *Institutes* set the pattern of much of his writing: "Without knowledge of self there is no knowledge of God."[23] Calvin emphasized the need for the unregenerate self to become aware of the horror of its complete and utter corruption in order that it might accept judgement, reject itself, and turn instead to God. This was what the sojourn in the wilderness was all about. This, according to scripture, was why "the Lord thy God led thee these forty years in the wilderness, to humble thee, and to prove thee, to know what was in thine heart" (Deut. 8.2). Clearly God, being omniscient, was not the one who needed to know "what was in thine heart." It was the children of Israel who needed to know the true nature of their own hearts. Self-knowledge was the first step of the journey of conversion. This was the purpose of the law, of the thunderings from Mount Sinai, not to frighten the people into doing good, but to give to those wandering in the wilderness the means to see the sinfulness of their own hearts, "for by the law is the knowledge of sin" (Rom. 3.20). And knowing one's own sin was the first step on the road to salvation.

Most human beings remain blissfully unaware of the selfish and cruel motivations that unconsciously control their behavior. They imagine themselves to be sincerely good and well-meaning. This illusion, according to Calvin, was the first idol that had to be destroyed, the first wall of defense that had to be battered down. Sinners who relied upon their own wisdom, what Calvin called "the stupidity of human understanding," those who were confident of their own virtue and ability, had to be forced to recognize the terrible truth. They had to have the rug of self-respect pulled out from under them. "Man's understanding," wrote Calvin, "is pierced by a heavy spear when all the thoughts that proceed from him are mocked as stupid, frivolous, insane, and perverse." Sinners naturally resisted this accusation, but all who would be converted had to first be "overwhelmed" by this "unavoidable calamity." Calvin could not have been more explicit in his insistence that sinners had to first "descend into themselves" and there be overwhelmed by the wrath of God. Sinners, he explained,

> because they murmur and kick against him and rant against their Judge, their violent fury stupifies them with madness and rage. But believers, admonished by God's scourges, immediately descent into themselves to consider their sins, and struck with fear and dread, flee to prayer. . . .[24]

The descent into the pit was not a voluntary act. Sinners had to be led into the wilderness, but there were many paths that lead there. A person who tried to apprehend God rationally, to learn the Truth intellectually, "to penetrate even to the highest eternity . . . casts himself into the depths of a bottomless whirlpool to be swallowed up; then he buries himself in innumerable and inextricable snares; then he buries himself in an abyss of sightless darkness."[25] The effort to apprehend God through the intellect lead only to the pit of the fear of God. According to Calvin, whether we descend into ourselves or attempt to ascend directly up to God, whenever we leave our tiny floating islands of self-confidence, we encounter surrounding us the chaotic wilderness of eternity, the wrath of God.

Calvin used the images of darkness, of the raging sea, and of the abyss that had all been long associated with the wilderness in Hebraic and Christian thought. Like the Hebrew's, his was an image of human consciousness barely able to hold itself above an awesome abyss, the wrath of God, that "is naturally inborn in all, and is fixed deep within, as it were in the very marrow." Nor could this wrath be ignored simply by clinging to the security of self, "for the worm of conscience, sharper than any cauterizing iron, gnaws away within." The sins which all human beings unavoidably commit are icy slides: "the impious are borne headlong into their own errors, the end of which is the pit."[26]

At times, Calvin described a state of mind significantly different from that empty desert wilderness described by the medieval mystics. Calvin's mental wilderness was not quiet emptiness but mad insanity. It was hell on earth. "The sinner," he wrote, "wounded by the branding of sin and stricken by dread of God's wrath, remains caught in that disturbed state, . . . hell, which [he] had already entered in this life." The state of mind which Calvin called people to, the wilderness he demanded they cross, was a form of madness; self-denial, to Calvin, meant going mad. It meant abandoning the security of rational consciousness and plunging through the waves out into the wilderness of the subconscious. There was no guarantee that a sinner, once having entered this wilderness, would emerge again either returned to Egypt or at rest in Canaan. The "carcasses" of many of the children of Israel were left to "rot" in the wilderness never to see the promised land. Calvin did warn his readers against despair, but it is hard to see just where the line is or how to know when one has crossed it:

Those who are really religious experience what sort of punishments are shame, confusion, groaning, displeasure with self, and other emotions that arise out of a lively recognition of sin. Yet we must remember to exercise restraint, lest sorrow engulf us. For nothing more readily happens to fearful consciences than falling into despair. And also by this stratagem, whomever Satan sees overwhelmed by the fear of God he more and more submerges in that deep whirlpool of sorrow that they may never rise again.[27]

Such warnings point out the dangers in Calvin's form of therapy, but they do not temper it. He did not tell sinners to forego the terrors of the wilderness. Instead he held out to those who were drowning the hope of salvation. He warned them not to look back to Egypt but to persevere through the wilderness in the hope of reaching Canaan:

We must regard the Egyptian bondage of Israel as a type of the spiritual captivity in which all of us are held bound, until our heavenly vindicator, having freed us by the power of his arm, leads us into the Kingdom of freedom.[28]

Hard though it may have been, and full of violent dangers, the only way to the "Kingdom of freedom" was through the wilderness of the depraved mind.

v

Calvin's English disciples in the sixteenth and seventeenth centuries were not as reluctant as their tutor to make full typological use of wilderness imagery. The Anglican establishment had no particular use for the theme; theirs was a rational religion in no need of refuge with no desire to subject its adherents to the terrors of the conversion process. But, according to George Williams, "by the seventeenth century the wilderness impulse appeared everywhere in the piety and ecclesiology of Puritan England." For these English Puritans, who unlike the Anglicans adopted the Radical Reformation's emphasis on the conversion experience, the word "wilderness" became "an almost incantational term" carrying "the full charge of all the biblical-nuptial connotations. . . ."[29]

The medieval tradition of typology, used only with cautious suspicion by the first reformers, became the medium of this renewal. Developed out of the manner in which the New Testament writers made use of the Old Testament prophecies, typology, by the time of the Reformation, had become an elaborate system for reading the Old Testament as a foreshadowing of the Christian dispensation. Persons and events in the Old Testament were seen as prefigurations of eternal truths embodied in the person of Christ. The Old Testament figures were called "types"; their New Testament counterparts which the types foreshadowed were called "antitypes." In almost all cases, the antitype was Christ. Jonah, for instance, in the belly of the whale three days before being cast up on the land, was a "type" of Christ, who spent three days in hell before his resurrection. Christ, then, was the "antitype" of Jonah. The belly of the whale was a type of hell, and Jonah's experience a type of conversion. This tradition, which had its roots in the early church,[30] eventually led exegetes into the temptation of finding types and antitypes everywhere. Old Testament figures with no clear relation to any New Testament counterpart were often labelled types of Christ. Rather than limit themselves to those persons or events actually acknowledged as types within scripture, Catholic typologists expanded their use of the term to include any symbol, even when such symbolic interpretations were wholly a product of their own imaginations. In the New Testament, Matthew 12.40, Jesus specifically acknowledges the typological validity of the story of Jonah: "For as Jonah was three days and three nights in the whale's belly; so shall the Son of Man be three days and three nights in the heart of the earth." But not all typologists restricted themselves to the few such acknowledged types. Through this broadening of the definition of "type," gradually typology merged into allegory and threatened to escape the bounds of scripture altogether.

It was against this human appropriation of a typological tradition based in scripture that Calvin and the early reformers objected. They were willing to acknowledge types that were clearly intended as types. But they resisted the temptation to make every Old Testament hero, for instance, a type of Christ. And they were adamantly opposed to the practice of reading spiritual allegories into any scriptural or even natural event.

This Protestant distrust of the extremes to which typology was being carried pushed Protestantism toward an often restricting literalism. The reformers were all too well aware of the dangers: on the one hand, a fanciful interpretation of scripture wholly removed from the divine intent; while on the other, the insidious danger of a mindless literalism. Symbols can be liberating only as long as they continue to point beyond themselves, but when the symbols become more important than that which they are supposed to symbolize, it becomes necessary to repudiate them. For the reformers, types which did not point to Christ were not true types, and all of the many symbols which were said to be types of Christ actually obscured a true sight of Christ. For this reason, the reformers emphasized the need to return to the literal word of scripture. Thus, their return to the literal was an attempt, not to repudiate symbolic consciousness, but to shift men's eyes from the symbols to the things they were meant to symbolize. Basically they agreed with Augustine that:

> There is a miserable servitude of the spirit in this habit of taking signs for things, so that one is not able to raise the eye of the mind above things that are corporal and created to drink in eternal light.[31]

No Protestant opposed the use of typology entirely. Even Calvin acknowledged Moses to be a type of the law, Joshua a type of Christ, and the flight from Egypt into Canaan a type of conversion.[32]

In England, the typological tradition enjoyed somewhat more freedom than it had in Geneva. In the Anglican tradition, and particularly in the work of such writers as John Donne and George Herbert, it became an important literary vehicle for portraying abstract concepts symbolically. Barbara Lewalski has observed that "typological symbolism became, in the earlier seventeenth century, an important literary means to explore the personal spiritual life with profundity and psychological complexity."[33] This application of the type-antitype motif to the individual was made possible by the dual nature of the antitype. Christ was both man and God, both the human person Jesus of Nazareth and that spiritual being called the Son of God. The antitype completes, or fulfills, the type, but Christ as antitype was more than the person Jesus. Christ is also the eternal being who continues to afflict and enliven sinners and saints in the present. To speak of a type of Christ was to speak of both the type and of Christ at once. Both continued to exist, just as a symbol is both itself and the thing that it symbolizes. So in speaking of the antitype, Christ, both the man and the eternal being were believed to exist.

Typology has been said to exist in three stages, the Old Testament, the New Testament, and the future kingdom.[34] It is in this continual unfolding of the kingdom that typological symbols could be applied by seventeenth-century Englishmen to their own lives. Even such a conservative typologist as the New Englander Samuel Mather insisted that typology had relevance beyond the Bible:

> The types relate not only to the person of Christ; but to his benefits, and to all Gospel Truths and mysteries. . . .
> I mention this the rather, because I have observed that it doth much darken the thoughts of many, that they study to accomodate every type directly to the person of Christ; because we commonly call them types of Christ. But that expression is not meant of his person exclusive to his benefits; but of both together, Christ and the good things of Christ.[35]

Calvin had brought to men's attention the significance and the urgency of conversion. The revival of the typological tradition within English Protestantism allowed theologians to apply the often communal wilderness imagery of both the Old and the New Testament to this renewed emphasis on personal conversion. The Exodus account of the flight from Egypt could now be read as a type of the crucifixion and resurrection of Christ, and as such it could be preached as a type of the conversion experience that every English man and woman was called to undergo. In this way, traditional wilderness imagery was carried into the English Reformation with all of its original symbolic power intact.

vi

Of those Puritans who brought the Reformation to England, William Perkins, fellow of Christ College until his death in 1602, was one of the most influential. According to Perry Miller, he was "a towering figure" in the eyes of the New Englanders, not because he was particularly original but because he was "a superb popularizer" who made plain sense of complex Calvinist doctrine. His "energetic evangelical emphasis" with its insistent call to the unregenerate to face the rigors of conversion contributed to the popularity of his works.[36] This emphasis on the need for conversion led to an emphasis on the wilderness as a type of the place where sinners must go in order to be converted.

Perkins' handling of wilderness imagery was not restricted to any single use. A wide variety of interpretations of the wilderness can be found throughout his writings. At times, he was as cautious as Calvin, qualifying his use of wilderness imagery with angry denunciations of monks who tried to withdraw from the world: "Whither was Christ led to be tempted? Namely *into the wilderness*, that is the place chosen of God for this combat," a wilderness, he insisted, not of the mind but of the world, the arena in which Christ must struggle against Satan. "In this estate of Christ in the wilderness, we may behold the condition of Christ's militant church; to wit, that it is in this world as in a wilderness, and desert of wild beasts. . . ." No monk, he warned, should use the example of Christ's temptation as justification for withdrawing into a monastery, for "the place of this combat is the present world."[37]

If the wilderness was at one time seen by Perkins as a type of the world, at other times he interpreted it to be a place of refuge from the world. But the wilderness sojourn, he still warned, must not be thought of as a model for monks who would hide in the wilderness from the world. The saints, he asserted, are driven only reluctantly into refuge by persecution.

> We must not think that they betook themselves voluntarily to this solitarie life, but only upon necessitie, being contrained by persecution to flie into the wilderness, for the saving of their lives and the keeping of a good conscience.

Perkins' primary emphasis, however, was upon the necessity of conversion. To this end he brought a third use of the image of the wilderness:

> As the Israelites went through the Red Sea . . . to the promised land of Canaan: so we must know that the way to the spiritual Canaan, even the Kingdom of Heaven, is by dying unto sinne. . . . If we would have [everlasting life], . . , then we must take the Lord's plaine way in this life; which is to die unto all our sinnes. So it is said, *They which are Christs have crucified the flesh with the affections and lusts thereof.*

To enter into the wilderness then also meant to die unto sin.[38]

As had Calvin before him, Perkins insisted that "every one of us" must "enter into our hearts and make a thorough search." There we must "quake and tremble at his pressence," for every natural man hangs perilously over the pit of hell. Here is the same image that Calvin used, that of the wilderness of hell that exists just below the surface, "under the feet," of every human consciousness. The unawakened sinner, said Perkins, is like a man crossing a bridge at night. If he should suddenly see the "violent stream and a bottomless gulf," he will awaken, and "then he seeth the fraile bridge of this narrow life, and how little a step there is between him and damnation, then he seeth hell open due for all his sinnes, and himself in the highway unto it: sin being the craggie rock, and hell the gaping gulf under it. . . ." The hell that existed at the end of life also lay waiting in the heart of man; it was there that sinners had to "die unto sinne." It was that wilderness that they had to experience if they were ever to enter into the promised land.[39]

John Preston, Master of Emmanuel College, was a close personal friend of several of the leading New England divines. Influential among English Puritans, his works were also "a mainstay of New England libraries" and a "prerequisite to any understanding" of the New England mind in the seventeenth century.[40] Like Perkins, he preached conversion to the unregenerate, warning them "that whosoever would be translated from death to life must first apprehend himself to be a child of wrath." Like many a modern psychologist, Preston urged men and women to let their corrupt practices be a guide to lead them back to the unconscious principles that gave rise to their behavior.

> Consider first, the greatness of thy sins in particular and make catalogues of them. And then secondly, let our actual sins lead us to our corrupt heart, which is the root of all. So God dealt with the children of Israel. Deut. 8.2. Where it is said *God led them forty years in the wilderness, to humble them and to prove them, and to know what was in their hearts.*

Here, clearly, can be seen what today we would call the psychological use made by the Puritans of the wilderness as a type of the unconscious mind.[41]

It was this act of learning what was in one's heart that was the first stage of the process of conversion. It was in this wilderness, explained Preston, that John cried "prepare the way of the Lord, etc. but how? by humility . . . : Humility which prepareth for Christ, diggeth down those high mountains and maketh plaine those rough wayes." John's cry, according to Preston, was directed not at men's habitations, nor their behavior, but at their hearts. The wilderness in which the way of the Lord was to be prepared was a "humble" heart.[42]

To those who thought the Puritan preaching of humility through terror a cruel, painful and dangerous practice, Preston had a ready answer:

> You had therefore no need to cry out against us, that our words are cruell words, for this is a doctrine full sweete: you must at first give us the leave to open the wound, though it be painful; . . . The surgeon that will not search the wound to the bottom, for paining the patient, at the first may be pleasing; but afterward in the end he shall have little thank for his labor.

As long as the wrath of God hangs over a man, Preston wrote, and "he sees his own nothingness . . . so that he must sink utterly," then and only then is there hope that he may be saved from the pit by casting himself on Christ "as a man that is faling into the sea, casts himself on a rock."[43]

William Ames may have been the English Puritan with the most influence on his contemporaries. His *Medulla,* or *The Marrow of Sacred Divinity,* was "the standard textbook survey of theology used by New England students."[44] In it, Ames defended the careful use of symbolic imagery as a tool for leading worldly men to an understanding of spiritual truths. Literal language, he realized, cannot reach beyond itself. Spiritual truths, being higher than the human mind can fully comprehend, cannot be explained in direct simple rational language. Symbols are therefore an important tool for approaching, or at least pointing toward those spiritual realities that are beyond the ability of mere language to articulate.

> Because man in this animal life doth understand by senses, and so is as it were led by the hand from sensible things to intelligible and spirituall, therefore unto that spirituall law were added unto man outward symboles, and sacraments, to illustrate and conform it.

One of the most powerful of these symbols was that of the journey of the Jews out of Egypt through the wilderness to Canaan. By this story the process of conversion was graphically illustrated:

> Redemption and the application thereof was extraordinarily signified.
> 1. By the deliverance out of Egypt by the ministry of Moses as a type of Christ. Mat.2.15.
> And by the bringing into the land of Canaan . . . the Red Sea . . . , by Manna from heaven and water out of the rock.[45]

Nor did Ames believe that the wilderness of the world was all that was signified by that typical wilderness of trial and affliction. Christ, he reminded his readers, had "a two-fold way of subsisting: one in the

divine nature from eternity, another in the humane." The body is afflicted in the wilderness of the world, but Christ's afflictions were "two-
fold," of the body and of the soul: "That subjection to the power of
darkness was not to bondage, but to vexation, which Christ did feele in
his mind . . . , a certain sense of supernaturall and spirituall death." In a
"sinner's being grafted into the likeness of his death," the nails of mor-
tification whereby "sinne is fastened to the cross . . . are the very nailes
whereby Christ was fastened to the cross, and not those materiall ones
which his murtherers did use for this purpose." Thus the mortifications
of the cross include both the trials of the body and "vexation, which
Christ did feele in his mind." The wilderness in which conversion takes
place is both the world and the humbled heart.[46]

Examples of this joining together of the wilderness type with a psychological understanding of the conversion experience can be found
throughout the literature of seventeenth-century England. It was not
restricted to those Puritan writers preferred by the New England migrants nor to the period of the migration. Whatever its effect on New
England theologians, the actual migration of New England Puritans into
the literal wilderness of America does not seem to have affected the use
of wilderness imagery by English authors. The wilderness theme crossed
the Atlantic unchanged.

There was, however, little consistency in the use of particular images.
Some wrote only of the wilderness of the world, some of the wilderness
of the heart, and some of both. For some, the wilderness experience was
the true type of conversion and the crossing of the Red Sea but a type of
the initial awakening to sin. For others, most notably those who did not
wish to emphasize the extreme suffering necessary to conversion, the
crossing of the Red Sea became by itself a type of conversion and the
forty years in the wilderness were reduced to a trial of faith and not a
part of the conversion process. In 1681, Benjamin Keach noted that
"God by a gracious condescension, [conveys] the knowledge of spiritual
things by preaching them by their respective earthly parallels: . . ."
Thus, "Moses led Israel through the Red Sea: Christ leads his church
through a sea of tribulation." But in the same work, Keach described the
gushing forth of water from the rock in the wilderness, an event which
took place after the Red Sea crossing, as a type of Christ's refreshing "the
souls of poor sinners that come unto him when they can find no help,
comfort, or refreshment anywhere else, but without him must perish
eternally." The exact point in the conversion process at which conversion
could finally be said to have taken place was never satisfactorily agreed
upon.[47]

But whether conversion was said to occur at the Red Sea or elsewhere
in the metaphor, none doubted that in fact conversion was an experience

of both mind and soul. John Welles in 1639 defined the wilderness alone as the place where the soul must be humbled prior to any affectual workings of Christ's grace. To establish this, he turned to the example of John the Baptist in the New Testament:

> Christ enters not into the heart by grace unless John Baptist first prepare the way by repentance. . . . [God] leads us first into hell by serious griefe that afterward he may bring us back by the sweete taste of his grace.[48]

The hell of "serious griefe" to which Welles referred was the very wilderness in which John Baptist prepares the way for the coming of Christ. This wilderness was neither the external world nor some metaphysical construct. Welles had a definite belief in hell as an ocean of terror that surges beneath the surface of rational consciousness. We are held out of this sea, he implied, by our attachment to the material world through our senses. Sense perception provides the webbing that holds the sane mind above the underlying sea of madness. He described the horror of falling into that sea by pointing to the terrors of a man on the verge of death:

> Now the miserable soul perceiveth her earthly body begin to dye; For as towards the dissolution of the universal frame of the great world, the sunne shall be turned into darkness, the moon into blood, and the starres shall fall from heaven, the aire shall be full of stormes, and flashing meteors, the earth shall tremble, and the sea shall rage and roar; so towards the dissolution of man, which is the little world, his eyes which are as the sunne and the moone, lose their light, and see nothing but blood-guiltiness of sin, the rest of the senses, as little stars, doe one after another fail and fall; his mind, reason, and memory, as heavenly powers of the soule, are shaken with dreadful stormes of despair; at first, flashing of hell-fire, his earthly body begins to shake and tremble, and the humours, like an overflowing sea, roar and rattle in his throat, still expecting the woeful end of his dreadful beginning.

The dying soul then calls out to each of the senses, hoping to stay in contact with the sensible world. But the senses do not answer, and at last the sinful soul slips back into the dark cave of consciousness alone with itself forever in "that bottomless deep of the endless wrath of almighty God."[49]

It is neither an exaggeration nor an anachronism to say that these Puritan theologians were dealing with the same mental experiences that are treated in our time by doctors of the mentally ill. As do Freudian and other psychotherapists today they believed that a thorough unveiling of all of the "filth" repressed or hidden in the subconscious was a necessary prelude to any possible salvation. As Perry Miller has stated, if we are to understand and appreciate what that terror was that so dominated the Puritans' lives, we must "appeal to psychology and to such techniques as the twentieth century has so far discovered for dealing with the unconscious and inaccessible depths of the human spirit."[50]

Some of the writings of these theologians sound a surprisingly modern note. Even then, there were disputes between those who believed that mental problems were organic in origin and those who believed some form of "psychotherapy" to be the only possible cure. In a book published in 1605, William Perkins objected to the practice of trying to find material causes of mental disorders:

> Some think that all trouble of mind is nothing but melancholy, and therfore think nothing needs but phisicke and outward comforts: but . . . nothing can properly trouble the mind but sinne. . . . So the good phisitian of the soul, must first of all search into the cause of his sicknesse, that is his sinnes, and must take them away, which if they doe not, then all their labor is lost.[51]

Richard Baxter, also a popular Puritan polemicist, did not shrink from the psychological implications of the Puritan demand that sinners enter into and suffer the annihilating terrors of the wilderness of the soul. He specifically called on the unconverted to enter into this wilderness and, with language foreshadowing that of R.D. Laing, he boldly answered the objections of those who would remain secure in Egypt:

> Object. 7. I think you would make men mad under pretence of converting them; it is enough to rack the brains of simple people, to muse so much on matters too high for them.

> Ans. 1. Can you be madder than you are already? Or at least can there be a more dangerous madness, than to neglect your everlasting welfare, and wilfully undo yourselves?
> . . . Is it a wise world, when men will disobey God, and run to hell for fear of being out of their wits?
> . . . I had rather be in the case of such an one, then of the mad unconverted world, that take their distraction to be their wisdom.

Baxter admitted the danger of entering into the wilderness. As had Calvin, he recognized that distraught sinners might there be driven to final despair. But the experience of grace was seen to be great enough to be worth the danger. It was, as Miller said, "better in Puritan eyes that most men be passed over by this illumination and left to hopeless despair rather than that all men should be born without the hope of beholding it, or that a few should forgo the ecstasy of the vision." If the wilderness was the place to go in order to experience God, then Baxter as a good Puritan was not about to shrink from his duty:

> Though a wilderness be not heaven, it shall be sweet and welcome for the sake of heaven, if from thence I may but have a clearer prospect of heaven. . . . May there be more of God, readier access to him, more flaming love . . . in a wilderness, than in a city . . . ; let that wilderness be my city . . . as long as I abide on earth.[52]

Certainly by the 1630s, when the first wave of English Puritans arrived in the wilderness of New England, the idea of flying for refuge into the wilderness was already clearly associated with the sojourn of the Jews in the Sinai desert. Moreover, it was typologically associated with the all-important experience of conversion. When the New England settlers first contemplated flying for refuge into the American wilderness, they surely had all levels of this cultural tradition in mind. It is therefore hard to accept Perry Miller's statement that "they attached no significance a priori to their wilderness destination."[53] Indeed their minds must have reverberated with all the symbolic importance of what they intended to do. For they were not only going to repeat the journey of the Jews, they were going to participate typologically—symbolically—in the conversion process itself. They were going to cross their Red Sea and enter into their own wilderness. And there, they knew, was where their ordeal was going to begin. Some surely imagined that the crossing of the sea would be enough, but those who knew their Bibles and who were familiar with the rich tradition of wilderness imagery knew better. They were as sinners fleeing out of Egypt and the whole conversion process was still before them.

2

New England
Canaan and the Wilderness

For the Lord's portion is his people; Jacob is the lot of his
inheritance.
He found him in a desert land, and in the waste howling
wilderness; he led him about, he instructed him, he kept
him as the apple of his eye.

Deut. 32.9–10

i

The first generation of Puritan settlers entered New England expecting
it to be a "howling wilderness." They did not expect a paradise, at least
not immediately. The pastoral traditions of English literature had little
influence on them. The advertisements of would-be colonizers did not
fool them. Even if New England had been a paradise, these Puritans
would have called it a wilderness, for their conception of their errand,
their imaginative sense of who they were, overpowered external considerations and shaped their perception of the new land.

As long as the Puritans thought of themselves as sinners pleading in
the wilderness for the showers of God's grace, then whatever land they
inhabited would be to them a "howling wilderness," a place of refuge
and of trial, of suffering and of hope, the scene of both their damnation
and their ultimate resurrection. Gradually, the New Englanders' sense of
who they were, their *identity*, changed, and then they began to think of
New England as a paradise and of themselves as flowers in that garden.
When they ceased to think of themselves as wholly sinful and began to
believe that they indeed had become God's elect, when they ceased to be
anxious about their "justification" and began to believe in their growing
"sanctification," their perception of their environment also changed.
Emphasis on the "desart solitarie wilderness" gradually was replaced by
an emphasis on the gardens and oases in that wilderness. Once they

46

ceased to be buffeted by demons and bitten by flying serpents in the wilderness, they began to think of themselves as a garden of holy flowers surrounded by the hedge of God's protection in the promised land of Canaan. In this process, the vital edge of Calvinist piety was lost.

Although this change in emphasis was a gradual development, the self-image that accompanied this change was by no means new. There had always been within English Calvinism a tension between those who saw themselves as sinners in need of wilderness trials and those who believed themselves safe and secure in the promised land of Canaan. The extremes of this division can be seen in the controversy in the Bay Colony in the 1630s between the "Arminians" and the "Antinomians." Those who distrusted claims of absolute assurance and who insisted on working to prepare a way in the wilderness for the future coming of Christ were labeled "Arminians." Those who distrusted the highly ritualized "morphology of conversion," who did not believe that all converts had to pass step by step through the trials of the law, who believed all "works" to be signs of hypocrisy, were called "Antinomians."

The term "Arminian" referred to the followers of the Dutch theologian, Jacob Arminius, who preached that works, that is, adherence to the moral law, could prepare the way for salvation. Arminius believed that grace could be earned through the performance of good works and the avoidance of sin. He saw no need for the tortures of conversion. Those labeled "Arminian" in New England in the 1630s were not true Arminians, but because of their insistence on wilderness trials preparatory to conversion, their Antinomian opponents unjustifiably labelled them Arminians. These Antinomians, literally those who are "beyond the law," rejected the performance of works as being in any way preparatory to conversion. Instead, they believed that conversion was wrought by God in the soul and nothing humans did could either enhance or retard it. They stressed God's sovereignty and man's absolute dependence.

The difference between these two attitudes is difficult to define. It cannot be neatly demonstrated by pointing to any particular dogmatic distinctions. Those much disputed doctrines, "works," "grace," "sanctification," "justification," were not the sources of this division but attempts to articulate and clarify already existing differences. Even after those points of doctrine have been explained, the real differences that divided the community remain unaccounted for. These had less to do with doctrine and more to do with individuals' trust in themselves and in their perception of reality.

The Arminians believed in the reality of original sin, in all humanity's utter depravity and inability to reach the truth. They perceived intuitively what Calvin meant by "the stupidity of human understanding."

They distrusted their feelings and perceptions and longed for a mystic wholeness they believed beyond the comprehension of human consciousness. They believed that all human belief is relative, that even emotions have unconscious sources, and they looked beyond the five senses for a way out of the trap. These traditionally "Puritanical" fixations on damnation and sin can be attributed to what has been called "their profound need to achieve a new basis for trust," that is, a new identity more reliable and satisfying than the old. Their sense of sin lead them to distrust individual human perception and to emphasize instead the community that each weak member was bound to through the covenant.[1]

The Antinomians, believing themselves already the recipients of mystic vision, dared to presume that they had received justification and were proceeding through conversion, that their perception was holy perception, and that they were in a state of grace. They believed that their hearts were faithful and that they really did have "the truth." The self-doubting Arminians thought of themselves as sinners still subject to the terrors and obligations of the law. The confident Antinomians, as their name implies, imagined themselves to be beyond Sinai, beyond the law, and already entered into Canaan. As individuals supposedly enlightened by the grace of God, they placed individual perception above communal authority or tradition.

Puritanism thus contained within its complex theology two apparently contradictory strains, a communal pessimism that looked to the wilderness of human depravity and an individualistic optimism that rejoiced at being one with God in the sunny vineyards of Canaan. The tension between these two strains can be discerned clearly in the history of New England in the 1630s. But this tension had a more than antiquarian significance, for the ripples then set in motion continue to spread. The struggle between doubt and affirmation, protest and celebration, denial and devotion has been an integral part of American culture ever since.

The "Augustinian Strain of Piety," in Perry Miller's characterization of the New England mind,[2] contained from the beginning both self-denial and divine affirmation, and both of them somehow at once. That perfect balance of those two emotional states exemplified by Augustine was rarely found in any one community or individual. Instead, at different times, an emphasis on one or the other prevailed. In the conversion process, self-denial had to precede any reception of grace. Yet in saints, both were supposed to exist together. The problem was that each attitude annulled the other. A person meditating on his or her own sinfulness could see only that total depravity, not the mercy of Christ. On the other hand, joy at being one with Christ often led to a loss of the humbling spirit that preceded it.

There was also the problem of assurance. Utter self-denial could open the way to an experience of divine affirmation. But how could a sinner know that this experience was not some Satanic delusion? Rather than one of the God's elect might not he or she be a deluded hypocrite? From the heights of mystic vision, a saint could be cast by such doubts back into the pit to be tormented by demons of self-doubt.

These two strains of piety came to New England already thoroughly entangled in the hearts of the immigrants. When, soon after Boston was settled, this tension burst forth, individuals who felt these divisions within themselves were forced to choose sides. Where they imagined themselves to be on the journey of conversion was a crucial factor determining their identity. Within a few years of their arrival in the new world, these Americans had to struggle with this question of identity, not yet as Americans but as Christians. Where they the children of Israel just entering onto the journey through the wilderness? Or were they God's chosen people, already elect, already justified, and protected in their purity in the garden of the promised land?

A careful reading of the literature left by the first generation of settlers reveals that, contrary to earlier studies, even before leaving England, the Puritans did think of themselves as participants in a recreation of the biblical flight into the wilderness.[3] They knew that New England would be no paradise. Indeed, their conception of themselves as sinners fleeing out of Egypt over the sea required a wilderness of trials and temptations for them to enter into. More important to them than material comforts was their sense of themselves as parallels of the biblical type. The wilderness was a state of mind, but just as the type was both literal event and spiritual symbol, so their recreation of the type required a literal wilderness that they too might have a symbolic as well as a spiritual conversion. They would have been disappointed had their destination been a fruitful garden. But just by being a wild and desolate wilderness, New England fulfilled their mythic desire and delighted them.

The Massachusetts Bay Puritans' public explanation for emigrating, *The Planter's Plea,* written in 1630 in England, looked forward to that time "when we shall be in our poore cottages in the wilderness, over-shadowed with the spirit of supplication, through the manifold necessities and tribulations which may not altogether unexpectedly, nor we hope, unprofitably befall us."[4] The anticipation of a redemptive wilderness experience is evident here. The note of hope is significant. The first generation may have expected New England to be a wilderness, but they also expected at the end of their wilderness sojourn to enter into Canaan. Some imagined that Canaan would be an England reborn in the image of New England. Others thought that New England itself might be the scene of that final reformation. But in either case, the hopeful references should not be allowed to obscure the basic perception, that New England would at first be a howling wilderness and only later after a typical forty years of hardships, trials, and testing, the promised land of Canaan.

This dual expectation of danger and deliverance was a common theme among the English migrants on the eve of their departure. Edward Johnson remembered explaining to a friend that he was leaving in order "to rebuild the most glorious edifice of Mount Sion in a wilderness" and that like "John Baptist" he could only cry "prepare yee the way of the Lord, make his paths strait, for beholde he is coming againe." John Eliot later claimed that "we chose" purposefully to settle in a harsh wilderness where nothing could be expected "but religion, poverty, and hard labour, a composition that God doth usually take most pleasure in." He made it clear that the emigrants wanted neither a paradise nor a neutral environment. They fully desired trials and temptations as searching as those undergone by the Jews in the Sinai:

> Assuredly the better part of our plantations did undertake the enterprise with a suffering minde, and whoever shall do such a thing, must be so warned or else he will not be able to hold out in the work: to part with our native country, a settled habitation, dear friends, houses, lands and many worldly comforts, to go into a wilderness where nothing appeareth but hard labour, wants, and wilderness-temptations (stumble not country-men, at the repitition of that word, wilderness-temptations) of which it is written, that they are trying times, and places, Deut. 8. There must be more than golden hopes to bear up the Godly wise in such an undertaking.[5]

It would be tempting to read these statements simply as the bravado of old men telling tales about the rigors of their youth. But within the context of the wilderness tradition and the recorded statements of the emigrants, there can be little doubt that the expectation of "wilderness-temptations" was authentic and not read back into the history after the fact.

John Winthrop's letters to his wife, written on the eve of his departure, reveal his awareness of New England as a type of the wilderness refuge. "My deare wife," he wrote in 1629, "I am very perswaded, God will bring some heavye affliction upon this lande, and that speedylye; but be of good comfort, . . . [i]f the Lord seeth it will be good for us, he will provide a shelter and a hiding place. . . ." Similar references to the wilderness as a place of refuge occur throughout Winthrop's writings of this period. He cited not only the Jews fleeing Egypt, but Abraham fleeing Ur, the "Waldenses" and the "albigenses" escaping into the wilderness, and he asked, "dothe not the history of the church give us many examples of the like, who hath been renewed by repentance?" In his carefully prepared arguments for removing to New England, he mentioned the woman who "was persecuted by the dragon, and forced to fly into the wilderness." In his "Objections Answered," he speculated that God may "by this meanes bring us to repent of our intemperance here at home, and so cure us of that disease, which sends many amongst us to Hell: So he carried many of his people into the wilderness, and made them forget the fleshpots of Egypt." Here, in one sentence, can be found the desire for wilderness trials, the parallel with the wilderness sojourn of the Jews, and an expectation of conversion in the American wilderness.[6]

It has been asserted that John Cotton, when delivering his sermon to the departing emigrants, "spoke of no American wilderness."[7] This is literally so; the word "wilderness" does not appear in *God's Promise to His Plantations*. However, there is evidence that Cotton did have the wilderness tradition in mind when he wrote that sermon. To illustrate his assertion that God will lead his people to a chosen land, Cotton quoted Exodus 19.4, "You have seen how I have borne you as on Eagle's wings, and brought you unto myself."[8] Although the "wilderness" is not specifically mentioned here, the parallel to Rev. 12.14 (as well as Deut. 32.11), the woman flying "into the wilderness" on the "wings of a great eagle," would not have been missed by those listening. Even without that, the scriptural context of this line, which also would have been familiar to Cotton's audience, makes the reference explicit:

> 1 In the third month, when the children of Israel were gone forth out of the land of Egypt, the same day came they into the wilderness of Sinai.
> 2 For they were departed from Rephidim, and were come to the desert of Sinai, and had pitched in the wilderness; and there Israel camped before the mount.
> 3 And Moses went up unto God and the Lord called unto him out of the mountain, saying thus shalt thou say to the house of Jacob, and tell the children of Israel:
> 4 You have seen . . . how I bare you on Eagles' wings, and brought you unto myself.

The wilderness tradition was so strong among these English Calvinists that specific mention of the wilderness was unnecessary. They all recognized the reference, they knew where Moses was, and they knew what Cotton meant.

Nor did the wilderness of New England disappoint the first settlers. It proved as hard and as rigorous a trial of their faith as they had wished. They had no need to alter their view of the land. Accordingly, wilderness

imagery abounds in the literature of New England in that first decade
without significant change. Francis Higginson, on the eve of his departure, had portrayed New England "as a refuge and a shelter." A year
later, in 1630, the wilderness tradition still dominated his perception of
the new environment. In a sermon preached on Matthew 11.7, "What
went ye out into the wilderness to see?," he once again reminded the
settlers "of the design whereupon this plantation was erected, namely
religion: and of the streights, wants, and various trials which in a wilderness they must look to meet withall."[9]

On the day that John Davenport landed at what would soon be the
colony of New Haven, he preached from the Gospel of Matthew, "Then
was Jesus led up of the spirit into the wilderness to be tempted of the
devil." Later that afternoon, Peter Prudden preached on "The voice of
one crying in the wilderness, Prepare ye the way of the Lord, make his
paths straight." The savage nature of the wilderness was no surprise to
these Puritan settlers. They knew exactly where they were, and they were
prepared, even before they landed, with the appropriate texts to describe it.[10]

Despite the Puritans' nearly unanimous expectation that New England
would be a recapitulation of the "howling wilderness" of scripture, the
two strains of Puritanism, labelled for convenience' sake Arminianism
and Antinomianism, were already effecting in subtle ways the Puritans'
perception of their new home.

John Davenport believed in the wilderness and the need for wilderness trials. The saints of the community he founded, New Haven, the
strictest of the Puritan colonies, harbored no illusion that they had
crossed over into Canaan. Davenport's belief that the settlers were still
under the rod of the law placed him on what has been called the
Arminian side of the spectrum of Puritan opinion. His was a stern sense
of himself as a child of wrath, "dead in trespasses and sins, altogether
filthie and polluted throughout in soul and body, utterly averse from any
spiritual good, strongly bent to all evil. . . ."[11] This sense of being on the
human side of the cross, "judging himself worthy to be destroyed," was
particularly strong among the generation that had fled England. These
emigrants were obsessed with an overpowering sense of their own sinfulness. In terms of the image, they identified not with the Jews of a
restored Israel, but with the Jews of the desert still subject to Moses and
the law. They prayed for and expected salvation, but they did not assume
it. They believed that they still had to cross the wilderness. Their ministers were used to preaching in England to "mixed multitudes" of saints
and sinners. Hence, theirs was an evangelical stance directed to the
unconverted, calling them to join the gathered church as it set out into
the wilderness in the hope of finding Christ.

This overwhelming sense of personal and communal depravity was rarely found untouched by at least occasional assumptions of grace. Puritan piety included the two strains of fear and hope, self-denial and mystic affirmation. There was no Puritan in whom both of these elements, in some degree, could not be found. Emphasis on one or the other had significant influence on a person's theological sympathies. Those who believed themselves to be sinners and felt the need for the law tilted toward the Arminian position; those who believed themselves to be recipients of Christ's grace tilted toward the Antinomian side. Moreover, through an almost unavoidable confusion between type and antitype, of the symbol and that which it symbolized, theological sympathies influenced perception of the New England environment. Puritans who saw themselves as sinners under the wrath of the law saw New England as a wilderness. Puritans who believed themselves already saved, already among the converted, saw New England as Canaan, as paradise, as the garden of the Lord.

It is characteristic, then, that John Cotton, who would later be accused of being too sympathetic to the Antinomian extremists, was the first generation minister most ready to believe himself already saved and New England a type of Canaan. Although able in *God's Promise* to allude to the wilderness condition, he was more explicit in his references to the promised land:

> God's people take the land by promise: And therefore the land of Canaan is called a land of promise, which they discern, first, by discerning themselves to be in Christ, in whom all the promises are yea, and Amen.[12]

Here lies the other strain of Puritanism, the belief that the gathered congregation of the saints is indeed already "in Christ" and that New England is a garden in the wilderness, not a wilderness of conversion but the garden of sanctification.

This is not to deny that Cotton preached conversion. "It is true," he asserted, "John Baptist was sent to subdue all flesh by a spirit of burning, which burneth up the covenant of Abraham, I mean their carnal confidence in it. . . ." It is even true, he wrote, that the application of the law to the conscience "many times doth, end in utter despair." Still, conversion, once accomplished, he believed to be final. The experience of God's wrath leads to the experience of faith, and "this faith when God gives it a convincing power in the soul . . . doth not only convince of sin and danger but it convinces us also of all the truth and goodness of all the promises offered to us in the Gospel, and satisfies the soul that there is pardon with God. . . ." Cotton thus acknowledged the terrors of the introspective journey, but he believed himself to be safely beyond them. Despite its acknowledged "deceitfulness," his heart was comforted by God's faithfulness:

> I now may expect some changes of miseries
>   Since God hath made me sure
> That himself by them all will purge mine inequities,
>   As fire makes silver pure.
> Then what though I find the deep deceitfulness
>   Of a distrustful heart!
> Yet I know with the Lord is abundant faithfulness,
>   He will not lose his part.

For Cotton, the wilderness had ceased to be the place of trial and testing. It had become the place the humbled soul came unto Christ "as a spouse to her husband, for seed." John the Baptist, according to Cotton, went into the wilderness not to undergo conversion but "that he might see more clearly not only the judgement of the great whore but also the coming down from Heaven of the chaste bride, the New Jerusalem . . ." The difference at first glance is not great, but the emphasis that Cotton puts on "the chaste bride" is significant. God has planted us, he affirmed, "not in the wilderness of the world, but in the garden of his church."[13]

ii

Cotton, however, was an exception. He pushed against the bounds of first generation orthodoxy and eventually was called to task by his fellow ministers for his transgressions. A more orthodox understanding of New England's identity can be found in the works of the so-called Arminians or "preparationists," for theirs was the classic Puritan position, crying in the wilderness, prepare ye the way of the Lord.

It is generally accepted that Thomas Hooker's writings "constitute the most minute and searching analysis of the soul and the process of spiritual regeneration, the most coherent and sustaining expression of the essential religious experience ever achieved by the New England divines."[14] It is to Hooker that the student of New England must turn in order to understand the piety that inspired the first settlers. Here is the voice of the evangelist calling on the unconverted to look upon their total depravity, to abandon their security and self-confidence, and to flee from that wrath to Christ. Here too is the searching word of the sophisticated Puritan psychologist discovering the hypocrisy both of sinners and of those who presume themselves "in Christ," demanding that both submit themselves to the wilderness of their depraved hearts. "There is," notes George Williams, "rarely a sermon by Thomas Hooker in which he does not deal with some type of hypocrite."[15]

Hooker's use of the image of the wilderness preceded his arrival in New England. In *The Poor Doubting Christian Drawn to Christ,* first published in 1629, using many of the themes that would later characterize his New England ministry, Hooker sought to reveal "the private wiles of our own hearts, and to hunt out all those mazes, and turnings, and windings of our subtle souls." He compared this "proud heart" that refuses to be humbled to that of the Jews who "spake against the Lord, when they said, Can the Lord prepare a table in the wilderness?" After he had preached on the meaning of damnation and the hope of salvation, he reminded his readers that "when thou art in the wilderness, this God is thy God, when thou art in persecution, this God is thy God."[16]

This condition of persecution in the wilderness preceding conversion was what Hooker meant by preparation. He was no true Arminian; he did not believe that works could earn grace. He insisted that the soul must be humbled before it could even understand the hope of grace. Only after "we have plucked away all our carnal props," he maintained, could sinners sincerely surrender themselves to God. To be brought into the wilderness of the heart and there humbled was what it meant to be prepared for the coming of Christ:

> You see how far the Lord hath brought us; how the soul hath been prepared, and cut off from sin and itself, if fitted for the Lord Jesus, by contrition and humiliation.

Nor was Hooker's preaching entirely devoted to the trials of the wilderness. He did hold out a hope for salvation, reminding the sincerely fearful that "the fiery serpents stung the people in the wilderness, but there was a brazen serpent to heal them."[17]

In *The Soules Preparation for Christ,* also written prior to his departure from England, Hooker grappled with the limited language available to him to try to define what we would call the psychological experience of conversion. God's battering of the sinful heart, he explained, could be defined by "no word in our English tongue . . . but only a shiverednesse of soule all to pieces." The sinner who would flee from God's wrath "cannot tell which way to drive away his fear. . . . His conscience is all on a flame within him." What Hooker could confirm was that this experience was typologically prefigured in the scriptural account of the flight of the Jews from Egypt, that "their being in the wilderness was a type of the saint's conversion." It was the typological tradition that provided him with a language with which to discuss conversion.[18]

Hooker's New England writings show no radical departure from either the themes or the imagery that he had used in England. Perhaps the image of the wilderness took on even greater evocative power in the new world than it had in the old, but if so this was a matter of degree and not of substance. Hooker continued to use the image of the wilderness as he had used it in England, as that state of mind, that "sea of misery and confusion in thy soule," in which "John Baptist was sent to prepare the way" for Christ. He warned his New England congregation not to "thinke you may climb up to heaven by your owne imaginations," especially if in their imaginations they saw themselves in Canaan in a state of grace, at ease in the promised land. More than once, Hooker made the correlation between conversion and the crossing into the wilderness totally explicit:

> There must be contrition and humiliation before the Lord comes to take possession; . . . This was typified in the passage of the children of Israel towards the promised land; they must come into, and go through a vast and roaring wilderness, where they must be bruised with many pressures, humbled under many over-bearing difficulties, they were to meet withal before they could possess that good land which abounded with all prosperity, flowed with milk and honey. The truth of this Type, the prophet Hosea explains, and expresseth at large in the Lord's dealing with his people in regard of their spiritual condition, Hos. 2.14.15. *I will lead her into the wilderness* and break her heart with many bruising miseries, and *then I will speak kindly to her heart.* . . .

Here can plainly be seen the full expression of the wilderness tradition in New England. This is the explicit typological use of the passage of the Lord's people into the wilderness of the broken heart.[19]

Both in England and later in New England, Hooker conceived of this wilderness state as a symbol of the depths of unconscious "confusion" that undermine the foundations of sanity. Unregenerate men may have thought themselves secure, but all the time they were resting perilously upon their "own crazie bottomes." The comfortable and contented could not see it, but there was in this analysis a thin line separating sanity from madness. Sinners had to cross this line, to be held, as they said, over the pit of hell, even at the risk of going mad, if they were to be shaken out of their complacency. Hooker, with his customary bluntness, made it clear that the condition labeled madness by the world was the very condition which sinners had to experience before they could hope for salvation:

> A broken battered soule, that hath been long overwhelmed with the weight of his corruptions, the Lord brings him to a marveilous desper-

ate low ebbe; you may see a man, sometimes in the torment of conscience that nature and natural parts begin to decay, his
understanding grows weake, and his memory fails him, and he grows
to be marveilously distracted, and besides himselfe, so that the partie
which was (before) a man of great reach and of able parts, and was
admired, and wondered at for his wisdome, and government; he is
now accounted a silly sot, and a mad man, in regard of the horror of
heart that hath possessed him.

Thus did John the Baptist prepare the way for Christ in the wilderness,
by turning worldly men into "silly sots" so they could be led away from
self-esteem, out of themselves, and into God. By his very use of such
imagery, Hooker made it clear that he thought his congregation and
himself to be still in need of more afflictions, to be still sojourners in the
wilderness.[20]

Peter Bulkeley, the first minister of Concord, was one of those who had
come down hard on the Antinomians in 1636. In *The Gospel Covenant*,
published in 1651, he held to the orthodox view that the Bay colony was
a community still undergoing the trials of conversion. For him, the
journey of the Puritans into the wilderness of New England was clearly
identified with the journey of the Jews into the Sinai wilderness. "God
hath dealt with us as with his people Israel," he reminded his congregation, "we are brought out of a fat land into a wilderness, and here
we meet with necessities. . . ." The Concord congregation in the 1640s,
when these sermons were preached, had settled deep in what was then
the frontier. Theirs was quite literally a wilderness condition, and for
Bulkeley the literal wilderness was an important correlate of that spiritual wilderness in which conversion takes place. In case any of the
Concord pioneers missed the comforts of old England, or even of
Boston, Bulkeley reminded them that

When the Lord will come to the soule, and draw it into communion
with himself: he will have his way hereto prepared in the Desert; not in
the throng of a city, but in a solitarie desert place, he will allure us, and
draw us into the wilderness, from the company of men, when he will
speak to our heart, and when he prepares our heart to speak unto
him. (Hosea 2)

This wilderness condition, he argued, is the only condition for sinners
who want to experience Christ's mercy. Echoing the English Puritan
Richard Baxter (Chapter 1, fn. 52), he affirmed that Christ will not come
to those "living in the throng of a city." There was no suggestion here
that the church members were in the wilderness as a gathered garden of

saints. They were in the wilderness in order to be converted, for it was there and only there that the soul could be "thus alone with itself and with God." The people in the wilderness, literal and spiritual, were sinners undergoing the process of regeneration.[21]

Here the type and the antitype, the symbol and that which it was meant to symbolize, became closely identified. The soul in a wilderness condition, originally a type of conversion, here became more than the symbol of a spiritual state. The literal wilderness became the physical location of the conversion process. It did not replace the heart; conversion remained a mental experience. But the presence of the sinner's body in the wilderness made conversion more likely. Regeneration may take place in the mind, said Bulkeley, but those actually dwelling in a literal wilderness have a better chance of experiencing conversion than those living "in the throng of a city." Nature did not convert, but the descent into nature did facilitate conversion. Bulkeley, although still a Puritan, faintly foreshadowed what would become of his religion two hundred years later in the town he founded.

Thomas Shepard, a third proponent of the orthodox position, described the New Englanders as having willingly undertaken the "cares and temptations" of their wilderness sojourn "onely in hopes of enjoying Christ in his ordinances." The reference was to the sacraments, but the parallel to the experience of conversion is unmistakable. New Englanders willingly forsook their English homes and comforts, passed over the "vast seas," and entered into the wilderness all for the sake of "enjoying Christ." As he did to the children of Israel in bringing them safely through the Red Sea, "The Lord at first conversion draws his people . . . gently." Afterward, preached Shepard, he leads them through "a wilderness of sins and miseries, that they might know what is in their own hearts."[22]

The wilderness was thus still a wilderness of mind as well as fact. Shepard used the same images that appeared throughout Calvinist literature. Human consciousness hung perilously over the pit of God's wrath, a wilderness of terror in the soul, a turbulent sea that raged under the fragile shell of consciousness. Behavior is not what constitutes sin, argued Shepard: "An actual sin is but a little breach made by the sea of sin in thine heart." Here was the oceanic chaos that surrounded human life, the chaos that preceded creation, that waited at death, and that undermined every waking moment:

> God is a consuming fire against thee, and there is but one paper wall of thy body between thy soule and eternal flames. . . . There is nothing but that between thee and hell; if that were gone, then farewell all. . . ; thou hangest but by one rotten twined thread of thy life over the flames of hell every hour.[23]

An experience of this hell was what had to precede true conversion. This, and not some literal adherence to a "covenant of works" was what the doctrine of preparation was all about. Shepard and his fellow "Arminians" were understandably concerned that the Antinomian extremists were preaching an easy, instantaneous conversion; they were threatening to make hypocrites out of potential Christians. The works these Arminians were preaching were not, as the Antinomians charged, meant to make moralists out of pious Christians. They were the works of the law that taught the unregenerate, not how to behave, but "the knowledge of sin." Eventually, the truly legal and rational tendencies in their theology did grow into full Arminianism, but the legal was only one strain of "Puritanism" and not, as is sometimes assumed, the only one.

Shepard shared John Winthrop's contempt for Antinomians like John Underhill who, "as he was taking a pipe of tobacco, the spirit set home an absolute promise of free grace with such assurance and joy, as he never since doubted of his good estate." Such a "faire and easy way to heaven, that men may pass without difficulty" was to the orthodox mind unscriptural nonsense. The Antinomian belief that "I know I am Christs . . . because I do not crucify [the flesh], but believe in Christ that crucified my lusts for me," meant to Winthrop "That believing in Christ, may ease me from endeavoring to crucifie my lusts in my own person." He found the notion "so grosse, that it needs no more confutation than to name it." An easy, instantaneous conversion could have no validity for a true Puritan.[24]

Winthrop touched here on an important theological difference between the two sides. The Arminians, being true Calvinists and heirs of the Reformation, believed that justification by faith meant accepting Christ's jusification *in place of* one's own. It meant accepting the possibility of one's own damnation and rejoicing, instead, in the eternal glorification of righteousness in Christ. The Antinomians, on the other hand, foreshadowed that flip in Protestant dogma which would have justification by faith refer to the justification of the sinner *because of* his or her faith in Christ. One interpretation stressed self-denial; the other led to self-exaltation, to the notion, as Winthrop said, "that believing in Christ, may ease me from endeavoring to crucify my lusts in my own person." It is no wonder that he found the notion "so grosse."

The Antinomian Ann Hutchinson's claim of a revelation of assurance directly from God to her soul, if justified, would have overridden the need for the kind of painful, introspective journey that ministers like Shepard insisted upon. And Shepard was not one to believe in an easy conversion. Rocked by self-doubt himself, forever unsure, as his journal readily reveals, of his own salvation, he did not agree with John Cotton's assumption that the New England saints were already "in Christ" and resting in the land of Canaan. What Shepard desired was not milk and honey, nor a sheltered garden, "but to be more humbled," to "fly out of self to the death of Christ." The emphasis in his writings is clearly on self-denial and not on the imagined glories of what Cotton called "wading in grace."[25]

Ann Hutchinson's Antinomian cousin, John Wheelwright, on the other hand, denied in his controversial *Fast Day Sermon* that there was any need for the New England saints to undergo a work of contrition. Only those who were without Christ, he claimed, had any need for fasting. He condemned "hungering and thirsting and the like" as a "work of sanctification." Like Cotton, he assumed that Christ was already in the community, and he warned the people not to do anything that might make him "depart from us." Believing himself safely in Canaan, he denied the applicability of the wilderness sojourn to his condition or to the situation of the New England saints: "the body of them [the children of Israel] were hypocrites. . . . They had the angel of God's presence to go before them, but they had not the Lord Jesus Christ in them." Many of those Jews died in the wilderness in a state of sin without ever having reached the promised land. Therefore, he argued, they are not a fit parallel to the Jews of this restored Canaan who already are in Christ.[26]

When the Antinomians were expelled from the Bay, Shepard and his fellow ministers believed that the question of New England's identity had been settled. New England Calvinists were not to presume themselves "in Christ;" they were not to be "at ease in Zion," but continually to repent their wickedness. They were the Jews of the wilderness. Shepard did not let down his guard when the crisis of 1636 ended. John Cotton had narrowly escaped being cast out of the church, but Shepard remained suspicious. "Mr. Cotton repents not, but hid only," he noted in the margin of his autobiography. "He doth stiffly hold the revelation of our good estate still, without any sign of word or work."[27]

Shepard's suspicions eventually went beyond John Cotton and focused on the broader community. It was not that the Quakers were slipping back into the Bay. What few Quakers did manage to breach the borders were discovered and expelled. More serious was the growing indifference among the rising generation to the necessity for suffering. Never having known the trials of persecution, nor the dangers of the Atlantic crossing, protected from the rigors even of their wilderness condition, young New Englanders growing up as members of prosperous churches in prosperous communities, were behaving as if they believed themselves not in Sinai but in Canaan. Shepard was alarmed:

New England's peace and plenty of means breeds strange security; and hence prayer is neglected here. There are no enemies to hunt you to heaven, nor chains to make you cry; hence the Gospel and Christ in it is slighted. Why? Here are no sour herbs to make the lamb sweet.

Even church members no longer doubted, as Shepard did, their own conversions. Self-denial it seemed to him was honored in name only. "Tell me," he cried to his congregation, "would you have all New England lie in security as well as yourselves?" The answer apparently was "yes."[28]

New England's problem continued to be one of identity. The parents had so often said that they were in the wilderness acting out the process of conversion that the children believed them and mistook the literal symbol of being in the wilderness for the spiritual experience it was supposed to symbolize. Their parents had undergone the wilderness trials and prosperity had resulted. Was not New England a land flowing with milk and honey, a Canaan? Had not Bulkeley said that their wilderness condition would bring them to Christ? Had not the expected transformation occurred? Were they not a community in covenant with God and didn't that covenant include every member of Christ's church? No, cried Shepard, we are still the Jews of the wilderness as long as we are in our sins. We may have some idea of what it means to know Christ, but until we have experienced conversion, we have not completed the journey. There is still a long way to go before any New Englander can rest at ease in Zion.

> That, look, as it was with Israel, they came out of Egypt and saw the wonders of God in the wilderness, and had his fiery law and tabernacle among them, yet they never came to the land of rest; so it is at this day with many: they have some glimpse of the excellency of Christ, and his grace, and some desires after it, and some tastes of it; they are pulled out of their woeful bondage, and seeing words of God are oft affected, yet their carcasses must fall in the wilderness, because they never came to rest; they fall off from God because they never know what this rest meaneth.

Shepard knew that for all of his scolding, the new generation had only "some sense of it, yet no awakening fear of the terror of the Lord." John Cotton may have been forced to acknowledge the orthodox line. But in the end, for reasons he had nothing to do with, his image of New England's identity prevailed.[29]

The declension from the anxious humility of the founders to the anxious assurance of their descendants was on the whole a gradual occurrence. It was, in Perry Miller's words, "a purely semantic evolution, which went on for years without registering itself in consciousness."[30] The process can be observed, however, in the work of at least one first generation settler, Edward Johnson.

The Wonder-working Providence of Sion's Savior in New England, published in 1653, contains both legal and Antinomian characteristics. No
other work reverberates so loudly with incantations to the wilderness.
There is barely a page without some reference to the "desert solitarie
wilderness," the feeding of God's people in the wilderness, "this wilder-
ness-work," and more. Johnson professed allegiance to the orthodox
ministers of the Bay. He sincerely believed that the wilderness was the
place for the conversion of humble sinners. Affirming that "the whole
will not see any need of phisicians [Christ], but the sick," he attacked the
Antinomians for saying that "God could see no sin in his people" and for
criticizing a saint "who beg'd for forgiveness of his sins." Like Winthrop,
he ridiculed the man who claimed "that the Spirit of Revelation came to
him as he was drinking a pipe of tobacco." Breaking into tears of
remorse as Shepard applied the word "so aptly" to his soul, he resolved
"to live and die with the ministers of New England."[31]

But for all of Johnson's orthodox use of wilderness imagery, he never
doubted that out of the wilderness afflictions eventually would come the
redemption of his community. He did not go to the extreme of ever
asserting his sanctification. Neither did he ever voice the fear that his
carcass might rot in the wilderness. The tone of *Sion's Savior* is confident
and secure, not anxious or fearful. He may have been in the wilderness,
but he believed that soon he would be in Canaan:

> As the Lord surrounded his chosen Israel with dangers deepe to make
> his miraculous deliverance famous throughout, and to the end of the
> world, so here behold the Lord Christ, having egged a small handful
> of his people forth in a forlorn wilderness, stripping them naked from
> all humane helps, plunging them in a gulph of miseries, that they may
> swim for their lives through the Ocean of his Mercies, and land
> themselves safe in the armes of his compassion.[32]

Recognizing that the metaphor was both "literall" and "mysticall," and
that "assuredly the spirituall fight is chiefly to be attended, and the other
not neglected, having a neer dependency," Johnson still tended to emphasize the literal over the "mysticall." There is a suggestion, as with
Bulkeley, that somehow "chusing rather to dwell on the backside of this
desert" assures that "our God will appear for our deliverance." There
was a clear correlation in Johnson's mind between "the Redemption of
the people of Christ" and "the great hardships Gods people have undergone in this wilderness-worke."[33]

Johnson was no Antinomian claiming assurance of salvation. He did
recognize the need for continual wilderness trials, but there is a growing
sense of self-confidence evident in his work that sets him apart from the
anxious sensibility of Hooker's or Shepard's preaching. He did not

confess himself "in Christ," but all of the evidence reveals a man who had few doubts of his own and his communities' eventual salvation. His exaggerated use of wilderness imagery can be read, perhaps, as unconscious compensation for this assurance. He used it as if the repetition of the word could make up for the nearly Antinomian self-confidence he felt. In a similar manner, his martial calls to "battell" can be read as a means by which he reassured himself of the strength and vigor of his faith.

Both of the strains that made up New England Puritanism thus can be seen in tension in this work. Johnson's emphasis on wilderness trials marked him as a member of the first generation. But his growing awareness that New England soon would be a garden revealed tendencies in his thinking that would blossom forth in the second and third generations.

iii

In the Antinomian controversy, John Cotton had managed to persuade his orthodox inquisitors that he would follow their interpretation of doctrine. Not willing to be a martyr for conscience's sake, he curbed his theology in order to remain in the relatively comfortable community of Boston. Unlike Bulkeley and Shepard, he felt no need for further wilderness trials. And as if to prove his orthodoxy he went a step further, waging in the 1640s, a pamphlet war against another mad enthusiast, Roger Williams. In this debate, Cotton became the champion of orthodoxy. The issue was the same one that had caused him so much trouble in 1636, but this time Cotton was more careful. He defended the orthodox position vigorously, and in the process he took the opportunity to articulate his new position.

Typology, as has been noted, had a tendency to merge into allegory and symbolism. Types became symbols not just of New Testament antitypes but of universal themes. The type was the literal Old Testament prefiguration of Christ, the personification of eternal truth. Thus the type pointed to the antitype, Christ, which in turn pointed beyond to Eternity. This is the importance of symbols, that they point beyond themselves to higher truths otherwise unapproachable by what Calvin called "the stupidity of human understanding." For instance, the symbolic importance of the figure of Jesus Christ was as a representation of the possibility of a fulfillment beyond the comprehension of rational human consciousness. "The human mind," so Jung confirmed, "can form almost no conception of this totality, because it includes not only the conscious but also the unconscious psyche, which is, as such, inconceivable and irrepresentable."[34] According to this position, there is a wholeness toward which human life is groping. But are we, as individuals or as a community, already in Canaan, or are we still in the dark groping for that ultimate fulfillment? That was the debate that divided the Antinomians from their opponents. It was also the question that divided Cotton and Roger Williams. In more secular terms, this same question continues to divide Americans today.

Roger Williams, like Ann Hutchinson and her followers, believed himself to be one of those "in Christ." Furthermore, he insisted from the moment of his arrival in New England that only such as he were truly Christian and worthy of membership in Christ's church. His expulsion from Massachusetts Bay stemmed from his insistence that the churches of the Bay were not sufficiently cleansed of unregenerate practices, members, and associations. So consistent was Williams in his belief that the church was a congregation of true believers only, that he objected to the preaching of conversion. What purpose is there, he asked, in urging conversion upon those already saved? It was a "most preposterous thing among a converted Christian people."[35] New England, according to Roger Williams, was clearly intended to be a Canaan and not a wilderness.

What must be understood, as Sacvan Bercovitch has shown,[36] is that Roger Williams denied the continuing validity of the type once the antitype had completed or fulfilled it. Once a person is truly converted and truly Christian, according to Williams, the Old Testament types no longer apply. The acceptance of Christ, the antitype, so Williams believed, liberated the faithful from the Old Testament types. Thus, these types could no longer be used, as Cotton used them, as a guide either for individuals or the commonwealth. Williams was for an "absolute separation of the literal and the spiritual."[37] For Williams, the Old Testament type was a literal object; its New Testament antitype the spiritual reality of which the type was merely a symbol. Believing himself "in Christ," he saw no reason to adhere any further to the type. The wilderness, to him, was a dead letter. All of the Old Testament had been replaced by the spiritual coming of Christ, and only the spiritual was Christ. Once one had embraced the substance, what need could there be for mere symbols?

What appeared particularly dangerous to the practical magistrates at Boston was that in denying the efficacy of Old Testament types, Williams was denying the validity of the social and political system they were trying to establish. His doctrine virtually invalidated the basis for the Puritan theocracy. It would have freed each Christian from the obligations of the covenant and would have transferred the seat of authority from the communities' interpretation of scripture to the individual.

Given the doctrine of Original Sin, such a move could be seen to produce nothing but anarchy.

To Puritans like Winthrop and Shepard, this assumption of individual sanctification must have seemed wholly absurd. But to Williams, their insistence on living at the level of the type, the mere symbol, seemed dangerously obtuse. Williams saw how his neighbors in Massachusetts, having clung to symbolic, typological thinking, already were mistaking the symbol for the spiritual reality. "Let none now think," he warned, "that the passage to New England by sea, nor the nature of the country can do what only the key of David can do—to wit, open and shut the consciences of men."[38]

Like most Calvinists, the ministers of New England realized the danger of an unimaginative literalism. They believed that eternal truth exists beyond this plane and that symbols are a necessary approach to that spiritual reality. At the same time, they agreed that ignorant sinners, mistaking the symbol for the reality, as Williams warned and the Papists proved, can confuse the symbolic with the real. Symbols, while necessary, clearly were dangerous. They agreed with Williams that it was in fact a mistake to confuse the literal journey into the New England wilderness with the spiritual journey of conversion.

However, they also knew that to abandon the use of symbols altogether led to the danger of allowing too much imagination. It was possible, the orthodox feared, that if typological symbolism was abandoned, earthbound sinners could easily mistake their own imaginings for the transcendent reality of Christ. Symbols, by pointing beyond the world to Christ, helped to prevent sinners from imagining that Christ was already come, that the passing moments of joy they occasionally felt were true salvation. They helped to maintain the distance between this world and the next. Williams was not unaware, nor unconcerned, about this possibility. But particularly in his younger days, Williams had been alarmed by the dangers of an unimaginative literalism that threatened, so he thought, to return to the idolatrous sacramentalism of the Roman Church. Types are only symbols, he warned. They should not be taken literally.

The confusion of the literal type with the spiritual antitype was the error that Williams rebelled against. Those who imagined themselves converted, or on the road to conversion, merely because they were recreating the sojourn of the Jews in the wilderness, were dangerously deluded. What is more, those, like Cotton, who argued that the laws and customs of ancient Israel could be translated literally into the laws of a Christian commonwealth, were by their actions denying that the antitype, Christ, had ever come and replaced the type. In his rebellion against this point of view, Williams backed into the other extreme and denied the continuing validity of Old Testament types completely. These, he argued, had all been replaced by the spiritual realities revealed in the New Testament. "God gave unto that national church of the Jews that excellent land of Canaan. . . . God's people are now in the Gospel brought into a spiritual land of Canaan."[39] Believing himself fully in Christ, Williams was determined to live as if the Kingdom of God had already come. Living at the level of the type implicitly denied that the community was in Christ and Williams was no doubter. He was sure of at least his own salvation.

Perry Miller, in his uncharacteristically flawed book on Roger Williams, wrote, "No other New England writer makes so much of an incantation out of the very word 'wilderness'. . . ."[40] This assertion is simply not borne out by the sources. Williams does use the word "wilderness," but his use of it does not match that of Hooker or Shepard, to say nothing of Edward Johnson. What is more important, when Williams does refer to the wilderness, he does so in a significantly different way.

The alternative image to the wilderness is Canaan, the land of milk and honey. But there was another image used to contrast the wilderness conditions, that of the garden in the wilderness, or of flowers growing in the wilderness. Christ's true followers, having survived the trials of the wilderness, were often described by Williams as "the garden of the church" and the members of the church as "the roses and lilies therein."[41]

Williams thought of himself as a flower in the wilderness. After he failed to build a visible church of the only true elect, he fell back on the idea that God's elect, "though scattered," made up an invisible church of which the visible church was only a shadow. His emphasis then, even when discussing the wilderness, was on the scattered garden of Christ's flowers in the wilderness and not on the trials and temptations of the wilderness condition. "As the same sun shines on a wilderness that doth on a garden," he explained, "so the same faithful and all sufficient God, can comforte, feed and safely guide even through a desolate howling wilderness." Here is the same howling wilderness of which Shepard and Hooker wrote, but the emphasis is on the Jews' safe passage and not on their trials.[42]

Williams did not adopt the evangelical stance of calling sinners to the wilderness to be converted. His ministry was directed to those he considered already Christian but who still had to come out of "the wilderness of the world" into the purity of Christ's spiritual garden. Writing to John Winthrop, soon after his expulsion from the Bay, Williams pointed out that Winthrop had already fled Egypt, and he urged him to continue his flight from sin:

Yet if you grant that ever you were as . . . Israel in Egypt or Babel, and that under pain of their plagues and judgements you were bound to leave them, depart, fly out, (not from the places as if the type) but from the filthinesse of their sins . . . , and if it prove, as I know assuredly it shall, that you have come far, yet you never came out of the wilderness to this day: then I beseech you . . . abstract yourself with a holy violence from the dung heap of this earth. . . .

It is characteristic of Williams that he urged Winthrop not to adhere too closely to the metaphor but to depart, not the wilderness of New England but "the filthinesse" of sin.[43]

To Winthrop's puzzled comprehension, Williams seemed to be falling into the errors of medieval monasticism, believing in an ascetic withdrawal from the world to some imagined purity. To the orthodox Puritan, the "dung heap of this earth" was the unavoidable site of mankind's ordeal and it could not be fled, except in death. Human nature was not considered capable of comprehending the glorious wholeness of God. Therefore symbols had to remain symbols. Was not Jesus Christ both man and God? Was not the Exodus both an historical occurrence and a spiritual type? Was it possible that Williams believed humans could attain perfection this side of the final resurrection? Williams argued as if the ideal had somehow replaced the real. But Winthrop, observing his own wayward soul as well as the world about him, saw the obvious evidence of corruption still abounding.

This was the argument that Cotton tried to impress upon Williams, that the literal type and the spiritual antitype cannot be separated in this life, that, as Bercovitch later wrote, "The acts both of Israel and of New England are simultaneously literal and spiritual."[44] But Williams imagined himself to exist on a transcendent plane above the "dung heap" of humanity. Christ was his. The spiritual had replaced the carnal types. Those who could not see it, whose eyes were on the mud and not the glory, were simply just not "there."

What finally distinguished Williams from his critics was an unwillingness to be damned. The true sight of sin was for him but a distant memory. He was at peace with himself, at ease in Zion. His writings do not exhibit the neurotic anxieties that distracted Shepard. On the whole, they reveal a man of great self-confidence, a man who felt not the raging sea of terror but what he imagined to be the serenity of Christ's grace. If he was aware of subconscious terror, his writings do not show it. His *Experiments of Spiritual Life and Health* is calm and reasonable. In it, he did not urge upon his wife the healing terrors of the surgeon's lance. "Godly sorrow," he assured her, is "not inconsistent but subservient to spiritual joy."[45]

Williams' eccentric assurance of his own salvation marked him as a
rebel against the sober theology of the founders. In the 1630s, he had
been a dangerous heretic. But his example, as it turned out, foreshadowed the direction New England was heading. By the end of the
century, there were few left who remembered what the fuss had been
about, and fewer yet who cared.

With the deaths of Thomas Hooker in 1647, Thomas Shepard and
John Winthrop in 1649, and John Cotton in 1652, the dominance of the
first generation ended. The second generation of New England Puritans, the first born and brought up in the new land, inherited their
parents' religion but not their experience. As Shepard had feared, this
new generation, raised in prosperity and security with "no enemies to
hunt you to heaven, nor chains to make you cry," never had to suffer the
trials that open up the worldly to the experience of the fear of God. As a
result, they, like the heretics of their fathers' day, confused time with
Eternity, the material with the spiritual, the symbols with their objects.
They forgot that the wilderness of the fear of God was still within and so
came to believe themselves true children of Israel at ease in the vineyards
of Zion.

Persons who are not sure of their security, who are forced to question
the economic, social, and intellectual assumptions of their native culture,
often are forced to justify themselves as well. Doubts about one's society
can often lead to doubts about one's personal values. Personal identity
and culture are closely associated and dependent upon each other. It was
just such an introspective process that originally led the first generation
into the wilderness of confusion and doubt. The social and political
instability that shook England in the late sixteenth and early seventeenth
centuries forced many "vexed and troubled Englishmen" to re-examine
their loyalties.[46] This look behind the veil of worldy security brought
many face to face with the wilderness within. External political chaos
helped to open the doors of perception and expose the internal chaos
that threatened the self-confidence of each individual and, once acknowledged, threatened the entire social structure. Convinced by experience they called the fear of God, they adopted the religion, Calvinism,
that spoke to their condition by trying to make sense of their fear.
Motivated by this profound anxiety and bouyed by a theology that
sanctified their terror, they ventured into the wilderness of New England in the hope of finding salvation.

But what of the second generation, that of the founders' children?
Never having experienced social and economic chaos, secure from the
chains of oppression and the dragons of persecution, they were welcomed into the covenant without ever having to suffer affliction. As
children of saints, they were even brought into the covenant without

having had an experience of conversion. There should be little wonder that these children, who listened week after week as their ministers extolled the virtues of the New England way, did not share their parents' pious anxiety. Even among the first generation, there had been those who thinking themselves in Christ had rejected the need for converting terror. Those who were brought up on a weekly dose of Peter Bulkeley's sermons could be excused if they imagined themselves to be, not sinners heading for damnation but members of Christ's church growing as in a garden in the wilderness. As Edmund Morgan has noted, "Instead of an agency for bringing Christ to fallen man, it [the church] became the means for perpetuating the Gospel among a hereditary religious aristocracy."[47] The fear of God was for the heathen; they were saints singing the Lord's song in the promised land.

This is not to say that the typical second-generation New England Puritan exhibited all the self-confidence of a Roger Williams; far from it. The assumption of justification implicit in their church membership obliged the children of the saints to undergo a continuous process of self-examination in order to verify their status. There is a certain consistency in assuming oneself a sinner in need of conversion. And there is a definite stability in believing oneself a converted saint. But there was an awful uncertainty in not knowing where one stood. This was the condition of the second generation, uncertain of their professed identity, anxious about their presumed status as saints. This is what lies behind assertions, such as Barrett Wendell's, that "As soon as children could talk, they were set to a process of deliberate introspection, whose mark is left in the constitution of melancholy and frequent insanity. . . ."[48] Out of this came a generation of rigid legalists who professed to be inhabitants of Canaan but secretly feared they might simply be wanderers descending in deeper spirals into the wilderness.

One manifestation of this uncertainty was a rigidly defensive insistence on the rightness of the New England way. The adoption of the Cambridge Platform in 1648 institutionalized the congregational practices that had developed in Massachusetts Bay. The Platform was at the same time an expression of the colonists' desire to affirm their identity, to establish once and for all time who they were and for what purpose they had set out into the wilderness. Not willing to question their inherited identity, they denied that there was any further need to descend into the wilderness. Being at ease in Zion, they denied the need for fear. It was with this attitude that congregationalism became, as Perry Miller said, "a reasonable and sober program" that "would not produce chaos, because those who called themselves saints would bind themselves, through the church covenant, to sobriety."[49]

It was with this sense of a need to affirm their identity as the children

of saints that the second and third generations went to "battell" for the
Lord against Quakers, against Indians, against witches, and against
themselves. To have to undergo conversion would be to admit that they
never had been saints, that they had no right to their parents' pews; this
ritual therefore was denied them. To prove their salvation, they could
only strive harder against the enemies of Christ. In binding themselves
to sobriety, they bound themselves to a set conception of who they were.
Too frightened to face their underlying doubts, they clung to this identity as if to save themselves from the wilderness.

After 1662, those who were willing to do no more than affirm their
allegiance to the New England way bound themselves to sobriety by
owning the covenant and were admitted into partial church membership. Such "half-way" members never had to pretend that they had
undergone conversion. But not all second generation Puritans were at
such ease in Zion. It has been suggested that many of the founders'
children and grandchildren were too "scrupulous" to own the covenant
without first having had an experience of grace.[50] There were some in
the second generation who believed that they at least were still sojourners
in the wilderness, not "wading in" but waiting for grace. Though most
Puritans of the second generation did succeed in convincing themselves,
most of the time, that they were "in Christ," there were a few who
retained a conscious fear of their probable damnation. This division was
on the whole generational. A significant minority of the great migration
survived long enough to denounce the "declension" of their successors.

Among these, Nicholas Street, 1603–74, John Davenport's colleague at
New Haven, objected strongly to the half-way covenant on the grounds
that it would be better to remain in the wilderness than to return to the
ways of old England and allow the unregenerate into the church. The
difference between a converted saint and a pious hypocrite remained for
him a real and important distinction:

> We have suffered many things in vain, in leaving such a country for
> this; our estates, friends, comforts there, to enjoy God, and Christ,
> and our consciences in the Congregational way, in a low afflicted
> condition in the wilderness, for so many years together; and now we
> must lose those things for which we have wrought, and may return to
> our former state when we please, which the Lord preserve us from.[51]

Both Davenport and Street held out stubbornly against the assumption,
implicit in the half-way covenant, that the grandchildren of the saints,
like their parents, were not in desperate need of conversion. They
feared that the churches would soon be filled with tares instead of wheat.

Those like Street and Davenport who dissented from the half-way covenant were making a stand for the wilderness tradition. They insisted that only those who had crossed the wilderness should become members of the New Zion. These pietists held the experience of grace to be so precious that they doubted even their own conversions and were willing to forego church membership themselves if it meant keeping the church, however tiny, pure. Although often church members and even ministers, these Puritans continued to live in the fear of God constantly questioning their own worthiness. Cotton Mather wrote of the reverend John Warham that he was so often thrown into "deadly pangs of melancholy" that he despaired of ever reaching heaven. "Such were the terrible temptations and horrible buffetings undergone sometimes by the soul of this holy man," explained Mather with astonishment, that when he was administering the Lord's supper to his congregation "he had forborne himself to partake at the same time in the ordinance, through the fearful dejection of his mind."[52] Here was a Puritan who did not imagine himself in Canaan but in the wilderness of trial and temptation, still struggling even to his death in 1670 toward the promised land.

Michael Wigglesworth, 1630–1705, revealed in his diary a soul tormented by a fear of damnation so overwhelming that it was rarely, if ever, alleviated by a glimpse of grace. Pride, he confessed, "is a grievious sin against myne own soul. It provokes God to lead me through a howling wilderness of fiery temptations to humble and to prove me and shew me what is in my heart. . . ; he . . . feeds me the Torment of emptiness, with vexation and rebuke where I hoped to have met with comfort." Wigglesworth made use of the traditional Calvinist image of "a bottomless gulf of vileness in my heart" to describe the depths of his corruption. This image of a bottomless pit undercutting human existence can also be found in his poetry:

> What mortal man can with his span mete out Eternity?
> Or Fathom it by depth of wit, or strength of memory?
>
> It is a main great ocean, withouten bank or bound:
> A deep Abyss, wherein there is no bottom to be found.

The bottomless pit of eternity that no man can fathom was no astronomical or philosophical curiosity to Wigglesworth. It was a feeling of bottomless terror that spread out like a wilderness from the "deep Abyss" of his heart.[53]

Jonathan Mitchell, 1624–69, was another second generation minister who retained a strong sense of personal depravity. His diary, excerpted in the *Magnalia,* shows a man still in the torments of the wilderness state. "Lord I am in hell," he cried, "wilt thou let me lie there?"

God hath put this fear in my heart. . . . that I shall never know God for mine in truth, but live and die in an unsound and self-deceiving way: that I should have many fears and prayers, and good affections, and duties, and hopes, and ordinances, and seemings, but never a heart soundly humbled, and soundly comforted unto my dying day: but be a son of perdition to the last, and never have God's special love revealed and assured to me! Lord, keep this fear alive in my heart!

The fear of self-deception and the complete absence of assurance here are strong echoes of the piety of the founders. Mitchell was anxious, not because he had doubts about his status as a saint—he was not that presumptuous—but because he felt he was in the wilderness of hell. Unlike so many of his neighbors, he was not willing to accept "seemings" in place of the real thing. Most characteristic of this piety was his desire, not for immediate assurance of salvation, but for more suffering: "Lord, Keep this fear alive in my heart!"[54]

This piety can also be seen in the *Narrative of the Captivity of Mrs. Mary Rowlandson.* In her narrative, Mrs. Rowlandson admitted that prior to her abduction in 1676, "Before I knew what affliction meant, I was ready sometimes to wish for it." She confessed to having been jealous of others "under many trials and afflictions, in sickness, weakness, poverty, losses, crosses, and cares of the world." But after her captivity she no longer had to be jealous. Dragged "into the vast and howling wilderness," forced to suffer in "a lively resemblance of hell," she abandoned all her worldly attachments and committed her children and her "self also in this wilderness-condition to him who is above all." "When the Lord had brought his people to himself," she continued, "then he takes the quarrel into his own hand: and though they [the Indians] had made a pit, in their own imaginations, as deep as hell, for the Christians," the Lord instead hurled them into it.[55]

In this way Mrs. Rowlandson finally had the conversion she had long desired. The experience she had heard so much about and yearned so hard for was finally hers. In her narrative, the literal wilderness and the symbolic wilderness came together with startlingly dramatic results. Here can be seen the way in which the literal wilderness of New England reinforced the mythic wilderness and brought the cultural symbols of the wilderness tradition home to the colonial populace with blood-chilling validity. The fact that Mrs. Rowlandson's experience in captivity was more a representation of spiritual conversion than the real thing does not appear to have troubled her. The terror was real, the loss was real, and the resulting "dependence" upon the will of God was sincere; that was enough. The difference between inner spiritual experience and outer symbolic experience had become vague. Mrs. Rowlandson's first-generation piety did not prevent her from sharing her own generation's preference for the literal side of the metaphor. As long as her experience fit the model, she could believe that she had undergone a "regeneration through violence." The ancient model may have taken on a new form in her captivity narrative, but the energy that gave life and power to that form was as old as Moses.[56] Indeed, it was Rowlandson's ability to clothe the spiritual with an outward form, to bring the type and the antitype together in a powerful symbol, that accounts for the impact of this masterpiece. "Afflictions I wanted," she wrote, "and afflictions I had." Such afflictions were just what many in New England still wanted. The literal reality of affliction in the wilderness touched the depths of the culture's consciousness. Mrs. Rowlandson did not regret the escape of her tormentors from the pursuing colonists. Instead, true to her Calvinist conscience, she praised "the wonderful Providence of God in preserving the heathen for further affliction to our poor country."[57]

As attention continued to shift from the "invisible world" of the soul to the worldly reality of the literal wilderness, the emotional experience of the fear of God became in the second half of the seventeenth century a rare wonder. Many second and third generation New Englanders assumed, as did Increase Mather, that they were beyond the wilderness, that "the Lord hath given us his good spirit to instruct us, and hath not withheld manna from us, but hath turned this wilderness into a Canaan, and here hath he given us rest. . . ." In this same sermon, Mather complained "O how rarely do we hear of a sound work of conversion." Only occasionally did it occur to him that the wilderness had become Canaan in the material sense only, that only the symbolic wilderness and not the wilderness of mind had been crossed. It was at such times that he could say,

> As the children of Israel went through the Red Sea, and through the wilderness, before they could enter into Canaan, so must we wade through a Red Sea of troubles, and pass through a wilderness of miseries, ere we can arrive at the heavenly Canaan.

Despite occasional references to the need for wilderness trials, Mather continued to believe New England to be Canaan. This inconsistency was reflected in his strong opposition, at first, to the half-way covenant, and his later acceptance of it. He keenly felt the loss of New England's original piety, but he was willing to use the rhetoric, and support the policies, that undermined the wilderness strain of piety with its insistence on depravity and the need for conversion.[58]

This contradiction between rhetoric and reality was no more apparent to Mather's colleagues in the 1670s than it was to him. The Jeremiads of that period repeatedly called for conversion and reform with language that assumed New England already to be the promised land. The dominant self-image no longer was that of the Jews of the wilderness. It had become that of Israel restored in the land of Canaan, in need not of conversion but of reform. The assumed identity was closer to that of Roger Williams than of Thomas Hooker. Its emphasis was on the Lord's garden and on his hedge surrounding and protecting that garden from the wilderness.[59] The call to enter into the wilderness was not to the unregenerate nor to backsliding Christians. It was directed to those members of Christ's churches whose status as saints was not radically questioned, to consider, as Samuel Danforth said,

> whether our ancient and primitive affections to the Lord Jesus, his glorious gospel, his pure and spiritual worship, and the order of his house, remain, abide, and continue firm, constant, entire, and inviolate.[60]

Here was no radical call to become transformed; here was a reformer's plea that New England try to improve. Danforth was simply asking the people to question whether they were still as good and holy as he presumed they had always been.

Urian Oakes, 1631–81, also pleaded with New England to reform, but the need for reformation did not alter his assurance that New England had been chosen by God to be a Canaan and that "what he thought in his heart he hath fulfilled with his hand, in bringing you to this good land." No longer was the journey into the wilderness a type of terror and affliction. Instead, Oakes claimed that "God hath . . . allured you into this wilderness . . . that you might set up his way and worship in the purity and gospel glory of it." He reminded the people, not of their sins, but of their blessings, that "this Canaan, though a wilderness," flows with milk and honey. Because God had sheltered and fed his people, Oakes reasoned, surely they had a greater duty to walk in his way. Yet for all of his exhortations to reform, Oakes was unable to abandon the metaphor that worked to defeat his efforts. As long as New Englanders continued to be told, and to believe, that "God hath fed us in this desert land, and compassed us about, and kept us as the apple of his eye," they could not be expected to walk in fear of him.[61]

The most revealing of these Jeremiads is Thomas Shepard's *Eye-Salve* of 1673. Shepard, unlike his famous father, did not desire to "be more humbled" in the wilderness of afflictions. The text he chose for this sermon was God's question, "Have I been a Wilderness to Israel?" God's answer to this question, according to Shepard, was an offended "NO!" Shepard defined wilderness as a place where men "meet with nothing but wants, and terror, and woe, etc. and it may seem to allude to the state of the children of Israel in the wilderness." To him, it was clearly a place to be avoided. His God was insulted by the very notion that He had been as a wilderness to his people:

> A wilderness is not hedged in, nor fenced about. . . . Have I been so to you? . . . Have you not been as an enclosed garden to me, and I a wall of fire round about you?[62]

Bemoaning the fact that the affections of God's people toward Him "alter with the change of their wilderness into a fruitful field," Shepard called on the people not to slide into disobedience but to cling harder to their inheritance. He advocated stricter adherence to the law and stricter repression. Here was the standard second generation Puritan, brought up in a fruitful paradise, convinced of his righteousness, and terrified by the possibility that his paradise might lapse back into wilderness:

> I say if after all this we will now turn our back, and revolt from God, we may then expect that the Lord turn this fruitful land into a wilderness again . . . , that God should be a wilderness, and a land of darkness to thee O New England!

What Shepard failed to realize was that in terms of the metaphor, New England was still in the wilderness and still in need of conversion. He mistook the type for the antitype and thought that New England's material prosperity was grace. When the elder Shepard had written, "New England's peace and plenty of means breeds strange security," it was his own son to whom he was referring.[63]

The younger Shepard tried to protect New England from the wilderness by calling for an increased militancy in support of the New England way. He urged stricter enforcement of the laws, more strenuous oppression of heretics, and greater discipline for the whole society. His need to be "preserved from a wild wilderness-state"[64] extended from his psyche to his theology to his society. Under all of Shepard's anger lay a vast sea of unconfessed anxiety. Unlike Wigglesworth, he could not interpret this to be Godly doubt about his own salvation. If anyone was making him doubt, it had to be the Devil. He responded to his fears, not as his father might have by welcoming them in the hope of conversion, but as one too scared of doubt to confess it. Having grown up with the belief that he was one of God's elect in God's own Canaan, a member of a community already past its wilderness trials, he no longer cherished a desire for affliction. His father's sense of identity had thrived on threats to its existence, but the younger Shepard could not tolerate such threats. Too unsure of his inherited identity to wear it confidently, he was too afraid of the wilderness within to surrender, as his father might have, to the fear of God. His was a tenuous assurance clinging desperately to itself. To him, the wilderness was not the hope of salvation; it was a Satanic threat to everything he believed in.

Certainly more complex than Shepard, though not altogether different, Cotton Mather also viewed the wilderness as a realm of Satanic threats. No ego in New England was ever bolstered by a greater sense of historical place and tradition. The grandson of John Cotton and Richard Mather and the son of Boston's leading minister, Increase Mather, Cotton Mather developed a personal identity indistinguishable from his understanding of his community's identity.

Mather never denied the validity of the wilderness as a type of conversion, nor did he deny the need for conversion, but like many of his generation, he assumed that New England had crossed the wilderness successfully. "A people are often brought into a wilderness of difficulties and emergencies," he confirmed in 1689, "but if God be with them he guides them to a good issue of them all."[65] Surely, God had been with New England in its crossing into the wilderness of America. The "good issue" was the obvious evidence.

For such a people, secure in Christ, already cultivating their vineyards in the promised land, the wilderness could only be a threat. Mather used the story of Christ's temptation in the wilderness, not to typify conversion, but as a "figure" of the converted Christian who is then "exposed unto the buffetings and outrages of" the devil, "producing a most horrible anguish of his mind." This was to him a clear prefiguration of the ordeal of those Christians "driven into the American Desert, which is now called New England, [who] have to their sorrow seen Azazel [the Devil] dwelling and raging there in very tragical instances."

> It is written concerning our Lord Jesus Christ, that he was led into the wilderness to be tempted of the devil; and the people of the Lord Jesus Christ, 'led into the wilderness' of New England, have not only met with a continual temptation of the devil there—the wilderness having always had serpents in it—but also they have had, in almost every new lustre of years, a new assault of almost extraordinary temptation upon them; a more than common 'hour and power of darkness.'

Here was a use of classic wilderness imagery, complete with serpents and temptations, in which conversion is never mentioned. It was assumed already to have taken place. The people being tempted, in Mather's analysis, were already like Christ assured saints.[66]

Mather did not doubt his own conversion, or that New England was the prefigured land of Canaan. Doubts concerning these basic tenets of his identity were perceived not as calls to convert from worldly attachments but as demonic assaults from Satan. Like Shepard, he defended an established identity against a hostile and doubting world. Both at home and abroad, economic, political, intellectual, and social forces threatened to destroy the structure of Puritanism that the second generation had labored so hard to fortify. Mather took it upon himself to be New England's defender.

Like Johnson's *Wonder-working Providence,* Mather's *Magnalia Christi Americana* echoes with reverberations of chanted incantations to the wilderness, but with a difference. Mather used the image of the wilderness repeatedly, on the one hand, to establish the scriptural authenticity of New England's identity as the recreation of the Israel of scripture. He did not use the wilderness image in order to preach conversion; he used it to verify the self-image he was writing to preserve. He adopted wilderness imagery in order to establish his own identity, through that of his community, as a part of the greater identity of Jesus Christ as it was portrayed in both books of scripture.

On the other hand, the wilderness portrayed by Mather was an almost wholly external place. Mather did not deal with the subtle psychology of Thomas Hooker. His wilderness was not of the mind but the literal forest of New England. And just as the wilderness became externalized in his thinking, so did the demons and serpents that inhabited that wilderness. As the devils and imps once crept around the walls of conscience, Indians and witches now crept through the forests in the night.

This is not to say that Mather was a complete rationalist. He was, as most critics agree, a transitional figure, studying Newton at the same time that he defended his belief in the "invisible world." Content, however, just to talk about the invisible world, he saw no need personally to descend into it and wrestle bare-handed with the demons there. He preferred to battle the externalized demons discovered in Salem than to face those that existed in his own subconscious. Content with the view from the fair side of the Jordan, he had no desire to descend into the wilderness: "It is a caution given us in Psal. xxxv.6: 'Thy judgements are a great deep, O Lord,' and we should be very cautious, lest we drown ourselves in such a deep, when we go to fathom it." Religion, for Mather, had become a fairly rational affair. He saw nothing holy in the behavior of a man he called a "mad" enthusiast.[67]

Mather's avoidance of the psychological implications of Calvinist theology was just one product of his need to defend his threatened identity with clarity and concreteness. He was trying to define what New England meant as clearly as possible. To have ventured beyond the borders of rationality would only have threatened to destroy that identity in the waste and howling wilderness. He imagined himself on the constructive, not the destructive side of the conversion process. He was more concerned with defining acceptable patterns of moral behavior, as he did in *Bonifacious: or Essays to Do Good,* than with crucifying his beliefs in the wilderness of the invisible world.

Even *The Angel of Bethesda,* an essay in which Mather sketched an outline of a theory of the subconscious, deals not with conversion but with worldly considerations. The "Nish-math-Chasim," or "the breath of life," a "middle nature between the rationale soule and the corporeal mass," functioned for Mather much as the subconscious functions in the theories of modern psychologists. It controls human behavior "despite conviction of reason," and it prevents us from doing things "which we have heretofore been horribly frightened at." The source of "splenetic and hysteric maladies," it is even the "key" to understanding the existence of witches. Its health is the source of the soul's, and hence the body's, health.

> Let this be remembered; moderate abstinence, and convenient exercise; and some guard against injurious changes of the weather, with an HOLY & EASY MIND, will go as far, in carrying us with Undecayed Garments thro' the wilderness, to the Promised and pleasant land, which we are bound unto, as all the prescriptions with which all the physicians under Heaven have ever yet obliged us.

Here is no mention of sin or the need to purge the soul of sin. Mather has taken the place of the Elizabethan doctors that the English Calvinist, William Perkins, had railed against. Perkins had called on sinners, if they were to gain true health, to suffer the afflictions of the tempest; Mather recommended, in effect, that they eat light, jog, and wear a raincoat.[68]

This loss of the psychological dimension of the meaning of the wilderness ordeal did not begin with Mather. There had always been those who believed themselves beyond the need for holy terror. But Mather was an important figure in the growing literalism and rationalism of the New England mind as it changed from Puritan to Yankee. The tradition of wilderness imagery that had originally carried a mixture of threat and promise quietly divided in the late seventeenth century into a "wilderness strain" and a more literal and self-justifying interpretation of religion. For pietists like Mary Rowlandson, the wilderness still symbolized the promise of conversion. To legalists like the younger Shepard and Mather, the wilderness had become a threat to their established state of grace. This legal and literal strain of New England Puritanism achieved dominance with the ascendency of Cotton Mather. In later years, it became possible for ministers like Thomas Prince to preach an election sermon on a wilderness text and give no indication that the Bible was referring to any wilderness other than the forests of a triumphant New England.

> There never was any people on Earth so parallel in their general history to that of the ancient Israelites as this of New England. To no other country of people could there ever be so directly applied a multitude of scripture passages in the literal sense as to this particular country; . . . one would be ready to think that the greater part of the Old Testament were written about us, or that we, tho' in a lower degree, were the particular antitypes of that primitive people.[69]

The symbol of conversion, the journey into the wilderness, at last replaced the spiritual reality. The literal type no longer pointed to a spiritual antitype. Presuming their land to be Canaan, these New England Puritans forgot about the subconscious wilderness of the fear of God.

Puritanism had arrived in New England bearing the dual strains of Antinomian self-righteousness and Arminian self-doubt. In the beginning, the two halves of this piety were held together in a dynamic tension. The majority of the first generation were neither without hope nor safely converted. They saw themselves as pilgrims on the road to salvation. But as members of the community began to emphasize one or the other extreme, the society became polarized, torn between the head's harsh demands for introspection and the heart's eagerness to wade in grace. In the ensuing struggle for control of the Massachusetts Bay colony, the erroneously labelled Arminians defeated their more enthusiastic rivals. But in a few years, they and their descendants began to believe the assumptions that had once characterized their Antinomian opponents. By the eighteenth century, most of the leaders of New England believed their community to be the sanctified Israel of Canaan building the new Jerusalem in the promised land. Reacting against a self-righteous Antinomianism, they backed into a legal self-righteousness, forgot the spiritual reality behind their fathers' creeds, and became the rigid, rational, repressed "Puritans" so unpopular in later American lore.

Once secure in Canaan, past the need for wilderness conversion, Israel assumed itself beyond justification and progressing steadily through the stages of sanctification. The faithful did not need to be converted; they only had to live up to the requirements of the covenant. In this way, legalism replaced piety. To a people truly in a state of grace so they believed, works could be preached without fear of creating hypocrites. Once salvation was assumed and sanctification begun, ministers believed it safe to preach the duties of holiness. The presumption of holiness thus led inevitably to a theology dangerously close to true Arminianism. The works of the covenant replaced the theology of grace. The doctrine of preparation, originally an insistence that converts suffer in the wilderness, had degenerated into ritual. Cotton Mather's *Essays to Do Good* had replaced Hooker's *Application of Redemption*. Christ's justification had become theirs.

New Englanders of the second generation had tried to live, like Williams, on the level of the antitype, as if Christ had already come and New England had ceased to be a wilderness. The impossibility of this presumption swept them back into legalism and literalism. Once their symbolic language no longer pointed to a higher reality beyond their worldly condition, they began to think of their earthly condition as the Kingdom come. This near-Antinomian presumption of righteousness solidified around a literal Arminianism. Presuming themselves the recipients of the spirit, they believed themselves justified and they tried to lock their santification into place. They thought that their material prosperity proved their spiritual elevation. Were they not in the land that flowed with milk and honey? Presuming their land to be Canaan, they forgot about the subconscious wilderness of the fear of God. The spiritual sense of a terrifying wilderness within the soul was lost.

PART II
Revolutionary Identity

3

The Great Awakening of Fear

"Isai. 40.3. Prepare ye the Way of the Lord, make strait
in the Desart a highway for our God."
from the title page of
Jonathan Edwards' *Some
Thoughts Concerning the
Present Revival of Religion
in New England,* 1742.

i

The Fear of God had burned like a fire in the souls of the first New
England saints. Foremost in their lives had been neither land nor trade
but their belief in the need to burn away the dross of everyday existence
in the crucifying fires of God's holy wrath.

Conviction of personal depravity and the temptation to destroy
oneself in the wilderness for love of God remained the heart and soul of
the Calvinist strain of New England culture. But by the middle of the
seventeenth century other visions vigorously contested the wilderness
strain. Calvinists, once they no longer feared God, could no longer be
called Calvinists; they became either Antinomians or Arminians. The
Antinomian strain was an enthusiastic presumption of sanctification, a
precursor of Oral Roberts and Billy Graham. Arminianism, the third but
rapidly growing strain, was the religion of a bourgeoisie increasingly
addicted to morality and steady profits, a belief that conversion was little
more than sober acceptance of rational doctrines and a resolve to live in
accordance with the moral law. These unorthodox Puritans, both
pietistic Antinomians and legalistic Arminians, had become full of self-
righteousness; by 1700 much of New England had embraced one or the
other extreme. These, whom Jonathan Edwards' grandfather, Solomon
Stoddard, called "legal" and "evangelical" hypocrites,[1] had come to be-

lieve themselves the redeemed of Israel living in righteousness in the promised land.

By the late seventeenth century, the official practice of Puritanism had largely degenerated into a legal Arminianism of laws and ritual. Believing themselves bound as a society to obey God's covenant, the leaders of New England had felt safe in promoting duty and law at the expense of emotional experience. Children born into this covenanted society had self-consciously assumed their place in church and had grown up trying to adhere to the teachings of the law. This trend toward Arminian rationalism had been reinforced by the temptations of a growing commercialism under which order and duty proved highly profitable.

A crisis of identity was in the making. The original identity of New England as the Israel of the wilderness undergoing conversion was being challenged, as it had been from the beginning, by a growing confidence, especially on the Arminian right, that New England already was the Promised Land, that its institutions, if not wholly sanctified, were at least secure, and that the status quo was grace. These "Canaanites" preferred the wordly pursuits of shipping and land speculation to the pursuit of holy feeling. Believing themselves already regenerate, they only needed a weekly diet of moralism to maintain their continued ease in Zion.

Nevertheless, as the society succumbed to the dual temptations of legalism and evangelicalism, the wilderness strain, however subtle, remained alive, undercutting the majority's smug assumptions. From beyond the borders of rational consciousness, the voice of one crying in the wilderness could still be heard over the hedge that protected the New England garden. However the social and economic factors may have generated and sustained this uneasiness, there remained in the culture a yearning to go beyond the established frontier and to plead in the wilderness for the showers of Christ's redeeming grace.

Not all New Englanders at the close of the century accepted the myth that theirs was the promised land and their children God's elect. Aside from those ministers already discussed, Cotton Mather himself acknowledged that the half-way covenant, Congregationalism's compromise with worldliness, had the support only of the leading clergy. The lay members of the church, he confessed, were "stiffly and fiercely set the other way." It has been suggested that many who refused to own the covenant did so not out of indifference but out of an overly "scrupulous" conscience. Within Puritan culture, there remained a nagging sense of sinfulness begging for rebuke, a consciousness of the day-to-day reality of human vanity as a sacrilegious lie. And as Mather's statement indicates, this was a social as well as a mythic division. For it was the leadership of New England that was most willing to conform to the world and the common people who clung stubbornly to the identity of their fathers.[2]

The wilderness fire thus fed on the dry twigs of conscience scattered on the floor of New England's prosperous forest. At times it burned underground, on the roots, almost invisibly. Occasionally it burst upward and ravaged a whole section of forest before being brought under control. The Puritans had brought the fire with them from old England, and their descendants, however much they liked the price of timber, were not willing to let it entirely die out.

The early history of New England is the history of a people torn between two visions: a mysticism that longed for regeneration in the wilderness of soul and a materialism devoted to the planting and nurture of the vineyards of Canaan. Money and morality competed with the ancient demand for an introspective journey into the wilderness of self. It was the tension between these two forces, and the dynamic synthesis of them forged by Jonathan Edwards, that eventually touched off the raging conflagration of American nationalism and, a half century later, fueled the fires of American Romanticism.

ii

That worldly compromiser, Cotton Mather, may have dominated the pulpits and printing presses of Boston at the turn of the century, but he still had to confront the smoldering opposition of those diehards who refused to compromise the Calvinist identity of New England. Caught between the worldly Brattle Street rationalists and the increasingly provocative pietists, Mather strove to protect his New England Canaan from those on the right who would dilute it out of existence and those on the left who would distil it down to the purity of the last drop. As the society slowly divided into rational and pietistic factions, he tried to reaffirm the unity that had characterized his father's society.

But New England had begun to change. The Restoration in 1660 had signalled the end of the autonomy by which the legislatures of the New England colonies had been able to maintain to some degree the exclusive Puritan identity of their communities. In Massachusetts, the Charter was lost, nonchurch members received the right to vote, Baptist and Anglican services were conducted in Boston, and the impulse toward commercialism, already an internal threat, was given a great thrust forward.

From his pulpit in commercial Boston, Mather tried to prevent the complete destruction of the Puritan dream by compromising with the new social and political forces in the hope of preserving at least the memory of the magnificent acts of Christ in America. He made room in his father's creed for the science of Newton and the rationalism of the European Enlightenment. He broke bread with the Boston merchants and agreed to cooperate, to a degree, with Royal authority. Despite Mather's efforts to accomodate, the number of extremists who would abandon Puritanism altogether, or who refused to compromise at all, continued to grow. Mather's complex synthesis did not outlive him.

The Salem witch trials of 1692 have been defined as "a mortal conflict involving the very nature of the community itself." Across New England, at the turn of the century, an older largely rural Puritanism was struggling against the encroaching culture of a growing class of merchants, who, as Bernard Bailyn said, "took the pattern for their conduct not from the Bible or from parental teachings but from their picture of life in Restoration England." Those responsible for the witch trials were trying to strike back at the "invisible" forces that they believed were threatening their traditions and their institutions. The witch trials were part of a growing protest against the abandonment of New England's religious identity to the invisible forces today called "capitalism" or sometimes "modernism." Cotton Mather at first believed that the trials were a necessary purgation that could judiciously be controlled. In the end, he found that passions had been unleashed which threatened to rage out of control. By the time the Governor's wife was accused of witchcraft, Mather was forced to do what he could to put an end to the procedures. But he could not stifle the growing social rebellion of which the trials had been an opening shot.[3]

The boldest challenge to Mather's compromise of the New England way came from the Connecticut Valley when in the 1680s Solomon Stoddard had refused to accept the myth implicit in the half-way covenant that unconverted grandchildren of saints were to some extent elect. By opening full church membership to anyone of decent morals who would own the covenant, regardless of their parent's standing in the church, Stoddard effectively repudiated the official identity of New England's churches as congregations of God's pure saints. By denying any recognizable difference between the elect and the damned, he uprooted the hedge that Puritans like Mather imagined protected their holy garden from the wilderness. By rejecting the assumption that there was any correlation between church membership and election, Stoddard's church abandoned the pretense of piety and became a congregation of sinners traveling the harsh wilderness road of conversion. By denying that New England's church members had any special claim to holiness, Stoddard prepared the way for a renewed emphasis on the evangelical preaching of conversion. Once again the thunder of damnation rumbled across New England as whole congregations were called back into the wilderness of contrition, humiliation, and terror. Where lightning hit dry timber, flames lit up the darkness.

Stoddard did not hesitate to define the problem with characteristic

bluntness: "Some ministers speak a great deal to saints to comfort congregations: the body of the people are in a perishing condition; and
there is ten times more need that men be awakened and terrified."
Stoddard, like Hooker before him, spared neither saint nor sinner. He
believed that a minister, if he intended to bring men and women to
Christ, "had need speak piercing words." And Stoddard used words
most piercingly:

> Men in their natural condition live in a world of sin. . . . Some live in
> ways of sensuality, and wallow like swine in the mire. Some live in ways
> of injustice; they are beasts of prey. Some are mere earth-worms,
> seeking an heaven upon the earth: they are under the curse of the
> serpent; Dust shall be the serpent's meat. And such of them as are
> addicted to morality and religion, are serving their lusts therein. The
> most orderly natural men do live an unGodly life.

Here was the challenge thrown down by pietists like Stoddard to the
orderly ways of the city of Boston, addicted though it may have been to
"morality and religion." Those who imagined themselves saints and who
thought their wordly town the New Jerusalem received no better treat-
ment at Stoddard's hands than did common criminals. Even religion, he
reminded them, can be an idolatrous substitute for grace, as much a
worldly attachment as land or trade, as much an addiction as any expression of pride. Even the religious remain sinners, struggling in the
wilderness under the judgment of the wrath of God.[4]

All hypocrites, Stoddard insisted, whether "legal" or "evangelical," had
to undergo the terrors of preparation before they could expect to be
converted; they had to cross the wilderness before they could enter the
promised land. Just as Israel was led by Moses through a land "of pits
and droughts, and fiery flying serpents, before they were brought into
Canaan by Joshua," so must all sinners be "led into the understanding of
their own hearts." It was not enough, he reminded them, simply to have
an intellectual understanding of sin; they had to have "the experience of
the deceitful turnings and windings of their own hearts." To know
oneself, as Calvin had said, was the first step of conversion.[5]

Sinners, Stoddard affirmed, have good reasons to fear the wrath of
God. The sense of this wrath "is wont to fill them with terror." Individuals forced to confront their undeniable depravity experience a deep
"trouble of mind" and often are "over run with melancholy," and yet
there was no certainty that a descent into this wilderness would lead to
salvation: "Many went out of Egypt that never reached Canaan." Many
went mad and remained there, unable to return to Egypt, unable to go
forward. Their carcasses rotted in the wilderness.[6]

For those who did survive the wilderness and finally reached Canaan, the experience of grace was considered enough to justify the pain. A new being, with new feelings, new thoughts, new perceptions was born in the new land. To Stoddard, this ecstatic experience, like the experience of divine wrath, was a deep experience of mind and soul beyond the ability of language to articulate. Stoddard could only affirm that they who have grace know that they love God "by intuition, or seeing of grace in their own hearts. It is by consciousness."[7]

Once Stoddard revived the evangelical preaching of conversion and reaped "harvests" of new converts, the cracks in New England's self-confident identity began to spread. Mather denounced Stoddard for daring to tear at the hedge that protected New England's garden from the wilderness. "You cannot rationally imagine to attain any other ends," he wailed, "but only to throw all into confusion and contention." Seated comfortably in the New Jerusalem, Mather saw no need for a return to terror. Even in the literal wilderness of western Massachusetts, Edward Taylor looked up from his contemplations of

> Zion's paradise, Christ's Garden Deare
> His Church enwalld, with Heavenly Crystall fine

to protest Stoddard's return to the desert. Although living in a literal wilderness condition, Taylor was one who did not doubt, in the final stanza, that he was truly elect and worthy of Christ's communion table. These protests had little effect on Stoddard and his followers in the Connecticut Valley. Their ancient identity, long dormant, was beginning to awaken. Stoddard reaped five harvests of new converts—in 1679, 1683, 1696, 1712, and 1718—before his death in 1729. But in 1735, and most notably in 1740, his grandson and successor, Jonathan Edwards, took up where his grandfather had left off, preaching conversion with a power that was felt throughout not just New England but the entire English nation.[8]

In 1741, in the fires of revival known as the First Great Awakening, the tension between self-assurance and wilderness self-denial finally broke, and New England split into two warring factions. Those who believed themselves in Canaan stuck by their complacent, worldly moralism; those who believed themselves sinners in the wilderness embraced a vision of the purging fires of the tormented mind. Properly labelling their legalistic opponents "Arminians," the leaders of the Awakening preached the covenant of grace through terror as the only means of regeneration, calling the complacent back from worldliness and morality, urging them to abandon their neat New England gardens in order to embrace the terror of the wrath of God.

Beginning with the arrival of George Whitefield and spreading rapidly through the farms and towns of British North America, the enthusiastic response of the population to the revival stunned the establishment. Whole communities were disrupted as farmers deserted their fields, craftsmen left their shops, wives left their kitchens and church members rejected their ministers in order to be terrified by the preaching of itinerant evangelists. It appeared to the Old Lights as if the entire countryside was going mad. Many did experience extreme distress; the greater the sorrow the wilder seemed to be the visions and the more joyful the deliverance. But there were also those who entered the wilderness and never recovered from despair. The 1735 Northhampton revival ended suddenly when Jonathan Edwards' uncle, Joseph Hawley, at the height of the enthusiasm, "laid violent hands on himself and put an end to his life by cutting his own throat." Melancholy, noted Edwards, was "a distemper that the family are very prone to."[9] Many died in the wilderness who never reached Canaan.

The political and social changes of the 1730s and 1740s—the land bank crisis, the diphtheria epidemic, the disruption of older communities and the creation of new ones, the population boom, the endless legal disputes over land—did contribute to the development of the Awakening, but they did not "cause" the Awakening. These events contributed to the developing crisis by reinforcing the growing realization that New England had forgotten its errand. They were the evidence of God's disfavor, the proof that New England was not God's protected garden after all, and thus they helped to create a crisis of identity. Faced with the reality of a society in which the values and beliefs of Puritanism were gradually giving way to the antagonistic spirit of commercialism, loyal New Englanders were forced to admit that theirs was not a Christian community in need of reform but a community of sinners. The further New England grew from the purity and simplicity of the original vision, the stronger grew the desire to return to the faith of the founders; the greater the changes in society, the greater the sense of sin and the need for forgiving grace.

The Old Lights, who saw no need for madness, followed the lead of ministers from the more commercial towns. The New Lights, individually and then collectively as "Separates," threw themselves into the wilderness, literally and emotionally, in the hope of experiencing salvation and returning with New England to God. The split however was not a political or geographical but a mythic division. Bostonians who believed themselves sinners and in the wilderness in need of salvation rallied to the Awakening.[10] Those who thought themselves secure in Zion, wherever they lived, opposed it. The issue was New England's identity. Was New England the Israel of the desert under the rod of the law, living in tents and sojourning toward the promised land? Or was she the Israel of Canaan, planted in the vineyards of the Lord and free to prosper in the land of milk and honey?

iii

Richard Bushman has successfully placed Jonathan Edwards in the tradition of Erik Erikson's Luther as a "Great Man" whose personal identity crisis mirrored that of his society and whose resolution of that crisis provided the solution to his generation's collective identity crisis.[11]

According to Erikson, the man responsible for introducing the term into modern psychology, an "identity crisis" occurs when an individual's sense of who he or she is no longer provides the basis for a consistent pattern of belief and behavior. Every individual personality is structured around some set of beliefs about the world and that personality's place in the world, but this identity is not wholly conscious. It reaches down into the subconscious and provides the fundamental orientation every functioning personality requires.

Moreover, individual identity is tied to some larger "collective mentality." Just as individuals, communities require cohesive identities if they are to function and prosper. Culture and personality thus go together and reflect each other. According to Erikson, "we deal with a process 'located' in the core of the individual and yet also in the core of his communal culture, a process which establishes, in fact, the identity of those two identities." Identity can be spoken of as "psychosocial":

> The 'socio' part of identity, then, must be accounted for in that communality within which an individual finds himself. No ego is an island to itself. Throughout life, the establishment and maintenance of that strength which can reconcile discontinuities and ambiguities depends on the support of parental as well as communal models. For youth depends on the ideological coherence of the world it is meant to take over, and therefore is sensitively aware of whether the system is strong enough in its traditional form to be confirmed by the identity process, or so rigid or brittle as to suggest renovation, reformation, or revolution. Psycho-social identity, then, also has a psycho-historical side, and suggests the study of how life histories are inextricably interwoven with history.

Individual personality is thus sustained by the existence of a larger cultural identity to which it is tied. Supporting each individual consciousness there is, to use Jung's term, both a collective consciousness and a collective unconscious. Together, these contain all that is meant when we speak of a culture's identity.[12]

That societies require such unifying patterns of belief is, according to the sociologist Robert Bellah, "one of the oldest sociological generalizations." Moreover, these cultural identities "must also in turn rest upon a common set of religious understandings that provide a picture of the universe. . . ." Religion can thus be said to provide the basic building blocks of identity. It is in a person's religion, and in a culture's religion, that can be found the primary beliefs that hold personality and culture together; "that which a man gives his heart to," as Edwards said, "may be called his God."[13]

An identity crisis occurs when an individual can no longer reconcile his or her received identity with the actual demands of life in a particular society. When the values at the foundations of identity no longer correspond to the conscious beliefs of the structure of identity, the house, divided against itself, cannot stand. This crisis, as Erikson implies, can be the result of "parental and communal models" that fail to support the individual's actual behavior and beliefs. According to Bushman, Edwards' generation was faced with just such a crisis. The evolving reality of a commercial culture could no longer be reconciled with the official lie of New England's holy righteousness. The demands of a commercial society, and the disputes engendered, forced people into behavior that all of their received religious values told them was sinful. They believed themselves holy, yet their behavior declared them liars.

> The whole society suffered from a painful confusion of identity. People were taught to work at their earthly callings and to seek wealth; but one's business had to remain subservient to religion and to function within the bounds of seventeenth-century institutions. The opportunities constantly tempted people to overstep both boundaries, thereby evoking the wrath of the powerful men who ruled society. Even relations with neighbors deteriorated as expansion multiplied occasions for hard feelings. At some indeterminate point social values and institutions stopped supporting the man who placed his confidence in worldly success and instead obstructed and condemned his actions. The pleasureable rise which prosperity afforded carried one at last to destruction.[14]

Jonathan Edwards shared his generation's anxiety over the growing split between rhetoric and reality. His personal feelings of guilt were alleviated through confession of his utter sinfulness and helplessness, by yielding himself to God for punishment. This model, already a well-established part of New England's religion, provided a whole generation with a way to adapt their ancient religious beliefs to the reality of eighteenth-century life. By believing themselves, not the righteous Israel of Canaan but the Israel of the wilderness in need of redemption, they could reconcile their lives and their religion; they could keep their faith and earn a living too.

"To believe your own thought," said Emerson, "to believe that what is true for you in your private heart is true for all men,—that is genius; speak your latent conviction and it shall be the universal sense." Edwards spoke his latent conviction and his words struck to the hearts of those who heard him. He participated in their experience and articulated it for them in the familiar language of scripture. Consider, he said. "the great things God did for us at our first settlement in the land; and how he had followed us with his goodness to this day, and how we have abused his goodness; how long we have been revolting more and more (as all confess), and how very corrupt we were become at last." He thus persuaded them that he understood their guilt, and they accepted his identification of New England with the children of the wilderness as a sure foundation for a new identity. No longer self-assured saints, nor sinners in Zion, they became converts on the road to Zion. Edwards did not have to spell out this identity; his very language and emphasis displayed all of the mythic identity with convincing power. His own stance, firmly in the Fear of God, was a fit model. "There is a language in actions;" wrote Edwards, "and in some cases much more clear and convincing than in words." Edwards' own actions, undergoing the trials of conversion, preaching as had Moses the need for repentance, welcoming the wilderness of fear, communicated his meaning.[15]

The Great Awakening thus was a reaffirmation of New England's original identity. The assumption of a pre-established covenanted relationship with God was no more. New Englanders could no longer rely on the communal covenant to save them. Each individual had to face God in the wilderness alone. The sons and daughters of New England's saints, particularly, had felt the hypocrisy of their parents' faith. As often is the case, discrepancies between pious parental rhetoric and social reality were a scandal to the young. For them, mammon was no substitute for Jehovah. They thirsted for the heavy sense of purpose that had sent their great-grandparents into the wilderness one hundred years before. It was primarily the young who, as Erikson said, depend "on the ideological coherence of the world," who stared for a moment into the pit beyond belief and then embraced their new identity with enthusiasm.

The youthful nature of the Awakening was apparent at the time. Edwards noted that as with the Jews of the desert and the "Babylonish captivity," the Awakening "has been chiefly among those that are young; and comparatively but few others have been made partakers of it." And once again the model for the Awakening was the familiar one of the sojourn of the children of Israel:

> God by his aweful judgements that he executed in the wilderness, and the afflictions that the people suffered there, convinced and humbled the younger generation, and fitted them for great mercy. . . ; but he destroyed the old generation: 'he swore in his wrath that they should not enter into his rest,' Heb. 3.11. 17–18.

Edwards did not ignore the older members of his congregation. He repeatedly urged them into the wilderness, but they proved stubborn, and he was forced to warn them to cease their objections "lest while God is bringing their children into a land flowing with milk and honey, he should swear in his wrath concerning them, that their carcasses shall fall in the wilderness." The formula was thus repeated until the identification of the children of the Awakening with the children of Israel in the wilderness was made complete.[16]

In Salem in 1692 the terrifying experiences of a few young girls had been interpreted by the entire community as the work of witches. In Northampton in 1735 and 1741 when several young girls experienced similar terrors, the community interpreted the event as the beginning of a work of conversion. As Boyer and Nissenbaum have shown, the difference between the two episodes was "the interpretation which the adult leadership of each community placed upon physical and emotional states which in themselves were strikingly similar."[17] The difference between the two communities was one of identity. The residents of Salem Village had believed themselves a beleagured community of saints in no further need of holy terror. As had Mather, they interpreted the afflictions to be the work of Satan and his hordes. For a community secure in Canaan, there could be no other explanation.

On the other hand, Northampton under the preaching of Stoddard and Edwards had by 1735 become used to thinking of itself as a community of sinners in need of conversion. This change in self-image provided a different context in which to interpret behavior remarkably similar to that which had occurred in Salem. The people of Northampton, believing themselves in an unconverted state, were ready to welcome the afflictions that struck their community as the first signs of conversion. No longer certain of their election, but convinced of their active sinfulness, they required alleviation of their guilt through punishment. Terror no longer threatened an established holiness; it now promised a way out of decline into a state of unparalleled greatness. The authorities had been able to contain the Salem rebellion. In the Great Awakening they were not as successful. The people ran and embraced terror, for it both alleviated their guilt and provided them with a new identity that charged their lives with the enthusiasm of a cosmic sense of purpose.

This re-awakening of New England's ancient identity, if Bushman is correct, owed a great deal to Edwards' own interpretation of that identity and his ability to articulate it. As the Puritanism of the founders receded into the past, supplanted by a mercantile economy and an Arminian, almost Anglican, theology, young New Englanders, no longer secure in their received identity, responded enthusiastically to Edwards' preaching. Torn between pious rhetoric and worldly prosperity, between ancient dogma and the contemporary learning, between an exhausted dogmatics and the excitement of an expanding society, they found Edwards' synthesis of the ancient rhetoric with the latest science, of Calvinism with an expansive nationalism, to provide an irresistible solution to their cultural identity crisis.

It was Edwards' fate to be Calvinism's most articulate champion in the face of its decline under the dual onslaughts of rationalism and enthusiastic revivalism. At a time when men were learning how to govern themselves, Edwards preached the slavery of predestination under the sovereignty of God. As men began to view the universe with growing security, Edwards preached the irrational nature of the human mind. For these crimes against the enlightenment, he has been labelled a reactionary, "the last medieval American," a man "crippled by his Puritan heritage" who "merely wasted himself reimprisoning the mind of New England." Even those in the forefront of today's revival of interest in Edwards praise his "aesthetics," as if he could be respected, as one critic said, only "if the theology can be wiped clean of our reading of his works."[18]

To slight Edwards' theology, however, is to miss the point that, as Perry Miller stated, it was the liberals who "spoke in the language of outmoded science" and it was Edwards who "put his case upon a modern, dynamic, analytic psychology . . ." It was for this reason, because Edwards "brought the new science and the ancient regeneration together in an exhilarating union" that his rearticulation of Calvinism had such a powerful effect on his and on later generations of Americans. The Puritan tradition was channeled through Edwards and changed. A system of thought that had appeared doomed was instead restructured upon the new philosophical foundations provided by Newton and Locke. Because of Edwards' insightful reading of the new science and the old theology, Calvinism, albeit in a new form, was born again.[19]

Moreover, Edwards' insights continue to have relevance today. With the rediscovery of determinism in the twentieth century old questions have arisen to baffle a new generation. Not the least of these is the problem of the role of ideas and of moral responsibility in a thoroughly behaviorist system, a problem that historians and lawyers are particularly plagued by. It is possible that a study of Edwards' handling of these problems might provide more light than has commonly been recognized. For Edwards' system was thoroughly determinist, but ideas and feelings, rather than being discounted, were central to Edwards' understanding of how the will is determined by the environment; and much of his labor involved explaining how moral responsibility can be reconciled with a thoroughly determined universe.

According to George Bancroft, "he that would know the workings of the New England mind in the middle of the last century, and the throbbings of its heart, must give his days and nights to the study of Jonathan Edwards."[20] If we are to understand the "throbbings" at the heart of New England culture at the time of the Revolution as well as during the Transcendental Renaissance, it is to Edwards that we must turn in order to understand the dimensions of the new identity he established. And if New England's ancient religion is to be appreciated as "a modern, dynamic, analytic psychology," if the wilderness can legitimately be understood as the chaos of what today is called the subconscious mind, it is to Edwards that we must turn to prove it.

iv

We can conceive but little of the matter; . . . But to help your conception, imagine yourself to be cast into a fiery oven, all of a glowing heat, or into the midst of a glowing brick kiln, or of a great furnace, where your pain would be as much greater than that occasioned by accidentally touching a coal of fire, as the heat is greater. Imagine also that your body were to lie there for a quarter of an hour, full of fire, as full within and without as a bright coal of fire, all the while full of quick sense; . . . And after you had endured it for one minute, how overbearing would it be to you to think that you had to endure the other fourteen!

But what would be the effect on your soul, if you knew you must lie there enduring that torment to the full for twenty-four hours! And how much greater would be the effect if you knew you must endure it for a whole year! And how vastly greater still, if you knew you must endure it for a thousand years! O then, how would your heart sink if you thought, if you knew, that you must bear it forever and ever! That there would be no end!

This is the death threatened in the law. This is dying in the highest sense of the word. This is to die sensibly; to die and know it; to be sensible of the gloom of death. This is to be undone; this is worthy of

the name of destruction. This sinking of the soul under an infinite
weight, which it cannot bear, is the gloom of hell. We read in Scripture
of the blackness of darkness; this is it, this is the very thing. We read in
Scripture of sinners being lost, and of their losing their souls: this is
the thing intended; this is to lose the soul: they that are the subjects of
this are utterly lost.

This is what it meant to "die sensibly," to die and know it, to suffer in the
flesh all of the mental agony of Christ upon the cross, to yield to
annihilation and remain forever in the blackness of darkness, full of
quick sense, conscious of every burning second—alone—forever. This
was the terror of the void, the threat of eternal nothingness; this was the
wrath of God; this was the wilderness that had to be crossed.[21]

Jonathan Edwards preached terror not to scare people into being
good but "in a use of awakening to impenitent sinners,"[22] to force them
into the depths of panic beyond the walls of the self's defenses. He
preached terror as a means of forcing sinners to see themselves as God
must see them in the hope that this might drive them out of their minds
and be the means of their conversion from natural depravity to the
selflessness of the love of God. "Something will have the heart of man,"
and if it is the self, then it cannot also be God. The self must be destroyed
before there can be true love of God. Otherwise, that which is called love
is only a projection of self-love. Human beings cling so tightly to their
straw egos that it takes an extraordinary effort to make them let go and
lunge for the sure and steady rock that alone might save them from
drowning. It takes terror.

The experience of conversion, the experience that Edwards urged on
his congregation, was what today would be called a psychological crisis.
The wilderness that he called on sinners to cross was the howling desert
of the soul, and the experience of conversion, as he defined it, was the
destruction of the self, the ego, in the chaos of the subconscious mind.
This is not to say that God can be identified with the subconscious; it is to
say that what was called the wrath of God was made manifest to individual humans in that region today labeled the subconscious. The terror of
the wrath of God was the terror of psychic disintegration. But in Edwards' view, conversion could not take place until the old ego was yielded
to that terror; before this occurred, there could be no re-integration, no
discovery of wholeness, no psychic health. The Calvinist image of consciousness as a think layer of rationality suspended over howling chaos
can be found in modern psychology. C. G. Jung believed that humans
had to be exposed to the subconscious before they could achieve wholeness, and the subconscious he knew to be terror:

The opening up of the unconscious always means the outbreak of intense spiritual suffering; it is as when a flourishing civilization is abandoned to invading hordes of barbarians, or when fertile fields are exposed by the bursting of a dam to a raging torrent. The World War was such an irruption which showed, as nothing else could, how thin are the walls that separate a well-ordered world from lurking chaos. But it is the same with every single human being and his reasonably ordered world. His reason has done violence to natural forces which seek their revenge and only wait the moment when the partition falls to overwhelm the conscious life with destruction.[23]

Sanity, like civilization, is a fragile fabric. It is a rotten covering barely able to cover the seething cauldron below. Edwards was preaching the same message that the modern psychologists know: that the only way to get from the lies of the ego to a sight of truth is to plunge into the wilderness of insanity and to come out on the other side in the promised land of vision.

Edwards insisted that "preaching in a known tongue conveys something to the understanding which preaching in an unknown tongue doth not."[24] Edwards' own tongue, that of eighteenth-century theology, has in the twentieth century become an unknown tongue. It is therefore necessary, if we are to enter into Edwards' thought, to translate his language into modern terms, and the modern tongue that comes closest is that of modern psychology. It is the psychologists who have taken over where the theologians of Edwards' world left off.

There is nothing new in this; nor was there anything new in Edwards' use of human psychology as an entrance into theology. The first line of Calvin's *Institutes* states, "Without knowledge of self there is no knowledge of God."[25] God existed, not in space, not in time, but in consciousness. It was there that he had to be sought. That was why the children of Israel had to wander for forty years in the wilderness: "to humble thee, and to prove thee, and to know what was in thine heart" (Deut. 8.2). Natural men loved only themselves; these idols of vanity had to be pushed aside before there could be a sight of Christ. But before any persons would willingly accept the destruction of the self, they had to know the horror of their own complete depravity. Before they could clean the window to look out toward God, they had to know that the window was dirty.

The symptoms of suffering what Edwards called the fear of God are not unknown today. Instead of being perceived as a form of religious experience, such symptoms as thought and language confusion, disorientation, disorganization, illusion, "somatic, grandiose, religious, nihilistic, or other delusions," are categorized under the overarching term, "schizophrenia." This is not to argue that religious experience as defined by Edwards was simply undiagnosed mental disease. It could as easily be argued that what is today called a disease was once recognized as an essential part of a process of psychic regeneration. From whatever perspective one faces the problem, it is important to see that the reformed theologians and the psychologists are talking about the same human experience but looking at it from different intellectual contexts. Edwards did not invent the symptoms of conversion; he was talking about a real event. Modern psychology has simply taken over and given negative value judgments (as Cotton Mather did!) to what once was interpreted in a more constructive light. As Thomas Szasz has written, "with the decline of religion and the growth of science in the eighteenth century, the cure of (sinful) souls, which had been an integral part of the Christian religions, was recast as the cure of (sick) minds."[26]

An explication of Edwards in psychological terms should not be assumed to be a reduction of theology to psychology, as if the psychological language, being modern, had to take precedence. These can be thought of as two thought-systems each with its own internal validity and consistency. A comparison of them can be made because the two systems overlap. It is through this area of shared perception, in the analysis of human consciousness, that modern scholars most easily can enter into the thinking of Jonathan Edwards. For in Edwards' theological account of human nature and its relation to God can be found a behaviorist analysis of human consciousness remarkably similar to the behaviorism of B. F. Skinner. Moreover, coupled with this analysis can be found a therapeutic technique that foreshadowed many of the insights of Freud.[27]

To compare aspects of the works of different thinkers from different eras raises complex questions of influence and continuity in intellectual history. Skinner was brought up in the Presbyterian Church and there is evidence that he was introduced to Edwards while in college.[28] However, to stress the extent to which an early reading of Edwards may have influenced Skinner is to miss the point that each man developed his ideas within a separate worldview and for different ends. Edwards sought to rebuild a disintegrating theistic philosophy and to re-establish the Christian concept of conversion on the new foundations of Lockean psychology. He did this in order to provide a more effective means for the conversion of sinners from the tyranny of determinism to the freedom of regeneration. Skinner developed his behaviorism within the context of a materialistic science of human psychology in order to secure the greatest happiness for the hapless prisoners of a determined universe.

Yet, the analyses of mind with which both men began do overlap.

Crucial to each was a logical, systematic application of the law of cause and effect to human consciousness. But this alone cannot account for the parallels. There is, instead, an intriguing suggestion of continuities in man's understanding of mind that transcend cultural context, of a perception of consciousness recurring in different men of different eras that serves as the common root of trees bearing different fruit. Edwards and Skinner put their shared insights to different ends, but this does not alter the fact that they share a similar insight into what Herman Melville called that "Calvinistic sense of Innate Depravity and Original Sin, from whose visitations, in some shape or other, no deeply thinking mind is always or wholly free."[29] Understanding this shared insight should enable those of a modern, secular sensibility to understand Edwards and his concept of conversion in the wilderness of the depraved human mind.

A number of Edwards' works, notably *Religious Affections, Original Sin,* and *The Nature of True Virtue,* deal in a complex manner with questions of human nature. But of all his writings on human consciousness, Edwards' *Freedom of the Will,* the work by which he was known to friends and to foes, remains the most important. For the doctrine of determinism was the foundation of Edwards' psychology. Man's depravity and his utter helplessness before God are best displayed in the doctrines of predestination. No sermons are more affecting, said Edwards, "than those in which the doctrine of God's absolute sovereignty with regard to the salvation of sinners . . . have been insisted on." Nowhere was the truth of God's power felt more powerfully than here. He who saw the truth of this doctrine was truly awakened; he who felt the truth of this doctrine felt the full terror of the wrath of God.[30]

v

Edwards began by denying the existence of anything that might be called "free will." Every idea, every emotion, every response is determined, he said, before it is thought, or felt, or made. Human beings imagine that their wills are free, that they are in control of consciousness, but it is not so. To be awakened to this realization was to be pushed the first step beyond the wall that separates the well-ordered world from chaos. It was the first step into the wilderness of the mind.

"All exercises of the will," wrote Edwards, "are in some degree or other, exercises of the soul's appetition or aversion; or which is the same thing, of its love or hatred." Since human behavior is always a matter of making choices, he argued, all decisions must depend upon pre-established ideas, attitudes, and feelings; the law of cause and effect demands it. Also called the "affections," these "inclinations of the heart" are the "prejudices" of the personality. The understanding judges and decides, but decision is based upon the inbred loves or hatreds of the heart.[31]

Edwards never denied that people have liberty. People are free, he said, to do whatever they want; it is the *wanting* that is not free. Liberty

> is the power, opportunity, or advantage that anyone has to do as he pleases, or conducting in any respect according to his pleasure; without considering how his pleasure comes to be as it is. . . . Is not choosing, choosing as he pleases, conducting in some respect according to his pleasure, and still without determining how he came by that pleasure?

If every "free" decision is determined by some prior inclination of the heart, then having liberty simply meant being able without physical restraint to follow one's inclinations. Having liberty did not free the will from its dependence on the heart, and the heart, explained Edwards, derived these all-important inclinations from a process of environmental conditioning which ultimately was controlled by God. Thus every human act was determined ultimately by God.[32]

Edwards did not, of course, know the language of modern behaviorism, but he did define the environmental stimuli that elicits behavior as a "motive." It is, he said, that motive, whether "one thing singly, or many things conjunctly," which "as it stands in the view of the mind, is the strongest, that determines the will." The reason why some motives elicit a stronger response than others, he explained, lies in the "particular temper that the mind has by nature, or that has been introduced and established by education, custom, or some other means." The relationship between the perceiving mind and its object is what determines the relative strength of motive. Both contribute to the relationship, but it is the prior "state of mind," or "inclination of the heart," that determines what motive will appear strongest and thus determines behavior.[33]

There is no doubt that Edwards derived many of his ideas about human psychology from Locke, but it is clear that Edwards modified Locke adding to his strict sensationalism a belief in inherited instincts. His analysis begins, as did Locke's, with the belief that "opinions arising from imagination take us as soon as we are born, are beat into us by every act of sensation, and so grow up with us from our very births." But Edwards also believed in certain inherited "dispositions [which] may be called instincts," and that through the reactions of these instincts to the daily shock of sensation children acquire those ideas that make up the prejudices of the personality. Primary among these instincts was an inclination in favor of one's own preservation, a survival instinct. Edwards called it "self-love," and he considered it the instinct upon which all subsequent perceptions of love and hate were based. Because a child is born with this prejudice in favor of its own existence and comfort, it can make simple decisions and form the behavior patterns necessary for survival:

> Is there need of great degree of subtlety and abstraction, to make it out, that a child, which has heard and seen much, strongly to fix the idea of the deadly pernicious nature of the rattlesnake, should have aversion to that species or form, from self-love; so as to have a degree of this aversion or disgust excited by seeing even the picture and representation of that animal?

It is precisely here, in his understanding of how "the habitual connection" of these reactions "with the form and qualities of these objects . . . are impressed in the mind of the child" that Edwards' behaviorism most closely resembles Skinner's. In both systems, innate inclinations react with environmental stimuli to form patterns of response, the emotions and beliefs that then determine the later behavior of every individual.[34]

Skinner, studying the behavior patterns of pigeons, argues that human beings respond as pigeons do, with behavior that is habitual and not the product of free will. Edwards noted the same processes shaping the behavior of farm animals, and, like Skinner, he made analogies between animal and human behavior, arguing that behavior which appears self-willed in humans can more readily be recognized in animals as the product of determinism. Like Skinner, he found the roots of judgment to lie, not in the spontaneous activity of the mind but in the mind's prior interactions with positive and negative reinforcers in the environment. Here we find his most striking parallel with Skinner:

> Hence there is no necessity of allowing reason to beasts in many of those actions that many are ready to argue are rational actions—as cattle in a team are wont to act as the driver would have them upon his making such and such sounds . . . because they have been forced to do it by the whip upon the using of such words. It has become habitual so that they never do it rationally, but either from force or from habit . . . And those that they learn of themselves to do are merely by virtue of appetite and habitual association of ideas. Thus a horse learns to perform such actions for his food, because he had accidentally had the perceptions of such actions associated with the pleasant perceptions of taste; and so his appetite makes him perform the action, without any reason or judgement.

Human beings also learn behavior "by virtue of appetite and habitual association of ideas." As the horse learns by associating certain actions with the pleasant perceptions of taste, so humans by a "kind of reflex" acquire the prejudices of the personality from the association of their actions with the pleasant perceptions of an instinctual self-love. And these prejudices form the basis for later judgements and behavior.[35]

Here, Edwards' conception of human consciousness becomes important. The perception of conscious control of thought is the basis of most people's rejection of determinism. They "feel" that they are the sources of the ideas that arrive in their heads, and thus they call those ideas self-willed. But Edwards placed consciousness on the same level as the other five senses, as a sort of feeling:

> CONSCIOUSNESS is the mind's perceiving what is in itself—its ideas, actions, passions, and everything that is there perceivable. It is a sort of feeling within itself. The mind feels when it thinks, so it feels when it desires, feels when it loves, feels itself hate, etc.

The mind thus does not create the ideas that it thinks; it merely "feels" them as they are thought. It no more creates its ideas than it creates the sounds that it hears or the sights that it sees. Determinism did not mean that people react without thinking. Thought and feeling clearly are an indispensable part of the chain of conditioning that ties the determining environment to behavior. Ideas cannot arise out of nothing, for ideas are as bound, said Edwards, by the law of cause and effect "as the changeable motion of the motes that float in the air." Of course consciousness exists, but it is consciousness that is the thing determined. Edwards wanted to dispel the illusion that being conscious of one's behavior, even one's mental behavior, means being somehow in control of it.[36]

Modern social sciences, history included, are essentially behavioristic: the blind forces of urbanism, modernism, capitalism, etcetera, determine the behavior of people in the mass, just as they determine each individual of that mass. But even here, there is a tendency to forget that each individual has a mind that makes decisions. It is not the individual who is determined; it is the ideas, the beliefs, the emotions that are determined, and behavior is "freely" chosen as a result of determined ideas in the mind. Skinner too often gives the impression that people do not think, that they only react like machines. This our own experience tells us is false. But Edwards' argument is that despite our conscious decision-making we are still determined because it is not immediate choice but the mind with all its fundamental ideas and emotions that is the thing determined.

It would, however, be a mistake to assume that an analysis of Edwardsian theology in such psychological terms necessarily leads away from a theological appreciation of Edwards' thought. Edwards saw God as the ultimate determiner of human thought and thus of human behavior. He did not have to choose between environmental and divine determinism because he saw them as two aspects of the same process and tied them together. And yet he always believed that God was supreme.

Modern behaviorists accept the stimuli of sense perception from the environment as a given and work their way back to human behavior from there. Skinner realizes the regression involved in trying to arrive at the ultimate source of determined behavior. But rather than draw any theological conclusions, he uses this insight to criticize "mentalist" psychologists who try to locate such a place in the human mind. Instead, he prefers to stick to analysis of human behavior, because, he says, "there is no point going back beyond the point at which effective action can be taken."[37]

Edwards was not so cautious. By maintaining a consistent philosophical idealism, he avoided the charge of pantheism and pushed the regression all the way back to God. He did not, as a Pantheist would, identify the environment with God. Both the innate inclinations that are the long range foundations of conditioned behavior and the daily sense perceptions from the environment that are the immediate agents of determinism he believed to be communications from God. Both the objects of perception and the human minds that perceive them are, in his analysis, ideas in the mind of God:

> And indeed the secret lies here: That which truly is the substance of all bodies is the infinitely exact and precise and perfectly stable idea in God's mind together with his stable will that the same shall gradually be communicated to us and to other minds according to certain fixed and exact established methods and laws.

For Edwards, every rattlesnake seen is an idea in the mind of God communicated directly in each moment of time to men's brains, "which exist only mentally, in the same sense that other things do. . . ." Therefore, God remains the ultimate determiner of human behavior, providing both environmental stimuli and inherited instincts, all of consciousness, continually in every moment of time.[38]

vi

"Men either worship the true God or some idol," Edwards explained. "Something will have the heart of man, and that which a man gives his heart to may be called his God."[39] But according to Edwards' model of human psychology, men's hearts are naturally given over to self-love, and self-love is not the "true God" but an idol. That "true God" that underlies even the idol of self-love could be known only through an experience of conversion from natural idolatry through terror to truth. The first step of this conversion had to be a regression through the layers of conditioning into the subconscious where, below all of the personality's inclinations, the "fear of God" is felt. Under all of the conditioned layers of belief, beyond belief, lay the wilderness. Regeneration could not occur before all of the idols of the personality were surrendered to that pit.

The chain of association that makes up the unregenerate personality, according to Edwards, is dependent upon the idol of self-love. If not for this inherited instinct, the soul would have no basis upon which to order the stimuli that it is bombarded by from the moment of birth. It is only by judging objects good or bad in relation to self-love that the soul is able to make meaning out of what would otherwise be chaos. Self-love is the sand upon which the castle of the natural personality is built. To the extent that a person's perception of the world is governed by that person's initial judgements of love and hatred, his or her perception of reality literally is dependent upon maintaining the primacy of self-love. Without that foundation, all of the beliefs, or behavior patterns, that constitute the personality would be discredited. Personal identity could not exist without it.

Nor are speculative beliefs the only things threatened by such a disintegration of personality. According to Edwards, perception of the physical world is also a product of conditioning. The inclinations of the heart control vision as well as thought. Sense perceptions are not perceived as chaos and then consciously ordered by the intellect. The ordering, for those who are sane, is instantaneous. The principles governing that ordering are the inclinations of the heart; they are the program that control the human computer's response. Just as we believe what we want to believe, so we see and hear what we want to, and seeing it call it beautiful if it is "grateful" to our predispositions. The apprehension of beauty is not a rational choice but an emotional reaction. We see and hear what the "frame of our minds" leads us to expect. As long as the inclinations center on self-love, then only those objects that reflect the self will be seen to be beautiful.[40]

If a person's beliefs and prejudices constitute identity, then it can be said that identity actually controls perception. A man who believes himself in the wilderness in need of conversion sees the forest both as the arena of struggle and as the place of deliverance; it appears both frightening and promising. It has all the qualities of the "Numinous"; it is mysterious, frightening, and fascinating.[41] A man already sure of his conversion, at ease in Zion, sees the wilderness only as a threat to his imagined security. To him the forest appears as dark and dangerous and full of demons as it did to Cotton Mather. There is no appearance of the sublime in it.

Here we can begin to understand Edwards' analysis of conversion and the reason he preached terror. The awakening to the emotional apprehension of the totality of sin was the realization that all beliefs are built upon the idol of self-love. When all of the beliefs and behavior patterns that make identity are seen to originate from a sinful instinct, there is no way to avoid condemnation; even the most virtuous behavior can be shown to have originated in selfishness. Yet, without self-love and its attendant behavior patterns, there is only the void. Not only is justifiable, sinless behavior impossible, perception itself, because it is tied to self-love, comes into question. The natural sinner in love with self cannot know God and thus must cling tighter to self to avoid annihilation.

Once the patterns of behavior dependent upon self-love lose their foundation, both the moral and the physical world are perceived as chaos. Ideas, words, feelings, sights, and sounds all lose their meaning; there is either the idol of self-love or there is terror. When the walls of self-love crumble, the city of identity is doomed to destruction. Without self-love, even the fundamental loyalties of family and nation and tribe begin to distintegrate. "They that are the subjects of this are utterly lost."

Self-love is the wall that protects the self from the wilderness, the hedge around the garden. True self-interest is tied to a defense, not just of property and social status, but of belief. The destruction of belief is as much a threat to the self as the invasion of a foreign army. Many would rather die fighting an invader than give up fundamental loyalties. The loss of personal identity is the self's final defeat.

According to Edwards, the threat of the loss of identity is a constant part of consciousness. In every moment, nonbeing threatens being. This waiting terror creates anxiety and is felt in the souls of the sensitive few who cannot take the illusions of personal or communal identity for granted. Only a very thin, and rotten, membrane separates the sanity of natural men from the fear of God. This image was one of the most enduring products of the Calvinist mind. "Unconverted men," warned Edwards, "walk over the pit of hell on a rotten covering, and there are innumerable places in that covering so weak that they will not bear their weight."[42]

The world is an illusion maintained through each moment of time only by the will of God. Human beings are conscious of colors, distances, space, solidity, and order only because God wills it. If God's willing of these ordering principles were to be withdrawn—and it could be—there would remain only the complete terror of consciousness alone with itself in chaos. There would be only insanity, as painful and impossible to bear as the burning of the living body in an eternal furnace. Once awakened to this threat, the old personality clings desperately to itself for survival, struggling to keep from falling back away with the illusions of consciousness into the underlying, subconscious wilderness of God's wrath. It clings like a spider held over a fiery pit to the web of its own illusions. Only a fear greater than the loss of self could shake loose this grip. That is why Edwards preached terror, to convince sinners that Hell itself was hotter than the fear of hell, to convince them to let go and suffer God's wrath for the one great hope of receiving eternal salvation.

The unregenerate, explained Edwards, had to be "led 'into a wilderness' . . . and made to see their own helplessness and absolute dependence on God's power and grace. . . ." Self-denial literally meant abandoning the soul to the underlying pit:

> The duty consists in two things, viz. first, in a man's denying his worldly inclinations, and in foresaking and renouncing all worldly objects and enjoyments; and secondly, in denying his natural self-exultation, and renouncing his own dignity and glory, and in being emptied of himself; so that he does freely and from his very heart, as it were renounce himself, and annihilate himself.[43]

To Edwards, this was the crucifixion that had to precede regeneration. A person had to renounce his or her very identity and fall back through the layers of conditioned beliefs and feelings, as if from adulthood, back to childhood, to innocence, ignorance, and fear. It was Edwards' duty to force his congregation into this psychological crisis. Thus he preached terror, not to scare people into being good, but to put them in touch with the wilderness of fear in their souls, to push them through their defenses into terror. Like a modern psychotherapist leading patients through the agony of self-revelation, Edwards believed he was doing it for their own good:

> To blame a minister for thus declaring the truth to those who are under awakenings, and not immediately administering comfort to them, is like blaming a surgeon, because when he has begun to thrust in his lance, whereby he has already put the patient to great pain, and he shrinks and cries out with anguish, he is so cruel that he will not stay his hand, but goes on, to thrust it in further, until he comes to the core of the wound.[44]

The old personality, rooted to the self, could not be expected freely to renounce itself. Seeing only self-love or the void, it had to be forced to surrender. A minister could be an agent of the spirit that converts, but he could not implant those new inclinations of selfless love that were the mark of true conversion. That could only be done by God. The minister could push a sinner to despair, but there was no guarantee that a terrorized sinner would ever receive a saving sight of Christ. The carcasses of many of the children of Israel rotted in the wilderness; not all who went mad recovered in a state of grace.

Edwards' analysis may have been similar to that of behaviorism, but the therapy he advocated was closer to that of Freudian psychology, the rooting out of unconscious sources of "sinful" behavior in the hope that these might be replaced by more healthy inclinations. "Old inveterate wounds," said Edwards, "must be searched to the bottom in order to healing." Even the techniques he used to search out the bottom of consciousness anticipated the discoveries of Freud. In his Diary, he revealed his use of those two pillars of Freudian psychotherapy, both free association and dream analysis. Dreams he knew to be a guide to the unconscious:

Thursday, May 2. I think it a very good way to examine dreams every morning when I awake; what are the nature, circumstances, principles, and ends of my imaginary actions and passions in them, to discern what are my chief inclinations, etc.

And he used free association as a means of exploring his own psyche:

Saturday Morning, August 10—As a help against that inward shameful hypocrisy, to confess frankly to myself all that I find within myself, either infirmity or sin. . . .—When I find difficulty in finding a subject of religious meditation, in vacancies, to pitch at random on what alights to my thoughts, and to go from that to other things which that shall bring into my mind, and follow this progression as a clue, till I come to what I can meditate on with profit and attention, and then to follow that . . .

These quotations go far to substantiate the claim of Edwards' "modernity."[45]

In addition, in contrast to the stereotype of the repressed Puritan, Edwards maintained that to repress sinful inclinations was not only hypocrisy but was simply not possible. He used the same image to describe the unsuccessful results of repression that Freud would use a century and a half later. Nature, he said, is "like the stream of a river. It may be stopped for a while with a dam, but . . . it will have a course, either in its old channel or a new one." This was the grounds of Edwards' objection to Arminian moralism: "As long as corrupt nature is not mortified, but the principle left whole in a man, 'tis a vain thing to think to expect that it should not govern."[46]

For Edwards, conversion meant the elimination of self-love as the foundation of the personality and its replacement by a selfless love for all of existence without consideration for self or self-interest. Although he admitted it to be an "obscure metaphor," he identified this spirit as the spirit of Christ. To have this self-less love as the primal inclination of the heart meant the creation of a new personality based, not on an individual's "experiences," but on Christ, a "new simple idea" in the heart. This new inclination of the heart, by generating new patterns of behavior, would actually generate a whole new perception of the world. The unconverted saw the world through the distorted lens of self-love; things were beautiful only as they related to self and self-interest. But the new principle of love for "Being-in-General" provided for new contingencies of reinforcement and thus a new personality. A converted saint no longer loved himself alone. As the inclinations of the heart switched from self to "universal existence," the distinction between self and the universe disappeared. The despair of mortal separateness gave way to the ecstasy of abandoning the finite self for identification with the eternal glory of God. Self no longer mattered, only God did, and only after conversion had occurred could all of God's creation be appreciated in its true divine beauty.[47]

Not until the subconscious wilderness of confusion had been crossed, and the old Adam crucified, could there be a new Adam sincerely in love with God and God's creation. To this pilgrim only was given the "Divine and Supernatural Light," the vision of regenerate perception. With this perception one now sensed not only the Glory of God, but the fullness of His beauty in His creation. Herein was given the perception of Him in nature: "So the green trees and fields and singing of birds are the emanations of His infinite joy and benignity," explained Edwards. The proof of this was not speculative. Nor was it rational. It could be perceived only by the saints by "a kind of intuitive and immediate evidence." It could only be known, as Solomon Stoddard had said, "by consciousness."[48]

Perception of the beauty and excellency of God came only after the experience of annihilation. On this Edwards never wavered. It was the fundamental truth of the cross, the primary symbol of the Christian religion. His examples of true piety were chosen to show that only out of an experience of self-annihilating terror could come the perception of true joy:

> My soul hath been compassed with the terrors of death, the sorrows of hell were upon me, and a wilderness of woe was in me; but blessed, blessed, blessed, be the Lord my God.'

Only through destruction of the ego could a glimpse of Eternity be gained. Only through the disintegration of the patterns that control the mind could there be a vision beyond the finite island of human consciousness into the depths of that wilder sea.[49]

This liberty from the illusions of the self was true spiritual liberty, the "liberty in which Christ hath made us free." It was for this liberty that the saints entered into the wilderness; it was for this that they wished for affliction:

> The joy which many of them speak of as that which none is to be paralleled, is that which they find when they are lowest in the dust, emptied most of themselves, and as it were annihilating themselves before God, when they are nothing and God is all, are seeing their own unworthiness, depending not at all on themselves but alone on Christ, and ascribing all glory to God: then their souls are most in the enjoyment of satisfying rest. . . .

This paradoxical identification with God through the complete annihilation of self was—and remains—the foundation of orthodox Protestant piety. Only from the wilderness, from Mount Pisgah, could there be a true sight of Canaan. Self-destruction cleared the view for the sight of God, if only in passing. Thus the twentieth-century theologian, Karl Barth, has written:

> The judgment proclaimed in God's command concerning man—whatever else it may involve—is always the demonstration of his love for man, even if it is only an angry, burning and consuming love. If man were alien and indifferent to Him, how would this encounter come about? How would even its most negative outcome be explicable? The mere fact that it takes place at all, that God stands before man as his Lord, that man's existence can become his confrontation with God's command, always means that God does not will to be without us, but, no matter who or what we may be, to be with us, that He Himself is always "God with Us," "Emmanuel."

Self-knowledge leads to self-hatred and finally to the annihilation of self. This, said Edwards, is the only way to know God and to love Him and to enjoy Him forever.[50]

This also is what it meant to be justified by faith, not—as some enthusiasts have always imagined—that the redeemed sinner has somehow been made righteous, but that the sinner has given up on the possibility of attaining personal justification and accepted Christ's righteousness in place of his or her own. "And by that righteousness being imputed to us," said Edwards, "is meant no other than this, that that righteousness of Christ is accepted for us, and admitted instead of that perfect, inherent

righteousness that ought to be in ourselves."[51] Sinners in agony of guilt
had only to experience annihilation, to surrender their sanity, and accept
the invisible righteousness of Christ in place of their own. In this way,
they could participate in Christ, even if they found that they remained
sinners. Christ could lead them, despite themselves, if they had faith, to
the Millennial Kingdom of Freedom.

Edwards struggled to re-establish the primacy of the fear of God.
Reality, he argued, is not the world and its beauties, but the mind and its
fears. Beauty was truth only for those of regenerate perception. For
those still in the wilderness, the world would always appear ugly; the
perception to see its true beauty was still a future event, a promised land,
a second coming. Edwards called on those who had become at ease in
Zion to return to the pit of doubt and self-denial. To those who knew
themselves full of the guilt of sin, he affirmed that the world was not yet
a Canaan to be enjoyed but a wilderness to be endured by sinners still
struggling towards Canaan. And if the wilderness was endured, he
promised, then a land of promise, better than the squabbling towns of
New England, lay in the not too distant future.

In the Great Awakening, Edwards saw his vision come to life. The
sufferings of the awakened proved that the people were still in the
wilderness and that God still cared enough to make them suffer. And if
the wilderness was real, then the promised land could not be too far off.
"The New Jerusalem," Edwards affirmed, "in this respect has begun to
come down from heaven, and perhaps never were more of the preliba-
tions of heaven's glory given upon earth."[52] These, he thought, could
only multiply. And as they multiplied, surely there would gather together
a great union of God's people which would serve as the foundation of the
Millennium. And where else would the Millennium begin but in New
England? Here again, Edwards was not immune from the temptation to
translate the spiritual into the literal. Conversion was of the soul but the
Millennium would exist on earth and be made manifest in America.
What gave him hope and fueled his enthusiasm was the experience of
terror. He embraced terror as the one sure proof of the enduring love of
God. But if we are truly in the wilderness, he seemed to be saying, can
the New Jerusalem be far behind?

4

Revival and Revolution

And to the woman were given two wings of a great eagle,
that she might fly into the wilderness, into her place,
where she is nourished for a time, and times, and half a
time, from the face of the serpent.
And the serpent cast out of his mouth water as a flood
after the woman, that he might cause her to be carried
away of the flood.
And the earth helped the woman, and the earth opened
her mouth, and swallowed up the flood which the
dragon cast out of his mouth.
And the dragon was wroth with the woman, and went to
make war with the remnant of her seed, which keep the
commandments of God, and have the testimony of Jesus
Christ.

Rev. 12.14–17

i

The major impact of the Great Awakening of the 1740s was its reaffirmation of an evangelical American identity set in stark contrast to the
rational Arminianism that characterized Anglican England. Calvinists'
peculiar sense of themselves as a community of God's chosen people on a
holy errand to rebuild Jerusalem in the wilderness was given new emphasis and was spread by evangelical Protestants throughout the colonies
of British North America. Colonial hostility toward England began not
with the Stamp Act or the French and Indian War but with the flourishing of a new identity that required a contrast against which it could
define itself. The renewed Israel required an Egypt to escape from.
Arminian commercial England became that Egypt.[1]

Edwards had argued that New England was destined to be the location
of the final acts of the drama of world redemption. The Millennium, he
had declared, "will begin in America." Rising in stages from revival to
revival, millennial enthusiasm would build until all of the English colo-

111

nies were joined together in one union of God's people. Skeptics who doubted that such a glorious event would occur in such an obscure corner of the world were reminded by Edwards that "when God is about to turn the Earth into a paradise, he don't begin his work where there is some good growth already, but in a wilderness, where nothing grows and nothing is to be seen but dry sand and barren rocks." Even Edwards was not immune from the temptation to read the spiritual metaphor of conversion into the literal wilderness.[2]

Despite the tension between despair and elation that remained a part of Calvinism, the major result of the Great Awakening was an increased affirmation of America's elect status. Many who may not have been "convinceingly" saved nevertheless rushed to be included in the new Zion. As in the 1630s, many fell into the extremes of Antinomianism, imagining themselves in Canaan fully converted before they had suffered the preparatory trials and temptations of the wilderness.

Edwards did what he could to try to prevent a new outbreak of Antinomianism. "[A] great deal of caution and pains were found necessary," he wrote, "to keep the people, many of them, from running wild." But the exhilaration of the new identity could not be contained. Edwards had a carefully defined idea of what the new being was. But, as he ruefully admitted, many of the newly converted "never could be made to learn to distinguish between impressions on the imagination and truly spiritual experiences." Having experienced the excitement of the revivals and caught a glimpse of the new possibilities, they believed themselves in Canaan.[3]

Alarmed by the growing numbers of deluded enthusiasts, in 1746 Edwards wrote *A Treatise Concerning Religious Affections*[4] to defend the Awakening from its Arminian critics and Antinomian extremists and to help converts distinguish true religious experience from false. Not all who imagined themselves in Canaan were truly converted. Edwards himself went back and forth, at one point revelling in the grace of Christ, at another deeply concerned for his own salvation. The true Arminians had long since settled into a satisfied self-confidence, but among the adherents of the Awakening a certain ambiguity remained. Two visions competed for the loyalty of the newly awakened people. They were torn between the garden and the wilderness, between the presumption of election and the sight of sin, between an identity as God's Zion marching to the Millennium and one as God's Israel of the wilderness suffering the sublime violence of regeneration. The adherents of the Awakening, as *Religious Affections* makes clear, were split between those who clung to the wilderness and those who crossed over to Canaan. And these more enthusiastic evangelicals had this in common with their Arminian countrymen: they believed themselves to be the chosen Israel of God. However, whether Arminian or Evangelical, in the wilderness or in Canaan, when the time came to fight all believed it was essential that Israel be defended against the Egyptian dragon.

As early as 1740, Edwards had warned that the English Egypt was the source of the Arminian principles that were corrupting New England and threatening the work of redemption. He did not accept the Arminians as fellow Israelites but condemned them as traitors to the cause of God. He described England as a nation sunk in depravity where Christ is laughed at in the streets and even "among those who still profess Christianity, Arianism, Socinianism, and Arminianism prevail." Moreover, people in those English fleshpots, he proclaimed, "are not ashamed to be open in their vices, and vice and sensuality even in gross acts is pleaded and stood up by great men." It was, he was saying, the English elite, the "great men," who were principally responsible for destroying England, for their example "seems to have corrupted all sorts." It was, he implied, up to the common people of America to resist the corruption being introduced by those who were supposed to be their betters.

Now I say this has a very threatening aspect upon this land. We are [a] country dependent upon them, we are such to their government, we have our books and our learning from thence, and are upon many accounts exceeding liable to be corrupted by them. This country is but a member of the body of which they are the stock, and shall naturally derive, be assimilated, and likened to them.

If America was to retain its ancient purity, if it was to become the New Jerusalem, it was clear that somehow the corruption pouring in from England had to stop. If the contamination, already obvious among the commercial classes, could not be contained, then Israel would have to depart from Egypt and head out alone into the wilderness.[5]

Edwards' successor, Joseph Bellamy, the man primarily responsible for popularizing his views, carried Edwards' warning against English corruption to a larger audience. In 1750 in his most widely read book, *True Religion Delineated*, Bellamy warned against "a flood of Arminianism and immorality, ready to deluge the land." In 1758, he described the Arminianism that infected England and declared that "from this source it is that infidelity begins to creep into New England, which if divine grace prevents not, may in half a century make great progress."[6]

Bellamy's warning did not go unnoticed. Harriet Beecher Stowe later reported that her grandmother's "Blue Book," *True Religion Delineated*, was "heedfully read in every good family in New England, and its propositions were discussed everywhere and by everybody." This, she said, was one "undoubted fact: the other is, that it was this generation who fought through the Revolutionary war." In 1773, upon learning of the Boston Tea Party, Israel Holly, a preacher of the Gospel in Suffield, Connecticut, defined the purpose of the coming struggle with an echo of Edwards' rhetoric:

> O! What a deluge of impiety has overspread Britain, at this day so much drench'd in all manner of debaucheries & wickedness? How doth intemperance, drunkenness and sensualities of all kinds prevail? . . . What licencious doctrines and damnable heresies are imbibed, while the glorious truths of the gospel are rejected? Doth not arminianism, arianism, deism, and infidelities of the grossest kind prevail? . . . And if we cast our eyes over the American land, and colonies, and even New England in particular, once renowned for piety, and purity, and with the apostle should ask the question, *are we better than they?* must we not with him answer, *no in no wise.* . . . Have we not now reason to expect the frowns of Heaven, a storm of vengeance to be sent upon us? And are not the clouds now gathering? And have been for some time both thick and dark? And what does this portend but a storm at hand? People now in New-England begin to feel the effects of despotic power and are alarm'd thereat, but yet entertain hopes to evade the force of it, but whether they can or no, heaven only knows.

Thus, resistance to foreign corruption not only helped to define America's own emerging identity, it led directly to the outbreak of hostilities in 1775. The reaffirmation of America as the new Israel led to the need to defend Israel. As the regulations of English bureaucracy tightened, Americans, recognizing the intrigues of Satan, rose to defend the woman from the dragon.[7]

The eighteenth-century outpouring of evangelical enthusiasm thus came together in the form of an intense American nationalism, but in doing so it violated the tenets of the Great Awakening. The possibility of universal love was sacrificed to the achievement of national salvation. The participants thought that they were furthering the Kingdom of God. To be the chosen builders of God's New Jerusalem seemed to them to be justifiable cause for pride. But in fact they were creating, not the Kingdom of God, but only the United States of America.

The rise of American nationalism in the eighteenth century occurred as a result of continued externalization of the central metaphor of American Calvinism. Just as seventeenth-century New Englanders had imagined their literal journey into the wilderness to have been a suitable substitute for the spiritual journey of conversion, eighteenth-century adherents of the Great Awakening imagined the excitement they felt at revival meetings to be the true spirit of grace. At both times, people allowed external phenomena to become a substitute for internal experience. They forgot that the type is not the antitype, that the symbol is not the thing it symbolizes. Edwards had warned against the dangers of a deluded enthusiasm, but those who had undergone conversion did not doubt that their enthusiasm would rebuild Zion. Edwards himself fed this delusion by daring to suggest that a truly converted American nation, joined together into a union of believers, might usher in the Millennium.

Those who had been awakened believed themselves if not in Canaan then very close to its borders. Once they experienced the trials of war and emerged victorious, there remained little element of doubt. A presumptuous identification of the American nation with the New Jerusalem fueled the fire of American nationalism. As one observant Anglican noted, their enthusiasm stemmed from "too strict an adherence to the metaphor."[8] Once more the duality of the Augustinian legacy was lost. Edwards had briefly held the two strains in rough balance. But even before he was gone, the people, forgetting once again that they were sinners in the wilderness, rejoiced at their entrance into Canaan.

ii

To descend into the wilderness of the wrath of God meant to go mad. That is why Edwards preached terror. One hundred years before, in England, Richard Baxter had defended this practice with the question, "Can you be madder than you are already? Or at least can there be a more dangerous madness, than to neglect your everlasting welfare, and wilfully undo yourselves?" Thomas Hooker approvingly described a "broken battered soule" in the jaws of conversion as "marveilously distracted" to the point of appearing "a silly sot, and a mad man, in regard of the horror of heart that hath possessed him." These Calvinists did not recoil from madness; they encouraged it.[9]

But the terror of conversion involved much more than simply a lapse into madness. Edwards defined conversion as a breakdown of the "inclinations" of the heart, the basic emotional patterns of response which are the basis of the human personality. The "opinions" that "from the moment of birth are beat into us" create a cohesive pattern of belief that can be called "identity." Every person requires some conception of who he or she is in relation to the external world. The mind simply cannot operate without an internally consistent pattern of belief by which decisions and opinions can be justified. As Edwards said, "something will have the heart of man. . . . It is impossible it should be otherwise."[10]

Identity as it has been defined here is not always a conscious creed or ideology. For some the professed "religion" is in fact the real religion, the God that is worshipped is the self's true God. But most of the assumptions of identity are hidden in the subconscious. According to Jung, many of these underlying "patterns of the human mind . . . are transmitted not only by tradition and migration, but also by heredity."[11] Even without going this far, it is possible to see that the loss of "inclinations" and behavior patterns would be thoroughly disorganizing. Without these, there would be only the terror of the void. These patterns reach into the subconscious roots of culture; they were the idols that had to be destroyed. It was to free humanity from these idols that the Calvinists encouraged madness.

"All people," according to Erikson, "because of their common undercurrent of existential anxiety, at cyclic intervals and during crises feel an intense need for a rejuvenation of trust which will give new meaning to their limited and perverted exercise of will, conscience, reason, and identity." But if the trust is not rejuvenated, there remains only that underlying "existential anxiety." Paul Tillich has called this existential dread the threat that nonbeing constantly poses to being. The psychologist Rollo May has written:

> Anxiety . . . is rather an ontological characteristic of man, rooted in his very existence as such. It is not a peripheral threat which I can take or leave, for example, or a reaction which may be classified beside other reactions; it is always a threat to the foundation, the center of my existence. Anxiety is the threat of imminent non-being.

It is thus presumed in modern psychotherapy as in Calvinist theology that underlying all human rationalizations is a vast sea of terror. From the perspective of rational consciousness, this sea is the void that exists beyond the borders of identity. If the self and its Gods are idols, if all belief is a lie, then this is the very emptiness that Karl Barth called the NO of God's judgement. From the human standpoint there is only the lie of identity supported by the lies of the collective subconscious and under them the void. God is presumed to exist because the patterns exist and must come from somewhere as must His condemnation of those idols. He exists, but His face cannot be seen.[12]

That is why human beings cling to the web that holds them over the fiery pit. They can see nothing but the pit and the web of their own identity. In this, they are supported by their community, and their community's identity is supported by history. Like it or not, consciously or not, every personality reflects the identity of the culture in which it developed. As Sidney Mead has stated, "if we are to understand an individual's unique personhood (even our own) it is necessary to study the complex of traits that make up his community." Or as Erikson said, "the term identity points to an individual's link with the unique values fostered by a unique history of his people." This is the ideological web that sinners were said to cling to.[13]

The concepts discussed here have been described for many years but have been known by different names. Studies of "nationalism," "national character," "culture," "myth," "ethnicity," and most recently "mentalité," have all looked at these same phenomena from different angles. I prefer the psychological term, "identity," not because I find it more correct, but because I find it more useful. More than the others, it suggests a close connection between personal and cultural belief and thereby helps to illuminate the connection between collective mentality and individual psychology. The role of ideas in history is primarily here, not in the speeches and pamphlets of the articulate elite, but in the "collective mentality" of the people.

What occurred in the Great Awakening can be analyzed from this perspective. An established identity, clearly articulated, was being threatened by an alien identity. As the society divided into two antagonistic groupings, young persons at the stage of adolescence at which such decisions are made, had to choose between their parents' worldly Arminianism or the original identity that their culture seemed to be abandoning. They had to choose between a worldly ethic devoted to material gain and a theistic world view centered on the demands of spiritual regeneration. The process by which they rejected Arminian worldliness and reaffirmed the ancient identity of New England took the traditional pattern of crucifixion and regeneration. The abandoning of the old self and the assumption of a new personality paralleled the experience of identity-loss and the acceptance of a new identity. The rhetoric of damnation, hell-fire, and regeneration served to tie individual experience into the larger historical and transhistorical framework.

Edwards had envisioned a conversion from personal identity to an identity centered entirely on the eternal beauty and excellence of God. Justification by faith alone meant that neither the old personality of the sinner nor the new personality of the Christian could be justified—both were only human identities and therefore false—justification was Christ's and Christ's alone. Humans could participate in that justification only vicariously by identifying with Christ through faith. The self had to remain in the wilderness, blessing God for its damnation.

This was the ideal. The reality, as Edwards soon realized, was that sinners assumed all sorts of delusions to be evidence of the new birth. With or without the true spirit, they retained the rhetoric of Calvinism to describe their new identities and they used the language of Calvinism to justify, not Christ, but their new selves. The adherents of the awakening, momentarily terrorized, did not remain in the wilderness. Instead, the Calvinist identity forged by the first generation was rebuilt with stronger, more powerful steel.

The unconverted sinner, as has been said, could not want to be destroyed. The self had to defend itself against annihilation; identity had to be protected, the web secured. It was all that held the soul out of the pit. It could not be otherwise. This was as true for the new self as it had been for the old. Once having crossed the wilderness of despair and having reached, so they believed, the promised land, the converted sinner clung to his new identity with even greater force than he ever clung to the old. The commitment to the new identity, having been made consciously and proclaimed before the community, was far greater, if sincere, than was the attachment to the old.

Hadley Cantril has described how the ego's need to protect itself can be a powerful motivating force in history. Erikson has noted that "the rage aroused by threatened identity loss can explode in the arbitrary destructiveness of mobs, or it can serve the efficient violence of organized machines of destruction." Because the larger identity of the community is tied into the self's own identity, the defense of communal traditions and beliefs is a part of self-defense. Wars are *caused* by many factors, but it is in defense of the self and its identity that wars are *fought*. This was particularly true of the American Revolution.[14]

Too often historians have thought of the difference between self-interest and altruism as the distinguishing difference between material and ideological theories of causation, as if ideological self-interest was somehow more noble than financial self-interest: "To fight to defend beliefs is patriotic—to fight to protect profits is obscene." This association of ideological motivations with a virtuous patriotism has caused many scholars to view ideological arguments with understandable distrust. The suspicion of other historians that intellectual considerations are only pertinent when discussing "intellectuals" has also been responsible for much of the skepticism intellectual history has endured. But as Edwards knew, belief is neither altruistic nor elitist. It is the fundamental support of the self. It does not matter if the individual or group in question is college educated or illiterate, rich or poor, male or female, black or white. Even when called "peasants," farmers whose lives are governed by the rhythms of the seasons have beliefs and behave according to the ideas that exist in their minds. For all human beings act in response to their "inclinations" and beliefs. Identity is the last line of self-defense. Money and property contribute to the security of the individual. But even if these are destroyed, belief remains as the last wall of self-interest.

Those colonists who became rebels in order to defend New England's identity against the encroachments of an alien culture were no more altruistic than those who fought to protect their farms, their families, or their shipping routes. It could be argued that those who fought to protect their money would not have done so if their religious beliefs had not coincided with their financial interests. Many a Tory lost everything in order to be true to the crown and the Anglican Church; many a rebel sacrificed everything, not out of altruistic patriotism—though some may call it that—but to preserve the culture and support the ideology that nurtured and protected their identity. Patriotism, as Edwards had said, "cannot be of the nature of true virtue." Any love that does not extend beyond nation and ideology (and whose does?) but falls short of the "universality of existence" is merely an extension of "self-love."[15]

This is the importance of the American rhetorical tradition of the wilderness sojourn. The very use of the symbols of this tradition conjurs up the whole of the mythic identity of the culture. "It is, then," writes Mason Lowance, "a biblical impulse that defines America's purpose, not only in the prominent errand theme, but also in the application of language to the expression of that theme. . . ." In America, the cycles of personal and historical development became fused with the biblical pattern, and this association of the personal and the historical with the transcendent created a powerful and enduring identity. It was in the story of the children of Israel and their forty years in the wilderness, "whose whole conduct exemplifies our nature to the life and in which glass we may behold our faces," that New Englanders found and held onto an identity that gave their lives and their errand meaning.[16]

However powerful, this identity, after the restoration of Anglicanism and monarchy in 1660, was not secure. Threatened by political and economic forces, it maintained a defensive and suspicious posture. Because it was, so New Englanders believed, the true Christian identity, Satan could not allow it to live. God's people had to stay alert in order to protect what they repeatedly called their "liberty." The woman, the Christian church, had been driven into the wilderness, but that was not the end of the story. As foretold in *Revelations*, the dragon would "make war with the remnant of her seed, which keep the commandments of God, and have the testimony of Jesus Christ."

The American Revolution thus should be seen not as a protest against taxation or arbitrary government, not as a revolt of the poor against the privileged, and not as the defense of constitutional principles. Gordon Wood argues that it is necessary to look beyond the "refined and nicely-reasoned arguments" of Franklin and Jefferson to the "enthusiastic extravagance—the paranoaic obsession with a diabolical crown conspiracy" to understand the deeper motivations of the patriots.[17]

The "ideological" arguments that were put forward by the ruling elite of New England society were the equivalent of the "speculative notions" that, as Edwards knew, were determined by the deeper "inclinations of the heart." Those deeper inclinations are part of the identity that is threatened. The Whig and neo-Whig historians are not wrong in looking at belief, but they err in looking only to conscious, political, speculative belief. The unconscious is made of beliefs, too, and these are often the most important. As Wood has written:

> By implying that certain declared rational purposes are by themselves an adequate explanation for the American's revolt . . . the neo-Whig historians have not only threatened to deny what we have learned of human psychology in the twentieth century, but they have also in fact failed to exploit fully the terms of their own idealist approach by not taking into account all of what the Americans believed and said.

What we need to do is to look at even "the irrational and hysterical beliefs" of the people for that is where their true motivations are to be found.[18]

What is to be found in such an investigation is a consistent pattern of identity-defense. An alien culture based on an antagonistic Arminian Anglicanism was threatening to destroy a culture based on Calvinist principles. This was the cause of the revolution. It was not just the evangelicals who wore their identity on their sleeves who fought to defend Zion from being retaken by the Egyptians. Both the radical Antinomians and the conservative Arminians shared a belief in America's millennial promise. They differed only on how to get there and how close the Millennium was. Even the rationalists, at least in New England, had Calvinist hearts under their Arminian heads. Calvinist pietism may have meant little to them, but filio-pietism was very much alive. Their ties to their heritage went beyond their professions of faith. John Adams knew as well as anyone that the threat to establish a bishop in the colonies struck deeper into American paranoia than any of the other acts of Parliament:

> If any gentleman supposes this controversy to be nothing to the present purpose, he is grossly mistaken. It spread an universal alarm against the authority of Parliament. It excited a general and just apprehension, that bishops, and dioceses, and churches, and priests, and tithes, were to be imposed on us by Parliament. It was known that neither king, nor ministry, nor archbishops, could appoint bishops in America, without an act of Parliament; and if Parliament could tax us, they could establish the Church of England, with all its creeds, articles, tests, ceremonies, and tithes, and prohibit all other churches, as conventicles and schism shops.[19]

Popular pietism and cosmopolitan Arminianism should not be thought of as two totally separate and antagonistic cultures in colonial America. The difference between them was real, but it was a difference of emphases not enemies. To a large extent the two overlapped, particularly during the Revolution when, in coalition against the common enemy, the pietists shouted the slogans of political liberty and the cosmopolitan merchants wore homespun.

One of the factors that allowed the easy alliance of evangelical and liberal interests in the cause of the Revolution was their common belief in "liberty." In fact, each side interpreted the word differently. The liberals fought primarily for "Civil Liberty," the liberty of the political state to control its own affairs. The evangelicals also cherished civil liberty but not as an end in itself. For them, civil liberty was an essential protection for "Christian liberty," that mystic state of grace for which all Protestants yearned. To the religiously minded and, as John Adams indicated, even to some of the liberals, both were worth fighting for.

Many a political tract and sermon of the Revolutionary era quoted St. Paul's command to the Galatians to "Stand fast therefore in the liberty wherewith Christ hath made us free."[21] The theological reference was to the covenant of grace in opposition to circumcision, a mere "work." This Christian liberty was nothing less than salvation itself, liberty from the condemnation for sin, the liberty that Christ purchased on the cross. The Protestant doctrine of Justification by Faith was the doctrinal equivalent of this "liberty." The threat posed by a return to the legalisms and rituals of the Anglican Church, to say nothing of the Roman, was the loss of just this Christian liberty. Arminianism, by preaching a covenant of works, made the sinner's whole-hearted surrender to the mercy of Christ less likely. The preaching of morality instead of grace was the mark not of Calvin's "Kingdom of Freedom" but of a community still enslaved to the law. This calamity had to be prevented at all costs.

The first settlers had arrived in the wilderness of New England in order to develop their church, the collective body of Christ, without having to fear Anglican or Roman persecution. Their children had carried their errand into the second half of the century, but they and their children had allowed the flame to die down. In the Great Awakening, the flame was rekindled, and the community of God's people in the wilderness with the vision of Canaan before them was determined that the dragon would not prevent their entrance into the promised land. The American Revolution was the war brought on by the dragon. The rhetoric of that war was often secular, but its passions were religious. John Adams' priorities were clear: arbitrary taxation was a danger because it might lead to the destruction of New England's religion—not the other way around.

iii

The process by which the renewed American identity of the revivals fueled the fires of revolution was rarely made explicit. Only in Connecticut did the religious division enter directly into politics with the emergence of a "New Light" and an "Old Light" Party. And it was in Connecticut, during the Stamp Act riots, that it was said that "a man's religious principles are made the test or shall I rather say the badge of his political creed. An Arminian and a favourer of the Stamp act signify the same man."[20] But such direct evidence of correlations between religious and political allegiance are rare. Historians of this period are hampered by the fact that the Arminian elite had easier access to printing presses and could perpetuate their viewpoint but that the Calvinist populace lived in an oral culture which emphasized the spoken over the written word. Much of the literature of the Revolution articulates only the legal reasons for rebelling because it was the literature of the elite and reflects the impact of the Enlightenment on that class.

By the 1770s, a rough division can be discerned in the mainstream culture of British North America; a rational, politically-oriented elite culture, the remains of which constitute the bulk of the historical record, overlapped with a largely rural, largely oral culture that remained faithful to an older, traditional religious identity. This other popular culture, though it left fewer written records, encompassed the larger part of the colonial population, church members, members of the congregation, dissenters; even some who no longer attended church (like the "scrupulous" souls who abhorred the half-way convenant) still believed in the guiding religious identity of their community.

This split between a latitudinarian elite and an evangelical populace, so obvious in 1741 in the Great Awakening and in 1800 at Cane Ridge, did not simply vanish in the years between. For the sake of the struggle against the common enemy, these competing groups joined in implicit coalition. The clergy echoed the political arguments of the elite; the patriotic elite threw off the wigs and donned homespun. The differences between them remained in the background, but they remained. This split was a crucial element in the history of American culture; it remains so to this day. And no history of the Revolution is complete that fails to take it into account.

In *The Ideological Origins of the American Revolution*, published in 1967, Bernard Bailyn did not ignore religion, but he accorded it a minor role. Nor is this surprising. For Bailyn's influential book is a study of "the dominant or leading ideas of those who made the Revolution," the Revolutionary elite, whom he referred to with what he admitted is the often misleading phrase, "the colonists." By concentrating on the rhetoric of these leaders, Bailyn implied that the farmers who actually fought at Bunker Hill either shared the motivations of their political leaders or, in eighteenth-century fashion, deferred to these gentlemen and dutifully followed their lead.[22]

It would be wrong to challenge Bailyn's analysis of John Adam's fear of a political conspiracy. But it would be equally hard to demonstrate that the common soldiers and farmers who made up the bulk of the Revolution's supporters shared such cosmopolitan concerns. It is not necessary to refute Bailyn in order to argue that the patriotic populace supported their leaders' efforts but did so for different reasons. The Revolution was less a consensus and more a coalition of different ideological and material interests united behind the same slogans against the same enemy. Nor were political, religious, or material motivations restricted to particular groups; again, it was a matter of emphases. Though he stresses the moral rather than the metaphysical and the elite rather than the common man, in the latest comprehensive account of the Revolution, Robert Middlekauf acknowledges the motivating force of religion on even the most secular of the Revolutionaries:

> The generation that made the Revolution were the children of the twice-born, the heirs of this seventeenth-century religious tradition. George Washington, Thomas Jefferson, John Adams, Benjamin Franklin, and many who followed them into revolution may not have been men moved by religious passions. But all had been marked by the moral dispositions of a passionate Protestantism. They could not escape this culture; nor did they try. They were imbued with an American moralism that colored all their perceptions of politics. After 1760 they faced a political crisis that put these perceptions to an agonizing test. Their responses—the actions of men who felt that Providence had set them apart for great purposes—gave the Revolution much of its intensity and much of its idealism.[23]

Yet even these leaders were merely warmed by a fire that burned fiercely beneath them.

Only rarely did the published rhetoric reflect the concerns of the people who actually fought the revolution. But when it did, the impact of the publication was felt and the response electrifying. Tom Paine's *Common Sense*, which attacked King George as "the hardened sullen-tempered Pharoah of England," achieved much of its influence from the fact that it was written in an evangelical style familiar to the common people. In a like manner, Patrick Henry achieved success as an orator because he spoke to the evangelical Baptists of Virginia in a manner reminiscent of the style of itinerant preachers. The Great Awakening had come to the South with the waves of Scotch-Irish Presbyterians, and it was to this group that Henry directed his rhetoric. As Rhys Isaac has written, "Henry had brought into the politics of the gentry world an adaption of that popular oral form, the extempore sermon, which had been setting different parts of Virginia ablaze ever since the coming of the New Side Presbyterians in the 1740s."[24]

Popular, religious culture in this period can thus be characterized as much by its literary style as by its religious concerns. In the seventeenth century, the Puritans had consciously distinguished themselves from the more aristocratic Anglicans by their use of the "plain style." Their language tended to be straightforward, even confrontational, direct explanations of ideas, expressed with homely metaphors and rustic language that even simple persons could appreciate. But the main purpose of the evangelical sermon, even with its plain and logical application of theology, was not to impress the mind but to move the heart. In their often simple directness of image and style, these sermons were intended not to stir the intellect to thought but to stir the passions to action. To do so, they drew upon the rich tradition of symbolic biblical imagery. In the process, they raised fears deeper than those aroused by merely political or economic threats. The language of religious paranoia reaches beyond the state house, beyond even the church, to the soul.

There are, however, existing documents which do illustrate the manner in which the enthusiasm generated in the Awakening burst into flame in the Revolution. One such document, not published at the time, provides important insights into the way that the evangelical identity of the Awakening became the foundation for the rebellion of the 1770s. Although a farmer and carpenter and not an intellectual, Nathan Cole kept a private account of his "Spiritual Travels" from Arminian apathy in 1740 to evangelical patriotism in 1770. The language of this document is particularly interesting for it reveals how the Calvinist themes of conversion in the wilderness were perceived by at least one representative member of the general populace.[25]

Originally an Arminian, carelessly believing, so he tells us, that his good works would earn him salvation, Cole was first shaken from moral complacency during the Great Awakening. After listening to Whitefield preach in his native Connecticut, Cole was beset by doubts about his own salvation. The fears generated by these doubts threatened his self-confidence, and he withdrew to his room, neglecting both his farm and his family, in order to contemplate the horror of his condition. Unable to bear the ordeal, he became physically and mentally incapacitated. His brain, he said, seemed to burn: "Hell fire Hell fire ran swift through my mind and my distemper grew harder and harder upon me and my nature was just wore out—poor me—poor soul." He stared into madness, and, at long last became, so he thought, "swallowed up in God" and "set at liberty." After this occurred, he arose from his sickbed and, going out, he "saw with new eyes; all things became new, A new God; new thoughts and new heart . . . everything had a new countenance and seemed to praise God, all things seemed to be new." It was, he wrote, "as if I really saw the face of heaven by an eye of faith."[26]

On the basis of this experience, Cole dared to believe that he might truly be converted, that he was in Canaan and the trials of the wilderness were behind him. But "an old Christian" whom he met explained to him:

> you stand upon the top of mount pisgah, and you see the promised land and you think you shall presently be there; but you will find you must come down of/f/ of this mount, and must travel through a Rough wilderness yet and have the Sons of Anak to encounter with yet; before you get there.[27]

As predicted, Cole was soon beset by renewed temptations. A reading of Thomas Hooker's *The Poor Doubting Christian Drawn to Christ* only increased his doubts. Driven again to a state of despair, he even contemplated suicide. But after much soul searching, at last a "divine ray broke into" his soul and he went home "rejoycing."[28]

Cole's wife then began to show signs of distress and soon she became "raving distracted." According to Cole, "Satan came with many temptations to her, as his manner is to young Christians in the wilderness they are lead into." She finally confessed to her husband that she feared for her salvation for she felt that she never would be converted. Only after she had thus given up all hope for her own redemption, "the love of God broke clearly into her soul" and she too "was set at liberty."[29]

In 1747, discovering that "the old standing churches were not in a Gospel Order" since "every unconverted person that came there did solemnly lye unto God," Cole "came out or separated or dissented from them." This was the beginning of his struggle with the colony and with the local authorities. The process that had begun with a surprised recognition of his own personal sinfulness now broadened to include a recognition of his society's sinfulness. The complacence that had almost ruined him also threatened the wider community; it too was in need of conversion. What had begun as a rebellion against his own self-confidence was becoming a rebellion against the country's unconverted state.[30]

On several occasions, "in order to stand a witness to the cause of God," Cole risked prison by refusing to pay his taxes for a "hireling ministry." Continuing to struggle both with his own recurring doubts and with the established order, Cole began to realize that he had undergone a significant change. He was, he realized, different from what he had been and from what many of his neighbors still were. In an attempt to explain that difference, he was forced to conclude that the rich and powerful leaders of the colony, men whom he had once treated with sincere deference, were no longer worthy of his respect. If the New Jerusalem was to be built in America, the job could not be left to such leadership. Cole's own faith, his new identity, overpowered what feelings of deference still remained. He looked about him and realized that "honor plagued some men; and some were plagued with pride; and some with riches and others with covetousness, selfishness, malice, and envy." Clearly, the leaders of New England had strayed from the paths of righteousness. The task of defending the "cause of God" had become the responsibility of a new order of Christians. In the aftermath of the Great Awakening, the mantle of responsibility fell upon the shoulders of the common people.[31]

In 1765, ordered to pay his tax "out of obedience to the civil authority," Cole instead publicly confronted the local minister as he was conducting service. "I had rather have my head cut off than brake God's law," he declared. The congregation, moved by Cole's appeal, voted to abate his taxes. It was a telling blow:

> Now one says the minister lookt pale; and others say it killed the minister stone dead; but a certain Esqr. said I wonder he would come to us in such a spirit as he doth; to reflect so hard upon us—. . . the faces and eyes of the assembly turned as I went round, with a sober amaze in the countenance; as if I had been some strange creature from some other nation or world.

Cole had dared to defy the local authority in the name of what he considered true religion, and with a majority of the congregation on his side, he had won![32]

That same year, the year of the Stamp Act crisis, the Separates of Connecticut endured another round of persecution as the embattled establishment fought for its power and privileges. "There is," said Cole, "a dreadful storm of vengeance on the land; all being in a confusion like the troubled sea; writs and executions flying about the country after men." For Cole, and for many like him, the revolution against un-Godliness had begun. It was clear to them that the establishment, including both local magistrates and British administrators, were corrupt and that a cleansing was in order.[33]

The final section of Cole's narrative, written in 1771, recounts briefly the growth of the Separate Churches in Connecticut. Then Cole tells how in 1763, when he was ill, his sister had told a "reich man" who her brother was and how sick he was. The rich man replied that "this is a judgement upon him for leaving our Church and other words as if he rejoysed that . . . we shall gett red of all the separates fire." Cole thought about this remark in "a sort of visionary trance" and it came to him,

> that it was so I was left alone and was as a poor old coal buryed up in the ashes as if there was no more to be seen but the Lord seemed to show that in time a little spark of fire would come out of these ashes from that coal and catch fire to a brand that was neer and that brand catches fire to some brands that lay here and there and the fire began to burn more and more and keept increasing until it arose to a much greater height than ever it was before in Kensington etc:[34]

Cole was predicting, in this final section, nothing less than social revolution. The coals created by the fires of the Great Awakening, he punned, though temporarily dormant would soon burst into revolutionary flame, burning away the old order and creating the perfect world of his first ecstatic visions. These new men, new born in a new spirit, had suffered humiliation in the wilderness. The meaning of their experience was clear. Surely Canaan would soon be theirs, surely the day soon would come when the old world would be burned away and the newly converted American community would find "liberty" in the wilderness.

iv

Nathan Cole opposed not the British but a more local establishment. Yet from his perspective, both were carriers of the same corruption. He had no way of knowing that it would be easier to topple the mighty British Empire than to overthrow the entrenched power of more local elites.

Edwards had made the association between American and English corruption explicit, articulating what less learned men like Cole could not express. Surveying the feuds that had shattered Northampton's communal cohesion, Edwards had compared the split in his town to the division in English politics. One faction, made up of the "chief men in the town, of great authority and wealth, that have been great proprieters of their lands," he compared to the Court Party in England. His own less wealthy supporters, the other faction in town, he compared to the Whig or "country party" opposition. The identification of political with religious interests, whether justified or not, began early. To the Calvinists of New England, politics and religion, both local and international, were all part of one unbroken web.[35]

Nevertheless, the relationship between the British Anglican establishment and the Colonial Arminian establishment should not be over-emphasized. When the time came to take a stand, the rationalists of Boston who had not become Anglicans stood with the ghosts of their fathers in defiance of the British. Despite their flirtation with English ways, they were Americans. Those who had taken the extreme stand of rejecting the religion of their native land quickly filled the boats leaving for Nova Scotia. America meant little to them. Any ties they once had to American culture were severed when they abandoned the faith of their ancestors for a foreign Anglicanism.

American hostility towards Great Britain had existed long before the imperial administrators began to tighten their control over their colonial subjects. The roots of that hostility were cultural, and because the roots of American culture were religious, this cultural animosity was at heart religious. Two nations with different assumptions about their roles in the drama of history were subject to a single political administration. It was inevitable that this political entity, divided against itself, would not be able to stand.

If, as has been suggested, popular behavior is "usually rooted in popular culture," then the "suggestion here is that although by mid-century the old [Puritan] order was moribund in New England, popular culture included a real disposition toward resistance to change away from it." The populace of New England was not about to allow an unconverted ministry and a mercantile elite to lead them away from the "popular culture" of "Puritanism." Instead, they struggled in the face of vast historical changes to preserve the vision that had first inspired the saints. They fought invisible forces, "modernism," "capitalism," "bureaucracy"; but they believed that one central sinister force was responsible for all the changes that threatened them. They believed that theirs was a struggle between Satan and Christ.[36]

The cultural alienation that lay at the heart of the Revolution was thus nothing new to the eighteenth century. One can say it began in 1634 when John Winthrop first fortified Boston Harbor against an expected assault by Archbishop Laud. John Adams certainly believed that the origins of the Revolution "ought to be traced back for Two Hundred Years, and sought in the history of the country from the first plantation." From the beginning, a new identity, called "Puritanism," had been on the defensive against England. In 1664, after the Restoration, the Massachusetts General Court, threatened once again, had pleaded with the King to "let our government live, our patent live, our magistrates live, our lawes & liberties live, our religious enjoyments live . . ." New England's resistance to the Royal Commissioners and finally to Governor Andros in 1689 was, at root, resistance to the imposition of an alien religious culture and a defense of New England's peculiar identity. From this perspective, it can even be said that the Salem witch trials were part of the struggle that eventually led to war.[37]

As more and more people abandoned Puritanism for the ways of Restoration and Georgian England, the loyal inhabitants of New England, viewing the spread of Anglican culture with alarm, felt justifiably threatened. Satan, they knew, intended to destroy New England. If in the French and Indian War the dragon could not destroy the woman with Papist troops and their heathen allies, then Satan would have to work more subtly from within. Calvinist intellectuals, like Edwards and Bellamy, were deeply suspicious of British designs on their Protestant liberties. The populace of New England, predominantly Calvinist, took the lead in resisting the spread of the antagonistic culture. The enlightened John Adams may have articulated the grievances of the lawyers and merchants, but it was the Calvinist Samuel Adams, converted in the Great Awakening in 1741, who stirred the people to rebellion.

The American colonists believed that there was a conspiracy against them. The British officials may have been conscious agents of that conspiracy, but they need not have been. Satan did not require the conscious cooperation of his human tools in order to use them for his own ends. The colonists' assertion that all of the different events of history were somehow being manipulated by a master hand has appeared fantastic and paranoid. But to a people who believed in determinism and who believed that the determining environment is not neutral but controlled by supernatural forces, it was evident—even if the British did not realize it—that their actions were part of the Devil's larger plans. In the woodcuts of the period, the figure of Satan whispering in the ears of the British and their allies was more than just a symbol of evil.

Evidence of motivation is difficult to obtain. It is far easier to figure the cash value of a trading route than the psychological value of a beleagured identity. But evidence does exist that Americans at the time of the Revolution did view their struggle as a defense of Canaan against the encroachment of Egypt. Both Evangelicals and rationalists carried in their heads images of themselves as warriors defending Israel from the Satanic hordes. As Joel T. Headley wrote in 1861,

In our Revolution, the religious element was not paramount, and hence did not give shape and character to the whole physical structure and organization. It kept more within its appropriate sphere, and stood behind and sustained the political and military organizations of the land, rather than formed a part of them. But it is not on that account to be overlooked. He who forgets or underestimates the moral forces that uphold or bear on a great struggle, lacks the chief qualities of a historian.[38]

Headly was simply reflecting a viewpoint that had been commonplace during the struggle when he said that religion was "the deep, solid substratum that underlaid the Revolution." Peter Oliver's charge that the "black regiment," loyal to the traitor Cromwell, stirred the ignorant masses to rebellion was not far off the mark. Francis Kinloch, a delegate to the Continental Congress from South Carolina, later blamed the hostilities on

> the disappointment of a few smugglers in New England worked upon by the ancient Oliverien Spirit, that panted to suffer once more for the "good old cause," the idle opulence of the Southern provinces, where something was wanted to employ the heavy hours of life, the stupidity of two or three British Governors, and the cruel impolitic behavior of their government . . .

These leading figures were simply reflecting an assumption that most considered a commonplace. Popular participation in the Revolution owed more to the example of the Old Testament than to John Locke. Perry Miller concluded that "among the masses the Hebraic analogy was at least as powerful an incentive as the declaration of inalienable right." As evidence, he quoted "a typical communication" in the Boston *Gazette* for May 6, 1782. "My dear countrymen," it read, "my sincere wish and prayer to God is, that our Israel may be saved from the rapacious jaws of a tyrant."[39]

Such references to America as Israel abound in the literature of the Revolution. To try to dismiss them as "mere rhetoric" is to overlook the importance of "mere rhetoric" as a historical force. It is by just such rhetoric, repeated until it becomes an unquestioned part of consciousness, that collective identity is created and reinforced. Nobody had to explain the reference; everybody in Colonial America knew the typological significance of the sojourn of Israel out of Egypt into the wilderness. The use of such "buzz words" tapped a deep reservoir in the culture's collective unconscious. By using them, and using them repeatedly, the people by their language revealed just how important their religious identity was.

Letters such as the one quoted by Perry Miller are among the few means historians have to generalize about the motivations of people who were not engaged in public debate. Some letters to friends and relatives in England have been collected and published, and these reveal just how important religion was in the revolutionary mind. Many Tories shared Peter Oliver's belief that Cromwellian radicalism was responsible for the strife. One writer said, in 1774,

> The inhabitants of New England are the descendants of Cromwell's elect, and they not only inherit their sentiments in civil and religious

matters, but they have copied after them during the contest they have had with the Mother Country . . . the northern people, I mean the New Englanders and the Congregationalists, and the Presbyterians everywhere, are not only inimical to us, but determined to break off all connections with us as soon as they can.

Another, less polite, writer called the American Army then camped in Cambridge, "nothing but a drunken, canting, lying, praying, hypocritical rabble, without order, subjection, discipline, or cleanliness." Another reported with amazement that the "country people" believe and say that "the King of England was turned Papist." A number of writers noted that the Scotch-Irish in the colonies all supported the rebels and that they had "all the qualifications for a New England Saint of the first order." Clearly, these British sympathizers recognized that it was a religious sympathy that lay at the heart of the antagonism of the Americans to England.[40]

Among the letters supporting the American cause were a number that were explicit in their religious imagery. "Surely the people at large in Great Britain," wrote one Philadelphian in 1775, "are involved in worse than Egyptian darkness, while their rulers are madly rushing, like Pharoah and his host, through a sea of blood, on their utter destruction." And a writer from New York closed his letter in 1775 with the statement that "we trust in that arm that lead the armies of Israel through the wilderness, for our redemption."[41]

Thus, the use of the rhetoric of the Old Testament served to inspire the people to revolutionary zeal. It tied personal identity to communal identity and tied them both into the larger cosmic identity of scripture. Anne Holton, the daughter of a British Commissioner, witnessed the Liberty Riot of June 10, 1768. "All was ended," she wrote, "with a speech from one of the leaders concluding thus, 'We will defend our Liberties and property by the strength of our arm and the help of our God. To your tents, O Israel.' This is a specimen of the Sons of Liberty." We have no reason not to take Ms. Holton's word for it. But the Sons of Liberty were not the only ones to stir the feelings of the common people by applying religion to the political situation. As William McLoughlin has said, the Deists' and rationalists' "cool, judicious, scientific arguments for republicanism did not carry enough weight with the average man to lead him into rebellion." It was the preaching of men like the Reverend Judah Champion of Litchfield, Connecticut, who inspired men to take up arms against the British Army. According to Headly, Champion preached passionately on the British

enmity, to the American church, and the ruin to religion which their success would accomplish; of congregations scattered, churches burned to the ground, and the Lord's People made a hissing and a by-word among their foes, till his own feelings and those of his hearers were roused into intense excitement in view of the wrongs and sufferings designed for them and the church of God.

Many ministers, it was reported, when they heard the news of Lexington and Concord, preached to their congregations and then after calling for volunteers were seen "marching at the head of their parishes, with guns at their backs."[42]

As if persecution from Anglican Bishops was not a great enough threat, many saw their old antagonist, the Pope, behind the Anglican mask. Fear of Roman tyranny, whether justified or not, was very much a part of British popular culture. Ebenezer Baldwin, a Congregational minister from Connecticut, was explicit in his contention that the British ministry, in 1774, had "a settled fix'd plan," as the Quebec Act proved, "to establish in America, the same arbitrary government that takes place in France." Those British kings, he warned, who have been most disposed to "trample upon the rights of the people" and to support arbitrary government "have ever caressed the Papists and shewn a favourable disposition towards the bloody religion of Rome, as that religion is the surest prop to tyranny and despotism." And, he continued, when "our civil rights and privileges have thus fallen a sacrifice to tyranny and oppression, our religious liberties cannot long survive." If the British ministry is successful in its efforts, he warned, "Robberies, rapes, murders" will be the certain outcome.[43]

Israel Holly was even more inflammatory. Noting a "kindred and likeness" between despotic government and "Popery," he spelled out the reasons why the colonists had to resist British tyranny:

> Not only to have temporal property at the disposal of arbitrary power, but conscience bound by Popish chains, which, when thoroughly fastened upon us, away must go our bibles, and in lieu thereof, we must have imposed upon us, the superstitions and damnable heresies and idolatries of the church of Rome. Then we must pray to the Virgin Mary, worship images, believe the doctrine of purgatory and the Pope's infalibility, and such like. And last of all, the deepest plot of hell and Rome, the holy inquisition, must guard the Catholic faith of the church of Rome, and bind us thereto with all its terrors and cruelty. O! who that is awake, with any sensibility thereof, had not rather loose their blood and lives too, than leave posterity in such a situation!

It was through sermons such as these that the need to defend a religious heritage, the very heart of the popular Revolutionary movement, made its way into the public debate.[44]

Carl Bridenbaugh in *Mitre and Sceptre* has documented the importance of the debate over the creation of an Anglican bishopric in America. It was this debate, as John Adams stated, that "spread an universal alarm against the authority of Parliament." The threat of religious oppression seemed real, even to the enlightened John Adams. If Parliament can tax us without our consent, he reasoned, then they can establish the Church of England over us. And if the Church of England becomes established, he warned, it could "prohibit all other churches, as conventicles and schism shops." It was not taxation by itself that so terrified these American dissenters. It was the threat of what the exercise of such arbitrary authority might lead to.[45]

In his examination of *Revolutionary Politics in Massachusetts,* Richard Brown looked into the responses of the rural towns to the Boston circular of 1773 to see whether these towns were acting on their own impulses or simply reacting to Bostonian leadership. The results were instructive. The responses of the towns did not simply repeat the arguments of the original circular but often added touches of their own which revealed the evangelical emphasis of their anger. "God will not suffer this land," came one response, "where the Gospel hath flourished, to become a slave of the world." Another town declared that their ancestors "chose a wild Desert with Liberty Rather than the Fruitful Fields and beautiful Gardens of their Native Land with slavery." The need to defend their religious heritage was clearly enunciated.[46]

Not only did these towns show that they were acting in defense of their fathers' religion, they did so within the context of the biblical story. The town of Marlborough, according to Brown, "translated the whole matter of political conduct and political salvation into biblical terms." Attleborough specifically compared itself to the "Israelitish nation." In the towns of the colony, Brown concluded, "liberty was cherished as a kind of temporal salvation, public virtue was seen as part of the broad category of Christian virtue, while political apathy and acquiescence had their counterparts in religious backsliding and corruption." The Boston Committee, he noted, "had touched a super-sensitive area of popular belief." In this way, the traditional religious beliefs of the communities were "intertwined" with revolutionary action.[47]

The unlettered pietists were not the only revolutionaries to be caught up in the imagery and rhetoric of Old Testament typology. Samuel Adams, the man who did more than any other single person to keep the revolutionary flame burning, has been described as a diehard Puritan who was fighting to return Massachusetts to his imagined ideal of a Christian cooperative commonwealth. His "Christian Sparta" was not based on the model of England, Rome, or Greece but on the Israel of the time of the Judges. "The child Independence is now struggling for birth," he wrote from Philadelphia in 1776. "I trust that in a short time it will be brought forth, and in spite of Pharoah, all America will hail the dignified stranger."[48]

Adams' friend and ally in the Massachusetts legislature, Joseph Hawley, had been an Arminian during the Great Awakening and had led the fight to oust Jonathan Edwards from his pulpit in 1750. He later had a change of heart and begged Edwards for forgiveness. During the revolutionary turmoil of the Seventies, he fought alongside Adams and when Adams was in Philadelphia in 1776 wrote urging him to "strike while the iron is hot. The people's blood is so hot as not to admit delays . . ." He was fearful that the people might lose their enthusiasm for liberty and, "as they did in England after Cromwell's death," might call for a return to the old order. He wrote to Elbridge Gerry with the same message and added his prayers that Americans would "not be cajoled by Lord Howe and carried back to Egypt." He did not have to explain the metaphor.[49]

Samuel's cousin, John Adams, although no Calvinist, was enough of a New Englander to share his cousin's sympathies. Both he and his wife, Abigail, understood the meaning of the Exodus. In 1775, Abigail wrote to John and expressed the ancient Calvinist belief that afflictions are a desired prelude to salvation: "Great events are most certainly in the womb of futurity," she wrote, "and if the present chastisement which we experience have a proper influence upon our conduct, the Event will most certainly be in our favor." The particular chastisement she referred to was the British occupation of Boston, and the plight of the refugees fleeing that city called up the expected parallel:

> One day their household furniture is to come out, the next only wearing apparrel, and the next Pharoahs heart is hardened. and he refuseth to hearken unto them and will not let the people go. May their deliverance be wrought out for them as it was for the Children of Israel.[50]

In a letter dated June 11, 1775, John wrote to Abigail about a sermon he had heard from "Mr. Duffil, a Preacher in this City whose Principles, Prayers, and Sermons more nearly resemble those of our New England Clergy than any that I have heard."

> His Discourse was a Kind of Exposition on the thirty fifth Chapter of Isaiah. America was the Wilderness and Solitary Place, and he said it would be glad, rejoice and blossom as the Rose.

This was not the only occasion when Mr. Duffield "fill'd and swell'd the Bosom of every Hearer" with this theme. A year later, John wrote again to Abigail about one of Duffield's sermons: "He run a parallel between the Case of Israel and that of America, and between the conduct of Pharaoh and that of George," and he concluded "that the Course of events, indicated strongly the Design of Providence that We should be separated from G. Britain." John Adams was not one to let the parallel stop here. If America was Israel in the wilderness, then what of the leaders of this American Exodus?

> Is it not a saying of Moses, who am I, that I should go in and out before this great People? When I consider the great Events which are passed, and those greater which are rapidly advancing, and that I may have been instrumental of touching some Springs, and turning some small Wheels, which have had and will have such Effects, I feel an Awe upon my Mind, which is not easily described.

Thus the Puritan identity still influenced both the evangelical and the rational strain of New England thought. Even such a rationalist as John Adams dared to suggest that he might be a second Moses.[51]

The identification of America with the Israel of the Exodus was thus not a peculiarly New England theme. Calvinists throughout the colonies carried the image with them, and the Presbyterian Scotch-Irish, along with migrating New Englanders, carried the rhetorical assumptions of evangelical Calvinism into the South and the West. Among these, Joseph Montgomery, a Presbyterian minister who would later become a delegate to Congress, in 1775 in Philadelphia published *A Sermon Preached at Christiana Bridge and Newcastle.* In this sermon, an extensive parallel of America and Israel, he recalled the words of Moses as he lay dying on Mount Pisgah: "Keep, therefore, the words of this covenant and do them, that ye may prosper in all you do." America was within sight of the Promised Land; it was not a time to abandon the faith. The underlying "inclinations" that inspired the New England Calvinist also inspired the Scotch-Irish community. As one historian wrote in 1826, "the old hatred and animosity against high church authority and arbitrary government . . . became, as it were, infused into their blood and breeding; and it is supposed, even to this day, that there is not a descendant of that steadfast community, who could, even by accident, beget a Tory or an Arminian."[52]

There were numerous sermons preached throughout the South and the Middle Colonies which showed that the theme of America as the new Zion was not a peculiarly New England or Puritan theme. These even included sermons by Patriotic Anglicans such as John Lewis' *Naboth's Vineyard,* preached in Charleston, South Carolina, and David Griffith's *Passive Obedience Considered,* preached in Williamsburg, Virginia. Even in

Georgia, according to a recent study, all of the political pamphlets of the Swiss Reformed minister, John J. Zubly, who in 1776 turned from Patriot to Loyalist, "embodied the theme of America as the New Canaan and the Americans as the chosen people of God." The same forces at work in New England produced in the South a similar externalization of the originally spiritual metaphors of conversion in the wilderness. In *The Transformation of Virginia*, Rhys Isaac has written:

> While the fields became scenes for collective redemption, the woodland wilderness became the proper setting for individual spiritual quests. Jesse Lee's father, "one day when his conviction [of his lost state] was deep, and his distress very great, went out into the woods, and continued travelling about, and mourning for his sins." His sons, in their turn, took themselves off into the wilderness. Indeed such solitary wandering seems to have been an expected preparation for conversion. John Taylor sought out "a lonesome mountain, where nobody lived," and James Ireland constantly sought "solitude and retirement in the woods." . . . For these men the wild forest had become the appropriate haunt of the isolated individual and a symbol of his quest.

Thus in the South as in the North, the religious emphasis on conversion, brought to new importance in the Great Awakening, helped to create the impression that the natural American wilderness would be the scene of salvation, their's and the world's.[53]

It was, however, the articulate New England clery who made the most of the traditional typological imagery. The use of biblical imagery and language was so widespread that it even became an object of ridicule and satire among proponents of the loyalist cause. Benjamin Church, who later was revealed to have been a traitor, published a sermon in 1765 titled *Liberty and Property Vindicated; and the St-pm-n burnt.* The purpose of the sermon, so he said, was to "compare the time present with the former," that is, to compare the experience of the Americans with that of Israel. He specifically identified Ingersoll, the Connecticut Stamp agent, as "an emblem of the molten calf made by Aaron of old in the wilderness" and he called on the freemen of Connecticut to "stand fast in the liberties granted you by your royal charter." Church may have thought he was being funny, but apparently he did not understand his audience. According to Bernard Bailyn, Church

> seized the opportunity both gently to mock the Biblical pedanticism of rural New England and, parsonlike, to 'improve' the occasion politically by publishing this pamphlet. If so, it was his greatest literary success, for despite its exaggeration of the genre . . . it appears to have been taken with full seriousness.

The loyalists never could comprehend just how seriously the "fanatics" of New England took their own rhetoric. To them, it was all just words; to the Calvinists it was the stuff of life. Church, without intending to, had touched a "super-sensitive area of popular belief."[54]

Perhaps if Church had read Stephen Johnson's sermon of 1765 published in Newport, Rhode Island, he would have understood more clearly why the public took his satire seriously. In that sermon, Johnson took as his text, "I have seen, I have seen the affliction of my people which is in Egypt, and I have heard their groanings, and am come down to deliver them." He denied that British oppression must drive the colonies to independence, but it is possible, he said, "that, sooner or later, it may happen to the British colonies." His conclusion was a clear statement of New England's religious mythology:

> Israel was called and set apart for God, in the peculiar engagement of his covenant, that they might be to him a holy people, for a name and praise; and he subjected them to his yoke and redeemed them out of Egypt, and brought them to Canaan . . . And let us never forget, that our forefathers left the dear delight of our native country, and fled into the inhospitable desarts of America, not for worldly wealth or honors, pomps or pleasures; but for the glorious cause of liberty, and undefiled religion.

It was only as long as religion remained "undefiled" that there could be any hope for the preservation of "liberty." The two were inseparable and it was to defend them both that the revolution was fought.[55]

Of all the possible examples of the importance of religious identity and particularly of the Great Awakening as an underlying factor in the Revolution, none is more striking than the story of General Arnold's preparation for the expedition to capture Quebec. According to Headley, Arnold "felt that the perils of the untrodden mysterious wilderness, they were about to penetrate, might be too great for human energy and endurance," so he called on Samuel Spring to preach a sermon over the assembled troops. Spring preached in the Presbyterian Federal Street Church in Newport directly over the spot where the leading evangelist of the Great Awakening, George Whitefield, lay buried. According to Spring,

> I preached over the grave of Whitefield. After the service, the general officers [among whom presumably was Colonel Aaron Burr, Jonathan Edwards' grandson] gathered around me. Someone requested a visit to Whitefield's tomb. The sextan was hunted up, the key procured, and we descended to his coffin. It had lain in the tomb six years, but was in good preservation. The officers induced the sextan to take off the lid

of the coffin. The body had nearly all turned to dust. Some portions of his graveclothes remained. His collar and wristbands, in the best preservation, were taken and carefully cut in little pieces and divided among them.

So un-Protestant an act as dividing up the relics of a saint demonstrate how far from the principles of the Awakening those who fought to defend its legacy had fallen. Again symbols had become more important than the things they were meant to symbolize. But the need to defend an inherited identity was as strong, if not stronger, than ever. Arnold's troops were unable to endure "the perils of the untrodden mysterious wilderness" and were defeated long before they reached Quebec. Perhaps because they had fallen to idolatry, an angry God poured his vengeance upon them in the wilderness.[56]

On July 4, 1776, John Adams, Thomas Jefferson, and Benjamin Franklin, three secular rationalists each representing a different region of the new country, met in Philadelphia for the purpose of designing the Great Seal of the United States of America. Adams made an effort to defer to his non-New England neighbors and suggested Hercules resting from his labors as a fit symbol. But Franklin and Jefferson both insisted on the rightness of the biblical parallel. Franklin wanted to depict the Red Sea swallowing Pharaoh's army, and Jefferson suggested the pillar of smoke that led the Children of Israel toward the Promised Land. In the end, none of these was chosen, but the fact that they were suggested indicates just how widespread the biblical image was. The enthusiasm of New England sent waves across the American pond; the final ripples were secular but the original rock was religious. Even Thomas Jefferson, despite his own Deistic sympathies, knew what symbolism would be most effective in tying the allegiance of the people to the new government.[57]

v

For most evangelicals, the revolution provided one more opportunity to be tried in the wilderness. The experience of war, as it had been for Mrs. Rowlandson, was another opportunity for a literal regeneration through violence. But the wilderness of war also proved ambiguous, reaffirming the sanctity of the elect who already presumed themselves in Canaan as it reaffirmed the conviction of others that there were still many miles of wilderness to cross.

After the battle of Lexington and Concord, the use of the biblical parallel increased. Jonas Clark, the minister of Lexington, commemorated the first anniversary of the battle with a sermon on the text, "Egypt shall be a desolation, and Edom shall be a desolate wilderness, For the Violence against the Children of Judah, because they have shed INNO-CENT BLOOD in their land."[58] But other ministers were able to go beyond the basic parallel and to develop more complex themes that tied into the whole Calvinist tradition of wilderness imagery and its relation to the conversion process. Within the metaphor of America's parallel with Israel, two separate visions of the new American community competed for the loyalty of the people. One identified with the Israel of the wilderness still under the rod of the law and suffering for its many sins. Adherents to this more orthodox view leaned heavily on the jeremiad tradition to remind Americans of their sins and of the many miles left to travel before theirs truly was a Godly community. Adherents of the other, the more "liberal," view believed that the wilderness had been crossed and that America was the Israel of Canaan, at ease in Zion, secure in the assumption of God's grace. This division is of course too neat. These two emerging American cultures, as has been said, were not always distinct but overlapped. Most orthodox jeremiads ended with a vision of the millennial glory that could, or even would, follow the expected reformation, and no Protestant sermons, however liberal, neglected to mention the sins of the people. Nevertheless, sermons could be distinguished by their emphasis. A close examination of two of these provides insights into the enduring potency of the wilderness tradition in the American mind.

Samuel Sherwood's *The Churches Flight into the Wilderness* provides an important example of the way in which popular association of America with the biblical Israel contributed to the revolutionary spirit as well as to the growth of American nationalism. Uncomplicated by doubts about America's redeemed status, the sermon, published in New York in 1776, reflects the near Antinomian enthusiasm that had engulfed the nation in 1775. It begins by reminding the people that the political troubles of the day were the manifestations of deeper and darker conspiracies. These were not the intrigues of cabinet ministers but more sinister intrigues that dated back to the beginnings of time. New England's ancient enemy had simply reared its head in a new guise, using new instruments to attain its ends. The old serpent

> has ever been using his subtlety and malice to defeat the purposes of divine grace, and to destroy Christ's Kingdom on Earth; and has, in all ages of the world, been successful in stirring up agents and instruments to accomplish this diabolical and hellish design.

King George and his ministers and agents were themselves only fronts. The true forces of evil were invisible.[59]

Having placed the machinations of local bureaucrats in their proper cosmic perspective, Sherwood reminded his readers of America's affinity with the children of Israel in the wilderness. But he pointedly denied that the word wilderness should continue to mean "danger and affliction." It was our father's task, he said, to subdue the wilderness. Since their time, the wilderness had been made to "blossom like the rose." The parallel with the children of Israel was no longer with their wilderness sojourn but with God's "delivering them from the tyrannicall power of the haughty, cruel monarch of Egypt, and conducting them to the good land of promise in Canaan."[60]

America, for Sherwood, was truly and surely God's redeemed Israel. Though it suffered affliction, he was convinced it would be victorious. He reminded his readers of Isaiah's promise that "when the enemy shall come in like a flood, the spirit of the Lord shall lift up a standard against him." The flood, he explained, was already upon the land, consisting of

> all the subtle temptations, artful schemes, and machinations of our enemies and adversaries, to ensnare and corrupt us, and to destroy our liberties and privileges, that we might be embarrassed again under the old tyrant, the dragon, and patiently submit to the iron yoke.

But the flood, like the flood of Noah and the sojourn in the wilderness, was also a symbol and a promise of coming redemption.[61]

Satan's attempt to prevent the establishment of Zion in America was an old story. Readers of the Bible knew that the woman who fled into the wilderness "as on Eagle's wings" was pursued by floods that issued from the mouth of the dragon. It did not need to be said that America was that woman; the parallel was clear:

> Everyone acquainted with the history of our country, of the New England colonies in particular, must know, that there have been floods issued from the mouth of the old serpent, after the woman, to affect her destruction and overthrow.

The old serpent's agents, "frogs," were in the process of hatching their slimy schemes. Citing two historical examples of corruption, Andros in Boston and Cornbury in New York, Sherwood warned that once again Satan's agents

> have been slyly creeping into all the holes and corners of the land, and using their enchanting art and bewitching policy, to lead aside, the simple and unwary, from the truth, to prepare them for the shackles of slavery and bondage.[62]

Identifying "the administration" in Great Britain as what "seems here described," Sherwood ended with a call to arms to defend Christ's kingdom. But his was more than a simple defensive posture. Victory over the beast, he prophesied, would result in the establishment of God's kingdom over not just the united American colonies but all the world:

> . . . it is to be hoped, that the dragon will be wholly consumed and destroyed; that the seat and foundation of all tyranny, persecution and oppression, may be forever demolished; that horns, whether civil or ecclesiastical, may be knocked off from the beast, and his head receive a deadly wound, and his jaws be effectually broken; that peace, liberty and righteousness might universally prevail; that salvation and strength might come to Zion; and the kingdom of our God, and the power of his Christ might be established to all the ends of the earth.

Here were all the elements of the developing American myth. America, the renewed Zion, would conquer the agents of Satan and millennial glory would spread from the American shores throughout the globe. For Sherwood, not the French and Indian Wars but the American Revolution loomed as the first American war to end all wars. Here was millennial enthusiasm unleashed in the name of God and in the service of American nationalism; here was the first American struggle between the children of liberty and the evil empire. The cause of America had become unmistakably the cause of God. As in former periods of revival, once the initial shock of awakening was over, an enthusiastic presumption of righteousness completely overwhelmed any lingering doubts. The people were truly God's Israel, the wilderness had become a garden, and Zion blossomed like the rose.[63]

If Sherwood's rhetoric was typical of evangelical preachers of the revolutionary era, committed wholly to the presumption that America had become Canaan, there were still others who, though they may not have retained the full psychological meaning of wilderness imagery, did remember that there was a wilderness and that it had not yet been crossed. Nicholas Street, a Connecticut minister and a descendant of John Davenport's assistant of the same name, was one of those who tried to restore the balance. In a sermon too long overlooked,[64] he reaffirmed America's identity as the new Israel and branded England the new Egypt, but he was less willing than Sherwood to proclaim the wilderness sojourn at an end. To fulfill her role in history, America he believed had to leave Egypt and plunge through the wilderness of war, re-establishing her ancient identity through a new round of affliction, humiliation, and conversion. America was not yet Zion, he insisted, and her people not yet converted. Street feared that the orthodox balance between joy and despair had been lost and he attempted to restore a sight of sin to Zion.

Nevertheless, the wilderness that Street called the people to return to was a wilderness not of the mind and soul but of battle. Even for one who held to the wilderness tradition, the literal symbol proved more compelling than that which it was meant to symbolize. If true spiritual conversion could not be had, Americans were ready once again to accept a literal substitute for the real thing.

The title of Street's sermon tells the story almost by itself: *The American States Acting Over the Part of Israel in the Wilderness, And thereby Impeding Their Entrance Into Canaan's Rest; or, The Human Heart Discovering Itself Under Trials.* The trials under which the human heart would discover itself would be, not the introspective journey through the insanity of self, but the trials of war. The process was the same, but material symbols had replaced spiritual reality. The wilderness, explained Street, was "a state of troubles and difficulty"; the British, the Egyptians; the Red Sea, "a sea of blood"; the British "Tyrant," another "Pharoah king of Egypt"; and even the Tories had their predecessors in "those of Nehem. 2.19 who tried to prevent the building of Jerusalem."[65] For Edwards, the human soul had been the wilderness in which sinners found the truth about themselves; for Street, the wilderness of war would suffice.

Yet for all of this literal parallelism, Street's main purpose in this sermon was to warn people that the reason God led Israel into the wilderness was not to make them proud of their holiness but "that they and others may see what corruption there still remains in their hearts unmortified and unsubdued."[66] The people may be Israel recreated, but they should not therefore imagine themselves out of the wilderness and already at rest in Canaan.

Britain may be the recreation of Egypt, he warned, but that does not make America the Israel of Zion. Many went into the wilderness who never saw the promised land.

> And 'tis likely God will keep us in this wilderness of trouble to humble us and prove us, that we may see our errors, and know that God had a righteous controversy with us at this day. We are apt to think that our cause is so righteous with regard to Great Britain, that I fear we are ready to forget our unrighteousness towards God.

In case any had forgotten, Street listed in remarkable detail exactly what evidence there was for this charge. With an understanding of the economic motives of "natural men" that would do credit to any Progressive historian, he catalogued the sins of the people—war profiteering, hording, exploiting labor, trading with the enemy, serving self before nation and God. The true state of the nation's heart was being brought out by the trials of war, declared Street. "Be ashamed and confounded for your own ways, Oh house of Israel!"[67]

Street's purpose may have been to chastise the people for their arrogant presumption of holiness, for daring to believe themselves saints even as they profited from the war. But as did most Jeremiads, his only served to heighten the illusion. If they were not yet in Canaan, they were certainly still God's Israel. Not only did Street spell out in detail parallels between the American struggle with Britain and the Jews' struggle with Egypt, but in chastising the Americans for their sins, Street assumed the role of Moses in the wilderness. It would not be the wilderness and they would not be Israel if a Moses was not there to remind them of their sins. Is it any wonder that Americans continued to believe themselves Israel, especially after the war was won? Why did the war occur, asked Street? To expose the people's sins! "And what is the end of this discovery? Why to humble us, and to bring us to repentance and a general reformation."[68] The Revolutionary War was thus seen as one more instance of the ancient symbol of regeneration in the wilderness of violence. And those who survived it became convinced that they could put self-doubt behind them for theirs was the New Jerusalem come at last.

vi

For Americans today, the religious identity portrayed in these sermons has a more than antiquarian interest. The nature of the movement which gave birth to the United States remains a crucial part of American identity. Our politicians and pundits constantly return to the Revolution and the Founding Fathers for expression of what America is or should be. The idea is still popular that the American Revolution was the product of the rational Enlightenment, and people with an interest in what they believe to have been the values of that movement continue to argue that America is essentially a rational, secular nation in the image of Jefferson and Franklin. But it is a fact that King George III with his attempt to "rationalize" and centralize his empire had more in common with the Enlightenment of Voltaire and the Enlightened Despots he endorsed than did the American colonists with their anachronistic talk of charter rights and local liberties. It is not surprising that many secular academics, themselves partisans of the Enlightenment, have with considerable success portrayed the Revolution as a secular, rational, political movement. Nor is it surprising that adherents of the religious interpretation of the Revolution have, as often as not, been personally more sympathetic to religion and more willing to define the national purpose in religious terms. Surely, both of these existed and continue to exist. The argument over the identity of the Revolution is an argument, at bottom, over our identity today. Its significance endures.

The significance of the debate is not all that endures. The very language of these sermons continues to echo through our culture. It is surprising, only at first, to read Sherwood's description of the Revolution as a war to end all wars. His further division of the world into an evil empire of dark, satanic despotism and regions filled with the light of liberty is unnervingly familiar. It has, he proclaimed,

> been the constant aim and design of the dragon, sometimes called the beast, and the serpent, Satan, and the Devil, to erect a scheme of absolute despotism and tyranny on earth, and involve all mankind in slavery and bondage—, and so prevent their having that liberty and freedom which the Son of God came from heaven to procure for, and bestow on them.[69]

When he writes, a few pages later, that it is "the administration" that seems here described, the relevance of these sermons for modern American culture is brought sharply home.

For here is the American character. Jefferson and Franklin were not our only ancestors. Here are other passions that also drive us. Here is the language that reverberates through our historical consciousness. We have been trying to convince ourselves that the practical, worldly, rational side is the only side. But it is not so. This too, with its frightening paranoia and its ecstatic millennial vision, is also us.

After the Revolution the wilderness was not completely forgotten. But with the victory over Britain most Americans enthusiastically accepted the belief that their republic was the recreation of the land of Canaan. In New England, the image of the American Israel retained some of its original ambiguity. The split between Arminian rationalism and Calvinist piety had remained hidden during the war. The further division among the Calvinists between those who were at ease in Zion and those who remembered the wilderness of sin also remained hidden. But once the war was over, with the Tories either fled or quiet, the whole spectrum of opinion shifted to the left. No longer did a significant portion of the elite endorse Anglicanism. Even Virginia severed its legal ties to its Anglican establishment. Thus when the split did re-emerge, it did so within a broad consensus loyal to the originally Calvinist identity of America as Israel whether as the Israel of the wilderness or of Canaan. Asked who was the author of Independence, John Adams replied,

> The only true answer must be the first emigrants, and the proof of it is the charter of James I. When we say, that Otis, Adams, Mayhew, Henry, Lee, Jefferson, etc., were authors of independence, we ought to say they were only awakeners and revivers of the original fundamental principle of colonization.[70]

What had originally been a New England identity thus became an American identity. The belief that America was not just a "land of opportunity," but figuratively the Promised Land of the Bible became a part of the developing American consensus that has been called America's "Civil Religion."[71] But if for the majority America had become the Promised Land, there remained those who thought it still a wilderness.

At the beginning of the nineteenth century, in New York and South to the Kentucky mountains, evangelicals like Charles G. Finney stirred up the fires of democratic reform. As one observer noted, travelers who carried the revival fire "from the paternal altars of New England to the 'new country'" of the West "have found it more dangerous among the more combustible materials" there.[72] On the frontier, the presumption of personal and national righteousness raged out of control.

But in New England, Federalist evangelicals like Lyman Beecher, who had some memory of the Fear of God, maintained a political alliance with their equally-conservative Unitarian adversaries. New England was not ready for perfectionism, not yet. The New England mind remembered, however vaguely, that the metaphor was not the reality, that the real was not yet the ideal, that America was far from being the recreation of Zion. It distrusted the human passions unleashed by the more enthusiastic revivalists as much as it distrusted Jefferson's faith in human reason. The unconverted human personality was not to be trusted. Despite the claims of the revivalists and the self-assurance of the enlightened rationalists, there were still many miles of wilderness to cross before the human heart or the human brain could be trusted.

In other parts of the nation, evangelicals could rejoice at being saved. Christ's justification, through the magic of revivalism, had become theirs. But in New England, even the Second Great Awakening was a more sober affair. The image of Canaan was still caught up in its ancient tension with the image of the wilderness. The human heart was felt to be a place of dread as well as joy. New Englanders knew themselves to be Israel, but they were not certain where Israel was. Assumptions of righteousness and temptations to emotional abandon were still constrained by memories of Calvinism's insistence that the self was a lie and its perceptions illusions. The New England soul, beneath its shell of smug self-confidence, was still haunted by the ancient call to suffer in the wilderness and be purged in the fires of the wrath of God.

PART III

The Literary Remains

5
The Transcendental Growth

In the church of the wilderness Edwards wrought,
Shaping his creed at the forge of thought;
And with Thor's own hammer welded and bent
The iron links of his argument,
Which strove to grasp in its mighty span
The purpose of God and the fate of man!
Yet faithful still, in his daily round
To the weak, and the poor, and sin-sick found,
The schoolman's lore and the casuist's art
Drew a warmth and life from his fervent heart.
Had he not seen in the solitudes
Of his deep and dark Northampton woods
A vision of love about him fall?
Not the blinding splendor which fell on Saul,
But the tenderer glory that rests on them
Who walk in the New Jerusalem,
Where never the sun nor moon are known,
But the Lord and His love are the light alone!
And watching the sweet, still countenance
Of the wife of his bosom rapt in trance,
Had he not treasured each broken word
Of the mystical wonder seen and heard;
And loved the beautiful dreamer more
That thus to the desert of earth she bore
Clusters of Eshcol from Canaan's shore?

Whittier, "The Preacher"

i

The Calvinist spirit of Hooker and Edwards, the call for self-destruction in the wilderness of subconscious fear, did not entirely die out in the nineteenth century. The fires of an optimistic Arminian evangelism filled the western forests; in the East schoolroom poets like Whittier used the language and imagery of the wilderness tradition to sustain a purely sentimental Christianity, but the old embers survived underground,

almost forgotten, until they flared up in unexpected form, burning the
soles of surprised nature buffs out for what they thought would be
innocent nature walks through the woods. Especially in New England,
the wilderness fire continued, however subtly, to singe the cultural consciousness, no longer from the pulpit but in literature.

The influence of Calvinism's introspective terrors on the American
Gothic tradition can easily be shown.[1] But the sunshine side of American
Romanticism was no less influenced by Calvinism. Its very assertion of
hope and meaning was a "YES" shouted with enough force to hold the
wolves of the wilderness at bay. In most cases they remained at bay; but
they remained.

Nor should the Transcendental debt to European Romanticism be
allowed to obscure the fact that much of Transcendentalism was, in
Stephen Whicher's words, "essentially 'reminiscent Puritanism' thinly
disguised as philosophy." The foreign ideas, as Perry Miller has shown,
merely "stirred native propensities" by providing a new language with
which the Transcendental revivalists could disguise their regression—
even from themselves—to the spirit of the Great Awakening and the
Antinomian crisis. Coleridge and Kant, Carlyle and Cousin did not
introduce romanticism into America. They simply provided the language with which the heirs of Edwards could "rephrase the ancient
religious pre-occupations of New England." In *Freedom of the Will,* Edwards had argued that the "inclinations of the heart" precede the "speculative notions" of the head, that the loves and hates of youth determine
the intellectual decisions of maturity. Certainly the European romantics
were important sources of the specific ideas with which the Transcendentalists articulated their new beliefs, but the attitudes, the inclinations,
that prepared the way for those new ideas were the effects of closer
causes.[2]

Nor was the optimistic emphasis of romanticism a foreign import
altogether alien to the native Puritanic gloom. Calvinism, after all, did
have an enthusiastic side. The Calvinist image of wilderness was never
just a symbol of darkness and sin, but combined both terror and joy,
crucifixion and resurrection, the sojourn through the desert and the
entrance into Canaan. New England Calvinists had always held that the
beneficiaries of the conversion experience received a heightened perception of beauty, a new appreciation of divine truth, and an intuitive love of
moral excellency. Emerson's "divine light of Reason" was but a distant
reflection of Edwards' "Divine and Supernatural Light Immediately
Imparted to the Soul by the Spirit of God." Edwards' grandfather,
Solomon Stoddard, had said quite clearly that saints know their election
"by intuition, or seeing of grace in their own hearts. It is by consciousness." Edwards had "seen" the immediate presence of Christ in the

beauties of the woods and fields. The Transcendentalists, as Octavius Frothingham revealed, could not deny their ancestry:

> Indeed, whenever orthodoxy spread its wings and rose into the region of faith, it lost itself in the sphere where the human soul and the divine were in full concurrence. Transcendentalism simply claimed for all men what Protestant Christianity claimed for its own elect.[3]

This much is not new. The parallels between Edwards and Emerson, their love of the natural world, their philosophical idealism, their symbolic consciousness have been pointed out by numerous authors. Long before Perry Miller published his famous essay, "From Edwards to Emerson," Harriet Beecher Stowe had noted that "Waldo Emerson and Theodore Parker were the last results of the current set in motion by Jonathan Edwards." Henry Bamford Parkes, in the year Miller's essay was published, went even further than Miller dared go and claimed that almost "all the ideas of Transcendentalism can be found in Edwards." Miller's essay, like much of this other criticism, had merely pointed out to those who were looking elsewhere the true mountain source of the mighty stream that was American Romanticism. Most critics have been content with little more than a repetition of the news of his discovery. They have not tried to penetrate that wilderness. For Miller left no map, and there are no obvious paths up the mountain from Emerson back to Edwards.[4]

Had Emerson studied Edwards more carefully than he did, and left clearer records of his borrowings, there would be little problem.[5] If Emerson had been brought up by Calvinist parents, the job would be much simpler. But without such specific trails to follow, the argument would have to be made in terms of general cultural inheritances, that Emerson, as Parkes argued, "seems to have absorbed ideas which Edwards put into circulation rather than to have studied Edwards himself."[6] This could be done, but there is at least one trail, one clear Calvinist influence on Emerson, that largely has been ignored: the influence of his aunt, Mary Moody Emerson.[7]

A true mystic and a true New England Calvinist, Mary Moody Emerson was one of her nephews' earliest and certainly their most impressive teacher. She did not define her faith by creed or catechism, she lived it. To her "the fiery depths of Calvinism, its high and mysterious elections to eternal bliss, beyond angels, and all its attendant wonders" was not dogma. It was an attitude that knew man to be but flesh, a wind that passeth away and cometh not again. She held human endeavor to be worthless, human pretensions absurd. Whatever point of view anyone put forward she took delight in destroying. She never denied the vain satisfaction this gave her, but she also insisted on a serious intent, to prove to the worldly that all human speculations fall short of the absolute, that the glory of God forever stands above and against all human idolatry, that despite all pretensions Israel remained in the wilderness. "If she found that anything was dear or sacred to you," wrote Van Wyck Brooks, "she instantly flung broken crockery at it."[8]

Emerson was well acquainted with his aunt's eccentricities. No one reading his letters to her, or his essay commemorating her life, can deny that he loved her. When his father, William Emerson, died in 1811, "Aunt Mary," as she was always known, was asked to come to Concord to help care for the four small boys. She agreed, as long as she could take over not just the household chores but the spiritual education of her nephews. She had disapproved of her brother's Unitarianism, unable even to grieve his death remembering his "defective theology."[9] She gladly replaced him as the chief spiritual guide and authoritative "father figure" to the fatherless boys. When she arrived, it was to make sure, as Emerson himself put it, that her nephews should be "bred to purify the old faith of what error and narrowness adhered to it, and import all its fire into the new age." She was determined that her nephews should rekindle the spiritual flame and set their generation afire with the faith once delivered to the saints.[10]

Born in 1774, the heir of "six generations of a sovereign priesthood," Mary was, as she later told Lafayette, "in arms" at the battle of Lexington and Concord. Her filio-pietism was as strong as her pietism. She once rebuked Waldo for citing classical examples of heroism and ignoring his own more noble ancestors. Her father had died of a fever while serving as Chaplain to the army at Ticonderoga, and her widowed mother had sent the infant to Malden to be raised by an ageing uncle and aunt. Tried by harsh poverty and ill-tempered guardians, forced to care for a second "insane" aunt, she found solace during her hours of lonely drudgery in the doctrines of self-denial and divine sovereignty. Later, when she had access to books, she gave herself to study. Her earliest reading, according to Emerson, "was Milton, Young, Akenside, Samuel Clarke, Jonathan Edwards, and always the Bible." Her treasured copy of *Paradise Lost* lacked a title page and not until years later did she learn who its author was. In this setting, she saturated herself with the moods and the language of orthodox Calvinist piety. In time she passed these on to her nephews. "In my childhood," recalled Emerson, "Aunt Mary herself wrote the prayers which first my brother William, and when he went to college, I read aloud morning and evening at the family devotions, and they still sound in my ear with their prophetic and apocalyptic ejaculations." Throughout his life, he continued to consult her letters for inspiration. "In reading these letters of M.M.E.," he wrote in 1841, "I acknowledge (with surprise that I could ever forgot it) the debt of myself & my brothers to that old religion."[11]

Scholars have not found it easy to characterize Mary Moody Emerson's faith. She was far too imaginative and lively for those who know only the literal and legal side of Calvinism. She was certainly no Transcendentalist. And she scorned the negations of Unitarianism. Phyllis Cole has defined her as "Arian but not Arminian." She consciously defied characterization. Even her favorite Calvinists felt the sting of her tongue. She did have her intellectual heroes, but she followed no earthly leader. Her God stood beyond the horizon of human speculation. Many a pompous balloon (and there were many in Concord) was punctured by a shard of her broken crockery.

Neither steadily to port or starboard, nor sailing that impossible course straight into the wind, but tacking back and forth between a daring exuberance and a sublime humility, between righteous exertion and a pious waiting on the call of God, she defied consistency. More often than not her letters shouted with the boastfulness of an assured saint marching through Canaan with sword on high, but there is enough evidence of the darker moods, especially in her journal, to justify the suspicion that in long periods of winter loneliness her soul wandered in the wilderness of contrition, humiliation, and fear.

Her letters emphasize the need, not for a specific experience of conversion, but for continual solitude and suffering. For her, life was a continual conversion, a never-ending crucifixion of the flesh and a constant turning toward God and His Christ.

Edwards had preached the necessity of men's crucifying their innate self-love in the typological wilderness before they could hope to enter Canaan. Calvinism had always held that human beings must crucify their self-love and accept in its place what Edwards had called love for "Being in general, or the great system of universal existence." This was Mary's faith, a willingness to be damned for the glory of God. If God should cast her off, she wrote, she would cling to her faith that "at some moment of His existence, I was present: that, though cast from Him, my sorrows, my ignorance, my meanness were a part of His plan." Faith in her own continuing crucifixion inspired her: "I would not write with so much confidence if I did not know that I am willing to give up everything to His will." If God required crucifixion, then her suffering put her in touch with God.[12]

One of Calvinism's highest attractions was the meaning that it gave to human suffering. By denying the necessity of suffering, by preaching that Canaan could be gained without a sojourn in the wilderness, the Unitarians and their sentimental allies had taken away that cosmic sense of purpose that Calvinism had claimed for the sufferings of humanity.

Mary valued her own despair because it assured her of the existence of God. Being in the wilderness put her on the road to Canaan and gave her life an eternal, biblical context. Hers was the paradoxical spirit of Calvinism that found in the darkest despair the most arrogant presumption of holiness, that embraced rejection and turned it into an identification with Eternity. Hers was that balance, though it never balanced but rocked wildly back and forth, that Augustine and Edwards had achieved. For her, the wilderness and Canaan, suffering and ecstacy, the shabby real and the cosmic ideal, were all bound up in the bundle of life together.

This dualistic desire for self-denial and for the substitution of God in place of self was what defined her Calvinism. In one of her earliest journal entries, Mary resolved to forgo self and lie in the dust: "Alive with God is enough—'tis rapture." To suffer was to be crucified unto Christ: "Oh let my miseries be arguments with God to bless me!" And she made a vow, at the age of 25, "of contrition, submission,—(oh how sweet) to His will, wherever recognized, of joyful silence that has nothing to utter before Him." Years later in Maine, at her farm, "Elmvale," she held to her original insight, embracing suffering as her one tangible connection to God:

> The problem still the same, how one soul cast out from all books, society, & health, sicken of its own follies & narrow limits, can love to adore the creation, rejoice in His infinite joy, and ask nothing but the conviction that pain is immediate from Him as His decree.[13]

Proud as she was of her trials in the wilderness, Mary was able to confess herself "a striking specimen of egotism." She regretted it, but she was not about to deny it. She did it for God. And she accepted the moments of regenerating grace as a free gift not to be questioned or denied. Here was the other side of the cross. There was the wilderness, but there was also the vision of the heavenly bridegroom coming into the wilderness:

> The rapture of feeling I would part from, for days more devoted to higher discipline. But when Nature beams with such excess of beauty, when the heart thrills with hope in its Author . . . it exults—too fondly perhaps for a state of trial. But in dead of night, nearer morning, when the eastern stars glow, or appear to glow, with more indescribable lustre, lustre which penetrates the spirits with wonder and curiosity,—then, however awed, who can fear? . . . I shall delight to return to God. His name my fullest confidence. His sole presence ineffable pleasure.

The presumption of assuming oneself a recipient of grace, as Hooker had tried to explain to Anne Hutchinson, as Edwards had tried to warn the enthusiasts, was a dangerous thing. Mary was a good enough Calvinist to know that enthusiasm is "a delight, but may not always be a virtue." She thought of herself as a sojourner in the wilderness, but like Moses she had climbed Pisgah and had visions of the paradise to come. When God calls, when the emptiness suddenly is filled with waves of supernatural love, who can but answer?[14]

Nevertheless, the dominant note in her writings continued to be one of self-denial. Believing life to be futile, knowing herself unable to reach God, she prayed constantly that she might lose herself in Eternity. She took to wearing a shroud and complained bitterly of death's delay. Irritated by the daily frustrations of being human, she could not wait to lose her individual existence in universal existence, her idea of what it meant to be one with the blowing clover:

> There is such an abyss of capacity to live; of falling short of the plainest duty, that I could live all *without,* that is, in God's agency—lose myself. O wise and sublime theology of the ancient Hindoos who sought to lose themselves!

But if life was futile and full of pain, still there was a God, an Existence, a universal Being-in-General whose acts and thoughts were not futile. For His sake, she endured: "I keep going round and round like the squirrel on a wheel, but I revolve about the center of infinity."[15]

This was her goal: "the desire of being absorbed in God, retaining consciousness" seemed to her more real than the vaunted "usefulness" of "action." This was the vision at once of her own damnation and of Christ's glorification. This was the point of balance between Canaan and the wilderness, what Edwards called the "Beauty in the Divine Character" of His "Vindictive Justice." This was the joy discovered in despair, the Bridegroom discovered in the desert. For the Calvinist, the human being in the lonely depths of despair who turns to the heavens to accept the justice of God's judgement and thereby receives grace, is the complete human being, fully damned, fully justified, and on fire with the vision of Christ. "Never," wrote Mary, "do the feelings of the Infinite and the consciousness of finite frailty and ignorance harmonize so well as at this mystic session in the deserts of life." Like Augustine, she rejoiced Not I, but Thou, Oh Lord, "Let the whole prosper—no duration for me."[16]

Despite her exhaustive learning, Mary's temptation was to spiritual, not intellectual, pride. "That my mind is not formed for a Plotinus, or

Edwards, I never dared repine; only sought that awe, that concentrating
fervor, which is the boon of small ones." To be with God was the one
reward she craved: "Away with knowledge—God alone." She denied
herself the satisfaction of an intellectual belief in truth deeming it better
to *feel* at one with truth than to pretend to know it. She confessed her
inability to "think God," but she proudly proclaimed that at times she felt
Him "through all the little compass of mind and soul."[17]

One specific intellectual gift that Mary did bestow on her nephew,
Waldo, was an interest in Hindu philosophy. Another was an introduction to the moral sense philosophy. According to Joel Porte, it was Mary
who first suggested that young Waldo read Richard Price, and it was
from his reading of Price that Emerson first received his appreciation of
the concept of God's indwelling in every human soul in conscience.
Although they used philosophical argument as their means, these philosophers emphasized the priority of intuition, of felt sense, over intellect. It was, Emerson would come to believe, through this innate "moral
sense" that men and women could become one with the Oversoul.[18]

It is true that the moral sense philosophers taught that it is possible for
men, through conscience, to have an intuitive appreciation of God's
moral law. Emerson read them correctly. But this was not the message
that Mary intended. Had she known what his reading in Price would
lead to, she would never have suggested it. For Price believed that the
moral sense is something that all human beings in their natural state have
access to. Mary also believed in conscience, "this primitive faculty inde-
pendent, though modified by circumstances without," but she believed
that the ability to know God intuitively was a gift given exclusively to "the
good" and was higher than mere natural conscience.[19]

Edwards, who had read and appreciated Hutcheson, also believed that
all men, no matter how depraved, have some shadow of the moral law
within them. But he had distinguished such "common grace" from the
supernatural sense of God's excellency which was given exclusively to the
saints. Mary too believed in natural conscience, but natural conscience
was not Christ. These stirrings of natural conscience, which all persons at
some time felt, though they might lead eventually to Christ, were not to
be confused with supernatural grace.

The moral sense philosophy, although a repudiation of Calvinism, can
be seen as an enlargement of the Calvinist conception of election to
include all mankind. The moral sense philosophers, and after them
Emerson, wrote as if they believed natural conscience to be the voice of
God. If this were so, then human beings did not have to undergo the
terrors of conversion in order to hear the voice of God; they had only to
go a short distance to their own natural hearts. They thus borrowed

from Calvinism the doctrine of regeneration without also taking the doctrine of crucifixion. They assumed that all humans were born with the ability to enter Canaan without having to cross the wilderness. As Frothingham said, they simply "claimed for all men what Protestant Christianity claimed for its own elect." For Mary, the elect were those who had a conscience awakened to the truths of original sin and the contrasting excellency of Christ. To have said that all people have such a conscience would have been to confuse the products of imagination with those blessings only Christ could give to those predestined to be saints. Like the Common Sense moralists, she believed in going to the heart and not to the head, but like Edwards she believed that what would be found there would be, not easy grace, but first an entrance into the wilderness of the fear of God, and only after crucifixion, resurrection.

Mary believed intuitively that life was a dance to an unheard tune, all striving and exertion spinning endless circles around infinity. She believed that a person desiring to hear the divine music could only return to the wilderness where, after forty years of suffering and self-denial, the soul might be led out of chaos to Pisgah to view the promised land. And she certainly believed the metaphor to be spiritual, that the wilderness was of the soul, in consciousness. But she was not immune from the temptation to believe that the physical creation was more than just a symbol of the invisible world. She loved the solitude and beauty of nature for itself and not just for its symbolism. Like Peter Bulkeley before her, she believed that the presence of the body in a literal wilderness, while not the same thing as conversion, nevertheless was a helpful prerequisite to conversion. From her wilderness Pisgah, she had her visions of Canaan. The feeling of being lost in God came to her most frequently, she admitted, at Elmvale where "the Divinity was felt as seldom elsewhere." She valued her "years of privation in . . . the beautiful wilderness, tho' famished" of "all social and literary advantages." Time, she wrote, is but "an image of Eternity," and "in the stillness of the wilderness where God hath built a midnight—it thus becomes undefiled."[20]

Her sojourn in the wilderness, in silent waiting on God, held out the hope that God yet might build on her, that despite her intellect and her pride God might make use of her. The Calvinist saint might wait piously for many years, eager for the first faint stirrings of something beyond human conception, before God's terrible swift sword suddenly cut across the warp and woof of time to call His saints to battle. My Aunt, wrote Emerson, is "the wierd-woman of her religion & conceives herself always bound to walk in narrow but exalted paths which lead onward to interminable regions of rapturous and sublime glory." To be made use of, with all one's sins, was the only way Calvinists could hope to obtain any participation in glory. Mary rejoiced when she remembered that there can be no contingencies, in "the nature and origin of things none but all that to us and by us is so, was forseen and met by weaving all the blunders and sins into a web of gathering beauty & happiness, like as the flower grows from . . . the dunghill." Thus she allowed herself to flow with the rhythms of the universe waiting and praying for God to call on her to serve creation and lead her onward to "regions of rapturous and sublime glory." When she first received a request from Concord to assist in the education of her nephews, surely she entertained the hope that finally her call had come.[21]

ii

Mary Moody Emerson began and ended her attempt to pursuade her nephew, Waldo, of the benefits of Calvinism with the wilderness tradition, literally and figuratively, urging him both to leave the city for the solitude of nature and to lose his ego in the psychic wilderness for the hope of divine perception. It was during his years at Harvard that Emerson's correspondence with his aunt was most intense. Having failed to instill in him when he was young her own love of self-denial, Mary then appealed to his intellect. But the very fact that his intellect had become the judge showed just how far from self-denial Waldo was.

Mere philosophical contemplation, Mary wrote to him in 1821, "cannot long actuate the mind." To endure life, "we must have some method of affecting the sense and imagination and must embrace some *historical* as well as *philosophical* account of the divinity." Fearing she might lose him to the pale speculations of Harvard's rational religion, Mary forcefully argued for the necessity not just of dogma but of feeling. As had Edwards in *Religious Affections,* she argued that the emotions and not just the intellect must be part of the worship of God. Emotional responses, she insisted, cannot be gained by reading books about philosophy. They come as the result of a process of self-examination, self-denial, and regeneration, of a crossing of the inner wilderness to the promised land of vision:

> Those who paint the primitive state of man's creation are sweet poets—those who represent human nature as sublimed by religion are better adapted to our feelings and situation; but those who point the path to the attainment of moral perfection are the guardian angels. But this is no easy poetic task. The lowly vale of penitence and humility must be crossed before the mount of vision—the heights of virtue are gained. Therefore we so often hear the warning voice of

high-toned morality against the seductions of the vagrant flower-clad muse. May yours if she should continue and prune her wings be sanctified by piety.[22]

Mary did not argue the doctrines of Calvinism with her nephew. "Of that system," she objected, "you know nothing but a few bare words." Instead, she continued to hammer away at her theme that "superficial science & false philosophy" cannot lead to God. "Away with your offerings at his shrine," she scolded him, "if they come not like the emblem of those laid up in the antient ark pure gold & polished without & celestial manna within."[23]

Surrounded by Harvard Unitarians, reading the latest from the advocates of rational and natural theology, Emerson valued the letters he received from his aunt. They breathed a spirit that he did not find in his daily school work. But he was unable to give intellectual assent to the doctrines they contained. He resisted their attraction and held himself aloof. Mary reacted to his continuing rationalism by accusing him of "collecting facts," of preferring "sensation" to "sentiment" when he should be "energising" his soul. She prophecied his fall but prayed that "your fall may call down some uncommon effort of mercy and you may rise from the love of deceitful good to that of [the] real." At the bottom of this letter is the inscription:

This letter is a most beautiful monument of kindness and high-minded but partial affection. Would I were worthy of it. Reread Dec. 1822 R. Waldo E.[24]

At this point, Mary's efforts were directed toward saving her nephew from philosophy and winning him for the religion of the heart. As he strove to externalize and objectify his understanding, she fought to bring it back to the heart:

As to words or language being so important—I'll have nothing of it. The images, the sweet immortal images are within us—born there, our native right, and sometimes one kind of sounding word or syllable awakens the instrument of our souls, and sometimes another. But we are not slaves to sense any more than to political usurpers, but by fashion and imbecility.[25]

Thus, with additional support from the European Romantics, Mary tried to save her nephew from Lockean rationalism. But as Mary soon began to learn there were dangers on the other side. By merely touching emotion and not diving deeply into the wilderness, one could become a slave to mere superficial "sense." By saying that "the sweet immortal images are within us," she had unwittingly played into the hands of the romantics.

In 1824, responding to Emerson's growing interest in the rhetoric of European Romanticism, Mary argued the benefits of Calvinist spirituality over those of the "flower-clad muse." "This deep and high theology," she proclaimed, "will prevail & German madness may be cured— The public ear[,] weary of the artifices of eloquence[,] will ask for the wants of the soul to be satisfied. May you . . . be among others who will prove a Pharos to your country & times."[26] But Mary was not able to persuade her nephew to look still deeper beyond the superficial "sensations" of his heart and surrender to the fear that she knew was there. Convinced of the errors of Lockean rationalism, unconvinced of the glories of Calvinism, Emerson found in Romanticism an alternative that allowed him to sing the praises of heart religion and retain his ego too. As Edwards had and as Freud would, Waldo constructed a rational defense of irrationality, an affirmation of the "all" in which the self still remained distinct and in control.

This transition was by no means immediate or complete. Emerson continued to ask for letters on "the dark sayings and sphinx riddles of philosophy and life." Despite his inability to accept her doctrines, he still respected his aunt's spirit, and he used her as a sounding board to help him clarify his own emerging philosophy. In particular, he continued to defend rationalism as a necessary balance to those feelings whose importance he could not deny. Does not Divinity make Himself amenable to our reason, he asked? What about Benjamin Franklin? "Don't you admire (I am not sure you do) the serene and powerful understanding which was so eminently practical and useful, which grasped the policy of the globe, and the form of a fly with like felicity and ease. . . ?"[27]

Mary blamed herself for Emerson's stubborn defense of his own condition. The encouragement she had given him in childhood had strengthened his natural self-love to an unreasonable degree. Now she tried to undermine the very self-confidence she had once helped to establish:

> It was pretty, it seemed best, to tell children how good they were,—the time of illusion and childhood is past, and you will find mysteries in man which baffle genius.

But Emerson was far too set in the self-confidence of his age. His nature rebelled at the very notion of self-denial; he could not see any benefit in yielding to insanity, and he was determined to remain comfortably sane. He was intrigued and revolted, fascinated and repelled:

I am blind, I fear, to the truth of a theology which I can't but respect for the eloquence it begets and for the heroic life of its modern, and the heroic death of its ancient defenders. I acknowledge it tempts the imagination with an epic (and better than epic) magnificence; but it sounds like mysticism in the ear of understanding. Paley's deity and Calvin's deity are plainly two beings, both sublime existences, but one a friend and the other a foe to that capacity of order and right, to that understanding which is made in us arbiter of things seen, the prophet of things unseen. . . . I can not help revolting from the double deity, gross Gothic offspring of some Genevan school.

By making his own "capacity" and "understanding" the ultimate criteria, of course Emerson could not see the benefits of a deity who would cast those central idols into chaos.[28]

Mary Moody Emerson was not one to give up easily. If Waldo would only keep his mind open, he might yet experience his understanding's depravity and accept the sovereignty of God over man's feeble "capacity." The Holy Ghost, she reminded him, comes not from human effort but is "the reward of prayer, agony, self-immolation!" And she added bitterly, "Dost not like the faith and the means? Take thy own—or rather the dictates of fashion.—" But still she held out hope that he might yet have a sight of sin and reject the authority of man's feeble, determined, depraved perception: "You have not had time to feel that this huge globe was but a web drawn round about us that the light the skies the mountains are but the painted vicissitudes of the soul. . . ." But when he did feel this, Emerson embraced not Calvinism but the doctrine of correspondence. He did not lose himself but saw himself in "the light the skies the mountains."[29]

When Emerson became ill in 1825, Mary saw his sickness as an opportunity for him to be held over the pit and forced to confess the folly of his dangerous self-confidence. But he recovered and her disappointment was bitter and unrestrained:

I say you are getting well too soon before you have seen the mystic visions which visit the sick;—before *thought* (O wonderful mysterious power which allies us to Him who passes wonder) has dispelled those mists which rested on some of your speculations.

She complained that he had not suffered enough. "Never mind," she consoled him, "you will, if you are destined to future eminence." And still she hoped that he might be brought over to the cause of God in time. "I rejoice," she wrote to him, "that you have been kept from launching till your anchor is stronger than I suspect it is, till the tide which you imagine is sweeping away old beliefs will ebb & return with full bearings of truth."[30]

To all this Emerson responded by agreeing, intellectually, with much of the thought but never by giving himself to the deed. "I agree," he wrote from his sickbed at St. Augustine, "to the sentiment of your letter that I shall be a wiser and better man. He has seen but half the universe who never has been shown the house of pain." He even acknowledged "a principle in human nature . . . that suggests and sanctions the crucifixion of the flesh before the mighty image of God within the soul." Nevertheless, he added, "we are not bound by suggestions of sentiment, which our reason not only does not sanction, but also condemns." Emerson's reason remained firmly in the saddle. But he was tempted. He found it pleasant, he admitted to his aunt, "to hover on the verge of worlds we cannot enter, and explore the bearings of piled mists I cannot penetrate." He would hover but never enter. He was not ready to sacrifice his reason for the sake of mystic promises he could not trust. Nor did he see the need. He was, he told her, "not curious to add to my genuine grief horrors for imaginary and remediless delinquencies." Would it not be a crime, he asked, to "surrender to the casual and morbid exercise of the sentiment of a midnight hour the steady light of all my days, my most vigorous and approved thoughts, barter the sun for the waning moon?" And yet he had to confess, in the privacy of his journal, that

> now and then the lawless imagination flies out and asserts her habit. I revisit the verge of my intellectual domain. How the restless soul runs round the restless orbit and builds her bold conclusion as a tower of observation from whence her eyes wander incessantly in the unfathomable abyss.[31]

If sickness could not force Emerson into the subconscious depths, there was always the possibility that a sojourn in the literal wilderness might be the needed catalyst. To this end, Mary continually urged her nephew to leave the city and return to nature. Apparently, at this stage of his life, Emerson was not altogether enamored of the country life. After a hike through central Massachusetts in 1822, he wrote to his aunt expressing his doubts about her enthusiasm for the wilds. He found much of nature enjoyable but not somehow divine:

> I cannot tell but it seemed to me that Cambridge would be a better place to study than the woodlands. I thought I understood a little of that *intoxication,* which you have spoken of; but its tendency was directly opposed to the slightest effort of mind or body; it was a soft

animal luxury, the combined result of the beauty which fed the eye; the exhilarating Paradise *air,* which fanned and dilated the sense; the novel melody which warbled from the trees. Its first charm passed away rapidly. . . . Perhaps in the Autumn, which I hold to be the finest season in the year, and in a longer abode the mind might, as you term it, return upon itself.

Mary had convinced her nephew that there was some spiritual benefit to be gained from going to nature, but he had not yet experienced it and he did not know what it was. In a letter to his friend, John Boynton Hill, Emerson expressed his frustration:

My aunt, (of whom I think you have heard before & who is alone among women,) has spent a great part of her life in the country, is an idolater of Nature, & counts but a small number who merit the privilege of dwelling among the mtns. The coarse thrifty cit profanes the grove by his presence—& she was anxious that her nephew might hold high and reverential notions regarding it (as) the temple where God & the Mind are to be studied & adored & where the fiery soul can begin a premature communication with the world. When I took my book therefore to the woods—I found nature not half poetical, not half visionary enough.

Clearly, the idea had begun to get through to young Emerson that there was something sacred to be discovered in nature. But what it was and how to obtain it remained mysteries.[32]

Mary did not try to argue the benefits of the pastoral life. She stuck closely to her central concern, the need to lose oneself in the wilderness. It was to this end that she urged her nephew to leave the city, not to improve his reading ability but to plunge him into the darkness of the solitude of his soul:

Then you find no necessary sacredness in the country, nor did Milton; but his mind & his spirits were their own place, & came when he called them in the solitude of darkness. Solitude . . . is to learning & genius the only sure labyrinth, tho' sometimes gloomy, to form the eagle wing that will bear one farther than suns & stars. . . . Would to Providence your unfoldings might be there.

Further attempts to lure Emerson into the wilderness were equally fruitless. But Mary had her call, and her stubborn determination to make him see the dark reflected the importance that Waldo had assumed in her lonely life. In her journal, when her spirits were low, she flogged herself back to the task:

Courage, and go on to the mortifying work of years,—transcending. . . . Yes I know I haste to the ocean, tho' this silly little wherry is aground. In Earth's ocean is many a treasure. . . . But to thy task slave! boat-woman, cabin-mother, book scavenger! Waldo lives and praises thy lines. There was no Waldo, no idea of society when thou wast up early & late to copy a sermon or scrap lent thee by a rustic. To it, to it!

Her efforts were to no avail. Emerson agreed that the wilderness was pretty, that it perhaps had a supernatural beauty in which the will of God could be discerned, but even that cold analysis was made from the relatively civilized precincts of Concord. When I go to the woods, she enticed him, "I shall not think . . . only feel pleasantly abroad." But she also confronted him demanding,

> But why are you in the city? They will buzz to you of music, of literature, of chemistry, of everything that will disturb the culture of your character, everything averse to that enthusiasm of piety,—of extensive benevolence of highminded principle which can alone support devotion to God and love to the race.

But Emerson never did see the wilderness, at least not in the Calvinist sense. His own strict self-control kept him and his deepest emotions quite separate. Even in the woods he saw, not wildness, but order, "nothing done at random, No accidents in nature . . . Never get out of God's city, Order, order everywhere. . . ." For Emerson the wilderness had become Canaan; he had only to stroll through the Concord woods to find himself in the promised land.[33]

Mary, saint though she may have been, soon wearied of her nephew's inability to understand her. When he wrote to her asking for more letters, "What from the woods, the hills, and the enveloping heaven? what from the interior creation—if what is within be not the Creator?" she sent back a polite reply. When he tried to explain to her his belief that nature itself was the voice of God, she shot back angrily, "if this withering Lucifer doctrine of Pantheism be true what mortal truth can you preach or by what authority should you feel it?" He did not comprehend how his going to the woods differed from her sojourn in the wilderness, and he complained of her "always fighting in conversation against the very principles which governed & govern her." Years later, in 1832, she wrote to his brother, Charles, that Waldo "is lost in the halo of his own imagination."

> As to Waldo's letter, say nothing to him. It is time he should leave me. His sublime negations, his non-informations I have no right in the world to complain of. His letters are always elegantly spiced with

flattery, which I love. What he thinks sound, or intends, time and report may unfold.

Time and report brought Mary news of *Nature* in 1836 and of "The Divinity School Address" in 1838. It was worse than she had feared. She had introduced him to nature and he had learned the wrong lesson there. She accepted defeat but she was not defeated. She continued to correspond with her favorite nephew, but the driving sense of purpose faded from her letters. She fell back on her own resources, back to "the mortifying work of years,—transcending." Her spirit remained to the end as fiery as it had ever been:

> The yesterday does never smile, as I would. Yet in the name of the Sheperd of mankind, I defy tomorrow. God himself cannot withdraw himself. Health feeble. alone. most alone, but I defy tomorrow.[34]

iii

By 1838, after Mary had abandoned all attempts to win her nephew for her truth, Emerson was launched on his career. His soul's "bold conclusions" had become fixed and from his tower he defended that "intellectual domain." The frontier of this domain was marked by the romantic affirmations of *Nature*, and the territory within those boundaries has been thoroughly surveyed. He repudiated original sin; the doctrine of innate depravity, he declared, "is the last profligacy and profanation. There is no scepticism, no atheism but that." He described a Calvinist as one whose "active powers are paralyzed" by fear, whose affections are cramped "and all its energies directed to an anxious exploring of ways of escape, a way of atonement." In contrast, he believed the new American, freed from paralyzing doubts, to have an unlimited future. The wilderness, he implied, is a false myth; grace is available to every human being. The human mind can attain all that the human heart deserves. There is only Canaan to be enjoyed by all Americans forever:

> If they have not the lamp of Aladdin, they have [in Pennsylvania and Ohio] the Aladdin oil. Resources of America! Why, one thinks of St. Simon's saying, "The Golden Age is not behind you but before you." Here is man in the Garden of Eden; here the Genesis and the Exodus.

It would be wrong however to picture Emerson's fortress as secure and steady. He had rejected the pessimistic view of human consciousness, but he must have suspected that the oil might not last forever. For Mary's arguments continued to haunt him, and the possibility of terror re-mained.[35]

If a revolutionary is one who successfully overthrows an established order, then Emerson was no revolutionary. It would be better to think of him as a rebel engaged in an ongoing battle, still trying to overthrow the old establishment. Emerson's self-reliant man was not a cooperative person helping to build a new order; he was an embattled figure stand-ing up against the universe. Whicher correctly described the early Emer-son as "a balked hovering affirmation searching for a safe landing-place."[36] He never did refute Mary; he only asserted his unwillingness to sacrifice his ego in a mystic quest.

Yet he wanted what Mary offered. He wanted grace; he wanted her mystic insight, her transcendent vision, her transcendent confidence. He never was wholly convinced that she was wrong to preach self-annihila-tion as the only path to transcendent vision. He never was an unqualified romantic; he was always both "The Skeptic" as well as "The Poet."

It would be going too far to say that Emerson remained in any way a Calvinist. He believed that God is available in the soul of every man and woman. The Calvinists, in contrast, believed that God stands apart from and against this world and that only the saints have even a glimpse, not of Him, but of His son. And yet, Mary's influence was there. Perhaps it would help to take a clue from Emerson's friend and biographer, Dr. Oliver Wendel Holmes, who said in those pre-Freudian days,

> There are thoughts that never emerge into consciousness, which yet make their influence felt among the perceptible mental currents, just as the unseen planets sway the movements of those which are watched and mapped by the astronomers. Old prejudices, that are ashamed to confess themselves, nudge our talking thought. . . .

Mary Moody Emerson was the unseen planet that continued to sway her nephew's thoughts, and the influence was not altogether unconscious. After her funeral, in 1863, Emerson wrote that he clung to her writings and that "her letters and journals charm me still as thirty years ago, & honor the American air."[37]

The sceptical side of Emerson is more apparent in his early and late writings, writings which reflect the doubts that lurked beneath the sur-face of his serenity, doubts which in his early years he had not yet out-argued and in his later years was unable any longer to deny. In his theoretic speculations, he maintained that in the human soul is to be found, not the chaotic wilderness of insanity that the Calvinists em-braced, but the very image of God communicated from the Godhead to the waiting soul of man. And yet, he was not always quite sure. "Love has an empire," he declared, "but fear has an empire too." Occasionally he made use of a model of human consciousness that resembled Calvin's more than Kant's. In 1832 he confessed in his journal that "It is awful to look into the mind of man and see how free we are, to what frightful excesses our vices may run. . . . Outside, among your fellows, among strangers, you must preserve appearances . . . ; but inside, the terrible freedom!"[38]

Emerson's early poem, "Grace," a poem that stands in stark contrast to the bulk of his published poetry, creates a clear picture of the Calvinist view of the mind as a conditioned reflex held over the mouth of a flaming pit:

> How much preventing God, how much I owe
> To the Defenses thou hast round me set;
> Example, custom, fear, occasion slow,
> These scorned bondmen were my parapet.
> I dare not peep over this parapet
> To gauge with glance the roaring gulf below,
> The depths of sin to which I had descended,
> Had not these me against myself defended.

Here is the same sentiment that Emerson expressed to his aunt when he wrote that he dared only go to the edge of his intellectual domain and let his eyes "wander incessantly in the unfathomable depths." Only custom, example, and fear, the means of conditioning, kept him from tumbling into the wilderness of sin that he clearly realized just below his ego's domain. If anything, this poem shows Emerson even more determined to avoid the pit. Here he dared not even peep at the abyss. He knew, as he confided to his journal, that "for every seeing soul there are but two absorbing facts,—I and the abyss." Mary was transfixed by the abyss; Emerson, though he heard her muse, clung stubbornly to the I.[39]

This poem reveals that Emerson did, despite his romantic affirmations, believe in the abyss. Despite all he wrote, he knew that there was a gulf between himself and God. He did not have the emotional experience he desired. He was, as Melville said of him, all intellect: "his brains descend into his neck and offer an obstacle to a draught of ale." Mary convinced him of the need for feeling, but she was unable to make him feel. He envied her passionate nature. "Can you not awaken a sympathetic activity in torpid faculties?" he asked. "Whatever heaven has given me or withheld, my feelings or the expression of them is very cold. . . ." When his son died, he wrote, "Alas! I chiefly grieve that I cannot grieve." In his writings he sang the praises of passion and emotion. But in his personal life he was as cold as any Unitarian cucumber, and he regretted his "torpid faculties."

I count and weigh, but do not love. . . . Yet would nothing be so grateful to me as to melt once for all these icy barriers, and unite with these lovers. But great is the law.

Trying to explain himself to Margaret Fuller, who all but despaired of getting a human emotion out of him, he begged her forgiveness describing himself as "a mute, not ungrateful though now incommunicable. . . ."[40]

Emerson affirmed to all the world the ability of every human being to partake of the Godhead. yet he was unable himself to break out of the prison of his own intellectuality. He wanted Mary's mysticism, but he was unwilling to go through Mary's ordeal to get it. He wanted Canaan without the wilderness. The question was "How?"

In *Nature,* he described the one time he felt "glad to the brink of fear." But he did not know how to reproduce this experience. "The power to produce this delight," he equivocated, "does not reside in nature, but in man, or in a harmony of both." Later he instructed his readers to "conform your life to the pure idea in your mind." He did not say how to do this. Nor did he get any closer in his later essays to describing just how one got in touch with the Oversoul. In "The Poet," he suggested that it was "some obstruction or some excess of phlegm in our constitution which does not suffer them to yield the due effect." It was to try to attain this experience, he suggested, that bards love "wine, mead, narcotics, coffee, tea, opium, . . . or whatever other producer of animal exhilaration." But he knew that this was the wrong approach. Instead he suggested that the poet put himself in touch with this "new energy . . . by unlocking, at all risks, his human doors, and suffering the ethereal tides to roll and circulate through him;" The answer seemed to have something to do with having to risk suffering. But every time Emerson urged his readers—and implicitly himself—to "break off your association with your personality, and identify yourself with the Universe," the frustrated reader can only cry out, "How?"[41]

Emerson did of course have one answer. And it is hard to avoid the conclusion that while he was unwilling to accept the spiritual meaning of the sojourn in the wilderness, he was ready to embrace the literal. Go to nature, he said. Go to the woods, and there you will find God. "The land is the appointed remedy for whatever is false and fantastic in our culture." It is the "sanitive and Americanizing influence."

He who frequents those scenes, where nature discloses her magnificence to silence and solitude, will have his mind occupied often by trains of thought of a peculiarly solemn tone, which never interrupt the profligacy of libertines, the money-getting of the miser, or the glory-getting of the ambitious. In the depths of the forest, where the noon comes like twilight, on the cliff, in the cavern, and by the lonely lake, where the sound of man's mirth and of man's sorrow were never heard. . . , is a shrine which few visit in vain.

Emerson went with Mary only as far as the trees; despite his affirmation that "Nature is the symbol of the spirit," he went only to the literal woods, not to the symbolic wilderness. As Whittier did in his poem "The Preacher," Emerson appropriated the Edwardsian wilderness tradition and transformed it into a sentimental sojourn with nature.[42]

The Puritan typologists of the seventeenth century had also forgotten the spiritual meaning of the sojourn in the wilderness and had confused the type with the antitype, the symbol with the substance, mistaking their sojourn in the literal wilderness for true conversion. As Mary Moody Emerson herself stressed the solitude of the woods as the locale of this transformation, Emerson, remembering his aunt's insistence that he return to the wilderness to see God, went to the woods and sat on a log and wondered why the mystic visions never came. Because he refused to accept the separation of the real and the ideal, of this world and the heavenly Canaan, like Roger Williams, the Antinomians, and even like Cotton Mather, he declared himself a citizen of Zion. He imagined himself reborn in Canaan, beyond the wilderness, and he elevated his worldly imaginings to the status of the divine.

The Unitarians, by denying in effect that this world is merely symbolic denied that there was anything higher beyond the veil. Emerson knew better, but his attempt to embrace the antitype brought the transcendent down to earth and led to a denial of the duality of symbol and substance. If symbol and substance are one, then there is no symbolism. The end result must be a materialism as cold and sterile as any tea the Unitarians served.

Edwards had reveled in the beauty of Christ in the fields and the clouds, but Edwards had passed through the wilderness of humiliation and terror. Emerson wanted Edwards' experience, but he was not willing to suffer for it. He wanted the experience here and now in this body, in this world, with his accustomed dinner at dinner time and his comfortable bed in the evening. To accept duality would have meant giving up the world for the spirit. This he was not willing to do. He wanted both.

In the thirties Emerson had ridiculed the evangelical mob. But in 1845 he wrote,

There must be the Abyss, Nox and Chaos, out of which all come, and they must never be far off. . . . This is the strength and excellency of the people, that they lean on this.

Toward the end of his life, before senility set in, as the mystic experiences tarried, Emerson grew even more skeptical. Clearly, he was beginning to accept the notion that Calvinist pessimism had its point. His own confidence in his ability to know the truth, intuitively or otherwise, had begun to wane. His essay "Experience" marks the turning of his life. "All things swim and glitter," he wrote. "Our life is not so much threatened as our perception." Edwards had seen the loss of habitual perception as the first step into conversion. It was the loss of such perception that Emerson had once fortified himself against. But now he saw it coming. If there was no easy woodland path to grace, then the violence of regeneration might be the only means after all.[43]

The Puritan soul with its anxious readiness to battle for the Lord had always been attracted to the terrible swift sword. War, Mary had said, is

> so much better than oppression that if it were ravaging the whole geography of despotism, it would be an omen of high and glorious import. Channing paints its miseries, but does he know those of a worse war,—private animosities, pinching, bitter warfare of the human heart, the cruel oppression of the poor by the rich. . . ? War devastates the conscience of men, yet corrupt peace does not less.

In the Civil War, Emerson saw that violence had a place in converting men and nations. The scriptures written on men's hearts, he said, "do not come out until they are enraged. They can be read by war fires and by eyes in the last peril." God still dwelt within, but getting to him had not been as easy as Emerson had hoped. Perhaps Mary had been right and the "lowly vale of penitence and humility," the terrifying violence of the crucifixion of the self in the wilderness, was "to learning and genius the only sure labyrinth . . . to form the eagle wing that will bear one farther than suns and stars."[44]

Ralph Waldo Emerson's attraction to nature, then, came not only from the influence of the European Romantics but from his own New England heritage, and more directly from his aunt, Mary Moody Emerson. The typological association of the wilderness crossing with the experience of conversion in the wilderness of the soul was much in the minds of the Emersons' ancestors when they came to New England, and this wilderness tradition was carried to Waldo through the agency of his aunt. That he forgot the spiritual meaning of the metaphor and confused the literal woods with the spiritual wilderness does not weaken the connection between the Transcendental religion of nature and the Calvinist wilderness tradition. The transcendentalists may have looked to nature to bring the self in touch with God while the Calvinists looked to the wilderness to destroy the self in favor of God. But both looked to the wilderness as a means of grace, however different these means may have been. The Transcendental love of nature as well as the sentimental nature worship that followed, was thus a product of a barely conscious fascination with the wilderness as the wilderness of the soul, as a projection of the antitype onto the type, of the spiritual onto the literal. Ralph Waldo Emerson sought an easy way to Canaan, but in the back of his mind were Mary Moody Emerson's "prophetic and apocalyptic ejaculations" and her warning that the "lowly vale of penitence and humility must be crossed before the mount of vision—the heights of virtue are gained."

iv

Mary Moody Emerson's enthusiastic Calvinism battered on the door of more than one Transcendental heart. Henry David Thoreau was fascinated by his mentor's aunt and engaged her in conversation for hours at a time. She was, he said, "the wittiest and most vivacious woman I know." She was one of the few persons in Concord who would actually listen to him, and, most incredible!, was a woman with a mind of her own:

> In spite of her own biases, she can entertain a large thought with hospitality, and is not prevented by any intellectuality in it, as woman commonly are. In short, she is a genius, as woman seldom is. . . . Thus she is capable of a masculine appreciation of poetry and philosophy.[45]

Although not descended from as lofty a Calvinist lineage as Emerson, Thoreau too was a New Englander. His maternal grandfather, the reverend Asa Dunbar, was as consistent a Calvinist as any in Emerson's family tree. The two aunts with whom Thoreau lived adhered to their father's faith, supporting the orthodox faction when it split from the more liberal Concord establishment. Although he left the church upon graduating from Harvard in 1837, it would be wrong to assume that the church and the orthodox precepts of his native culture, no longer nudged "his talking thought."

Upon reading Emerson's *Nature* in 1836 Thoreau embraced the new religion of Transcendentalism, but still he had had to struggle with such doubts and insecurities as led others to a less happy faith. His college essays reveal that his Transcendentalism did not develop spontaneously. As an adolescent Thoreau had had to choose between the competing visions of Canaan and the wilderness. Before he could become a Transcendentalist, Thoreau, like many of his generation, had had to banish the specter of the wilderness from his mind.

These college essays reveal Thoreau in the process of putting the doctrines of conversion through terror behind him. The idealist perception of the unreality of matter, the same perception that for Edwards had been a pathway to the pit, became for Thoreau the perception that distinguished the "superior" from the "common man." Edwards had warned that men walk over the pit of hell as on a rotten covering. The earth, echoed the young Thoreau, firm under the feet of the common man, for him of superior insight "affords only a frail support,—its solid surface is as yielding and elastic as air." His superior man, awakened from common confidence in the "infallibility of reason," has learned to doubt,

> to question even the most palpable truths. He feels that he is not secure till he has gone back to their most primitive elements, and taken a fresh and unprejudiced view of things.

The purpose of this questioning, however, was not to obtain a speculative understanding of truth nor, as it had been for Edwards, to force sinners to face their innate depravity. Instead, what Thoreau's "superior" man hoped to achieve was a heartfelt perception of "the sublime."[46]

In an essay titled, "The Sublimity of Death," Thoreau had argued against the orthodox view that terror "is the ruling principle of the sublime." That far he would not go. He was willing to admit that "obscurity, solitude, power and the like, so far as they are able to excite terror, are sources of the sublime." But, he argued, it was "that second birth, the resurrection . . . which we approach with a kind of reverential awe." The resurrection and not the crucifixion, Canaan and not the wilderness, became for Thoreau the true source of the sublime. Terror, he decided, is not eternal and therefore cannot produce eternal states of mind. The sublime, he said, is produced by a "ruling principle, an inherent respect or reverence, which certain objects are fitted to command. . . . The Deity would be reverenced, not feared." Taking his cue from the moral sense philsophers, like Emerson he endorsed the concept of a natural indwelling principle which "prompts us to pay an involuntary homage to the Infinite, the Incomprehensible, the Sublime," a faculty "which forms the very basis of our religion."[47]

Like Edwards and his Calvinist predecessors, Thoreau was motivated by a desire to be ravished by the grace of God, to "secure one new ray of light," to "feel myself elevated for an instant upon Pisgah." He believed in the existence of what Sherman Paul has called "naturalized grace" and he was determined to experience it:

> My desire for knowledge is intermittent; but my desire to commune with the spirit of the universe, to be intoxicated even with the fumes,

call it, of the divine nectar, to bear my head through atmospheres and over heights unknown to my feet, is perennial and constant.

But Thoreau was never able to experience this grace. Like Emerson, he did not know how to obtain it. His was the ancient cry of the awakened, What must I do to be saved? And as Paul says, "failing this Godlike emotion," he became "a desperate searcher for it."[48]

Walden has long been recognized as "a song of death and a paean of resurrection." Thoreau's journey into the woods to "live deliberately, to front only the essential facts of life" was the Transcendental equivalent of the Christian journey into the solitude of the wilderness of the self. But even more than Emerson, Thoreau was caught up in the literal interpretation of the ancient symbol. If grace was to be found in the wilderness, then "the poet must, from time to time, travel the logger's path and the Indian trail, to drink at some new or more bracing fountain of the Muses, far in the recesses of the wilderness." Thoreau's essay, "Walking," is evidence of the continuing incantational potency of the very word "wilderness." "In wildness is the preservation of the world," sang Thoreau. "From the forests and the wilderness come the tonics and barks which brace mankind." "Give me a wildness whose glance no civilization can endure." The wilderness still called from beyond the civilized hedge, but the difference between the literal and the symbolic had become blurred. Thoreau, at his best, knew the difference, but he also clung to the illusion that being alone, in the woods, might yield the due effect.[49]

The ambivalence of Thoreau's use of the wilderness metaphor can be understood in the light of his preference for the resurrection over the crucifixion. He wanted to believe that the "divine nectar" could be found on the forest trail by the uncrucified self. He knew the orthodox prescription but he rejected it. He refused to yield his identity, and he vigorously fought off any threat to it. He surrounded himself with a thorny hedge of assumed indifference, shunning even human friendship, male and female, when it came too close to his fortress. His was a consciousness, as Perry Miller said, "dedicated to self-justification," an ego defiantly unwilling to confess itself sinful. Even when he clumsily burned down the Concord woods, he could not admit that he had been wrong but continued to try to justify himself, even to himself, for years thereafter.[50]

As his interest in Eastern mysticism shows, Thoreau certainly admired others' capacity for self-denial. His attitude toward the wilderness of contrition must be understood in the light of Rudolph Otto's characterization of the "numinous" as possessing a mixture of fascination and horror. Thoreau praised the Eastern bards "uttering in silence the mystic 'OM,' being absorbed into the essence of the Supreme Being," but he also found them "infinitely wise, yet infinitely stagnant." He praised the doctrine of self-denial, but he recoiled in horror from the practice of it.[51]

Thoreau wanted both this world and the next, both mystic insight and the pleasures of the senses. This too was part of his legacy from Puritanism. Edwards had defined "the divine and supernatural light of God" as the perception of holiness through the medium of the senses. As William Drake has shown, "Edwards was essentially doing what Thoreau was to attempt a century later: pursuing the divine spirit in the very act of comprehension of natural fact." Thoreau wanted to hold the two worlds of the ideal and the real in union, "to integrate the idealism of the subjective, spiritual self with the objective natural world." He wanted Edwards' regenerate vision, but he was unwilling to accept the cross. He accepted only half of the Edwardsian Calvinist legacy. He was, in Drake's words, trying "to put himself in Eden before the Fall, and to claim grace as a natural prerogative, a divine right." His ego, too sensitive even for feminine hands, was not about to be risked in the howling wilderness of the fear of God.[52]

As he had shown in his college essays, Thoreau was no stranger to the anxieties of introspection. Not only was he aware of the call to stare into terror, but he did in fact travel into the wilderness and stare into the pit though he drew back from any final surrender. He did this, not literally or emotionally, but vicariously, in his imagination, in literature, and he recorded this journey in *Cape Cod*.[53]

Both *Cape Cod* and *The Maine Woods* often have been dismissed as "literally and simply, travel books." *Cape Cod*, however, is actually a record of Thoreau's journey into the desert of the self to determine if the death of self-denial might not, after all, be the way to achieve divine perception. It is the record of his attempt to test the claims of the wilderness tradition.[54]

The very first sentence of *Cape Cod* establishes a symbolic correlation between the sight of the ocean and that of "another world." As George Williams has shown, both ocean and desert were the two images used in scripture and in Christian theology to denote the chaos believed to lie just below the surface of consciousness. This is that other world that Thoreau hoped to glimpse. It is into the darkness of death and desert that he descended as he traveled into the Cape's howling wastes.[55]

At the beginning of the book, on his ride to the Cape, Thoreau stopped to examine the wreckage of the *St. John* and to view the bodies of the immigrants drowned just as they were about to reach their promised land. The author of a youthful essay on "The Sublimity of Death" now took an objective, "quite bloodless," look at death and found it not as affecting as he had expected. It was not sublime; the fact of death, itself, could not move him. Rather, he said, it is "the individual and the private that demands our sympathy." He thus signaled a turn inward away from the cold facts for a moment to a different region. The dead immigrants, he explained, "were cast upon some shore yet further west, toward which we are all tending, and which we shall reach at last, it may be through storm and darkness as they did." Just as these dead now headed for another world, so did Thoreau, interspersing through the narrative of his literal journey the story of a journey into the metaphoric wilderness of self.[56]

As he headed into the desolate autumn landscape of the Cape, Thoreau's spirits "rose in proportion to the outward dreariness." The more the landscape resembled a wilderness, the closer it came to his preconceptions, and thus, for the same reasons that his Puritan ancestors had fallen in love with the "howling wilderness" of New England, the more he thrilled to it. He made evident the religious nature of his quest by discussing the religious history of the towns through which he passed. The meeting houses, he noted hopefully, were like windmills "where another sort of grist is ground, of which, if it be not *plaster*, we hope to make bread of life."[57]

Passing through Eastham, he commented on the town's Puritan past and sneered at the shallowness of the revivalism that characterized more recent religion there, contrasting it to the rigorous theology of the town's original inhabitants. Thoreau made it clear that his sympathies lay, not with the evangelicalism of the contemporary church, but with the consistent, or Edwardsian, Calvinism of the founders, men who had sought the same vision which he pursued. Samuel Treat, the first minister of Eastham, had been, he said,

> a Calvinist of the strictest kind, not one of those who, by giving up or explaining away, become like a porcupine disarmed of its quills, but a consistent Calvinist, who can dart his quills to a distance and courageously defend himself.

To illustrate this assertion, Thoreau then provided a series of hell-fire quotations from Treat's sermons, beginning with, "Thou must erelong go to the bottomless pit."[58]

Although still unwilling to accept terror as the means of regeneration, Thoreau did acknowledge that the doctrine of terror "is naturally productive of a sublime and impressive style of eloquence" and quite affecting. At the conclusion of the chapter, he revealed the purpose of his errand:

Let no one think I do not love the old ministers. . . . If I could but hear the 'glad tidings' of which they tell, and which, perchance, they heard, I might write in a worthier strain than this.

To hear those "glad tidings" as those old Calvinists had said they had to be heard, in the wilderness, was the principal motivation for Thoreau's errand into the desert wilderness of Cape Cod.[59]

The further Thoreau traveled into the wastes away from civilization, the closer he believed he was to the object of his journey. He imagined that he was approaching Canaan. "In short," he explained, "we were traversing a desert, with the views of an autumnal landscape of extraordinary brilliance, a sort of Promised Land, on the one hand, and the ocean on the other. . . ." In the chapter titled "The Sea and the Desert," he said explicitly that "The ocean is a wilderness reaching round the globe, wilder than a Bengal jungle, and fuller of monsters, ..." The roar of the breakers became the voice of God out of the wilderness in thunder. He imagined the preaching of the Eastham Methodists competing with "the preaching of the billows" and felt certain that God could be heard more easily in the latter. The noise was loud and the feelings it engendered sublime, but its meaning was like the seaweed tossed in the waves, "symbols of those grotesque and fabulous thoughts which have not yet got into the sheltered groves of literature." God's message remained a mystery.[60]

Behind the beach, beyond the ridge of the great dunes, "Charity" or "Humane Houses" had been built to provide shelter for sailors shipwrecked along the outer coast. Like churches, which also had been designed to comfort the storm-tossed survivors of the ocean's wrath, these charity houses did not appear to Thoreau to be particularly comforting: "They appear but a stage to the grave." Thoreau had never been comforted by the sight of a church. But he was willing, for this particular journey, to take a closer look. In *Cape Cod,* the charity house became a symbol both of the church with its claim to be a shelter from the storm and of the human soul. In looking into the charity house with "the eye of faith," Thoreau symbolically looked into his own soul to try to "see" the mystic depths, to stare into that desert to see if Christ, the Bridegroom, might be there with the "glad tidings" he sought. This was as deep as he went into the wilderness; this was the climax of his symbolic journey. Looking into the charity house, he looked into both the church with its mystic claims and into himself to determine if those claims were valid. The passage is worth quoting in full:

However, as we wished to get an idea of a Humane House, and we hoped that we should never have a better opportunity, we put our eyes, by turns, to a knot-hole in the door, and after looking, without seeing, into the dark,—not knowing how many shipwrecked men's bones we might see at last, looking with the eye of faith, knowing that, to him that knocketh it may not always be opened, yet to him that looketh long enough through a knot-hole the inside shall be visible,— for we had some practice at looking inward,—by steadily keeping our other ball covered from the light meanwhile, putting the outward world behind us, ocean and land, and the beach,—till the pupil became enlarged and collected the rays of light that were wandering in that dark (for the pupil shall be enlarged by looking; there never was so dark a night but a faithful and patient eye, however small, might at last prevail over it),—after all this, I say, things began to take shape to our vision,—if we may use this expression where there was nothing but emptiness,—and we obtained the long-wished-for insight. Though we thought at first that it was a hopeless case, after several minutes steady exercise of the divine faculty, our prospects began decidedly to brighten, and we were ready to exclaim with the blind hero of 'Paradise Lost and Regained,'—

'Hail holy light! offspring of Heaven first born.
Or of the Eternal, co-eternal beam,
May I express thee unblamed?'

Here Thoreau finally achieved insight, but what he "saw" in the darkness was not the Christic Bridegroom, not even some "ruling principle" that reflected the divine, but only waste and chaos:

A little longer and a chimney rushed red on our sight. In short, when our vision had grown familiar with the darkness, we discovered that there were some stones and some loose wads of wool on the floor, and an empty fireplace at the further end; but it *was not* supplied with matches, or straw, or hay, that we could see, nor 'accommodated with a bench.' Indeed, it was the wreck of all cosmical beauty there within.

Unable to get into the house, unwilling to lose himself in that symbolic emptiness, seeing nothing to be gained by entrance, Thoreau concluded that the promises of theology were false. Rather than surrender himself to chaos in the hope of resurrection, he retreated from that vision to the world of sense leaving the church and its claims behind:

Turning our backs on the outward world, we thus looked through the knot-hole into the Humane house, into the very bowels of mercy; and for bread we found a stone. . . . So we shivered round about, not being able to get into it, ever and anon looking through the knot-hole into that night without a star, until we concluded that it was not a *humane* house at all, but a sea-side box, now shut up, belonging to some of the family of Night or Chaos, where they spent their summers by the sea, for the sake of the sea breeze, and it was not proper for us to be prying into their concerns.[61]

It would be too much to say that Thoreau actually plumbed the depths of his own soul here, that this is a true account of an experience of the spiritual wilderness. This is more a literary conversion, what Thoreau imagined might happen were he to leave his fortress and peer over the edge into the roaring gulf below.

In the last paragraph of this section, the last one of the chapter, the self-justifying Thoreau is back, protecting himself from his companion's charge that he had "not a particle of sentiment" and would not open himself to God, to fear, or even to his friend. The accusation is readily dismissed:

> I suspect he meant that my legs did not ache just then, though I am not wholly a stranger to that sentiment. But I did not intend this for a sentimental journey.

Thus did Thoreau turn a friend's honest invitation back with a sarcastic retort, protecting himself from having to feel and finally denying that emotional experience was anything that he had originally desired. Having failed to see God within, having seen only the wilderness without the Bridegroom, he closed the doors to his heart and turned from introspection to the counting of beach peas.[62]

Although from this chapter on, *Cape Cod* does become more and more a travelogue, Thoreau did continue to insert justifications for his refusal to dive deeper into the self. And each justification became an additional brick in his rebuilt fortress. He discussed religion with the Wellfleet Oysterman, but he did not try to get to the bottom of the man's faith. He only listened. Having made his decision to seek truth, not in the confusion of self but in the empirical world of objects, he was willing just to observe from the outside and take notes. He rejected mysticism and became instead a naturalist and reporter.

With this transition, Thoreau proclaimed his break with his New England heritage. This, if any, is the point of the final essay on the early French explorers of New England. The English, he is saying, have been given too much credit; let us look elsewhere. He did not want to resurrect the "ancient regeneration." He had no use for the "rusty flukes of hope deceived and parted chain-cables of faith." We should not, he said, "be Chatham men, dragging for anchors" lost long ago by other ships. The mystical promise of resurrection in the wilderness, the heart of New England's Calvinist theology, could not be trusted. There was, he determined, nothing there:

As we looked off, saw the water growing darker and darker and deeper and deeper the farther we looked, till it was awful to consider, and it appeared to have no relation to the friendly land, either as shore or bottom,—of what use is a bottom if it is out of sight, if it is two or three miles from the surface, and you are to be drowned so long before you get to it, though it were made of the same stuff with your native soil?—over that ocean, where, as the Veda says, "there is nothing to give support, nothing to rest upon, nothing to cling to." I felt I was a land animal.

Thus did Thoreau reject the metaphoric wilderness of self-denial, thus did he reject the need to lose oneself in the oceanic depths, and thus did he declare himself a being of the solid, material earth, a land animal.[63]

Edwards had argued that the hope of resurrection was worth the risk of drowning, of being lost forever in the wilderness, and he forced sinners into that wilderness to stare directly into the pit. Only out of such a crucifixion, he had preached, might there arise the "true virtue" of love for all being, all existence, without any qualification or exception. And this was grace. Thoreau was unable to break free of what Edwards would have called his natural self-love. He could love only within the fortress of his original determined being. "When I am condemned and condemn myself utterly," Thoreau confessed, "I think straightway, 'But I rely on my love for some things.' Therein I am whole and entire. Therein I am God-propped."[64] Edwards would have called this an extension of self-love to a few other objects. To love only "some things" falls short of the universal love of all Existence that is true love of God.

It is true, as has been said, that Thoreau was cool to mysticism, that, unlike such romantics as Hawthorne and Poe, he did not pursue truth "in the twilight fringe of mind." Staying in the house, Thoreau once noted, "breeds a sort of insanity always." Not wanting to go insane, not believing in the promises of the possibility of resurrection, he fled outside and clung tightly to the natural world of facts. Perhaps more deliberately than Emerson, he rejected the wilderness in favor of nature. "We must go out," he said, "and re-ally ourselves to Nature every day. We must make root, and send out some little fibre at least, even every winter day. . . ." These fibres, like the strand that held Edwards' spider over the fires of hell, kept Thoreau from falling into the pit. When he heard the wind whistling out of the desert of his soul, he rushed outside his house crying, "the solid earth! the actual world! the common sense! Contact! Contact!"[65]

6
Hawthorne, Very, and Dickinson
The Wilderness of the Mind

> Religion spells disruption, discord, and the absence of
> peace. A man at one with himself is a man still unac-
> quainted with the great problem of his union with
> God. . . . Those who are genuinely concerned to pre-
> serve their own peace of mind, to retain humanism on
> an even keel, and to assist the steady progress of
> culture—or barbarism!—will, with Lessing, Lichtenberg,
> and Kant, so long as they are able, do their best to
> prevent the intrusion of religion into this world. They
> will lift up their voices to warn those foolish ones, who,
> for aesthetic or historical or romantic reasons, dig
> through the dam and open up a channel through which
> the flood of religion may burst into the cottages and
> palaces of men, after first overwhelming those
> thoughtless pioneers!
>
> Karl Barth
> *The Epistle*
> *To The Romans*

i

Although Romanticism, Rationalism and Evangelical Arminianism
had by the 1830s replaced Consistent Calvinism, still the old faith survived. Those new beliefs were laid down on top of the old assumptions,
covering them over, but lying insecurely on their foundation, as conscious beliefs are said to lie on layers of unconscious thought. The new
creeds were on men's lips, but the ancient beliefs remained buried in
their hearts. The nineteenth-century American battle of the head
against the heart was in part a reflection of this division between heads
that assumed themselves in Canaan and hearts that remembered the
terror of the wilderness.

In times of rational contentment, the self-contented speculations of

180

the mind reigned unchallenged over consciousness. But when their emotions were deeply stirred, many enlightened Americans were surprised to find their hearts' ancestral Calvinism rising to command. After visiting the battle camps of the Civil War, Julia Ward Howe forgot her Unitarian beliefs as the evangelical language of "The Battle Hymn of the Republic" rose out of her heart before being transferred quickly to the page.[1] Emerson was not the only romantic to be swayed by unseen Calvinist forces. The optimism of both rational and evangelical America was never far from the darkness of the pit.

The evangelicals and Transcendentalists shared even with their Unitarian adversaries a confidence in their inherent righteousness. Like Roger Williams, Ann Hutchinson, and Cotton Mather, like Charles G. Finney and Lyman Beecher, most nineteenth-century Protestants believed that America was the promised land and that they were rightly citizens of Zion. Some, like Emerson and Thoreau, knew full well that the wilderness existed, but their loud celebrations of Canaan drowned out the howls of the desert wind. They protected themselves from the winds within by tightly sealing the doors to their hearts. Alone within their fortress selves, they celebrated the individual who could turn his back on fear. These rugged individuals had no use for the support and protection of society. The old Puritan communal ethic had fit the needs of a community of confessed sinners. No longer lost in that wilderness, these romantic Americans brashly stood alone before God and the world.

Not all of the American Romantics however, found it that easy to ignore the wilderness. Nathaniel Hawthorne shared his generation's conflict between a rational, hopeful intellect and a subliminal urge to surrender to the fires of the soul. But unlike Emerson, he remained caught between the two visions, wanting to affirm the light but too aware of the wilderness to deny the darkness. As he said of Melville, he could "neither believe, nor be comfortable in his unbelief."[2]

Hyatt Waggoner has said, "like Kierkegaard, Hawthorne believed all the more firmly because he had explored the depths of doubt. He understood and valued the light because he knew so well the degree and extent of the darkness." It might be more accurate to say, not that he "believed all the more firmly," but that because he had seen the dark he *struggled* all the more firmly to believe. Hawthorne's criticisms of the scientific mindset show how well he knew the dangers of closing the doors to the heart, but he also knew the terror of the wilderness beyond those doors, and he carefully kept his distance. Keeping one eye on the open door, he struggled to affirm the solid, human world of sense. *The House of Seven Gables* was to have been a cheerful romance, and compared to *The Scarlet Letter* it is. But Hawthorne's inclination, when he was

alone in his study with his conscience, was to look through the open door
and be transfixed, like Ishmael, by the flames. This according to Melville
was what gave Hawthorne his power as a writer. Echoing Edwards,
Melville wrote,

> this great power of blackness in him derives its force from its appeal to
> the Calvinistic sense of Innate Depravity and Original Sin, from whose
> visitations, in some shape or other, no deeply thinking mind is always
> and wholly free. . . . You may be witched by his sunlight, transported
> by the great gildings in the skies he builds over you, but there is the
> blackness of darkness beyond; and even his bright gildings but fringe
> and play upon the edges of thunder-clouds.

What Melville here called the "sense of Innate Depravity and Original
Sin" is the heart of the wilderness tradition. It is from the perspective of
this tradition that Hawthorne needs to be understood.[3]

The theme of "Regenerative Descent," the basic Christian pattern of
crucifixion and regeneration, can be found throughout Hawthorne's
writings. The call to the wilderness sounded in his ears, and in many of
his novels and short stories he repeated the descent into the wilderness
of mind. Yet contrary to the demands of the Consistent Calvinists,
Hawthorne never surrendered to damnation but repeatedly drew back
at the last moment to return to the leeks and onions of Egypt. He was
fascinated by the wilderness, but he knew the fear of fear too well ever to
let go. "Intrigued by non-identity but fearing non-existence," as Barton
St. Armand put it, Hawthorne entered the darkness, "had a true sight of
sin and an apocalyptic vision of the hell within his own being," but
remembered Cotton Mather's fear that insanity can be the work of
witches as well as grace. He remembered that the carcasses of many of
the Children of Israel rotted in the wilderness, and he dared not let go.[4]

Had he believed himself in the wilderness of sin in need of complete
regeneration, Hawthorne might have yielded to the fear of God. Had he
believed himself secure in Canaan, then, like Mather, he might have
resisted all attempts to lure him back into the wilderness. But caught as
he was between two competing visions, at home neither in Canaan nor
the wilderness, he could neither affirm nor deny. Beset by doubts he
could not silence, unwilling to follow where those doubts might lead, he
could only continue to approach his fears and then withdraw to safety.

In "The Haunted Mind," Hawthorne attempted to convince himself
and his readers that he had completed the cycle and experienced a kind
of secular conversion. On the edge of the "wilderness of sleep," he wrote,
"the dark receptacles are flung wide open" and the "tomb" that lies "in
the depths of every heart" is exposed. What follows is a "nightmare of
the soul," a "wintry gloom about the heart," an "indistinct horror of the

mind," as the mind, still awake, slides into the darkness. But the descent into darkness is never made. There is no letting go, no ego-loss, no acceptance of Christ in place of self. Instead, breaking from this vision, the eye "searches for whatever may remind you of the living world," and when it finds the solid earth again secure the mind comforts itself with sentimental thoughts until overcome by sleep. As St. Armand said, this pulling back was not "a restoration of psychic wholeness" but a return to the psychic separateness of normal consciousness. Unable to bear his soul's "deepest and most disturbing revelations," Hawthorne left his sojourn "dangerously unfinished." Like so many of his lesser contemporaries, he merely substituted sentimentality for "Truly gracious affections." But the sentimental mood he achieved was no substitute for true grace.[5]

Loosely following Bunyan's *Pilgrim's Progress*, "Night Sketches" is another secular conversion narrative in which, again, Hawthorne does not complete the journey but only ventures forth into the stormy night, "a black impenetrable nothingness, as though heaven and all its lights were blotted from the universe." In this impenetrable darkness, he becomes, not a participant, but a spectator, "a looker-on in life." Taking note while others head out into that "Slough of Despond . . . of unknown bottom," he watched a young couple fall "on a slippery remnant of ice." As they are "precipitated into a confluence of swollen floods" the reader is reminded, however purposefully, of the text of Edwards' Enfield sermon: "Their feet shall slide in due time." Hawthorne rejects the sunny Transcendentalists by calling the light of the surrounding Vanity Fair,

> an emblem of the deceptive glare which mortals throw around their footsteps in the mortal world, thus bedazzling themselves till they forget the impenetrable obscurity that hems them in, and that can be dispelled only by radiance from above.

Hawthorne did not forget the "impenetrable obscurity." He felt its presence but he could not—would not!—throw himself into it.[6]

At the end of the sketch, Hawthorne watches as a man with a tin lantern passes fearlessly into the unknown gloom "whither I will not follow him." This is another example of what Waggoner calls Hawthorne's "constant return to the literal." Once again, Hawthorne has withdrawn from a plunge into darkness explaining, "if we bear the lamp of faith, enkindled at a celestial fire" then we too might be able to head into the storm secure that the lamp's faith will "lead us home to that heaven whence its radiance was borrowed." Once again, Hawthorne substituted sentiment for the terrifying descent into darkness that once had been thought the only means of grace.[7]

Hawthorne's clearest use of the wilderness tradition with all its typological conversion imagery is in "Young Goodman Brown." Much of
the ambiguity of this story, and the resulting confusion of interpretations, could be cleared up if the story were read with the wilderness
tradition in mind. Goodman Brown's journey into a wilderness and his
discovery there of the world's inherent sinfulness falls into a pattern well
established in New England literature, that of the awakened sinner's
journey from Egypt into the wilderness in order "to humble thee, and to
prove thee, to know what was in thine heart" (Deut. 8.2).

On a "dreary road, darkened by all the gloomiest trees of the forest,"
the Devil reveals to Goodman Brown that all human beings are sinners
and fit only for damnation. Forced to confess his own evil, Goodman
Brown cannot accept the idea that all humanity is equally lost in sin. But
even his beloved Faith shows up at the witch's sabbath, and at last he
accepts the reality of what he has seen. As a result he becomes "mad-
dened with despair . . . in the heart of the dark wilderness." As one critic
said, "Goodman Brown is like the person who from perverse curiosity
experiments once with LSD and has a bad trip." Brown stared into the
heart of blackness, into the madness of the inner wilderness, and found
himself. By "the sympathy of all that was wicked in his heart," he
accepted his "brotherhood" with all sinners. "Welcome, my children,"
said the Devil to the new recruits, "You have found thus young your
nature and your destiny."[8]

Although he acknowledged himself one with the brotherhood of sinners, a spark of hope must have remained, for at the last moment Brown
cried out, "Faith! Faith! . . . Look up to heaven and resist the wicked
one." At this point his journey ended and he found himself suddenly
back in Salem Village. But no longer could he live a normal life. He
became a "desperate man," and he died in despair. Goodman Brown
thus repeated Hawthorne's pattern of entering the wilderness but pulling back from the complete surrender that might have meant salvation.
Instead of regeneration, his journey into the wilderness produced an
endless wandering in the psychological wilderness of despair. He became one whose carcass rotted in the wilderness never to enter Canaan.
If not a projection of Hawthorne himself, Brown at least was for
Hawthorne a symbol of the dangers inherent in the Calvinist command.[9]

Those who think Hawthorne's sympathy for such sinners as Hester
Prynne and Goodman Brown prove him to be unequivocally opposed to
his Puritan heritage need to consider the original meaning of the wilderness sojourn. Only those Puritans, like Cotton Mather, who believed
themselves saints in Zion, condemned other mortals for becoming
caught in sin. For Calvinist theology preached with St. Paul that all are
sinners and lost in the wilderness of sin. Even those who lead Godly lives,

as Solomon Stoddard said, "addicted to morality and religion, are serving their lusts therein." Only those forced to confess their complete depravity, or to wear it openly on the bosom or as a veil across their face, could have true Christian sympathy for their fellow sinners. Grace, as Edwards had defined it, was a love for all Existence including sinners and was not limited to visible Christian saints.[10]

If American Protestantism is to be defined by the hypocrisy of its most narrow-minded adherents, then Hawthorne indeed was attacking "Christianity" for having become a self-righteous religion. But if American Protestantism can be viewed from the perspective of the wilderness, then Hawthorne must take his place, despite his superficial secularism, alongside those Christians, from Calvin to Edwards, who tried to make their fellow men recognize that all human beings are of the brotherhood of sinners. "Whither, then," asked Goodman Brown, "could these holy men be journeying so deep into the heathen wilderness?" The answer lies with the realization that even holy men had to be damned before they could hope to achieve salvation.[11]

The "brotherhood of sinners," one of the constant themes of Hawthorne's works, stands in contrast to the individualism of the holy Transcendentalists and the sanctified revivalists. Degenerate humanity, alone together in the wilderness, have need of each other. Only those who have passed over to Canaan and received the grace of God can presume the arrogance of standing against all other men outside of human institutions. Only a convinced Antinomian, too sure of sanctification to fear the wrath of God, marches boldly into the wilderness alone to a different drummer.

ii

Although the wilderness haunted both Emerson and Hawthorne, they reacted in different ways to this same incipient fear. Emerson, in this respect, foreshadowed the future of American culture while Hawthorne reflected the past. They stood at the turning point between a religious and a secular sensibility, between a communal, cooperative moral ethic and a competitive, laissez-faire individualism, between the last remnants of the old order and the first full days of the new. A comparison of their separate reactions to the wilderness within reveals much about the origins of these external, cultural differences. And nowhere can these differences be seen as clearly as in their separate reactions to the Salem poet and transcendental mystic, Jones Very.

Although nominally a Unitarian and generally considered a Transcendentalist, Jones Very did not wage the battle of the bright new world

against the dark superstitions of the past. He accepted the traditional
Calvinist view of reality, and after a fierce struggle in the wilderness he
surrendered his will completely to the fear of God. In 1838, at the time
of this conversion, Very was a tutor of Greek at Harvard. At the height of
his trauma, while Harvard was still overreacting to Emerson's "Divinity
School Address," Very loudly commanded his class to "Flee to the moun-
tians, for the end of all things is at hand!" Quickly released from his
academic duties, he returned to his home in Salem.[12]

Believing that he had been crucified in the wilderness of his soul, Very
became convinced that his will had been replaced by the will of God. As
Anne Hutchinson had attacked John Wilson in 1636, as the New Lights
had attacked the "unconverted ministry" of the 1740s, Very confronted
the religious establishment of his day and tried to baptise several of the
leading ministers of Salem with the fire of the Holy Spirit. Not believing
him divinely inspired, his neighbors, led by the reverend Mr. Upham,
had him forcibly committed to McLeans, the insane asylum then located
at Charlestown. After his release, while still in the full passion of his
disorder, Very concluded that his own will had been completely sacrificed "in the wilderness of my heart."[13] Believing that God's will had
been made his will, he determined that henceforth, his only words and
actions would be those commanded to him by the Holy Spirit. Believing
himself to have become a vehicle of the Spirit, he put on the black robe
of Puritan God-consciousness and dared all who met him to look him in
the eye.

Had Very been born a hundred years earlier, he would have been
recognized as a converted sinner undergoing the trials of the wilderness
state. Had he been born a hundred years later, he would probably have
been locked up in Mcleans (more probably Mass. State) and would be
there today, heavily sedated with Thorazine. But because he lived in the
cusp between two worlds, no one quite knew what to make of him.
Margaret Fuller wrote to Emerson asking if Very really was insane.
Emerson wrote back:

> Very has been here himself lately and staid [sic] a few days con-
> founding us all with the question—whether he was insane? At first
> sight and speech, you would certainly pronounce him so. Talk with
> him a few hours and you will think all insane but he. Monomania or
> monosania he is a very remarkable person. . . .

During this visit, Emerson helped Very put together a small volume of
poetry, and he introduced his young friend, only a short time out of
McLeans, to other members of the Transcendental Club. "Jones Very,"
Emerson wrote in his Journal, "charmed us all by telling us he hated us
all."[14]

Tall and awkwardly skeletal, with a face stretched tightly on a bony skull, dressed in ministerial black, Very lived out his life alone in an upstairs room of his mother's house, writing poetry and taking long walks along the shore. It was, he thought, his calling to show his neighbors the possibility of resurrection in the wilderness of the mind. And so, when the Spirit commanded, he ventured out like an angel of terror to call others to follow his insane example.

One such soul, the Boston banker Samuel Grey Ward, was interrupted at his office by a visit from Very. As soon as Very had left, Ward took time to write down a full account of that remarkable meeting. Very came in politely and urged Ward to drop everything, to stop right there in the middle of the letter he was writing, to follow him on the spiritual journey of the crucifixion of the self that he too might attain the heavenly banquet. Ward remembered him saying,

> I come from the banquet where we are all together. I do not wish to come for myself. I am happy there—and it pains me to break my repose and to come into the world,—but I feel that we cannot live for ourselves alone; and so I do come to tell you how sweet the banquet is, and to beg you to come into it.

Ward politely thanked Very for his concern, but he declined the offer on the grounds that he still had some business to complete on Earth first.[15]

Very's manner was particularly unnerving when he tried to communicate thoughts deeper than language could express. Charles Brooks remembered a walk he took with Very:

> . . . what I remember the most prominent is the way in which he would stop after expressing some thought about nature, man, or God, that he seemed to fear might appear commonplace from its simplicity, and then turning around and fixing upon you an earnest look, as if he would show from his piercing glance that there was a depth in his thought concealed from superficial minds by its very transparency.

At such times, Very gave the impression of trying to lure his listeners into the pit with him. Most, understandably, refused. One of those in whom he tried to "promote the new birth" responded, "Mr. Very, I feel as if I could take your point of view—but I do not dare to—because if I did I am afraid I should lose my sense and could never recover myself again." On those walks which he did not take alone, he was more often accompanied by the children of Salem than by any adult.[16]

Very thus became a living emblem of the Puritanical command to surrender one's self to the emotional wilderness of the soul's deepest fears. To men like Emerson and Hawthorne, he became a walking

The Literary Remains

projection of that which haunted them, a symbol of the dangerous results of yielding one's rational intellect to the fires of the pit. Different New Englanders had different reactions to the vestigal Puritan anxieties that lurked in their consciences; these same New Englanders had different reactions to Jones Very. Emerson, almost alone, continued to befriend Very, even after Very's passion had subsided and he had retired to an uneventful life in his mother's house. But his attitude toward Very was never one of uncritical approval.

For one thing, Emerson never approved of Very's stubborn adherence to the language of Christian orthodoxy. He complained that Very "never got out of his Hebraic Mythology," and he even tried to edit the obvious Christian language out of some of Very's poetry.[17] But more important was Emerson's ambivalent attraction to Very's doctrine and practice of the surrendered self. Emerson preached the necessity of self-reliance, of trusting in the deepest impulses of one's own consciousness, even if these impulses "may be from below." The "self" of Emerson's "self-reliance" was not the rational ego but the spirit that revealed itself in the depths of the human soul. Yet Emerson could never bring himself to abandon those "defenses thou has round me set;/ Example, custom, fear. . . ." which protected him from the "roaring gulf below." For all of his talk of surrendering to the mystic waves of the spirit, Emerson remained a man of the world, occasionally regretting his cold worldliness, but never losing it. He wanted both the spirit and the intellect. Fascinated by Very's mysticism, and drawn toward it, he was still unwilling to pay the price that Very had paid for it. He wrote in his Journal:

. . . religion for religion's sake, religion divorced, detached from man, from the world, from science and art grim, unmarried, insulated, accusing; yet true in itself, and speaking things in every word. The lie is in the detachment; and when he is in the room with other persons, speech stops as if there were a corpse in the apartment.

He also wrote in his Journal, "Wherever that young enthusiast goes he will astonish and disconcert men by dividing for them the cloud that covers the profound gulf that is in man."[18]

How to uncover the profound gulf that is in man without losing everything in that black hole was the problem that beset Emerson. He never did resolve the dilemma of wanting to experience profound emotions—at a safe distance. Very paid Emerson several visits (Emerson never visited Very), and even after he began to weary of Very, he continued to show an interest in him and to encourage him. Eventually, the passion died down in Very, and as the Spirit no longer directed him to visit Emerson, he stayed away.

Most of Very's rigidly formal sonnets, written in the first person as if by the Holy Spirit, catalogue the rhythms of the natural world and preach familiar morals in the familiar language of scripture. But his best poems contain a depth of meaning and imagery that lift them above the bulk of his verses. His own conversion is relived with startling freshness in "The New Birth,"[19] a poem that reveals the wilderness from the inside:

> 'Tis a new life; thoughts move not as they did
> With slow uncertain steps across my mind;
> In thronging haste, fast pressing on they bid
> The portals open to the viewless wind
> That comes not save when in the dust is laid
> The crown of pride that gilds each mortal brow,
> And from before man's vision melting fade
> The Heavens and Earth; their walls are falling now.
> Fast crowding on, each thought asks utterance strong;
> Storm-lifted waves rushing to the shore,
> On from the sea they send their shouts along,
> Back through the cave-worn rocks their thunders roar;
> And I a child of God by Christ made free
> Start from death's slumbers to Eternity.

The poem begins at the moment of awakening, " 'Tis a new life." Something different is happening. No longer do thoughts move as they used to with "slow uncertain steps." The separation of thoughts from "mind" here is an echo of Edwards' contention that the mind is passive in regard to thinking just as it is to sights and sounds. The mind does not create the thoughts; they simply move slowly and stupidly across consciousness. In the third line, the pace of the rhythm begins to speed up. Thoughts now run across the mind too quick to follow, and in their rush they push open the "portals" to the wind, "viewless" because it comes, not from the land, but from the soul. The wind is the Holy Spirit, and the portals are the doors to the heart.

Here is a symptom that a good psychiatrist surely would label a sign of schizophrenia, a mind overflowing with uncontrollable ideas rushing fast upon each other creating panic and a sudden letting go. The Spirit, said Very, comes only when pride is finally laid in the dust, or as Edwards would say, when self-love finally is abandoned. Then, as all sense perception rushes together in a confused torrent and the solid walls and the granite cliffs collapse, the awakened sinner experiences the chaos of wilderness where there is only consciousness aware of itself in hell. The pace of the rhythm then slackens, as the thoughts, "fast crowding on," compel attention. In the tenth line, the rhythm regains speed as the image changes from steps and wind to ocean waves rushing through the "cave-worn rocks" of the mind. Ocean, it must be repeated, like wilderness was a symbol of primal chaos. The image of ocean waves is an even more powerful one than that of footsteps or of wind. The crashing of waves against the mind, the uncontrollable turbulence associated with breakers booming into the rocks, is an image of chaos and destruction against which there can be no resistance and no survival. This is the breaking point, the climax of the poem and the climax of the conversion experience.

At the start of the final couplet, the rhythm abruptly changes, as if the mind were suddenly lifted out of the wave-beaten rocks into a transcendent state above the confusion. The rhythm stops its relentless rush forward, it breaks. And the poet declares himself a child "made free," battered but rescued, translated from the chaos of time and circumstance to the peace of "Eternity."

The shift in the last two lines to traditional Christian imagery and language, Emerson notwithstanding, is significant. The poet here is saying that his old words were involved in chaos and confusion. But his acceptance of Christ's Spirit in place of his own included an acceptance of God's language as superior to any "mythology" created by the merely human mind. Very always insisted that his poems were written not by him but by God. He objected to Emerson's attempts to edit his words not because he had but because he had *not* written them. "Cannot the Spirit parse and spell?" teased Emerson. But after his conversion, Very did nothing, so he said, except at the command of the Holy Spirit, not even, he told a skeptical William Ellery Channing, lift his arm to put it on the mantle. No longer his, he had become God's.[20]

Living in the same town as Very, Nathaniel Hawthorne, despite his best efforts, was unable to avoid him. Indeed, it was his irrepressible future sister-in-law, Elizabeth Peabody, who introduced Very both to him and to Emerson. Between 1837 and 1840, Hawthorne had to endure a number of unannounced visits from Jones Very.

Direct evidence of Hawthorne's reactions to Jones Very is unfortunately limited. What little there is can be found in letters he wrote to Elizabeth's sister, Sophia, and since his future wife was a warm admirer of Very's unearthly pietism, Hawthorne was careful not to speak ill of him to her. His attitude toward Very manages to come through nevertheless.

In a letter written in 1830, he told Sophia of several interruptions he had endured and added, "Night before last came Mr. Jones Very; and you know he is somewhat unconscionable as to the length of his calls." By 1840, Hawthorne was already well acquainted with Very. Wishing to avoid him, he had once passed up a chance to spend an evening with his wife-to-be because of Very's presence. Sophia mentioned this in a letter dated 1838: "I told him we were all disappointed at his vanishing that night, and he laughed greatly. He said he should not be able to come this evening to meet Very, because he had something to read, for he was engaged Monday and Tuesday evening and could not read then. I am so sorry." Under most other circumstances, Hawthorne would have gladly put down his reading in order to spend time with Sophia, but as Emerson had noted, when Very was in the room casual conversation stopped "as if there were a corpse in the apartment."[21]

In another instance, Hawthorne complained that Very "wants a brother." But as Melville would later learn, Hawthorne was not interested in that kind of a relationship and was somewhat embarrassed by such familiarity.[22]

Still, Hawthorne and Very had much in common. Both were sons of Salem sea captains, both became fatherless at an early age, both were men of letters, both loners living in upstairs rooms in their mother's homes, both drawn to the introspective traditions of their Puritan ancestors, and both victims of the reverend Mr. Upham's zeal. But Hawthorne, for all of his introspective brooding, resisted the call to the pit with all his might. He did not pursue his fears as Emerson, however skittishly, did; they pursued him. More sensitive than Emerson to the emotional realities of "the roaring gulf below," he did not tempt the blackness. It was because he knew, intuitively, the meaning of Innate Depravity and Original Sin, and sought to repress them, that he sought to avoid Jones Very. He understood, better than Emerson, what Very represented; he respected it enough to avoid it.

Many of Hawthorne's best stories are arguments against the kind of obsessive surrender to the blackness of darkness of which Very was a symbol. "Young Goodman Brown" provided one example of what could happen in the wilderness. Roderick Elliston of "Egotism; or, The Bosom Serpent," is perhaps the closest Hawthorne came actually to portraying Very. Elliston, like Very, "became the pest of the city" as "he grappled with the ugliest truth that he could lay his hand on, and compelled his adversary to do the same." As with Very, "the city could not bear this new apostle," and his neighbors "placed him in a private asylum for the insane" from which he was soon released unchanged. But unlike Very, Roderick Elliston realized finally that it was "diseased self-contemplation" that nourished the snake in his bosom, and he was able to get rid of it, as Hawthorne tried to overcome his own fears, "in the idea of another." In this, Hawthorne foreshadowed what would become America's answer to the anxieties of the soul: romantic love conquers all despair, romantic love as the secular substitute for grace, the answer to all human problems.[23]

Hollingsworth in *The Blithedale Romance* also portrays some of Very's traits. "Prolonged fiddling upon one string," wrote Hawthorne, made him not only "mad" but a "bore." Like Very, Hollingsworth asked Coverdale to be his brother, and like Hawthorne Coverdale declined the offer.[24]

The struggle between the worldly affirmations of his head and the fears of his heart generated the power of many of Hawthorne's stories. He did not want to end up like Jones Very, a lonely fanatic scribbling away in his mother's attic. But the Calvinist impulses of his heart haunted him and he was too honest to deny them. Writing provided him with an outlet for exorcising those fears, as if by facing them on paper, as Thoreau had pretended to do, he could more easily overcome them.

One of the ways in which Hawthorne kept himself sane was by refusing to take himself or his situation too seriously. He knew himself to be one with the universal brotherhood of sinners and could not fall into the arrogance of assuming himself a saint. He was willing, however, to allow Very the "vanity" of sainthood. William Andrews recalled that

> Hawthorne speaks of his [Very's] limitations as arising from want of a sense of the ludicrous; but regarded his views as sanctified by his real piety and goodness. He added, however, that 'he had better remain as he is—one organ in the world of impersonal spirit—at least as long as he can write such good sonnets.'

Because he was sensitive to the demands of his own Puritan conscience, Hawthorne understood Very's fanaticism all too well, and he had to admit that it had its value. He avoided Very not because Very bored him but because he terrified him. Hawthorne felt that he already suffered from too painful an awareness of the pit. Emerson once said of Very, "To stand in true relation with men in a false age is worth a fit of insanity, is it not?" Hawthorne thought not.[25]

Jones Very was not the only fanatic Calvinist against whom the difference between Hawthorne and Emerson can be measured. In numerous cases Emerson showed himself innocently willing to tempt the wrath of God while Hawthorne wisely kept his distance. John Brown, the fiery abolitionist who carried Edwards' *Works* to Kansas and who preached from Edwards' sermons on the sabbath, was hailed by Emerson as a second Christ who would make the gallows as glorious as the cross. Hawthorne, on the other hand, denounced Brown as a "blood-stained fanatic" and said that "nobody was ever more justly hanged." In the same spirit in which he said he was willing to risk madness, Emerson said that he was willing to risk war if that trial should purge the nation of its sins. But Hawthorne remembered that the wilderness of war was only an outward projection, a type, of the wilderness of the soul. The violence of regeneration must take place in the heart, not on the battlefield. And even knowing that, he was not so rash as to risk insanity for the elusive object of the fiery hunt.[26]

Despite his severe apprehensions, Hawthorne was not unfriendly toward Jones Very. He held him at a distance, but from that distance he did admire him. After witnessing one of Very's attempts to persuade Hawthorne to join him at the mystic banquet, Elizabeth Peabody noted:

> Hawthorne received it in the loveliest manner—with the same abandonment with which it was given . . . and it was curious to see the respect of Very for him—and the reverence with which he treated his genius. There is a petulance about Hawthorne generally—when truth is taken out of the forms of nature . . . But in this instance he repressed it and talked with him beautifully.

And in "A Virtuoso's Collection," Hawthorne went out of his way to express his admiration for Very, calling him "a poet whose voice is scarcely heard among us by reason of its depth."[27]

Hawthorne, then, had the same ambiguous attitude toward Very as Emerson had, but with this difference: Emerson, fixed in the speculative rationalizations of his head, was attracted by Very's mysticism as he was drawn toward, but never fully encountered, the fears of his own heart; while Hawthorne, who felt all too close to the terrors that howled beneath the surface, respected but avoided Jones Very.

Hawthorne may not have had the intellectual abilities that Emerson had, and, as Elizabeth Peabody indicated, he was uncomfortable with metaphysics and abstract philosophy. But he was far more sensitive to emotion than was Emerson. Once, while visiting a friend, Hawthorne tried unsuccessfully to feed a baby bird that had fallen down the chimney. Its suffering, he wrote in his notebook, "distressed me a good deal; and I felt relieved, though somewhat shocked, when Bridge put an end to its misery, by squeezing its head and throwing it out of the window."[28] It should not be surprising that a man so sensitive should have sensed in Jones Very a manifestation of those wilderness terrors that he most feared in himself.

If the wilderness tradition of Calvinism endured, even in a secular literary form, beyond the age of faith, it is because its concerns are universal. Its portrayal of human consciousness is familiar enough that even today its basic philosophy is one, to quote Melville, "from whose visitations, in some shape or other, no deeply thinking mind is always or wholly free." Hawthorne would have recognized the spirit responsible for Karl Barth's admonition:

> Religion is not all to be 'in tune with the infinite' or to be at 'peace with oneself.' . . . Let simple minded Occidentals (!) retain such opinion as

long as they are able. But religion is an abyss; it is terror . . . Those
who are genuinely concerned to preserve their own peace of mind . . .
will lift up their voices to warn those careless ones, who, for aesthetic
or historical or romantic reasons, dig through the dam and open up a
channel through which the flood of religion may burst into the cottages and palaces of men, after first overwhelming those thoughtless
pioneers!

Emerson was one such thoughtless pioneer. He believed that he could
dig through the dam and still retain his balance, that he could "peep"
into the Calvinism of his depths and retain the Transcendentalism of his
senses. That is why he encouraged Jones Very. But Hawthorne had a
truer feeling for what "religion," in Barth's sense, meant, and he wisely
feared all religious zealots including Jones Very.[29]

For Very had become the living symbol of the Calvinist conscience, of
the ancient command to stare into the blackness and to suffer in that
wilderness. Hawthorne's writing retained that which inspired the best
Puritan writing, not boastful self-confidence but the passion of a convicted sinner crying in the wilderness for salvation. Yet he held back
from the destroying pit lest he become as much a monomaniac as Jones
Very.

Emerson wanted to unite the real and the ideal here and now, regardless of the dangers inherent in trying to reach across the gulf that
separates man from God. Emerson, who once told Very that he had
never suffered,[30] played foolishly with fire. Hawthorne knew more
clearly the awful terror of the void and he held back. Hawthorne crossed
the street when he saw Jones Very coming; Emerson welcomed him into
his home.

iii

> Remember, and care for me sometimes, and scatter a
> fragrant flower in this wilderness life of mine by writing
> me, and not forgetting, and by lingering longer in
> prayer, that the Father may bless one more!
> Emily Dickinson to Abiah Root

Emily Dickinson, like Mary Moody Emerson, a lonely heir of the
wilderness tradition, spun endless circles around infinity transfixed by
the abyss at the center. "This is to die sensibly; to die and know it,"
preached Edwards. "We read in Scripture of the blackness of darkness;
this is it, this is the very thing." Not fire, not torture, not eternal

nothingness, but consciousness of endless consciousness alone was the terror of the pit. To sleep, perhaps to dream—that was the rub. To be alone, without body, without perception, forever and forever, fully awake, facing "in lonely place/That awful stranger Consciousness—" this was the threat of immortality. "Looking at death," Emily Dickinson said "is dying."[31]

If Hawthorne was the last New England writer to struggle publicly with the wilderness, Emily Dickinson was the first New England writer in whom that tradition, though dominant, remained hidden. It is not just that she hid in her home and never published; these were but outward types of her spiritual seclusion. It was her Calvinist orthodoxy that she kept hidden. Even critics for whom her private life is an open book have not appreciated the extent to which Emily Dickinson's poetry was a personal response to the Calvinist conversion crisis. She was no dogmatist; the Calvinist theology is never made explicit. But the themes are there, consistently, forcefully, elegantly, everywhere.[32]

John Cody has argued that Emily Dickinson suffered a "psychotic" breakdown and that her poems "portray faithfully the terror of a mind collapsing under pressures that exceed its endurance."[33] This may be so. It is hard to read her letters and poems and deny that she did suffer a traumatic emotional experience of some kind or that her behavior was, at best, eccentric. But whatever the exact nature of this experience, whatever the causes, however analyzed in whatever discipline, Emily Dickinson would have understood it within the context provided by her culture. It is her poetry that is important to us, and if her poetry is her response to her experience, neither Freud, not Jung, nor Sappho can be the primary guide to help us understand what she wrote. To understand Emily Dickinson, it is necessary to be familiar with the New England Puritan tradition of belief in a psychological crisis of conversion from the spiritual Egypt of worldly bondage across the mental wilderness to the promised land of Canaan.

That Amherst, Massachusetts, in the middle of the nineteenth century, was a stubbornly Calvinist community, and that the Dickinson family was a pillar of that community, are facts that do not need to be proven. It is enough to recall that Amherst College had been founded in order to save orthodox Calvinism from the Unitarian heresy and that Edward Dickinson, Emily's grandfather, had been one of its founders. She was, as Thomas Johnson said, "nourished" by the "russet base" of her Puritan past.[34]

But there still remains confusion regarding Emily Dickinson's relationship to her ancestral religion. Richard Sewall has said that her "whole career may be regarded as a sustained, if muted, rebellion against this very inheritance." More recently, Karl Keller has stated that she

more than left the church, "she stood against, stood up *to* it." Albert
Gelpi has advanced the position that she was essentially a "Romantic
Poet" liberated from the restraints of her Puritan past by the refreshing
winds of Emersonian Transcendentalism.[35]

Much of this misinterpretation results both from a misunderstanding
of what it meant to be a Calvinist in New England as well as from an
inability to distinguish between the evangelical orthodoxy of the 1850s
and the spiritual Calvinism preached by men like Edwards, Stoddard,
and Hooker. Emily Dickinson was in rebellion, not against her ancestral
religion, not against Calvinism, but against the sterile and superficial
faith of her more immediate culture. If she revolted against the church,
it was in the name, not of Emerson, but of Christ. And her doing so put
her in the mainstream of the true Calvinist wilderness tradition.

The debate centers on the story of Emily Dickinson's lone refusal to
stand up and confess Christianity when she attended Miss Lyon's Semin-
ary at Mount Holyoke in 1847. Although sometimes interpreted as a
youthful rebellion against religion, the evidence indicates that she refused to conform not because she did not believe, but because she
believed too well. According to the one good account of this incident, she
did not reject Christ; she simply refused to lie and claim a conversion to
a *sincere* desire for Christ when she knew that the mystic promise had not
yet been made hers.

> To illustrate the independence and honesty of her convictions,—Miss
> Lyon, during a time of religious interest in the school, asked all those
> who wanted to be Christians to rise. The wording of the request was
> not such as Emily could accede to and she remained seated—the only
> one who did not rise. In relating the incident to me, she said, "They
> thought it queer I didn't rise"—adding with a twinkle in her eye, "I
> thought a lie would be queerer."

This alone might be considered ambiguous evidence. But placed next to
the letters she wrote during this period, it becomes obvious that her
rebellion was in the tradition of the seventeenth-century minister,
Jonathan Mitchell, who refused to accept "seemings" in place of the real
thing and of those faithful Christians who were "too scrupulous" to own
the half-way covenant.[36]

In 1846, as the revival at Mount Holyoke was just beginning, Dickinson revealed to her friend, Abiah Root, that she had briefly believed
herself one of the saved but that she had been mistaken:

> I was almost persuaded to be a Christian. I thought I never again
> could be thoughtless and worldly—and I can say that I never before
> enjoyed such perfect peace and happiness as the short time in which I

felt I had found my savior. But I soon forgot my morning prayer or else it was irksome to me. One by one my old habits returned and I cared less for religion than ever. I have longed to hear from you—to know what decision you have made. I hope you are a Christian for I feel that it is impossible for anyone to be happy without a treasure in heaven. I feel that I shall never be happy without I love Christ.

Her desire to believe remained sincere, but the lesson of this false conversion stayed with her, for she feared that she might "again be deceived and I dared not trust myself." Years later, still unwilling to trust herself, she remembered her youthful error and blamed, not fate, but herself "for entertaining Plated Wares/Upon my Silver Shelf—" (J-747).[37]

At home, in Amherst, in 1850, Dickinson again was caught up in a revival and again her attitude was one, not of derision or criticism but of hopeful expectation. "How strange is this sanctification, that works such a marvelous change," she wrote admiringly to Jane Humphrey. But at the same time she had to admit that the change had not affected her, that she was "standing alone in rebellion and growing very careless." It should not be imagined that the term "rebellion" had the positive connotations it carries today. If Emily Dickinson was a rebel, it was not by choice but by an unwelcome fate. The "still small voice," she continued,

certainly comes from God—and I think to receive it is blessed—not that I know it from *me*, but from those on whom *change* has passed. . . . You must pray when the rest are sleeping, that the hand may be held to me, and I may be led away.[38]

To her friend, Abiah, Emily Dickinson wrote of her growing fear that she was not destined for salvation. Her carnal spirit enjoyed the world too much. Her head believed but her heart did not seem able to grieve the acknowledged danger. She was not boasting but confessing when she wrote:

The shore is safer, Abiah, but I love to buffet the sea—I can count the bitter wrecks here in these pleasant waters, and hear the murmuring winds, but oh, I love the danger! You are learning control and firmness. Christ Jesus will love you more. I'm afraid he don't love me any!

Although willing intellectually to acknowledge the desirability of Canaan, Dickinson had to confess that the danger of the wilderness, of the sea, had a greater claim on her emotions. Preferring wilderness to the pretense of salvation, holding out—even at the risk of damnation—for true feeling, may have kept her from membership in the Amherst church, but it placed her in the center of the wilderness strain of Calvinism.[39]

Her refusal to profess a false salvation was considered "queer." The irony of her stance was not lost on her and she was able to observe the situation with humor, if only to mail her anguish. Of her family, she said, "They are religious, except me, and address an Eclipse, every morning—whom they call their 'Father.' "[40] The "sun" of her God in "Eclipse," twice passed over and barely touched by the Holy Spirit, she believed herself lost in the waste:

> I never lost as much but twice
> And that was in the sod.
> Twice have I stood a beggar
> Before the door of God!
>
> Angels—twice descending
> Reimbursed my store—
> Burglar! Banker—Father!
> I am poor once more!   (J–49)

Dickinson believed that she was without Christ and that her loved ones at least believed themselves to be in Canaan. For that, she was the better Calvinist and they the latitudinarian heretics.

It was not until years later, at some time in the early 1860s, that "Christ" did visit Emily Dickinson. It was then that she underwent the mental breakdown that John Cody analyzed, an event that stood out in her memory as the climactic moment of revelation. It was on a particular "Day," one that felt "Centuries" long, that "I first surmised the Horses Heads/ were toward Eternity—" (J–712). As William Sherwood has written, this was the "conversion that both her inclinations and her traditions had prepared her for. . . ."[41]

The developments that led to this traumatic event, for whatever reason, began years earlier. In 1846, when Dickinson was just sixteen, she wrote to Abiah that she was "alone with God, and my mind is filled with many solemn thoughts which crowd themselves upon me with irresistible force," as the waves "fast crowding on" had beaten into the caves of Jones Very's mind. "I feel," she continued, "that I am sailing upon the brink of an awful precipice, from which I cannot escape and over which I fear my tiny boat will soon glide if I do not receive help from above." In 1854, she wrote to Susan Gilbert about the ordeal of going alone to church and being frightened by a "phantom." The symptoms of paranoia are unmistakable:

I'm just from meeting, Susie, and as I sorely feared, my 'life' was made a 'victim.' I walked—I ran—I turned precarious corners—One moment I was not—then soared aloft like phoenix, soon as the foe was by—and then anticipating an enemy again, my soiled and drooping plumage might have been seen emerging from just behind a fence, vainly endeavoring to fly once more from hence.

She also expressed her growing fears and her yearning for some "New Land" to her friend, Mrs. J. G. Holland: "I often wish I was a grass, or a toddling daisy, whom all these problems of the dust might no more terrify." "Pardon my sanity," she pleaded, "in a world insane, and love me. . . ."[42]

In 1858 the tone of her letters began to change dramatically. No longer coherent and flowing, they began to take on the appearance of her poetry, cryptic, mysterious, choppy, and superficially disordered. They also dealt more and more with her own states of mind and showed a growing concern for her mental stability. For instance, in 1859, she wrote to Catherine Turner:

Insanity to the sane seems so unnecessary—but I am only one, and they are 'four and forty'. . . . I am pleasantly located in the deep sea, but love will row you out if her hands are strong, and don't wait till I land, for I'm going ashore on the other side—

The image of the sea, as used here, reappears constantly in Dickinson's writing. As it had been for the Old Testament prophets, as it had been for Puritan New England from the first coming over, as it continued to be for writers like Melville, the sea was an image of a state of mind beyond the borders of waking consciousness, of the wilderness within the soul. Like the wilderness that the children of Israel crossed, the sea was a type of that subconscious realm of terror that had to be crossed before there could be true salvation. It is clear that Dickinson imagined herself already floating away from "reality" into a space beyond ordinary frames of reference. When a friend's child died at birth, Dickinson wrote to her, "We don't know how dark it is, but if you are at sea, perhaps when we say that we are there, you won't be afraid." She knew, even then in 1860, that she was not one of the "Majority" but was sailing into "Madness" and would be considered "dangerous—/ And handled with a Chain—" (J–435). And then she sailed over the edge.[43]

It is not possible to date exactly the moment of Emily Dickinson's crisis. But that something happened, and that she remembered it happening on a particular day, is clear from her poetry. According to Cody, this "terrible sundering of the personality's connection with reality" is prob-

ably the "most terrifying" experience that a person can undergo. There
is a "dread of impending loss of control" followed by an apocalyptic
break.[44] Dickinson's poetic recreation of this event in 1861 echoes the
pattern of Jones Very's "New Birth" as a steady drumming breaks
through the thin covering that holds sanity over the pit:

> I felt a Funeral, in my Brain,
> And Mourners to and fro
> Kept treading—treading—till it seemed
> That Sense was breaking through—
>
> And when they all were seated,
> A Service, like a Drum—
> Kept beating—beating—till I thought
> My Mind was going numb—
>
> And then I heard them lift a Box
> And creak across my Soul
> With those same Boots of Lead, again,
> Then Space—began to toll,
>
> As all the Heavens were a Bell,
> And Being, but an Ear,
> And I, and Silence, some strange Race
> Wrecked, solitary, here—
>
> And then a Plank in Reason, broke,
> And I dropped down, and down—
> And hit a World, at every plunge,
> And Finished knowing—then—   (J–280)

Here, in a nondoctrinaire, nondogmatic form, are the classic Calvinist
images of the crisis of conversion as they apply to the sinner first
awakened to the terrors of the wilderness of the wrath of God. Here is
the beating on the mind like Christ knocking on the door to the heart,
here is the breaking of the rotten plank over the pit of hell as worldly
sense perception rots and consciousness plunges into subconsciousness,
here is the complete surrender of finite being to God's sovereignty, here
is the loneliness of the lost sinner who cannot hear the heavenly music,
and here is the complete destruction of reason. The Calvinist image of
human consciousness suspended over the pit of hell is a striking and
unmistakable aspect of Dickinson's poetry:

> A Pit—but Heaven over it—
> And Heaven beside, and Heaven abroad,

And yet a Pit—
With Heaven over it.

To stir would be to slip—
To look would be to drop—. . . .   (J–1712)

That this pit is of the mind is made clear when Dickinson says, "The depth is all my thought—." And in another poem, dated 1872, she reveals her understanding that the terror of the pit is in what today would be called the subconscious, repressed, silent, but waiting:

Its Hour with itself
The Spirit never shows.
What Terror would enthrall the Street
Could Countenance disclose

The Subterranean Freight
The Cellars of the Soul—
Thank God the loudest Place he made
Is licensed to be still.   (J–1225)

The day of revelation was a day of madness, a plunge into total depravity, an experience so powerful that two years later, in 1862, she recalled it with awe, and named it:

The first Day's Night had come—
And grateful that a thing
So terrible—had been endured—
I told my soul to sing—

She said her Strings were snapt—
Her Bow—to Atoms blown—
And so to mend her—gave me work
Until another Morn—

And then—a Day as huge
As Yesterdays in pairs.
Unrolled its horror in my face—
Until it blocked my eyes—

My Brain—begun to laugh—
I mumbled—like a fool—
And tho' 'tis Years ago—that Day
My Brain keeps giggling—still.

And Something's odd—within—
That person that I was—

> And this One—do not feel the same—
> Could it be Madness—this?   (J–410)

What we see here is the same confusion that had sent Jones Very briefly to McLeans, the same state of mind, the same uncertainty about its nature. By the middle of the nineteenth century, American evangelical Christianity had forgotten the profoundly disturbing reality of the conversion experience. But there was enough of the ancient spirit left, at least in the Dickinson house, for her to wonder, Was she mad? or was she being ravished by the Holy Spirit? And how could one know? When is "madness" a disease? And when is it a form of religious vision?

One way in which Emily Dickinson tried to express her own perception of her experience was by writing it out in poetry. In 1862, she wrote to Thomas Higginson, "I had a terror—since September—I could tell to none—and so I sing, as the Boy does by the Burying Ground—because I am afraid." At the time of her crisis, her strings "snapt," she could not sing, but in the "Quartz contentment" (J–341) that followed, she found her voice.[45]

The full conversion experience always had two aspects, crucifixion and resurrection, the wilderness and Canaan, and these often came together. The destruction of the self that was the crucifixion removed the blinders of self-interest and made possible a sight of Christ in the same blinding flash with which it damned the Old Adam to hell. With the ego removed, it suddenly became possible to glimpse, if only like Moses in passing, the not-self. And all that is not the self is Eternity. The vision was thus one of resurrection as well as damnation. The death of the self made possible the vision of Eternal life. The glory, however, was not immediately as apparent as the fear, and sometimes it had to be spelled out:

> One Year Ago—Jots what?
> God—spell the word! I—can't—
> Was't Grace? Not that—
> Was't Glory? That—will do—
> Spell slower—Glory—

Moreover, this Glory was, once again, a specific experience, that came only once and therefore had to be drunk of deeply and fully:

> I tasted—careless—then—
> I did not know the Wine
> Came once a World—Did you?   (J–296)

It was thus a sudden once-in-a-lifetime experience of Glory, of "Wine," as well as madness. The immediate—1860—effort to describe this apparently contradictory state produced some of Dickinson's finest poetry:

> A Wounded Deer—leaps highest—
> I've heard the Hunter tell—
> 'Tis but the Ecstacy of death—
> And then the Brake is still!   (J–165)

The conjunction of ecstacy and despair, of resurrection and of crucifixion, often served her as the subject of poetic imagery. But when Dickinson wrote the line, "Much Madness is divinest Sense" (J–435), she was trying to get beyond metaphor and symbol and to say directly that what people call madness is in fact the only way to heaven.

Dickinson also made wide use of traditional scriptural imagery. Like Mary Moody Emerson, she was saturated with the language of scripture, particularly of the Old Testament. "The Smitten Rock that gushes!" (J–165) is a direct reference to the typological symbol of Christ that followed the Children of Israel through the wilderness. Direct wilderness imagery appears less often in her conversion poems than does sea imagery, but it is there nonetheless.

For instance, whether recalling her one experience of Christ or waiting patiently for His return, Dickinson repeatedly compared herself to Moses looking from Pisgah to the promised land:

> Could we stand with that old 'Moses'—
> 'Canaan' denied—
> Scan like him the stately landscape
> On the other side—   (J–168)

Like Moses, she had been allowed a sight of Christ, from a distance, but had been denied entrance into Canaan. And as had Moses on Mount Sinai, she believed she had seen the face of God, if only in passing:

> "Am not consumed," Old Moses wrote,
> "Yet saw him face to face—"
> That very physiognomy
> I am convinced was this.   (J–1733)

At times, such a sight was deemed sufficient: "What would I give to see his face?/I'd give—I'd give my life—of course—" (J–247). At other time, "One hour—of her Sovereign's face" was not enough. She complained that Moses suffered worse than Stephen or Paul, "For these—were only

204 The Literary Remains

put to death—" while Moses was given a "tantalizing" sight of Canaan
"Without the entering—"(J–597). The sight of Christ from the desert
was not enough. She wanted the full experience of damnation and
salvation. Because of this the combined image of Christ as the Bridegroom in the wilderness appears again and again in her poetry. This, as
it had always been in the Christian mystical tradition, was where the
divine nuptials would take place:

> With Thee in the Desert—
> With Thee in the thirst—
> With Thee in the Tamarind wood—
> Leopard breathes at last!   (J–209)

The image appears repeatedly. There is an "Awe," she wrote, "that
men, must slake in wilderness" (J–525). Her sojourn through the world
was a sojourn "through Desert or the Wilderness" (J–711). The experience of the sight of the "Son" of God from deep in the wilderness of
madness was the hinge of her existence. Although the experience did not
recur, and even the memory of it lost its original intensity, the brilliance
of that flash changed everything:

> Had I not seen the Sun
> I could have borne the shade
> But light a newer wilderness
> My wilderness has made—   (J–1233)

The loss of sanity was a loss of control of sense perception; it was a
fading back from the world into the chaos of undifferentiated consciousness: "I clutched at sounds—/ I groped at shapes—/ . . . / I felt the
wilderness roll back. . . ." (J–430) described the unfolding of the inner
wilderness before her. But there was always the image of Christ in the
wilderness making the ordeal bearable:

> No wilderness—can be
> Where this attendeth me—
> No Desert Noon—
> No fear of frost to come
> Haunt the perennial bloom—
> But Certain June!   (J-195)

The wilderness thus served Dickinson as it had served generations of
Calvinists, as a powerful symbol of the depths of mental anguish, of the
terror waiting in the soul that must be faced and crossed. When Higginson's wife died, Dickinson wrote to her mentor, "The Wilderness is
new—to you. Master, Let me lead you."[46]

Although many of Dickinson's poems use images that suggest the combination of despair and joy, others range widely from bleak anguish to the "divine intoxication" of a "liquor never brewed." Noting this apparent lack of pattern, Albert Gelpi has explained that Dickinson "could be possessed only by the experience of the immediate moment, and so her art expressed itself in short lyrics each of which incarnated a moment." Hence, we get no poems that try to synthesize the whole of her experience but little fragments from different parts which, taken together, do make a complete picture.[47]

The apparently contradictory moods of these poems have suggested to some that Dickinson's native Calvinism was offset by Transcendentalism, that her heritage of darkness was being challenged by the new light of Romanticism. But such interpretation ignores the long tradition of Christian exultation in the joy of Christ and overlooks the regenerate Calvinist joy in nature as the Garden of Eden restored by Christ. Jonathan Edwards reveled in the beauties of nature and declared the woods, the fields, and the sky, in all their beauty, to be "emanations" of God's joy. His student, Joseph Bellamy, in *True Religion Delineated*, a popular text of orthodox Calvinism, tried to describe elect perception of the natural world:

Now here is a new made creature in a new world, viewing God, and wondering at his infinite glory, looking all round, astonished at the divine perfections shining forth in all his works. He views the spacious heavens; they declare to him the glory of the Lord: He sees his wisdom and his power; he wonders and adores; he looks around upon all His works; . . . ; all is genuine, natural and free, resulting from the native temper of his heart.

Here is a passionate love of the natural world, the elect perception that Emerson had tried to reproduce. But to try to fit Bellamy into any Transcendental category would be to stretch the definition of Transcendentalism beyond any practical use.[48]

Dickinson's joyous poetry came out of the mystical strain of New England Calvinism that looked to the image of Christ in the wilderness as a symbol of the recreated Eden of the land of Canaan. Her reading of Emerson may well have reinforced this tradition, but Emerson did not produce it. The Transcendentalists, as Frothingham said, "simply claimed for all men what Protestant Christianity claimed for its own elect." The poem, "Mine by the Right of the White Election" is one of the most powerful hymns of celebration in our literature, yet it is not inconsistent, given the Calvinist mind, with the madness of "The First Day's Night. . . ." Without the loss of self, there could be no sight of Christ.

Without a crossing of the wilderness, there could be no entering into the garden.[49]

The mental crisis of the early sixties passed, but Emily Dickinson never fully recovered. For the rest of her life she retained a complex perception of herself as a second Moses waiting either to enter into the land of vision or to die. There were moments of remembered vision and there were moments of the darkest despair. And both of these found their way into her poetry. "Life is so rotatory," she wrote, "that the wilderness falls to each, sometimes." The wilderness had fallen to her, and like Mary Moody Emerson she could only wait there for the call of God.[50]

The waiting was not serene. The paranoia that had first surrounded her remained. She withdrew into seclusion, afraid to face the world. Having tasted of the fruit of the tree of self-consciousness, she experienced a sight of sin; her nakedness was unbearable. "I was afraid and hid myself," she explained. When left alone in the house, she came close to panic. The terror floated just below the surface and she tried not to tempt it:

> The nights turned hot, when Vinnie had gone, and I must keep no window raised for fear of prowling 'booger,' and I must shut my door for fear front door slide open on me at the 'dead of night,' and I must keep 'gas' burning to light the danger up, so I could distinguish it—these gave me a snarl in the brain which don't unravel yet, and that old nail in my breast pricked me.[51]

She recognized that she had wrestled with God, but unlike Jacob she had lost. She was no longer in control but neither had she received a blessing. She still waited with fearful uncertainty for the divine event. It could be terror:

> Others, can wrestle—
> Yours, is done—
> And so of woe, bleak dreaded—come,
> It sets the fright at liberty—
> And terror's free—
> Gay, Ghastly, Holiday!   (J–281)

It could be joy:

> A Transport one cannot contain
> May yet a transport be—
> Though God forbid it lift the lid—
> Unto its ecstasy!   (J–184)

Not able like John Cotton to "wade in grace," she tired of the waiting and even thought of suicide as a means of breaking free:

> What if I say I shall not wait!
> What if I burst the fleshly gate—
> And pass escaped—to thee!
>
> What if I file this mortal—off—
> See where it hurt me—that's enough—
> And wade in Liberty!   (J–277)

But most of Dickinson's time was spent in the details of the wait. "[T]he infinite we only suppose," she wrote, "while we see the finite."[52] Her days thus were spent kneading bread, planting flowers, and writing poetry. If she could not obtain grace herself, perhaps these could for her. She prayed for her flowers as for herself:

> The Grace—Myself—might not obtain—
> Confer upon My flower—
> Refracted but a Countenance—
> For I—inhabit Her—   (J–707)

The wait dragged on. Like Mary Moody Emerson, she could rely only on her memories and her pain to keep the truth of God's existence alive: "God cannot discontinue himself. This appalling trust is at times all that remains."[53] Believing pain to be evidence of God's continuing "controversy" with His people, she "lived on dread" (J–770). But even prayer had its limits:

> There comes an hour when begging stops,
> When the long interceding lips
> Perceive their prayer is vain.
> 'Thou shalt not' is a kinder sword
> Than from a disappointing God
> 'Disciple, call again.'   (J–1751)

Implicit in this readiness to accept God's will was a surrender of self that had occurred as a result of the lost wrestling match. "My river runs to thee— / Blue Sea! Wilt welcome me?" (J–162) The Blue Sea was Eternity, the infinite depth of God personified by Christ. Hers was the classic position of the Christian mystic, betrothed to Christ. She was the bride waiting with her lamp lit for the arrival of her Lord. Uncertain of her worthiness, "I am ashamed—I hide— / What right have I to be a bride—" (J–472), she also felt that she had been given God's promise.

That "Day at Summer's full" had been "sufficient troth, that we shall rise— / . . . / To that new Marriage, / Justified—through Calvaries of Love—" (J–322). The image out of scripture was that of Christ coming out of the wilderness leaning upon His beloved.

> Given in Marriage unto Thee
> Oh thou celestial Host—
> Bride of the Father and the Son
> Bride of the Holy Ghost.
>
> Other Betrothal shall dissolve—
> Wedlocks of will, decay—
> Only the keeper of this Ring
> Conquer Mortality—   (J–817)

Those who believe that Emily Dickinson can only be understood if some supposed secret lover's name is revealed need to read that poem over again, and again. The attempt to find a male, or female, lover to explain the passion of Dickinson's existence is the empty quest of those who cannot believe in any motivation more powerful than lust and those who believe that all any woman wants is a man to fulfill her.

This is not to argue that Emily Dickinson did not revere, even love, Charles Wadsworth, Samuel Bowles, or Otis Lord. But these men served as human types of the spiritual antitype. They were not the content; they were symbols of more than themselves. She acknowledged her love for Otis Lord to be "idolatry," and she rejected his proposal of marriage with a clear statement of her perception of the difference between symbol and substance: "you ask the divine crust and that would doom the Bread." In much of her poetry, the type and antitype are so close that readers unused to such symbolism do not always understand as she did that the physical objects of her poetry were only types or shadows of the divine, that as Edward Taylor knew, the physical world is "slickt up in types." As Jonathan Edwards had written, "husbands, wives, or children, or the company of earthly friends are but shadows; but the enjoyment of God is the substance." This, even more than her madness, her conversion, or her wilderness imagery, is what marks Emily Dickinson as an heir of the wilderness tradition. She remembered that the wilderness is of the mind and that all outward objects are but projections, not of the human, but of the divine mind. The world is an allegory and the conversion of the soul from self to God is its theme.[54]

Dickinson wrote three mysterious letters to her "Master." These letters were never mailed. Any attempt to discover the identity of the "Master" is futile, for even if she did have a human figure in mind when she wrote the letters, it is clear whom she was really addressing:

Oh how the sailor strains, when his boat is filling—Oh how the dying tug, till the angel comes. Master—open your life wide, and take me in forever, I will never be tired—I will never be noisy when you want to be still.

The waiting did not continue entirely in vain. There was no return of vision, but there was something else, call it light, or love, or peace; it has no exact definition.[55]

Jonathan Edwards knew that "After great pain, a formal feeling comes," that this is followed by "the letting go" (J–341), and that only after these have occurred can there be a reasonable expectation of grace. "Oftentimes," he wrote, "the first sensible change after the extremity of terrors is a calmness, and the light gradually comes in." When her nephew, Gilbert, died, Dickinson wrote to Sue, "The first section of Darkness is the densest, Dear—After that, Light trembles in—." When Higginson's wife died, she wrote to him, "Danger is not at first, for then we are unconscious, but in the after—slower—Days—Do not try to be saved—but let Redemption find you—as it certainly will—Love is its own rescue, for we—at our supremest, are but its trembling emblems." In both of these quotations can be seen a recognition of what Edwards called grace, the slow coming of light to the truly broken and truly faithful. The light that trembled into Emily Dickinson's life can be named only because the darkness that terrified her can be named: "Costumeless consciousness— / That is he—" (J–1454).[56]

In England in the seventeenth century, John Welles had described the last moments of a dying man as his senses one by one let go leaving his mind, awake, alive, sliding down that long dark tunnel into "that bottomless deep of the endless wrath of almighty God." "This is it, to die and know it," said Edwards. And this always had been the wilderness, "that profounder site / That polar privacy / A soul admitted to itself— / Finite infinity" (J–1695). It is not death, itself, that gripped Dickinson's imagination but consciousness, and since for her, death meant an eternity of disembodied consciousness, the fact of death brought her to "dare in lonely Place / That awful stranger Consciousness / Deliberately face—" (J–1323). The sliding back of consciousness into the wilderness at death is a theme to which she constantly returned. The mind of the dying person watches and waits as the physical world dissolves around it: "And then the Windows failed—and then / I could not see to see—" (J–465).[57]

"What is man that thou art mindful of him?" asked the Psalmist. He might as easily have asked, "What is consciousness?" This is the question that underlies all true theology. This is the question that prevents otherwise healthy persons from taking it all for granted. The awareness of consciousness, and of the self being conscious, is not just consciousness of the pit; it is self-consciousness screwed to its tightest. There are times, as Dickinson knew, when the "Mind is so near itself—it cannot see, distinctly."[58] The attempt to look oneself in the eye without a mirror, to get behind the "I" and see the "I" that is acting, this is the first step sideways into the wilderness. Once there, the soul can only chase itself in endless circles until it drops exhausted in surrender:

> This consciousness that is aware
> Of Neighbors and the Sun
> Will be the one aware of Death
> And that itself alone
>
> Is traversing the interval
> Experience between
> And most profound experiment
> Appointed unto Men—
>
> How adequate unto itself
> Its properties shall be
> Itself unto itself and none
> Shall make discovery.
>
> Adventure most unto itself
> The Soul condemned to be—
> Attended by a single Hound
> Its own identity.   (J–822)

Eternal consciousness is what Dickinson meant by the word, "immortality," a word she used often. Writing to Higginson in 1868, she said, "A Letter always feels to me like immortality because it is the mind alone without corporeal friend."[59] The mind alone "without corporeal friend" is the consciousness that "will be the one aware of Death / And that itself alone / Is traversing the interval. . . ."

Given this perception of "immortality," the question became, would eternity be spent alone in darkness and in pain or at One with the eternal, universal consciousness that is God? According to the Calvinists, such participation with God in eternity required a prior conversion from self-centered consciousness to a love for "Universal Existence," from personal "identity" to God's universal identity. It required a willingness that the self be damned that the totality might prosper, a giving up of all hope for oneself for God. Such a conversion had to begin with the revelation of the self alone in the eternal void of space. Thus, Emily Dickinson described the day of her own conversion:

I touched the Universe—

And back it slid—and I alone—
A Speck upon a Ball—
Went out upon Circumference—
Beyond the Dip of Bell.   (J–378)

Immortality was consciousness because God was consciousness. The world, as both Edwards and Emerson affirmed, is an Ideal one; all matter is in the mind and the mind in God. The vision of Christ was thus a vision of God's total consciousness, the highest level possible. Of Christ on the cross, Dickinson asked, "Might He know / How conscious Consciousness—could grow—?" (J–622). Participation with Christ in the crucifixion was thus a parallel experience for the human convert, a brief glimpse, if only in passing, of the Not-Me that is Eternity. Dickinson received her "One Draught of life," and her life was the price she paid for it:

They weighed me, Dust by Dust—
They balanced Film with Film,
Then handed me my Being's worth—
A single Dram of Heaven!   (J–1725)

Christ was thought to be eternally present because God's consciousness was thought to be eternally present, holding the entire creation together in every moment of time. What human beings lacked was the perception to see the presence of Christ in this creation. Christ was present, but they lacked the means to see Him: "Not Revelation—'tis that waits. / But our unfurnished eyes" (J–424). Emerson thought that he could just go into the woods and see the divine presence. But it was not that easy. First there had to be a desire to discover consciousness. Then there had to be a recognition that the perceiving self is an obstruction, that the ego is not the ultimate source of consciousness but a tin God, "plated wares," a sham. The journey of this discovery is an ancient story, not invented by Calvin or restricted to Christ. It is *the* myth of humankind.

Finding is the first Act
The second, loss,
Third, Expedition for
The 'Golden Fleece'—

Fourth, no Discovery—
Fifth, no Crew—
Finally, no Golden Fleece—
Jason—sham—too.   (J–870)

To go in search of identity and to find oneself a sham was a prerequisite for proceeding beyond to totality. One had to, as Melville did, accept one's own annihilation and learn to live not for self but for Being. This was what Emily Dickinson was waiting for. This was the light that slowly trembled in. To know that Eternity exists and to be able to accept that in place of self was the final revelation of grace:

> Time feels so vast that were it not
> For an Eternity—
> I fear me this Circumference
> Engross my finity—
>
> To His exclusion, who prepare
> By Processes of Size
> For the Stupendous Vision
> of His diameters—   (J–802)

To experience the "stupendous vision" of Eternity was to participate in Eternity. The "Perished patterns murmur," as the Children of Israel "murmured" in the wilderness against their God and perished there. But their children did enter into Canaan and claim the promised land. In the end, "Man" is left out; it is God, the totality of Being, that does alone "proceed" (J–724). To be united to Christ thus meant to Emily Dickinson to be free of the single hound, her own identity, and to be united forever to the universal supreme identity, the consciousness that alone can "Conquer Mortality." To deny self and to receive the vision of God was to be in covenant with God, the promise sealed. It was true liberation from the world, from the flesh, from finite consciousness. It was Heaven:

> Mine—by the Right of the White Election!
> Mine—by the Royal Seal!
> Mine—by the sign in the scarlet prison!
> Bars—cannot conceal!
>
> Mine—here—in vision and in Veto!
> Mine—by the grave's repeal—
> Titled—Confirmed—
> Delirious Charter!
> Mine—long as Ages steal!   (J–528)

7
Herman Melville
The Watery Wilderness

An evil and adulterous generation seeketh after a sign;
and there shall no sign be given to it, but the sign of the
prophet Jonas:
For as Jonas was three days and three nights in the
whale's belly; so shall the Son of man be three days and
three nights in the heart of the earth.
> Matthew 12.39–40

This most persuasive season has now for weeks recalled
me from crotchety and over doleful chimeras, the like of
which men like you and me, and some others, forming a
chain of God's posts around the world, must be content
to encounter now and then, and fight them the best way
we can. But come they will,—for in the boundless, trackless, but still glorious wild wilderness through which
these outposts run, the Indians do sorely abound,
as well as the insignificant but still stinging mosquitoes.
> Melville to Hawthorne, June 1851

i

Herman Melville understood the spiritual meaning of the wilderness.
His works howl with the agony of loss and loneliness. And his cry,
echoing down the years, has found a sympathetic audience in modern
America.

Melville, we are told, belongs to the twentieth century. His works
represent "the alienation of modern man." They are "alive with intellectual impulses that anticipate modern movements of thought." They are a
product of the transition from religion to psychology and thus speak "to
the modern mind with profound pertinence." Melville was "the literary
discoverer of . . . the mythological unconscious. As a depth psychologist
he belongs with Doestoevsky and Nietzsche, the greatest in the centuries

213

before Freud." His religion was not Calvinism, or Protestantism, or even Christianity; it was "skeptical humanism."[1]

These critics are not wrong to emphasize the similarities between Melville's insights and those of the twentieth century. Nor can there be any doubt that the lost and lonely intellectuals of twentieth-century America see more of themselves in Melville than Melville's contemporaries ever did. But the critics suffer from a bias that assumes that modern culture possesses insights into human consciousness incomprehensible to the earlier ages of "blind faith" and "enlightened reason." Orthodox theology also dealt with the phenomena which these moderns mistakenly believe to have been first discovered by the high priests of "depth psychology."

Melville was the last visible ship of a mighty American fleet that sailed out of the seventeenth century, lost its way in the eighteenth century, and foundered in the nineteenth-century sea. Behind him, supporting him, inspiring him, bedeviling him, was an ancient tradition of thought reaching from Edwards back to Calvin to St. Paul. He did not look to the future to find his star; he steered by a light from the past.

Critics like T. Walter Herbert and Thomas Werge interpret Melville's willingness to plunge into the wilderness of doubt as a rejection of Calvinism and of orthodox religion. And it was; but only if by "orthodox religion" is meant that nineteenth-century American faith that had forgotten the reality behind the doctrine. It is important to repeat that rebellion against this kind of formal, legalistic religion was exactly what orthodox Calvinism of the Edwardsian tradition demanded. The sojourn into the wilderness of doubt and confusion was the primary experience of that religion. To question established assumptions of truth and virtue was the first step toward the freedom of the spirit. Even those who, "addicted to morality and religion," were merely "serving their lusts therein" had to be shaken from their self-righteousness and made to feel the terror of despair. It is thus misleading to say, without qualification, that Melville rejected Calvinism. In rejecting the sterile orthodoxy of his day, Melville, like Emily Dickinson, was rejecting, not Calvinism, but a hypocritical, Arminian evangelicalism in order to keep faith with the more rigorous orthodoxy of his ancestors. And he knew it.[2]

The "blackness of darkness" in which Melville wrote was not atheism nor was it "skeptical humanism." It was the wilderness to which Calvinist Americans traditionally had been called to experience temptation, annihilation, and—possibly—regeneration. It derived its force, as Melville said, "from its appeal to that Calvinistic sense of Innate Depravity and Original Sin, from whose visitations, in some shape or other, no deeply thinking mind is always or wholly free." It was because of their anachronistic adherence to those ancient doctrines that Melville referred to Hawthorne, himself, "and some others," as "a chain of God's posts . . . in the boundless, trackless, but still glorious wild wilderness."[3]

If Melville was not strictly, as he said of Ishmael, "born and bred in the bosom of the infallible Presbyterian Church," he was brought up in the equally Calvinist and more dogmatic Dutch Reformed Church. Thus, his earliest patterns of thought and behavior were formed within the context of a nominally Calvinist worldview. Calvinist orthodoxy, as Herbert has shown, provided him with "a fundamental idiom in which to comprehend himself and the world; the problems of doctrine were for him continuous with the problems of experience." Like Emily Dickinson, Melville understood his own emotional experience within the context provided by his culture. The conflict between rationalism and orthodoxy, Arminianism and Calvinism, served as the idiom in which he comprehended life. It was in orthodox religious terms, and not in the language of existential psychology, that Melville grappled with doubt and affirmation, fear and hope, the wilderness and Canaan.[4]

In America, by the middle of the nineteenth century, Protestants in New England and throughout the United States, had come to believe themselves in the promised land of Canaan, beyond the wilderness. Belief in God had come to mean belief in American righteousness. To doubt that America was the Promised Land or that nominal Christians were the renewed Israel was to doubt, so it seemed, all religion. Church members were assumed to be Christians. Such hollow imitations of spiritual conversion as the mourner's bench provided relatively easy paths to grace. Even in the less enthusiastic churches, where the emotionalism of the mourner's bench was abhorred, "Christian Nurture" replaced the radical conversion experience as the accepted means of becoming a Christian.[5] Piety might require the occasional stimulus of a revival, but the salvation of most churchgoers, of most "professors," was rarely questioned. In such a culture, Calvin himself would have seemed a doubting, alienated atheist. As H. R. Niebuhr so succinctly put it, in America in the nineteenth century, "A God without wrath brought men without sin into a kingdom without judgement through the ministrations of a Christ without a cross." It was this sterile orthodoxy, this degenerate form of Protestantism, that Melville rebelled against.[6]

The orthodox doctrines of original sin, predestination, and election remained a part of the professed creed at least of the Melvilles' Dutch Reformed Church. But belief in these doctrines contradicted the actual behavior of orthodox churchgoers. For in almost all respects, despite the efforts of conservative theologians and the words of the creeds, American Protestantism had in practice become Arminian. The result was moralistic evangelical Protestantism which had as positive a view of human nature and human potential as had the liberal Unitarians. The assumption of grace had replaced the need for converting terror; saints already saved need encouragement and moral lessons, not damnation. What remained of the conversion process amounted in many cases to little more than verbal acceptance of an outdated creed. In the faith of genteel New Yorkers like the Melvilles, duty, discipline, and education had replaced the emphasis on mystic experience.[7]

Because the perception of evil, as presented by orthodox Calvinist theology, seemed to lead to madness, Melville, according to Herbert, rejected the creeds of the family church because he "felt that the God of orthodox revelation was unfit for worship" and therefore he rejected Calvinism.[8] In Herbert's view, Melville's position is similar to Emerson's; he saw no advantage in yielding his sanity without the assurance of compensating gain. He saw no benefit in crucifixion without a guarantee of resurrection. In Melville's day, those Calvinist doctrines that provoked despair remained as part of the professed creed, but the insistence on the need for conversion from death to life across the wilderness of despair had been lost. The threat of terror remained a part of tradition without explanation or meaning, but only a few were sensitive enough to see it. It is no wonder that Melville was alienated and confused.

Most Protestant Americans of Melville's generation believed America to be God's chosen nation. Even doubters like Melville initially shared this common assumption. One notable passage from *White Jacket*, a remnant of Melville's youthful enthusiasm, gives full voice to this theme:

> Escaped from the house of bondage, Israel of old did not follow after the ways of the Egyptians. To her was given an express dispensation; to her were given new things under the sun. And we Americans are the peculiar, chosen people—the Israel of our time; we bear the ark of the liberties of the world. Seventy years ago we escaped from thrall; and, besides our first birthright—embracing one continent of earth—God has given to us, for a future inheritance, the broad domains of the political pagans, that shall yet come and lie down under the shade of our ark, without bloody hands being lifted. God has predestinated, mankind expects, great things from our race; and great things we feel in our souls. The rest of the nations must soon be in our rear. We are the pioneers of the world; the advance-guard, sent on through the wilderness of untried things, to break a new path in the New World that is ours.

Later in his career, with the full maturing of his doubts, Melville made an attempt to correct his youthful nationalism. In *Israel Potter*, he described his hero as a "bondsman in the English Egypt" lost for forty years in the wilderness of London, dreaming of his New England home in "the far Canaan beyond the sea." But when Israel finally, in advanced old age, returned to his home, he found that Canaan had decayed into a "type now . . . of forever arrested intentions, and a long life still rotting in early mishap," and he wondered if his dreams had ever been anything but dreams. Just as Israel Potter came to doubt the reality of his own memories and to wonder if Canaan were real or had only been imagined, Melville also came to doubt his youthful enthusiasm and to wonder if all of his perceptions and beliefs were real or only imagined.⁹

As Thomas Werge has pointed out,¹⁰ epistemology, the problem of knowing, was as important to Melville as it was to the whole Calvinist tradition. The division between the Antinomians and the Arminians in seventeenth-century New England had been a division basically between those—the Antinomians—who trusted their feelings and had confidence in the reliability of their perceptions, and those—called Arminians—who did not believe that their perceptions or their feelings could be trusted. The Antinomians had felt at ease in Zion; the so-called Arminians had stressed the continuing reality of fear. Belief in "that Calvinist sense of Innate Depravity and Original Sin" was not intellectual assent to dogma. It was just this awareness of the uncertainty of human perception, the limits of human knowing, and the conditional nature of perceived truth.

The conflict that split New England at the beginning of its errand into the wilderness was the same conflict that split Herman Melville's soul. It was his awareness of the extreme subjectivity of human consciousness that prevented him from accepting the evidence of his consciousness as ultimate truth. He would have liked to believe that he was indeed in Canaan, but the doubts of his head overruled the affirmations of his heart and forced him to confront the continuing reality of wilderness. Referring to the experience Romantics called living "in the all," Melville willingly admitted that "This 'all' feeling, though, there is some truth in." But, he wrote to Hawthorne, "what plays mischief with the truth is that men will insist upon the universal application of a temporary feeling or opinion." Melville, like his Calvinist ancestors, was too tough-minded to mistake a passing sensation, no matter how pleasant, for true insight. He would not accept "seemings"; his search was deeper than that.¹¹

Whether he knew madness to be the wilderness that had to be crossed, Melville did acknowledge madness to be a real possibility, one that he was painfully aware of. "This going mad of a friend or acquaintance," he wrote,

> comes straight home to every man who feels his soul in him,—which but few men do. For in all of us lodges the same fuel to light the same

fire. And he who has never felt, momentarily, what madness is has but a mouthful of brains.

Melville's quest led him away from sentiment to the deeper heart, and that heart opened up over the abyss within. He wanted to believe without madness. He wanted to be able to affirm the romantic faith in life. But he did not believe that the passing sensations of consciousness could be trusted. The mind was not pure and free and honest; it was ensnared in a web of self-deception. The romantic promise was an illusion, self-reliance a dangerous sham; the introspective terrors alone seemed real.[12]

Melville never said explicitly that he would have to go mad in order to discover truth. He never acknowledged the relationship of insanity to the Christian symbol of crucifixion and resurrection. But it is clear that he was drawn to the inner wilderness whether he realized why or not. If the truth should lead to insanity, he seemed to say, then so be it; and if insanity should lead to Truth, so much the better. "Wandering to-and-fro over these deserts," unable to bear the uncertainty, he preferred a "sane madness" to worldly contentment if that was the price to be paid. As Hawthorne said, he could "neither believe, nor be comfortable in his unbelief; and he is too honest and courageous not to try to do one or the other." Unable to delude himself into believing himself a saint in Canaan, he turned and headed instead into the wilderness.[13]

ii

Not only was Melville, like Hawthorne, torn between fear and hope, between Edwards and Emerson, with the call to madness echoing in his ears. His very career traced a pattern of conversion from the tropical paradise of *Typee* and *Omoo* through the wrenching struggle of *Moby-Dick*, the cynicism of *The Confidence Man* and the desperation of *Pierre*, to the final acceptance and resurrection of *Billy Budd*. If Melville did not undergo a classic Calvinist conversion experience in his life, he did in his novels. There and not on the mourner's bench or the psychiatrist's couch he laid out the inner struggles of his soul and transformed the dynamics of his conversion into literature.

In his first novel, *Typee*, Melville was still the romantic adventurer searching for Canaan in the land beyond the borders of civilization. Typee is paradise, not wilderness. The natives there are yet in a "state of grace," their natural purity uncorrupted by civilization. "The penalty of the fall presses very lightly upon the valley of the Typee."

In this secluded abode of happiness there were no cross old women, no cruel step-dames, no withered spinsters, no love-sick maidens, no sour old bachelors, no inattentive husbands, no melancholy young men, no blubbering youngsters, and no squalling brats. All was Mirth, fun, and high good humor. Blue devils, hypochondria, and doleful dumps, went and hid themselves among the nooks and crannies of the rocks.

In contrast, Christian missionaries are attacked in the novel for their pious hypocrisy. The supposed benefits of Christian civilization are shown to be a sham. The native "whom Providence has bountifully provided with all the sources of pure and natural enjoyment," what benefit can civilization offer him?

She may cultivate his mind—may 'elevate his thoughts'—these are I believe the established phrases—but will he be the happier? Let the once smiling and populous Hawaian Islands, with their now diseased, starving, and dying natives, answer the question!

The implications are clear: sin is the fault, not of the self, but of civilization. The natural heart, like the natural man, is the answer to the world's complaints.[14]

And yet *Typee* is not totally an Emersonian endorsement of Nature. Even in that valley paradise, there are hints of darker themes that cast doubt on the purity of natural man and the supposed superiority of unquestioned, uncomplicated perception. The very name, "Typee," we are warned, means "cannibal," and at the climax of the novel the "horrid revelation" of cannibalism persuades Melville to try to escape from the smothering embrace of his hosts and return to the safety of unhappy civilization. The natural human heart, although so good and full of love when first encountered, reveals deeper, darker aspects on closer inspection. Where then, if anywhere, can paradise be found?[15]

By the time *Mardi* and *Omoo* were published, Melville had achieved some success as a writer of popular romance, and he was ready to put a bit more of himself on paper. He wanted to go a step deeper and begin to explore some of the doubts and darkness that played about the fringes of his earlier work. The result was a rather clumsy mixture of South Sea adventure and philosophical dialogue. The public was not amused.

Mardi begins with a calm at sea. From the first, Melville makes clear the philosophical significance of the events of the novel. The calm is shown to be a state of mind, a quiet withdrawal from the world and the rush of everyday sensation. "At first," he wrote, "he was taken by surprise, never having dreamt of a state of existence where existence itself seems suspended." The calm continues, feelings of contentment give way to vague anxieties. "Thoughts of eternity thicken. He begins to feel anxious concerning his soul." But the worst part was "the consciousness of his utter helplessness."[16]

Here was the beginning of the conversion experience, the first step of awakening from the sleep of ordinary consciousness to the awareness of the fear of God. Of all the sermons he preached, Jonathan Edwards held that "those in which the doctrine of God's absolute sovereignty with regard to the salvation of sinners has been insisted on" were the most affecting.[17] Consciousness of man's true helplessness in the hands of an angry God was the best means for shaking sinners from their natural self-confidence. Melville's own inability to endorse the optimistic concepts of free will and natural virtue prevented his endorsement of the self-assurance that characterize his era. The gnawing suspicion that a sovereign providence did control all aspects of human life lured him into the wilderness. The end of the calm was only the beginning of Melville's journey. After sailing beyond the calm, he continued "to penetrate further and further into" what he aptly called "the watery wilderness."[18]

No longer a tropical island paradise like Typee, the islands of *Mardi* represented the world in all its complexity. In its several islands were contained allegories of the history of mankind. Narrating the history of one allegorical island after another provided Melville with the means to indulge in social criticism and philosophy. The debate building within Melville thus was transferred to the novel, and there, midst the action of the plot and the interactions of the different characters, the Calvinist doctrines of free will, original sin, and predestination could be debated with vigor:

> "I am not sure of that," retorted Media. "Methinks this doctrine of yours, about all mankind being bedevilled, will work a deal of mischief; seeing that by implication it absolves you mortals from moral accountability. Furthermore, as your doctrine is exceedingly evil . . . it follows that you must be proportionately bedevilled; and since it harms others, your devil is of the number of those of whom it is best to limbo; and since he is one of those that can be limboed, limboed he shall be in you."
>
> And so saying, he humorously commanded his attendents to lay hands upon the bedevilled philosopher, and place a bandage upon his mouth, that he might no more disseminate his devilish doctrine.
>
> Presently, however, they released him; when Media inquired how he relished the application of his theory; and whether he was still of old Bardianna's mind?

To which haughtily adjusting his robe, Babbalanja replied, 'The strong arm, my Lord, is no argument, though it overcomes all logic.'

Thus for the moment Melville ventured only part way into the wilderness. Like many of his contemporaries, he was "bedevilled" by Calvinistic doubts but rather than confront their full implications, he used force to "limbo" those doubts, "though it overcomes all logic."[19]

But the doubts remained. Pani spoke for Melville when he cried "Off masks, mankind, that I may know what warranty of fellowship with others may own thoughts possess. . . ." And lost in the labyrinth of subjectivity he howled, "I brood and grope in blackness; I am dumb with doubt; yet tis not doubt, but worse; I doubt my doubt." Pursued by the furies of determinism and depravity, Pani tried to escape. But at last the avengers of his "original" crimes caught up with him. Rather than submit to punishment for crimes over which he had no control, he made a last courageous romantic assertion of self. Steering his canoe into deadly breakers, he cried

And why put back? Is a life of dying worth living over again? Let me then be the returning wanderer. The helm! By Oro, I will steer my own fate, . . . Now I am my soul's emperor; and my first act is abdication. Hail! Realm of shades![20]

In *Mardi,* Melville escaped the jaws of his fears only by steering into the breakers. The one free act that he could still control was suicide, and rather than submit to the sovereignty of an angry God, he chose abdication. Finding no comfort in the blind optimism of liberal theology or the deluded piety of evangelical hypocrisy, Melville still tried to resist the only answer left to him: annihilation in the wilderness of the self.

The popular and financial failure of *Mardi* was a bitter disappointment to Melville. But the book's failure did not prevent him from diving even deeper into the darkness in *Moby-Dick.* "What I feel most moved to write," he told Hawthorne, "that is banned,—it will not pay. Yet, altogether write the *other* way I cannot." Because Melville was externalizing his own spiritual struggles in his work, to give up writing would be to give up the struggle. And as Hawthorne had written, he was too brave and courageous to do that.[21]

Moby-Dick's power derived from the heightened struggle within Melville between the two forces fighting for his soul. Ishmael and Ahab represent the two competing possibilities. Ishmael is the hopeful Romantic who wants to believe in humanity and who champions the liberal view of man: "But man, in the ideal, is so noble, and so sparkling, such a grand and glowing creature. . . . Bear me out in it, Oh God!" He has

little patience with the introspective terrors of dark and self-effacing
creeds:

> But when a man's religion becomes really frantic; when it is a positive
> torment to him; and when, in fine, it makes this earth of ours an
> uncomfortable inn to lodge in; then I think it high time to take that
> individual aside and argue the point with him.

Ishmael did get taken in, at first, in Ahab's mad quest, but he saw the
light and in the milky sperm washed his hands of it and survived.

Ahab, on the other hand, in all his sinful "fatal pride," was the classic
Calvinist sinner awakened to the reality of the fear of God who tragically
resists the call to the wilderness even as he sails to inevitable destruction.
The convicted sinner does not willingly suffer the trials of the wilderness
but must be dragged, fighting, into the abyss. The Old Adam struggles
fiercely to remain supreme; the self cannot, by nature, acquiesce in its
own annihilation. Calvin had understood Ahab. "Sinners," he had explained, "because they murmur and kick against him and rant against
their Judge, their violent fury stupefies them with madness and rage."
"So, awakened sinners, when under a deep and thorough conviction,"
preached Joseph Bellamy, "have comparatively a very clear sight and
great sense of God; but it only makes them feel and see their native
enmity which before lay hid. . . ." This was Ahab, the convicted sinner
who has suffered in the jaws of God, who has a great sense of the
enormity and power of that God, and whose "native enmity" was in full
rage against him. Ahab sailed on the downward curve of the conversion
process, heading into the wilderness abyss. Because he did not obey but,
like the Children of Israel, murmured against God, his carcass must rot
in the wilderness without his ever having glimpsed the promised land.[23]

Moby-Dick begins on a note of despair. "This is my substitute for pistol
and ball," said Ishmael. "With a philosophical flourish Cato throws himself upon his sword; I quietly take to the ship." The ship was a microcosm
of the world as well as an escape from it. The world "is a ship on its
passage out, and not a voyage complete." It was not a utopia, not a
Canaan, but a sojourn, and the sea on which it sailed was the "watery
wilderness." Lank Bildad, the pilot, made the biblical comparison explicit as he sang loudly and steadily from the bow:

> Sweet Fields beyond the swelling flood,
>   Stand dressed in living green.
> So to the Jews old Canaan stood,
>   While Jordan rolled between.

The ship was on its voyage out, but to the hopeful eyes of Ishmael, being on the wilderness meant the promise of Canaan. "Never did those sweet words sound more sweetly to me than then," he said. "They were full of hope and fruition." The voyage might be long and difficult but Ishmael, like a good nineteenth-century American, had faith in the future.[24]

But Canaan lay a long distance off, and not all of those who entered the wilderness survived the ordeal. Although Ishmael may have had faith in the future outcome, Melville knew the danger he was risking. But he also suspected that to obtain the "Kingdom of freedom," the risk had to be taken. The men in control of the ship, like Melville, first had to fight all temptation to remain in the security of a snug harbor. They had to sail away from the illusory safety of the shore into the winds, "for refuge's sake forlornly rushing into peril." Know ye now, asked Melville, "that all deep, earnest thinking is but the intrepid effort of the soul to keep the open independence of her sea . . .?"

But as in landlessness above resides the highest truth, shoreless, indefinite as God—so, better is it to perish in that howling infinite, than be ingloriously dashed upon the lee, even if that were safety! For worm-like, then, oh! who would craven crawl to land! Terrors of the terrible! is all this agony so vain? Take heart, take heart, O Bulkington! Bear thee grimly, demigod! Up from the spray of thy ocean-perishing—straight up, leaps thy apotheosis!

Here is the echo of the wilderness tradition. Here Melville clearly can be heard to say, Fear not, Oh Israel, to descend into the "howling infinite" of the wilderness, for only out of such descent might there be gained salvation![25]

Ishmael took to the sea to escape for a time from the world. Melville, too, withdrew into his Berkshire attic to let the spiritual battle be joined. But he did not go to battle without reservation. *Mardi* had been a commercial failure. Melville knew that another such ponderous book would be rejected by the public. He was a man with responsibilities, with a family to support. He did not take to the watery wilderness lightly. But despite the danger and the loss, he had to do it. He was too courageous not to.

This is the significance of Father Mapple's sermon. It was directed not at Ishmael, Ahab, or at the readers; it was directed at Melville himself. There are, as Father Mapple said, two strands of the sermon, one addressed to all sinners and a second addressed "to me as a pilot of the living God." The message to all sinners is the basic message of the need for conversion, as Jonah, a type of Christ, was three days in the belly of hell before being resurrected. Jonah, like Melville, had tried to flee from the wrath of God, from the growing awareness of his own depravity and helplessness. Conscious of his sinfulness—"he but too well knew the darkness of his deserts"—when God at last caught up with him he did not try to escape or beg for mercy. Rather, he accepted the verdict and in order to save the ship asked to be thrown overboard. "And here, shipmates," preached Mapple, "is true and faithful repentance; not clamorous for pardon but grateful for punishment." Here too is the heart of the wilderness tradition, an insistence on suffering, a willingness, even a desire, to be damned for the glory of God. This is what Shepard felt; this is what Mary Rowlandson longed for; this is what Edwards gloried in. Jonah, according to Mapple, is "a model for repentance," an example of true conversion from a life centered on self to one that is given entirely to God. In writing *Moby-Dick*, Melville, like Jonah ready to face his God, was throwing himself into the watery wilderness.[26]

But it is the other strand of Mapple's sermon that was directed at Melville alone. Jonah, "bidden by the Lord to sound those unwelcome truths in the ears of a wicked Ninevah," fled from his mission. He ran from his responsibility to "preach the Truth to the face of falsehood!" And it was for this reason that he was thrown overboard into the belly of the whale, that type of the crucifixion, where he was made to suffer the full horror of the wrath of God. Melville also was torn between the dark truths that he did not want to confront and the profitable illusions of paradise. To tell his heart's truth in another dark book would ruin him. But the fear of God had caught up with him and he dared not disobey. Father Mapple's warning was meant for Melville's ears:

> Woe to him who this world charms from Gospel duty! . . . Woe to him who seeks to please rather than to appal! Woe to him whose good name is more to him than goodness! . . . Woe to him who would not be true, even though to be false were salvation!

And woe to Melville if he did not tell the truth about the fears that continued to batter relentlessly on the doors of his heart.[27]

The action of *Moby-Dick* provided Melville with more effective opportunities for philosophical argument that had the crude dialogues strung together in *Mardi*. The chapter on the masthead is Melville's strongest attack on the fantasies of Romanticism and the folly of believing in the pleasant illusions spun by the self. An invisible eyeball afloat in mystic revery has no place on a whaling ship. There is, he insists, a harsh reality that does not suffer fools. Beyond personal identity is not the oversoul but the pit. The look-out on the mast-head

lulled into such an opium-like listlessness of vacant, unconscious revery . . . that at last he loses his identity; takes the mystic ocean at his
feet for the visible image of that deep, blue, bottomless soul, pervading
mankind and nature. . . . In this enchanted mood, thy spirit ebbs away
to whence it came; becomes diffused through time and space. . . .

But while this sleep, this dream is on ye, move your foot or hand an
inch; slip your hold at all; and your identity comes back to you in
horror. Over Descartian vortices you hover. And perhaps, at mid-day,
in the fairest weather, with one half-throttled shriek you drop through
that transparent air into the summer sea, no more to rise forever.
Heed it well, ye Pantheists![28]

If the Pantheists were not mindful of the horrors of the fear of God,
Ahab was acutely conscious of them. His pursuit of Moby Dick was his
attempt to strike at if not destroy those fears. He fought to protect his
helpless self from the cosmic forces of determinism and depravity. He
was not a monster but an heroic human being, a Romantic hero, fighting
for his dignity against a universe that does not indulge the vanity of
human dignity.

Ahab felt "some unreasoning thing" hidden behind the mask of the
random cruelties of life. There, "some unknown but still reasoning thing
puts forth the moldings of its features from behind the unreasoning
mask." Sometimes, he said, "I think there's naught beyond," but he felt
the presence of conscious malice in a universe that created men sinners
and then punished them for their sins, that determined their behavior
and then damned them for their acts. Moby Dick was the symbol of this
Calvinist God. He was the mystery that Moses saw, in passing, on Mount
Sinai. "Thou shalt see my back parts, my tail, he seems to say, but my face
shall not be seen. But I cannot completely make out his back parts; and
hint what he will about his face, I say again he has no face." It was this
incomprehensible, omnipotent, invisible Calvinist God that Ahab hated.
This does not mean that he believed in some other God. No, he believed
in Edwards' God and it was for that reason that he hated Him:

I see in him outrageous strength, with an inscrutable malice sinewing
it. That inscrutable thing is chiefly what I hate; and be the White
Whale agent or the White Whale principal, I will wreck that hate upon
him.

Like Calvin's awakened sinner, Ahab knows God. He felt the power and
the dread. But he would not, could not, let himself go to be destroyed by
those omnipotent jaws. The pain was too great, the self's resistance too
strong, and the terror too profound.[29]

The white whale thus symbolized all of the terror of the fear of God.

"Was not Saul of Tarsus," asked Melville, "converted from unbelief by a similar fright? I tell you the sperm whale will stand no nonsense." Ahab saw him "as the monomaniac incarnation of all those malicious agencies which some deep men [like Melville] feel eating into them. . . ." The whiteness of the whale, particularly, symbolized all of the terrors encountered during the depths of conversion. By its very "indefiniteness," he wrote, the color white "shadows forth the heartless voids and immensities of the Universe, and thus stabs us from behind with the thought of annihilation." It was this same "indefiniteness" that Edwards saw as the fog that covers the abyss.[30]

In Edwards' metaphysical idealism, there was no external world, no colors except in the mind, no solidity except in the resistance of objects, no resistance that was not itself a perception of mind. Creation was consciousness; it existed only in the mind of God. The physical world, one's body included, were but ideas in the mind which itself "exists only mentally." The world was an illusion and the source of this illusion lay beyond the impenetrable veil. For the Emersonian, passage beyond that veil offered the promise of participation in the "Oversoul," but for the true Calvinist, passage beyond the veil meant the loss of self in a terrifying descent into wilderness.[31]

This was the significance of the color white. Beyond the comforting illusion of solid reality waited not mystic reverie but a terrifying "indefiniteness." The loss of solidity and certainty was the breaking of the dam that previously kept insanity from flooding into the soul. When the natural man suddenly discovered that "reality" was not what he had always assumed, when the certainty of sense perception dissolved in a mist, when the walls crumbled and the hills lost their solidity, the result was terror. Not only did the determined beliefs of personal identity disappear in the chaos of the wrath of God, all of the determined patterns of behavior, learned and inherited, disintegrated, and there was only consciousness alone with itself in the bottomless immensity. This was the apocalyptic vision that grabbed the imagination and turned worldly men into Calvinists. This was the experience that Emily Dickinson called her "white election." This was what the English Calvinist, John Welles, described as the last vision of a dying sinner as his consciousness slid into "that bottomless deep of the endless wrath of almighty God."[32]

It was to rid himself of the awful terror that waited with open jaws beyond the veil that Ahab set out on his fiery hunt:

And when we consider that other theory of the natural philosophers, that all other earthly hues . . . are but subtle deceits, not actually inherent in substances, but only laid on from without; so that all deified nature absolutely paints like the harlot, whose allurements cover nothing but the charnel house within; and when we proceed further, and consider that the mystical cosmetic which produces every one of her hues, the great principle of light, forever remains white or colorless in itself, and if operating without medium upon water, would touch all objects, even tulips and roses, with its own blank tinge—pondering all this the palsied Universe lies before us a leper. . . . And of all these things the Albino whale was the symbol. Wonder ye then at the fiery hunt?

Ahab's "fiery hunt" was his attempt to wreck his vengeance upon God, to strike through the mask of white terror at the invisible foundations of existence. The hunt was the rebellion of helpless humanity against the inevitability of sin and death and the sovereignty of fate. "Wonder ye then at the fiery hunt?"[33]

Ishmael, while at the helm, true to his romantic type, also looked for a brief moment into the fire until the "continual shape of the fiend shapes before me . . . at last begat kindred visions in my soul." Seeing his own internal hell thus projected into the flames, he became for a moment transfixed, and in that moment he almost lost control and capsized the ship. Coming suddenly back to his senses, he wrenched his gaze away from the try-works to the safety of the world of sense. Back in control, he warned all others against temptation:

> Look not too long in the face of the fire, O man! . . ; believe not the artificial fire, when its redness makes all things look ghastly. Tomorrow, in the natural sun, the skies will be bright; those who glared like devils in the forking flame, the morn will show in far other, at least gentler, relief; the glorious, golden, glad sun, the only true lamp—all others but liars!

Unlike Emerson, Ishmael did dare to glance at the "roaring gulf below," but like Hawthorne he drew back at the last moment and clung to the known security of Egypt.[34]

It was Pip, the black boy who fell overboard and was left alone on the infinite sea, who plunged into the depths and became utterly consumed in the watery wilderness: "The intense concentration of self in the middle of such a heartless immensity, my God!" The sea was Pip's abyss, his wilderness. His body stayed afloat as his soul was carried into the depths where he lost his mind seeing God:

> . . . among the joyous, heartless, ever-juvenile eternities, Pip saw the multitudinous, God-omnipresent, coral insects, that out of the firmament of waters heaved the colossal orbs. He saw God's foot upon the treadle of the loom, and spoke it; and therefore his shipmates called him mad. So man's insanity is heaven's sense; and wandering from all

mortal reason, man comes at last to that celestial thought, which, to reason, is absurd and frantic; and weal or woe, feels then uncompromised, indifferent as his God.

The similarity between Pip's insanity and Ahab's is made explicit by the relationship that developed between the Captain and the boy. Only they understood and drew comfort from each other, for only they shared the experience of the wrath of God. Ahab reacted madly and Pip surrendered, but they still recognized in each other the bond of a common experience.[35]

As the Children of Israel wandered for forty years in the wilderness, so Ahab, as he bitterly lamented, had seen "Forty years of continual whaling! Forty years of privation, and peril, and storm-time! Forty years on the pitiless sea!" He knew that he would never enter Canaan, that his carcass would rot where it fell. When at last the battle is joined, Ahab knew that he could not win. But he would see it through. As Stubb said, "And damn me, Ahab, but thou actest right; live in the game, and die it!" Ahab's death paralleled the romantic assertion of self at the end of *Mardi*. He died trying to defend human will by striking his lance into that "predestinating head." All that could be seen in the whale's "whole aspect" were "Retribution, swift vengeance, eternal malice." How could such a God be loved? Scorning Father Mapple's command that all sinners be grateful for punishment, but paradoxically reaching out to God, Ahab made a last desperate stab of human defiance:

> Toward thee I roll, thou all-destroying but unconquering whale; to the last I grapple with thee; from hell's heart I stab at thee; for hate's sake I spit my last breath at thee. Sink all coffins and all hearses to one common pool! And since neither can be mine, let me then tow to pieces, while still chasing thee, though tied to thee, thou damned whale!

When finally dragged down to hell, there is no chance that Ahab, like Jonah, might be resurrected, for unlike Jonah he never surrendered but went overboard cursing God.[36]

Finally, there is only Ishmael, saved by the coffin, a symbol of death, like the cross, turned into the means of survival. Ishmael did not say why he survived or whether the voyage cured the "drizzly November" in his soul. We have only the evidence provided in the chapter of Pip's ordeal: "In the sequel of the narrative, it will then be seen what like abandonment befell myself." There is thus opened up the possibility that Ishmael, because he too was left alone, adrift, on the enormous immensity of the sea, experienced the same terrors that drowned Pip's soul. But we are not told. Melville left the ending ambiguous.[37]

The ending had to be ambiguous. The two forces battling for Melville's soul met on the pages of *Moby-Dick* and lived out the game. Ishmael survived to tell the tale. But Ahab had the satisfaction of at least thrusting his harpoon deep into Moby Dick's side. It can only be said that if there was resolution of the tension within Melville, it was at the expense of Ishmael. And the evidence for this is to be found not in *Moby-Dick*, but in the book that Melville immediately began to write, *Pierre*.

Pierre is Melville's autobiography, his own story of the young romantic's fall from pastoral bliss into dark despair. It is the reverse American epic, the voyage of a soul from Canaan back into the wilderness. The incidents of Pierre's early life, as Henry Murray has shown, roughly paralleled Melville's youth. What is most important is that Pierre, like Melville, felt compelled to explore the darker side of human consciousness, and this led to his destruction.[38]

The book opens with lengthy descriptions of young Pierre's idyllic life in the country and of his romantic faith in nature, in human goodness, and in all the pious virtues: "gentle whispers of humaneness, and sweet whispers of love, ran through Pierre's thoughtveins, musical as water over pebbles."[39] The sentimental tone of this romanticism is too extreme to be anything but sarcasm from the man who had just finished writing *Moby-Dick*. Melville was venting his scorn for a public that preferred the sentimental mush of popular romances over his more complex works.

As the plot of the book develops, doubts begin to invade Pierre's consciousness. The reader is led, slowly but inevitably, into the wilderness of Pierre's disintegration. A serene and contented self-confidence is slowly undermined as the world, in all its familiar solidity, begins to give way:

> But now! -now! -and again he would lose himself in the most surprising and preternatural ponderings, which baffled all the introspective cunning of his mind. Himself was too much for himself. He felt that what he had always before considered the solid land of veritable reality, was now being audaciously encroached upon by bannered armies of hooded phantoms, disembarking in his soul, as from flotillas of spectre-boats.

Nor were these unidentifiable anxieties of unspecified origin. Melville deliberately tied much of Pierre's confusion to fears arising from serious contemplation of the Calvinist doctrines of predestination, determinism, the nonmaterial existence of matter, and the absolute sovereignty of God. As in *Moby-Dick*, the warning is clearly sounded that, however true they might be, such speculations lead to madness. Truth was not salvation but chaos: "enthusiastic Truth, and Earnestness, and Independence" lead a mind "fitted by nature for profound and fearless thought" into a region where "the most immemorially admitted maxims of men begin to slide and fluctuate. . . ."

> But the example of many minds forever lost . . . amid those treacherous regions warns us entirely away from them; and we learn it is not for man to follow the trail of truth too far, since by so doing he entirely loses the directing compass of his mind.[40]

Repeating the theme established in *Moby-Dick,* Melville set up a conflict in *Pierre* between worldly success and devastating truth. And even the established church sides with the world against Pierre and the truth he knows he must follow. Pierre has to choose between marriage to Lucy or his responsibility to his half-sister, Isabel. He is faced with "this all-including query—Lucy or God?" Put in these terms, there can be little doubt, despite ministerial advice, which he must choose, and he flees with Isabel to the city to try to make a living there as a writer of fiction.[41]

But Pierre must confront the same problem that faced Melville. He had been commissioned by a publisher to produce a popular romantic novel, but romance was no longer in his heart. He decided instead, despite the risk, to tell his heart's truth:

> . . . at last the idea obtruded, that the wiser and profounder he should grow, the more and the more he lessened the chances for bread; that could he now hurl his deep book out of the window, and fallen to some shallow nothing of a novel, composable in a month at the longest, then could he reasonably hope for both appreciation and cash.

Nevertheless, he wrote his "deep book" and the deeper he got into it the more disturbed he became. "Shivering thus day after day in his wrappers and cloaks, is this the warm lad who once sang to the world of the tropical summer?" As indeed Melville himself had once sung to the world of the tropical summer of *Typee.*[42]

In the end, Pierre became another Taji, another Ahab, breaking against the rocks in mad despair, but by his own hand and in the bottom of a jail. Less defiant and certainly less heroic than either Taji or Ahab, Pierre ended his life, not in destructive triumph, but in helpless, hopeless insanity:

> His soul's ship saw the inevitable rocks, but resolved to sail on, and make a courageous wreck. Now he gave jeer for jeer, and taunted the apes that gibed him. With the soul of an Atheist, he wrote down the Godliest things; with the feeling of death and misery in him, he created forms of gladness and life. . . .

This was no "courageous wreck," no stare-Him-in-the-eye-and-damn-Him defiance such as Ahab's. The words he wrote down were as much lies as his life was a lie. *Pierre* was the expression of Melville's own bitter despair, the destruction of his hopes and his surrender to the wilderness, not in the hope of resurrection but in the full expectation that his carcass would rot there forever. With *Pierre* he announced to himself and the world that he saw no other way out; the self could not be saved. As he said later to Hawthorne, he had "pretty much made up his mind to be annihilated." His mental state was such that after *Pierre* was published, Melville's family asked Dr. Oliver Wendell Holmes to examine him for insanity.[43]

With the contest essentially over, Melville's later works lack the driving power of his best efforts. But in the *Piazza Tales,* particularly, the sense of uncertainty, the perception of the world as illusion and of human beings as deceitful is effectively expressed. In "The Piazza," the opening story of this collection, Melville chooses the "illusion" of the view from his cottage over the drab reality of the distant mountain cottage. Acknowledging the distance between perception and reality, no longer in pursuit of truth, he prefers to remain with his illusory dreams; "But every night, when the curtain falls, truth comes in with darkness. No light shows from the mountain."[44]

In *Benito Cereno,* the illusory quality of perception, the untrustworthiness of humankind, and the foolishness of trusting innocence, are presented with greater clarity and impact than in the whole of that other bitter portrait of humanity, *The Confidence Man.* Captain Delano is portrayed as a cheerful American innocent who cannot see beyond appearance, who accepts the world as given and does not choose to look behind the veil. After boarding the slave ship and viewing its inhabitants, he is so completely taken in by mere appearance that he actually muses upon the natural subservience and "easy cheerfulness, harmonious in every glance and gesture" of the negro slaves. The possibility that things might not be as simple as they seem is dismissed by this simple accepting Christian as "an atheist doubt of the very watchful Providence above." His "piety," explains Melville, made him "incapable of sounding such wickedness" as actually did exist. At last, even Captain Delano has "a flash of revelation" and sees the terrible truth of the situation. The happy, docile blacks turn out to be aggressive murderers and the suspicious Benito Cereno their victim.[45]

Captain Delano's certainty that "piety" meant a faith in God's benevolence and human goodness is an indication of how much the meaning of the word "piety" had changed since the seventeenth century. But Melville remembered the old meaning. Jonathan Edwards had warned sinners that they walked "over the pit of hell on a rotten covering and there are innumerable places in that covering so weak that they will not bear their weight, and these places are not seen." Benito Cereno said to Captain Delano after he had been saved. "Do but think how you walked this deck, how you sat in this cabin, every inch of ground mined into honeycombs under you." The ship was Melville's image of the world, a place where appearances are lies and evil is in control behind closed doors, where danger lurks behind every lying smile, and where the deck is so rotten that at any moment the unaware stroller might suddenly plunge from the sunny air into the foul and chaotic depths. As Calvin knew, as Wigglesworth, Hooker, and Edwards knew, as Emily Dickinson clearly said, it is a very rotten plank indeed that separates sanity from insanity and keeps the worldly from crashing into the bottomless pit.[46]

iii

The *Piazza Tales* were published in 1856, *The Confidence Man* in 1857. *Battlepieces* in 1866 was followed by *Clarel* in 1876, a quest, in the words of one critic, "in which his pilgrim, Clarel, finds in place of the Promised Land only a dusty wilderness of broken dreams."[47] Then for fifteen years Melville was silent. This was the period of his surrender; the struggle was over. He had as he told Hawthorne accepted annihilation. But not all of those who descend into the wilderness leave their carcasses to rot there forever. There was always the possibility of resurrection, of a vision of Christ in the wilderness to outshine the sight of sin. Melville did complete his conversion. His entrance into the promised land is the underlying theme of *Billy Budd*.

Billy's acceptance of his annihilation with grace, and not with the bitterness of Pierre or the defiant resistance of Ahab, is what makes *Billy Budd* a novel of resurrection. Billy is innocence and virtue itself. But Billy, reacting involuntarily to a threatening act, kills a man; politics and military discipline require that he pay for the crime with his life. It does not matter that the man deserved to die. It does not matter that Billy acted involuntarily without forethought and might not be considered morally responsible. As with the Calvinist's relation to God, the sin is predetermined and the punishment is foreordained. There is nothing that can be done to prevent it; as Stubb said, "live in the game and die it!" To try to stop the execution would be, according to Melville, "as idle as invoking the desert." There can be only defiance or acceptance.[48]

Captain Vere is cast in the role of the Calvinist minister who must voice the commands of a sovereign God. He has no choice but to condemn

Billy to death. But he does it with love, with compassion for the victim, as God Himself "so loved the world that he gave his only begotten Son. . . ." and allowed him to be crucified. Billy died shouting, "God bless Captain Vere," and then, "Billy ascended; and ascending took the full rose of the dawn."[49]

Edwards had defined true virtue as love for all being without any consideration for self or self-interest, a willingness to forgo self for the sake of Being-In-General. True virtue, for him, meant what we might call self-less love that understands and accepts and forgives. Selfishness turned into universal love was the mark of grace, the fruit of the promised land.[50]

Ahab felt the pain of being a helpless, determined human being tossed about mercilessly in the jaws of a sovereign providence. Hating that determining force with all his might, he resisted and struck back. Pierre went to his death full of bitterness and confusion and resentment. But Billy learned how to accept pain and annihilation and to love despite it. Like Mary Moody Emerson, who cried, "Let the whole prosper—No duration for me," he was willing to die for the sake of the whole, and he was able to die blessing the man who had condemned him to death. He was a Calvinist saint. In *Billy Budd,* Melville's own despair and defiance became acceptance. He had learned the meaning of justification by faith, a willingness to be damned, as the Calvinists liked to say, for the glory of God, an acceptance of personal annihilation for the sake of the whole.

When Captain Vere announced to the crew the news of Billy's crime and sentence, he was listened to, wrote Melville, "by the throng of standing sailors in a dumbness like that of a seated congregation of believers in Hell listening to their clergyman's announcement of his Calvinist text." Next to this sentence, in the margin of the manuscript, in Melville's hand, is written the name, "Jonathan Edwards."[51]

The cruel condemnation of determined sinners to hell was one of the Calvinist doctrines that most bedeviled Melville. He could not see, at first, what Edwards called "The Justification of God in the Damnation of Sinners." In *Typee,* he rejected Calvinist morbidity and pessimism. In *Mardi,* he toyed with it. In *Moby-Dick,* he fought with it. In *Pierre,* he succumbed to it. And in *Billy Budd,* he announced his final acceptance and transcendence of it. It is not that he finally understood it or that he discovered some intellectually acceptable explanation for it. Rather, having abandoned the attempt to comprehend truth rationally, he threw himself into the deep sea of his emotions, and there in the watery wilderness, the self's need to understand had been drowned and he had learned to love that which he could never comprehend. He had learned to be "comfortable in his unbelief." Having given himself over to the wilderness and having accepted annihilation, he had received, in the end, the grace with which to love that which stands forever beyond the grasp of rational understanding, simply because, despite everything, it is.

The reference to Edwards was Melville's final acknowledgment of the tragedy of determinism, the tragedy not of Calvinism but of life, that human beings *are* held helplessly over the pit in the hands of an angry God.

8
Wilderness Lost
Oliver Wendell Holmes and the "One-Hoss Shay"

Have you heard of the wonderful one-hoss shay,
That was built in such a logical way
It ran one hundred years to a day,
And then, of a sudden, it—ah, but stay,
I'll tell you what happened without delay,
Scaring the parson into fits,
Frightening people out of their wits,—
Have you heard of that, I say?

i

The mystic vision of Calvinism's wilderness tradition flickered visibly in the nineteenth century in only a few great souls. The literal rigidity of Calvinism's well-known legal strain was more tenacious. But by the end of the century, both strains of American Calvinism had been supplanted by liberal Protestantism on one hand and evangelical revivalism on the other.

Optimistic faith in human potential, either to perform good works through the aid of moral reason or to make a commitment to God with the aid of Jesus, replaced the earlier emphasis on the need to cross the wilderness of despair before good works or a sound conversion could be possible. The communal ethic, based on the need of humble sinners for each other's support, was replaced by a buoyant individualism that preached the glory of the self-reliant American. For the multitudes, both unwashed and well-pressed, worldly expectations replaced the vision of a New Jerusalem in which regenerate perception would reveal to newborn eyes the eternal presence of Christ, the perfection of love, the beauty of beauty.

Though the fear of God may have been forgotten, it had not been hunted to extinction. The great leviathan still lurked deep beneath the waves. The nagging voice of conscience continued to "bedevil" even those worldly souls who had declared themselves liberated from the "hebraic mythology" that had for centuries, so they said, darkened the lives of their ancestors. Children and grandchildren of Calvinists turned from doubt and repressed their fears, but those fears remained, buried in the depths of their individual and the culture's collective subconscious. Even the evangelicals who clung to the outward forms of their ancestors' religion chose those aspects that seemed most flattering as they externalized the symbolic meanings. But the words of the creeds were supposed to be interpreted spiritually, not literally; the Kingdom of God was supposed to be, not in North America, but "within you."

This betrayal of their grandparents' faith created a nagging sense of guilt that had to be confronted, repressed, or argued down. Deep in the consciousness of even the most rational Unitarian beat a subliminal urge to turn and stare into the fire and be consumed in the violence of regeneration. Heads that were committed to the world were plagued by hearts that remembered the spirit. The tension toward which this division contributed had to be alleviated through the outlets of war, of nation-building, of strenuous action, and of literature.

Such great artists and obvious "Puritans" as Nathaniel Hawthorne and Herman Melville were not the only authors in whom the fires of the wilderness provided the energy that produced literature. Even such lesser lights as Oliver Wendell Holmes were "bedevilled" by their inability to "limbo" the old religion. Holmes's example demonstrates the manner in which Calvinism supposedly was refuted. In him, we can see how the terrors of the wilderness were denied, repressed, satirized, and finally banished to the back of the barn, lost to a nation that had forgotten the meaning of crucifixion in the wilderness of the Fear of God.

ii

"The Deacon's Masterpiece, or, The Wonderful 'One-Hoss Shay,'" first appeared in print in September, 1858, as part of the *Atlantic Monthly*'s serialized publication of Doctor Oliver Wendell Holmes's "Autocrat of the Breakfast Table." The witty Dr. Holmes, to everyone's great satisfaction, had done it again. He had provided the nation with a heartwarming piece of pure hilarity, "a witticism illustrating itself in action, a pseudo-logical demonstration leading to an absurd and merry end." That at least was the unanimous judgment of Holmes's contemporaries, one of whom, the reverend Theodore Parker, blamed his sore throat on the laughter it provoked.[1]

Literary critics, no braver than other human beings, seldom dare to introduce new interpretations of a popular work until the one person who could authoritatively refute them is safely dead. So it was with Holmes. Until the year of his death, 1894, his critics and admirers consistently placed "The Deacon's Masterpiece" high on the list of his humorous poems.

Although Barrett Wendell is properly credited with having introduced in 1900 the now standard interpretation of "The Deacon's Masterpiece," it was the dean of the faculty of Princeton in 1895 who broke the interpretive ice by suggesting that there were pious lessons to be learned even from the skeptical writings of the Unitarian, Dr. Holmes:

> His well known poem, "The Deacon's Masterpiece, or, The Wonderful One-Hoss Shay"—a more delicious bit of humor never found its way into verse,—may not be thought to have any theological bearings. But when I have heard or read occasionally some logical discussions of those aweful themes, where the finite merges in the infinite, I have recalled this 'logical story' with its closing lines:
> End of the wonderful one-hoss shay.
> Logic is logic. That's all I say.

It would be a minister, a Calvinist Presbyterian at that, who first read a deeper significance in that seemingly innocent verse.[2]

But it was, all agree, Professor Barrett Wendell of Harvard who first read "The Deacon's Masterpiece" as an allegory of the fall of Calvinism. In his *Literary History of America,* published in 1900, Wendell wrote,

> In 1857, nearly a hundred years after the death of Edwards, the most familiar and unanswerable comment on his system appeared. Often misunderstood, generally thought no more than a piece of comic extravaganza, Dr. Holmes's "One-Hoss Shay" is really among the most pitiless satires in our language. . . . Holmes . . . recoiled from the appalling doctrines which had darkened his youth. He could find no flaw in their reasoning, but he could not escape their conclusions.

In support of this interpretation, Wendell argued that "the dogmas of Calvin lurked constantly in his [Holmes's] mind; and he never failed to attack them." To Wendell, the shay represented the perfect logic of Edwardsian Calvinism, and Holmes's portrayal of the shay's collapse was intended as a satire of that system's demise. This interpretation became gospel almost overnight.[3]

Although Eleanor Tilton has been credited with the creation of the first significant modification of Wendell's interpretation, the credit properly belongs to (Senator) S. I. Hayakawa and Howard Mumford Jones. Their 1939 edition of *Oliver Wendell Holmes: Representative Selections* footnotes Wendell's interpretation and then adds:

The total effect . . . is a parable showing the limitations not only of one logical system, but of all systems in which problems are worked out in intellectual vacuums—without, that is, 'primary relations with truth.'

For Hayakawa and Jones, the poem was an argument against deductive reasoning regardless of the particular system it was being used to defend.[4]

This modification was then broadened in Eleanor Tilton's biography of Holmes published in 1947:

It is traditional to regard this poem as an intentional attack on Calvinism, although its context in the *Autocrat* and the headnote in *Poems* do not warrant so limited an interpretation. The poem applies quite as well to any "system" that of the homeopathist, Hahnemann, for instance. . . . A letter by Justice Holmes to a correspondent who inquired about the verses, says that he never heard his father give them such a meaning. . . .

According to Tilton, the poems should be read as "a scorn of logic *per se*" that "satirizes any logical system (not necessarily Calvinism) supposed by its authors to be perfect, uncorrectable, and, therefore, everlasting."[5]

The next contributor to this debate was George Arms who diplomatically acknowledged the value of both Wendell's interpretation and Tilton's variation without committing himself to either. What troubled Arms about Wendell's strict application of the allegory to Edwards was that the dates given in the poem, 1755 and 1855, have no relevance to the history of Edwardsian theology:

Had Holmes caused the shay to be built in 1754 (the date of Edwards' *Freedom of the Will*) instead of 1755, the major direction of the satire would have been clinched. Still it has been pointed out that the poem appeared in the centennial of Edwards' death.

Arms does suggest an additional possibility. He quotes Whittier as having once complained of his own poems,

My vehicles have been of the humbler sort—merely the farmwagon and buckboard of verse, and not likely to run as long as Dr. Holmes's "One-Hoss Shay". . . .

And later Arms notes, "the reference is not only to the logic of a tightly constructed system but as well to that of a well-made shay and poem." Arms here suggests that Holmes meant the shay to refer to his own poetry, which, as Holmes lamented, would be forgotten by the time "the next century rounds its hundredth ring."[6]

In 1962, in a new biography of Holmes, Miriam Small tried to resist the "burden of allegory" but she was forced finally to succumb to logic:

> . . . reluctant as the reader may be to accept the tale as an account of the downfall of Calvinism, the stress on *logic*—the subtitle is "A Logical Story" and the last line "Logic is Logic. That's all I say"—surely points in that direction, especially as the principle of Calvinism as developed by Jonathan Edwards and rejected by Holmes was its irrefutable logic.[7]

In the *Explicator,* October, 1965, Howard Webb substantially added to the allegorical understanding of the poem by demonstrating that Holmes didn't merely attack the Calvinist system. He also pointed the way to its alternative, an organic system that can "break down but doesn't wear out." Noting Holmes's medical profession, Webb assumed, justifiably, that Holmes's perfect system would resemble nature's perfect mechanism, the human body:

> . . . a sound religious system is not one which wears out and must be discarded; rather, when it breaks down, when time and knowledge reveal weaknesses in it, the system should be capable of being repaired, healed, and thus continuously maintained in accord with fact.

It was the Deacon's attempt to construct a system that would never need repair that was to blame for the sudden collapse of the shay. Holmes, according to Webb, was championing inductive reasoning over formal logic.[8]

In 1968, Hyatt Waggoner concluded that the poem is a satire on "any logical system containing clear thinking that appears to lead inevitably to a conclusion repellent to one's sense of truth." Holmes's point was that "once we scrutinize the premises, the system falls apart." Holmes, however, never did scrutinize the premises; he simply rejected a conclusion that did not agree with his own "sense of truth." As Waggoner quotes Holmes:

> I reject . . . the mechanical doctrine which makes me the slave of outside influences, whether it work with the logic of Edwards, or the averages of Buckle. . . .

Believing the poem is "of course" a satire on Calvinism, "the best illustration of a system at once perfectly logical and perfectly mistaken," Waggoner also reinforces Tilton's argument that the poem can be read as a satire on any logical system.[9]

But until J. Stanley Mattson published his article in *The New England*

Quarterly in 1968, no one had seriously challenged the basic allegory first outlined by Wendell in 1900. Mattson's critique centers on what he sees as a contradiction within previous interpretations of the poem:

> If the poem is to function as an allegorical vehicle for the con-
> demnation of the logic of Calvinism, it cannot simultaneously be taken
> as a "practical lesson" in praise of that logic used in the construction of
> a "well-made shay."

According to the traditional interpretation, the Deacon was a figure of scorn, justifiably ridiculed for his attempt to construct a perfect system. But, according to Mattson, it is the parson at the end of the poem who is made to look foolish. The Deacon, in contrast, was an admirably prac-tical, worldly man who set out to build the best carriage in the county and who did just that. The parson who eventually inherited the shay, because he was "preoccupied with revelation, . . . ignored the practical" and blindly accepted the reins of the ancient shay oblivious to telltale signs of decay.[10]

Thus, the Deacon, in this reinterpretation, no longer represents a discredited Edwards. Instead, he represents the more practical worldly men of the eighteenth century whose logical minds were superior to the otherworldly minds of nineteenth-century parsons. The shay, even in collapse, now symbolizes "the triumph of the forces of the world, of materialism, and 'logic.'"[11]

In 1972, a short article in *American Heritage* ignored Mattson and proved the durability of Wendell's interpretation by calling the poem a "burlesque of Edwards."[12] And the latest published word on the subject comes from Jill Perkins in the *American Transcendental Quarterly*.

Perkins repeats the arguments already mustered against the tradi-tional interpretation, that the dates are meaningless, that Calvinism's demise was gradual and not sudden, and that in his two published introductions to the poem, Holmes gave no hint of any allegorical intent. She adds a new piece of evidence, a statement by John T. Morse, the poet's nephew and biographer, to bolster her skepticism:

> Of course it is easy to see how it could be construed as a "satire or skit
> on Calvinism." But I must say that I think such a suggestion would
> astonish the good doctor very much. Its ingenuity would tickle his
> fancy immensely. But I would be willing to wage a considerable sum
> that he would say that no such thought was in the back of his mind. . . .

Having said all this, Perkins did not provide an alternative reading. Instead, she indicated a willingness to let the traditional allegorical interpretation remain if only because it "furnishes an entertaining little glimpse of the persistent liveliness of scholarly myth."[13]

When, finally, all of the arguments have been weighed and the poem considered within the context of Holmes's life, Wendell's original interpretation holds up fairly well. The arguments in support of his interpretation outweigh those that have been offered in opposition.

Mattson's intriguing, inverted analysis suffers from its own internal contradictions and does not fit into the context of Holmes's known beliefs. Mattson, however, is correct in pointing out that the Deacon and the shay are not the objects of ridicule many critics have made them. But recognizing this does not require a repudiation of the traditional allegory. Holmes did object to Puritan theology, but much of his writing reveals a filial attachment to his Puritan past that is deeply sentimental. He was capable of loving the past at the same time that he gently satirized it.

Holmes rebelled against his Calvinist father, the reverend Abiah Holmes, but he did not hate him. He did not believe Calvinism altogether the wrong creed for its time and place. What he objected to was the attempt to carry that creed into the middle of the modern 1800s. Holmes, after all, believed in progress and evolution. Edwards had not been proven wrong; New England, like the "frail tenant" of his chambered nautilus, had simply "left the past year's dwelling for the new." The shay was a wonderful creation, as Mattson said, but "Little of all we value here/Wakes on the morn of its hundredth year/Without both feeling and looking queer." There was a time for logic and a time for change. Holmes made this clear in his discussion of Edwards' *Freedom of the Will:*

> Does not the present state of our knowledge compel us to consider the narrative . . . as a disproved, or at best an unproved story, and to consign it to the nebulous realm of Asiatic legends. . . ? The change of opinion is coming quite rapidly enough. . . . For what we want in the religious and in the political organisms is just that kind of vital change which takes place in our bodies,—interstitial disintegration and reintegration; and one of the legitimate fears of our time is that science . . . will be too rapid in its action on beliefs.

The "one-hoss shay" of Edwardsian Calvinism was, to Holmes, a system that did not evolve with the age. It was incapable of change. If anything, we can detect some sympathy for the unfortunate parson for whom science was "too rapid in its action on beliefs."[14]

The most persistent argument made in objection to Wendell's interpretation has been that the shay did not represent Edwardsian Calvinism but that the "poem applies quite as well to any 'system.'" Waggoner's response to this objection is the correct one: "But of course it does." Holmes was obsessed with the need to refute, or in some manner do away with, the doubts and the guilt that Edwardsian Calvinism stirred up in him. Because of this, it is reasonable to assume that Holmes had Edwards somewhere in mind when he wrote the "One-Hoss Shay."[15]

Holmes, in perpetual rebellion against the doctrines taught him by his own Calvinist father, repeatedly tried to refute the logic of *Freedom of the Will.* He was, he said, "long engaged in the study of the writings of Edwards," whom he called "so remarkable a logician." Convinced that Edwards had to be wrong, he could find no faulty reasoning nor false premises in his logic, but neither could he yield to the terror that logic led to. Nagged by persistent doubts, uneasy in his filial rebellion, he wanted simply to be rid of the Calvinistic doubts that gnawed at his conscience.

> We find our wills tied up hand and foot in the logical propositions which he knots inextricably about them; and yet when we lay down the book, we feel as if there were something left free after all. . . . We are disposed to settle the matter as majesterially as Dr. Johnson did. 'Sir,' said he, 'We know our will is free, and there's an end on it.'[16]

Much has been made of Holmes's supposed antipathy to logical systems of any kind. But there is little evidence that logic *per se* was his intended victim. He did object to homeopathy and Calvinism, and these were total systems. But Holmes objected to these systems for specific reasons. Homeopathy he saw frankly as quackery; it did not work. Calvinism's main sin, he said, was that it imputed moral responsibility to those it considered completely determined and unable to alter their condition. Holmes's Victorian sensibilities were particularly upset by Edwards' consignment of unconverted infants, "little vipers," to hell. The bulk of Holmes's prose writings are efforts to free the victims of determinism from the imputation of moral guilt. We doctors, he wrote, "have nothing but compassion for a large class of persons condemned as sinners by theologians, but considered by us as invalids." It is hard to avoid the suspicion that Holmes was trying to get out from under a more personal sense of guilt, one brought on by his apostasy from the ancestral religion that continued to "bedevil" his soul.[17]

There will still be those who object that Holmes, who was nothing if not verbose, left no evidence of allegorical intent. There are two possible reasons for this. Holmes, it must be remembered, was known to his contemporaries primarily as a humorist. He did attempt serious poetry, but none, with the possible exception of "The Chambered Nautilus," ever received as much acclaim as "The Deacon's Masterpiece." To admit to a serious, allegorical intention would have only embarrassed the many admirers who toasted Holmes for having produced such a witty piece of pure humor. It might even have detracted from the quantity and the enthusiasm of those toasts. And Oliver Wendell Holmes was a man who valued praise and adulation.

For the other possible explanation, we have only to note that Holmes has been called a forerunner of Freud because he believed in the power of unconscious thoughts and associations over human behavior. His own words provide the best explanation:

> There are thoughts that never emerge into consciousness, which yet make their influence felt among the perceptible mental currents, just as the unseen planets sway the movement of those which are watched and mapped by the astronomer. Old prejudices, that are ashamed to confess themselves, nudge our talking thought. . . .
>
> We all have a double who is wiser and better than we are, and who puts thoughts into our heads, and words into our mouths.

Even the poet, Holmes admitted, "always recognizes a dictation *ab extra.*" Holmes's "old prejudices" against Edwards may have been "ashamed to confess themselves," but Holmes, despite the rash bet his nephew was willing to make, would never have been so naive as flatly to deny their influence.[18]

A more positive piece of evidence linking Holmes's famous carriage allegorically to Calvinism can be found in *The Professor at the Breakfast Table,* where Holmes used the image of a cart having its linchpins removed to contrast the different ways that Dr. Channing and "T'other fellow" set about dismantling the old religion:

> Parson Channing strolled along this way from Newport, and stayed here. Pity old Sam Hopkins hadn't come too;—we'd have made a man of him,—poor, dear, good old Christian heathen! There he lies, as peaceful as a young baby, in the old burying ground! I've stood on the slab many a time. Meant well,—meant well. Juggernaut. Parson Channing put a little oil on one linchpin, and slipped it out so softly, the first thing they knew about it the wheel of that side was down. T'other Fellow's at work now, but he makes more noise about it. When the linchpin comes out on his side, there'll be a jerk, I tell you! Some think it will spoil the old cart, and they pretend to say that there are valuable things in it which may get hurt. Hope not,—hope not.

The reference here is not directly to Edwards but to Samuel Hopkins, the theologian who produced the adaptation of Edwardsian Calvinism

that was most popular in New England. For many Americans, Hopkin-
sianism was but another name for Calvinism of the strictest kind. Who
"T'other fellow" refers to is not clear. The reference could be to the
Arminian revivalist, Charles G. Finney, who did more to discredit Edwardsian Calvinism than did the Unitarian Channing. One could even
suppose, from this piece, that it was "Parson Channing" who took the
spill and thereafter became the main advocate of Unitarianism.[19]

But once having established that Holmes did mean his poem to be an
allegory of the demise of Calvinism, there is still more that needs to be
said. For the very suggestion that Holmes's allegorical intent may have
been unconscious reveals how the children of the Puritans dealt with
their latent fears. Julia Ward Howe was only one of many "modern"
Americans who had the embers of their ancestral Calvinism stirred to
flame by the passions of the Civil War.[20] The essentially Calvinist attitudes, hopes and fears, that they thought they had outgrown had never
been lost but instead had gone underground where they continued to
influence thought and behavior unconsciously.

In *The Inner Civil War*, George Frederickson wrote,

> It is curious to see emancipated Unitarians, of rationalistic, almost
> positivistic beliefs, like Norton and the elder Oliver Wendell Holmes,
> writing in 1861 like seventeenth century Puritans. Holmes, whose
> urbane and amusing "One Horse Shay" had put forth the claim that
> Calvinism was dead, was now writing poems like the "Army Hymn," a
> fervent appeal to the Puritan God of battles.

Nor was Frederickson alone in recognizing Holmes's latent Calvinism. As
early as 1859, a letter writer to the *Boston Recorder* noted,

> The Professor is Augustinian in the great red working muscle under
> the ribs, but Arian in the pale substance under the skull. When he
> rationalizes, he is warped from rectitude; but no sooner does he begin
> to sing than he rights up.

The existence of a split between a Unitarian head and an Orthodox
heart cannot be stated more clearly. It was just this split that created the
anxieties that "bedevilled" Holmes.[21]

Holmes continued to be frustrated by his failure to deal Edwards a
fatal blow and thereby heal the split in his own psyche. He could not
accept the terrifying doctrines of determinism and original sin, but his
efforts to disprove Calvinism only forced him further into the jaws of its
irrefutable logic. In trying to dispel his intellectual and emotional
doubts, he merely went from the Puritan idea of predestination to a

psychological determinism. In the end he had to admit that "we are getting to be predestinarians as much as Edwards or Calvin was."[22]

Those who see the fact of Calvinism's gradual decay as evidence against Wendell's interpretation of "The Deacon's Masterpiece" have their answer here. They are after all right. Calvinism did decay gradually. The sudden collapse portrayed in the poem occurred only in Holmes's imagination. Unable to defeat Calvinism in logical argument, Holmes turned to literature to vent his frustration and he defeated Edwards there through poetry. In reality, Calvinism was alive enough to bedevil him relentlessly. It was by laying the blame for his feelings of insecurity and guilt on the inherited remains of Calvinism that he was able to sustain his remarkable self-confidence. It was by telling himself, over and over again, that Calvinism had collapsed, and by recreating that collapse in satirical verse, that he was able to keep his doubts, and ultimately his fears, at bay. Yet, as he confided to Harriet Beecher Stowe, "I do not believe that you or I can ever get the iron of Calvinism out of our souls."[23]

Holmes was by no means alone in his desire to be rid of the one-hoss shay. Many Americans in the Victorian era, refusing to acknowledge the sovereignty of fear, were in rebellion against Calvinist fathers. Many were engaged in the effort to construct new philosophies that would serve to bolster their growing personal and national self-confidence. Evangelical Protestants were able to point with pride to the material evidence of the fruits of their supposed conversions. But the liberals, by rejecting the creeds as well as the substance of orthodoxy, needed something more to fill the void.

Perhaps the most prominent of these rebels was Henry Ward Beecher, a man with the particularly difficult task of overcoming the paternal dominance of the mighty Lyman Beecher in order to escape from the doctrine of the fear of God. As a minister of his father's faith, he had the additional difficult task of having to articulate his rebellion in his father's idiom. His solution was to forge a synthesis of transcendental romanticism and evangelical Protestantism. Rejecting the morbid introspection of Edwardsian Calvinism while retaining some of its rituals and symbols, this synthesis proved to be just what liberal Protestants were looking for. And it even earned the respect of such staunch Unitarians as Holmes. In the words of William McLoughlin:

> Beecher's answer to the contemporary crisis of belief was to preach to the throbbing human heart, to reaffirm its faith in Christianity, and yet to do so without undermining . . . science, education, and learning,—in short, to harmonize religion and science not through meta-

physical speculation (as his father . . . had done) but by appealing to emotional experience.[24]

Every inch as much a Victorian American liberal as Beecher, Holmes also championed the ascendancy of the sentimental heart over the logical head. It was merely a nuisance to him that he found his will "tied up hand and foot in the logical propositions" of Edwardsian theology. What was important, in the end, was that "when we lay down the book, we *feel* [emphasis mine] as if there were something left free after all." As a professor of medicine at Harvard, Holmes was no enemy of science. But as a romantic Victorian he would always believe, when they did conflict, that the sentiments of the heart were superior to the reasonings of the head. None of Holmes's medical school knowledge could refute Edwards, but his heart told him that Edwards had to be wrong. And that, he managed to persuade himself, was an end on it. Justification by the feelings of the heart replaced justification by the logic of the head. (Justification by Christ alone had long since been forgotten!) The one-hoss shay of Edwardsian Calvinism thus never was destroyed; it was simply banished to the back of the cultural barn, forgotten and replaced but never refuted, limboed, "though it overcomes all logic." Unable to defeat Edwards in debate, Holmes defeated him in literature. He put him on the page and imagined the collapse of his system, not because it was wrong but because he did not like it, and that, he felt, was sufficient.[25]

iii

It is never possible to know with certainty the intention of an author. The interpretations we give to our literature are a reflection of our culture and not always that of its authors. To deny any generation the right to reinterpret its literary heritage would be to deprive that literature of its vitality and importance. How we understand our past is a reflection of how we understand ourselves. The interpretations we give to our literature reflect the meanings we give our own lives.

It is therefore significant that Barrett Wendell's interpretation struck such a lasting chord in the generations of American critics that followed him. It is Wendell's interpretation that has saved Holmes's poem from obscurity. For with Holmes, popular belief today dismisses the pessimism once associated with Calvinism as an outmoded philosophy of a darker day. The frontier, that edge of civilization that borders on the wilderness, was thought to have disappeared by 1890 when the government officially declared that the last remnants of the wilderness had been civilized. Today, existential despair is popular only among the thin layer of literati; the mass of Americans still imagine themselves in Canaan in the promised land. Not even those who use the words believe any longer in the fear of God. There is no popular belief in the need to deny the self and plunge into insanity in order to achieve psychic health. Health foods and jogging are currently considered sufficient. We carefully watch each other for signs of "madness," and those who do not conform to accepted standards of behavior are institutionalized until they can be taught to behave normally. We see no need to deny the world. We would like to believe that the one-hoss shay "went to pieces all at once," and that there is no longer any reason for staring into the flames. But still the "bright gildings but fringe and play upon the edges of thunderclouds."[26] The inner wilderness remains a bottomless pit of subconscious fear.

The significance of the continued interest in Wendell's interpretation lies in the fact that the one-hoss shay never was completely forgotten. It was merely banished to the back of the cultural mind, where, as Holmes himself said, "Old prejudices that are ashamed to confess themselves, nudge our talking thought." Deep beneath its optimistic surface, America's national self-confidence hides a Calvinist conscience. The literal wilderness may have been civilized by 1890, but the spiritual wilderness was never conquered. There, the doctrines of total depravity and regeneration, the call to descend into the wilderness, continue to bedevil the American soul. There, the vision of a spiritual "Kingdom of freedom" somewhere over the wilderness still drives us on.

Had belief in Melville's "Calvinistic sense of Innate Depravity and Original Sin" actually collapsed in the manner that Holmes imagined, we could securely forget about the wilderness and write off our anxieties as the vestigial remains of inherited nonsense, symptoms of organic illness, or the product of chemical imbalance. They would not continue to "nudge our talking thought." But the old shay is still out in the barn, and the wilderness of fear is still in the mind. Our rationalizations are still only rationalizations and true self-consciousness a terror. There remains a need to relive the descent into the desert, or to destroy the one-hoss shay over and over again in our imaginations, our journals, and our literature.

President Kennedy said that space would be the "New Frontier." Perhaps contemplation of that "heartless immensity" will awaken answering echoes in the American soul. Perhaps some behaviorist, frustrated with the confusion of modern psychology, will be the first to bring the old shay back into the open. Perhaps some psychotherapist will rediscover the wilderness and the hope of regeneration and name it. Emerson thought that the American "Garden of Eden" would be fueled by the "Aladdin Oil."[27] Perhaps we will have to wait until the fuel runs out and the electric sockets sit empty, technology having run its optimistic course, before "self-reliance" will be abandoned. Whenever the day comes, the one-hoss shay will be out in the barn waiting as sound as ever.

9
Conclusion

"What corner of Canaan in this?"
Isaac McCaslin to Lucas Beauchamp
William Faulkner, "The Bear"

"Men," wrote Jonathan Edwards, "will either worship the true God or some idol: it is impossible it should be otherwise; something will have the heart of man. And that which a man gives his heart to may be called his God."[1]

According to the anthropologist, Victor Turner, what he calls root paradigms "reach down to irreducible life stances of individuals, passing beneath conscious prehension to a fiduciary hold on what they sense to be axiomatic values, matters literally of life and death."

> . . . "structure" and "system," "purposive action patterns" and, at deeper levels, "categorical frames." These individual and group structures, carried in people's heads and nervous systems, have a steering function. . . .[2]

Call them Gods, idols, root paradigms, myth structures, or the content of "mentalité." Study eighteenth-century theology or twentieth-century anthropology. The message is the same: The behavior of human beings is largely programmed by the thoughts that are in their heads. These thoughts do not spring fully developed out of nothing. They exist in layered structures variably called paradigms, archetypes, myths, behavior patterns, inclinations, or the ideas of the subconscious. They are a living part of each person; together they define a culture. And like legs, eyes, and ears, they have evolved into instruments to be used when needed. Changes in external material circumstances more often than not are responsible for forcing changes in thought and behavior. But when a decision must be made, the mind relies on the cumulative evidence of

249

these earlier decisions and received forms as a basis for choosing. It is impossible it should be otherwise.

This organizing system of beliefs is rarely perceived by any individual in its entirety. Instead it is made manifest in consciousness in symbols like the American flag and "buzz words" like "Freedom" and "Liberty." Together, these beliefs and their symbols may be called "identity." It is our sense of identity, of who we are, that controls our reactions in ways more powerful and subtle than any externally controlling political or economic structure can. Identity determines perception as well as behavior. It is inevitable; we cannot live without it. True liberation means liberation from ourselves.

Identity is necessary and identity controls, but there are many possible identities and numerous possible variations within particular identities. No one way is absolute and it is certainly possible to be converted from one to another. There are those who mistake such conversion from one controlling identity to another for freedom: "Capitalism is corrupt, let us be socialist"; "Macho is unnatural, feminine is exploitive, let us be androgynous"; "Religion is oppressive, let us be free." But to shed one identity for another, though temporarily renewing, merely means in the end to shed one cage for another. True freedom exists in that moment between identities, that void between one certainty and another, in what the anthropologists call "limitas." That is the moment during which individuals can see beyond the idols of identity to what Emerson called the "terrible Freedom" beyond relative truths. This was what it meant to stare out into the openness of absolute possibility, to stare "fixedly and without relief into the very center of the blazing sun of glory."[3] This was the wilderness. It existed before life, it continued after death, it was always present under the relative identities and false Gods of the ego. It was the pit and the path to freedom.

The Puritans originally believed that all of the possible identities available to human beings are equally vain and idolatrous. They desired not the lies of human affirmation but "Truth" that they believed exists beyond the limits of human perception. They wanted neither Egypt nor Jerusalem but the wilderness with all its horrors, for there and there alone existed the possibility of transcending identity and participating in the Eternity of God "in Canaan." To be in the world but not of it meant to live in an idolatrous identity with an eye on Eternity, to live in the flesh but to live for the Spirit, turning constantly from the illusion of life to hunt in the consuming emptiness what Calvin called the "Kingdom of freedom."[4]

The first American settlers came to New England in the hope that in the literal wilderness they could find the liberty to pursue spiritual freedom. Political liberty was but a means to that end. Their descendants forgot the spiritual aspect of the quest, mistook the literal wilderness for the spiritual, the means of liberty for the end of freedom, and imagined themselves released from bondage without its being so. Despite their literal misinterpretation of the central cultural symbols, these same descendants did receive a legacy of yearning and a willingness, however subtle or subconscious, to break out of inherited structures and head into the wilderness, despite the risk, in the expectation of reaching some promised land. This legacy continues to exist on two levels, the type and the antitype, the literal and the spiritual, and these are bound so tightly together that they reinforce each other. Americans are still seeking liberty in the wilderness.

In 1959 in Rhode Island, President Ronald Reagan, then a private citizen, gave an impromptu talk to a group of students in a hall of the Rhode Island State House. One who remembered called his speech "part Jack Kennedy, part William Jennings Bryan." In the speech, Reagan said,

> If we believe nothing is worth dying for, when did this begin? Should Moses have told the children of Israel to live in slavery rather than dare the wilderness? Should Christ have refused the cross? You and I, my young friends, have a rendezvous with destiny. If we flop, at least our kids can say of us that we justified our brief moment here. We did all that could be done.[5]

Here is the latest externalization of the metaphor. Here is the crossing of Moses into the wilderness typologically identified with the crucifixion of Christ and both used as a rallying cry in the secular twentieth century by a major political figure to inspire the young to have faith in America.

But even in the twentieth century, the wilderness tradition has retained its more spiritual content, and it can be clearly seen in such major works as William Faulkner's "The Bear" as well as in the work of minor figures such as Robinson Jeffers. Robert Frost, a Californian who adopted New England culture, knew that the metaphor was of the soul. It has been noted that in his famous poem, "Stopping by Woods on a Snowy Evening," the attractiveness of the woods is due to an "irrational impulse, . . . one of several significant expressions of a major theme in American literature," namely, "fascination with the wilderness as wilderness. . . ." In another poem, even more clearly a part of this ancient tradition, Frost wrote,

> They cannot scare me with their empty spaces
> Between stars—on stars where no human race is.
> I have it in me so much nearer home
> To scare myself with my own desert places.

The modern mind is by no means the first to have stared into space, and into the empty spaces in the self, and be struck dumb with awe and terror.[6]

Although the wilderness tradition continues to have an ambiguous legacy, it has been interpreted literally more often than not. There are complacent souls today who believe that America is the Promised Land, a "city on a hill," and there are reformers who believe that America is still crossing the wilderness, that a political Canaan is still in the process of being constructed. Both of these, like the environmentalists with their Emersonian love of nature, are caught in a literal reading of the metaphor. But the true heirs of the wilderness tradition are those who have inherited the American faith that despite the dung heap of this world, something is, and, for those who are willing to suffer and endure, the perception to see it yet shall be.

For the Fear of God, as that concept was understood by the adherents of the wilderness tradition, was not a superstition but a fact of consciousness, one that "modern" man is only now slowly, reluctantly beginning to rediscover. "God" was the word for that ultimate reality, as yet unknown to us, that exists beyond the idolatry of our separate identities. And in that wilderness between idolatries, his eternal NO thunders the terror of our undoing.

The evasions of a Holmes and the confidence of an Emerson no longer work. The confident identity of the self-reliant individual is growing weaker. Even science has "caught a glimpse of our incomprehension" and begun to doubt.[7] The rotten cover over the pit is growing thinner. Americans may yet have to face the dilemma of realizing that their famous self-confidence is based upon the mistake of a literal reading of a spiritual metaphor. We are not the chosen people; this is not the Promised Land, nor is it about to be reformed into one. Americans may yet become aware of the content of their own consciousness, and when they do, they may find themselves not the Israel of Canaan but a community of sinners alone together in the wilderness, held helplessly over the pit in the hands of an angry God.

When they do, they may be comforted, as Emily Dickinson was, by the knowledge that others have been there before, that the major writers of our culture's literature have addressed themselves to just this theme, and that their works thus speak directly to our concerns.

For this is what characterizes the best American writing, not a serene acceptance but the frantic alienation of wanting to break free from false identity and idolatry, even red-white-and-blue idolatry, even at the risk of madness if that is what it takes to reach the promised land. The best American literature recognizes that the ideal has yet to be realized, that the worldly type has yet to be replaced by the spiritual antitype, that substance is still only symbolic and we are caught in the "dung heap" of this earth. It recognizes the existence of something better beyond the horizon of human consciousness from which we are helplessly separated. It does not strut the calm assurance of the scientific optimist or the self-righteousness of the fundamentalist. It does not assume salvation but looks from Pisgah to a better form of being and will not rest until it is attained. It prays in the desert for the showers of Christ's redeeming grace.

It is an awareness that human consciousness is still ensnared in the fleshpots of Egypt and that the "Kingdom of freedom" can only be obtained by a descent into the violence of the inner wilderness where it must be crucified if it is to be converted out of self and into God.

Notes

Introduction

1. Karl Barth, *Church Dogmatics: The Doctrine of the Word of God* (New York, 1936), I–1, pp. 252, 187.

2. See Michael Zuckerman, "The Fabrication of Identity in Early America," *William and Mary Quarterly* 34, no. 2 (April 1977).

3. Richard Slotkin, *Regeneration Through Violence* (Middletown, Conn., 1973) p. 13. I find Slotkin's definition of "mythology" (p. 6) adequate for my purposes: "A mythology is a complex of narratives that dramatizes the world vision and historical sense of a people or culture, reducing centuries of experience into a constellation of compelling metaphors." If for "world vision and historical sense" one would substitute "cultural identity," "paradigm," or "mentalité," I would not argue with the change in terminology (See chapter 4, part II.)

4. Jonathan Edwards, *The Works of President Edwards in Eight Volumes* (Worcester, Mass., 1808), 8:9.

5. Lewis Thomas, "Debating the Unknowable," *The Atlantic Monthly*, July 1981, 49.

6. Perry Miller, *Errand into the Wilderness* (Cambridge, Mass., 1953), p. ix.

7. Thomas L. Haskell, "Deterministic Implications of Intellectual History," in *New Directions in American Intellectual History*, John Higham and Paul Conkin ed. (Baltimore, 1979), p. 141. See also Gordon Wood, "Intellectual History and the Social Sciences," ibid., pp. 27–41.

8. James Bryce, *The American Commonwealth* (New York, 1908), p. 7; Emerson, "Self-Reliance," in *Selections from Ralph Waldo Emerson*, ed. Stephen Whicher (Boston, 1957), p. 147; George Bancroft to Jared Sparks, letter, 28 November 1832, Houghton Library, quoted in Donald Weber, "The Image of Jonathan Edwards in American Culture," unpublished thesis, Columbia University, 1978.

Chapter 1. The Wilderness

1. Northrop Frye, *The Great Code: The Bible and Literature* (New York, 1982), p. xviii.

2. Rollo May, *Symbolism in Religion and Literature* (New York, 1960), p. 16.

3. Ulrich Mauser, *Christ in the Wilderness* (Chatham, 1963); George H. Williams, *Wilderness and Paradise in Christian Thought* (New York, 1962).

4. Mauser, pp. 97 n, 19.

5. Mauser, p. 21.

6. C. G. Jung, "The Symbolic Life," in *Collected Works* (Princeton, N.J., 1976), 18:286.

7. Williams, p. 4.

8. Williams, p. 14.

9. Mauser, p. 52.

10. Williams, p. 18.

11. Ibid., p. 19.

12. Ibid., p. 4.

13. Mauser, pp. 87–88.

14. Williams, p. 47.

15. Ibid., p. 47.

16. Ibid., p. 56.

17. Ibid., p. 67.

18. Ibid., p. 68.

19. Perry Miller, *The New England Mind: The Seventeenth Century* (Boston, 1961), p. 92.

20. *The Geneva Bible,* 1650, (facsimile edition), p. 30.

21. Jean Calvin, *The Institutes of the Christian Religion,* ed. John T. McNeill, trans. Ford L. Battles (Philadelphia, 1960), 1:593.

22. Quoted in Williams, p. 65.

23. Calvin, *Institutes,* 1:35.

24. Calvin, 1:969, 290, 661.

25. Ibid., 1:968–969.

26. Ibid., 1:46, 664.

27. Ibid., 1:596, 608–9.

28. Ibid., 1:381.

29. Williams, p. 73.

30. Ursula Brumm, *American Thought and Religious Typology* (New Brunswick, N.J., 1970), provides a good account of the origins of typology and its importance in early American literature.

31. Augustine, *On Christian Doctrine,* (New York, 1958), p. 84.

32. Calvin, *Institutes,* p. 381; Calvin, *Harmony of the Pentateuch* (Edinburgh, 1852). 1:289.

33. Barbara Lewalski, "Typological Symbolism and the 'Progress of the soul' in Seventeenth Century Literature," in *Literary Uses of Typology From the Late Middle Ages to the Present,* ed. Earl Miner (Princeton, N.J., 1977), p. 81.

34. Joseph A. Galdon, *Typology and Seventeenth Century Literature* (Paris, 1975), p. 48–49.

35. Samuel Mather, *The Figures or Types of the Old Testament* (London, 1683), pp. 71–72.

36. Perry Miller, *Errand into the Wilderness* (Cambridge, 1956), p. 57.

37. William Perkins, *Works* (London, 1618), 3:375, 378, 373.

38. William Perkins, *A Cloud of Faithful Witnesses Leading to the Heavenly Canaan* (London, 1622), pp. 522, 430–431.

39. Perkins, *Works,* 1:411; *Works,* 3:412.

40. Miller, *Errand,* pp. 58–59.

41. John Preston, *A Liveless Life* (London, 1633), p. 65.

42. Preston, p. 60.

43. Ibid., pp. 100, 23, 73.

44. Miller, *New England Mind,* p. 48.

45. William Ames, *The Marrow of Sacred Divinity* (London, 1643), pp. 47, 173.

46. Ames, pp. 71, 88; Ames, *Cases of Conscience* (London, 1643), bk. 2, p. 26.

47. Benjamin Keach, *Tropologia: A Key to Open Scripture Metaphors* (London, 1681), pp. A2, 417, 434.

48. John Welles, *The Soule's Progress to the Celestial Canaan* (London, 1639), p. 181.

49. Welles, pp. 110–11, 116.

50. Miller, *New England Mind,* p. 489.

51. William Perkins, quoted in Paul Kocher, *Science and Religion in Elizabethan England* (San Marino, 1953), pp. 298–300.

52. Miller, *New England Mind,* p. 34; Richard Baxter, *Miscellaneous Works* (Springfield, Mass., 1814), originally published 1657, pp. 114, 209.

53. Perry Miller, *Errand*, p. 12 n. See also David Williams, "New Directions in Puritan Studies," *American Quarterly* (Spring, 1985).

Chapter 2. New England

1. Zuckerman, "Fabrication," p. 193.

2. Miller, *New England Mind*, chap. 1.

3. See Alan Heimert, "Puritanism, the Wilderness, and the Frontier," *New England Quarterly* 26 (1953). Heimert argues that the concept of the wilderness was not carried to New England "on the Arbella, but came out of that wilderness itself." He argues that the settlers first thought of New England as a paradise and only later as wilderness.

4. John White et al., *The Planter's Plea* (London, 1630), pp. 9–10.

5. Edward Johnson, *The Wonder-working Providence of Sion's Saviour in New England* (New York, 1910), p. 53; John Eliot, "The Learned Conjectures of Mr. John Eliot Touching the Americans," in Thomas Thorowgood, *Jewes in America* (London, 1660), pp. 22–23.

6. John Winthrop, in *Winthrop Papers*, Massachusetts Historical Society (Boston, 1931), 2:91–92, 122, 125, 135, 136.

7. Heimert, "Puritanism," p. 361; John Cotton, *God's Promise to His Plantations*, Old South Leaflets, no. 53, p. 5.

8. Cotton, *God's Promise*, p. 5.

9. Francis Higginson, in Cotton Mather, *Magnalia Christi Americana* (Hartford, 1853), pp. 362–63.

10. Albert Van Dusen, *Puritans Against the Wilderness: Connecticut History to 1763*, (Chester, Conn., 1975), p. 39.

11. John Davenport, "Profession of Faith," in *Letters of John Davenport*, ed. Isabel Calder (New Haven, Conn., 1937), pp. 69, 72.

12. Cotton, *God's Promise*, p. 7.

13. John Cotton, *The Covenant of Grace* (London, 1665), p. 53; Cotton, *The Way of Life* (London, 1641), pp. 306–7; Cotton's poem is in John Norton, *Abel Being Dead Yet Speaketh* (London, 1658), p. 29; Cotton, *A Brief Exposition on the Whole book of Canticles* (London, 1642), p. 92; Cotton, "Introduction," to John Norton, *The Answer to Appolonius* (London 1648), quoted in Williams, *Paradise*, p. 102; Cotton, *A Brief*, p. 139.

14. Thomas Johnson and Perry Miller, eds., *The Puritans* (New York, 1963), 1:xlix.

15. Williams, *Paradise*, p. 89.

16. Thomas Hooker, *The Poor Doubting Christian Drawn to Christ* (Boston, 1743), pp. 81, 31, 102.

17. Hooker, *Doubting*, pp. 139, 138, 8.

18. Thomas Hooker, *The Soules Preparation for Christ, or A Treatise of Contrition* (London, 1632), pp. 128–29, 141, 190.

19. Thomas Hooker, *The Soules Humiliation* (London, 1637), pp. 2, 78; Hooker, "The Unbelievers Preparing for Christ," in *Redemption: Three Sermons* (Gainesville, Fla., 1956), p. 37; *Redemption*, p. 55.

20. Hooker, *Soules Humiliation*, pp. 45, 117.

21. Peter Bulkeley, *The Gospel Covenant* (London, 1651), pp. 209, 340.

22. Thomas Shepard, "Preface" to *A Defence of the Answer* (London, 1648), in Miller, *Puritans*, 1:121; Shepard, "Parable of the Ten Virgins," in *Works* (New York, 1853), 2:177.

23. Shepard, "The Sincere Convert," *Works*, 1:30, 35.

24. John Winthrop, "A Short Story of the Rise, Reign, and Ruin of the Antinomians," in *The Antinomian Controversy*, ed. David Hall (Middletown, Conn., 1968), pp. 203, 246.

25. Thomas Shepard, "Meditations and Spiritual Experiences," in *Works,* 3:409, 415; Cotton, "Wading in Grace," in Miller, *Puritans,* p. 318.

26. John Wheelwright, "A Fast Day Sermon," in *Antinomian Crisis,* ed. David Hall pp. 161, 169, 167.

27. Thomas Shepard, *God's Plot: The Paradoxes of Piety: Being the Autobiography and Journal of Thomas Shepard,* ed. Michael McGiffert (Boston 1972), p. 74.

28. Shepard, "Parable," pp. 170, 383.

29. Shepard, "Parable," p. 476.

30. Perry Miller, *The New England Mind: From Colony to Province* (Boston, 1961), p. 429.

31. Johnson, *Wonder-working,* pp. 123, 126, 129, 136.

32. Ibid., p. 151.

33. Ibid., pp. 270, 145, 130.

34. C. G. Jung, "Psychology and Religion," in *Collected Works* (Princeton, N.J., 1969), 11:156.

35. Roger Williams, in Edmund Morgan, *Roger Williams: The Church and the State* (New York, 1967), p. 41.

36. Sacvan Bercovitch, "Typology in Puritan New England: The Williams-Cotton Controversy Reassessed," *American Quarterly* 19 (1967). In this article, Bercovitch corrects Perry Miller's argument that Williams used typology but that Cotton did not. He shows that both Williams and Cotton used typology but that Cotton held the types and the antitypes to have continuing application whereas Williams believed that the antitype had completely replaced the type.

37. Bercovitch, p. 177.

38. Roger Williams, in Perry Miller, *Roger Williams: His Contribution to the American Tradition* (New York, 1974), p. 142.

39. Miller, *Williams,* p. 150.

40. Ibid., p. 52.

41. Williams, in Miller, *Williams,* p. 137.

42. Roger Williams, *Experiments of Spiritual Life and Health* (London, 1652), p. iv; Williams, *Key Into the Language of America,* ed. Teunissen and Hinz (Detroit, 1973), p. 153.

43. Roger Williams, "Letters," in *Works* (New York, 1963), 6:10–11.

44. Bercovitch, "Typology," p. 174.

45. Williams, *Experiments,* p. 51.

46. Carl Bridenbaugh, *Vexed and Troubled Englishmen: 1590–1642* (New York, 1967). See also Zuckerman, "Fabrication," *William and Mary Quarterly* (1977).

47. Edmund Morgan, *The Puritan Family* (New York, 1966), p. 174.

48. Quoted in Emory Elliott, *Power and the Pulpit in Puritan New England* (Princeton, N.J., 1975), p. 65.

49. Miller, *Colony to Province,* p. 70.

50. Robert Pope, *The Halfway Covenant* (Princeton, N.J., 1969), pp. 134–36.

51. Quoted in David Hall, *The Faithful Shepherd* (Chapel Hill, N.C., 1972), p. 203.

52. Cotton Mather, *Magnalia,* p. 442.

53. Michael Wigglesworth, *The Diary of Michael Wigglesworth* (New York, 1946), pp. 104–5; Miller, *Puritans,* p. 606.

54. Mather, *Magnalia,* p. 90.

55. Mary Rowlandson, *Narrative of the Captivity of Mary Rowlandson,* in *Narratives of the Indian Wars, 1675–1699,* ed. Charles Lincoln (New York, 1915), pp. 166–67, 122–23, 121, 126, 160–61.

56. In *Regeneration Through Violence* (Middletown, Conn., 1973) Richard Slotkin argues that the Captivity Narrative of Mrs. Rowlandson was the first of a new genre of literature in America, which he credits with more than it can support. He claims that even the success of

Edwards' revival sermons "is testimony to the evocative power of the captivity-myth imagery" (p. 103). In this, he has the cart and the horse reversed.

57. Rowlandson, *Narrative,* pp. 167, 159.

58. Increase Mather, "Preface," to Samuel Torrey, *An Exhortation Unto Reformation* (Cambridge, 1674), pp. 1, 11; Increase Mather, *The Day of Trouble is Near* (Cambridge, Mass., 1673), p. 3.

59. A. W. Plumstead, *The Wall and the Garden* (Minnesota, 1968), and particularly Peter Carroll, *Puritanism and the Wilderness: The Intellectual Significance of the New England Frontier, 1629–1700* (New York, 1969) stress the Puritan use of the image of the garden surrounded by the "hedge" of God's protection. These, like Roderick Nash's *Wilderness and the American Mind,* fail to develop the theological and psychological implications of wilderness imagery. Even Nash sees the theological implications only in terms of threatening sins. He concentrates on later Puritan avoidance of the wilderness to the neglect of the more significant embrace of the wilderness outlined here.

60. Samuel Danforth, "A Brief Exposition of New England's Errand into the Wilderness," in Plumstead, *Wall,* p. 65.

61. Urian Oakes, *New England Pleaded With* (Cambridge, 1673), pp. 17, 19, 20.

62. Thomas Shepard, *Eye-Salve* (Cambridge, 1673), pp. 3, 5.

63. Ibid., pp. 8, 33; see n. 28.

64. Ibid., p. 95.

65. Cotton Mather, "The Way to Prosperity," in Plumstead, *Wall,* p. 122.

66. Mather, *Magnalia,* pp. 447, 490.

67. Mather, *Magnalia,* pp. 383, 392.

68. Cotton Mather, *The Angel of Bethesda* (New London, 1722), pp. 1, 9, 14, 12, 17.

69. Thomas Prince, "Election Sermon of 1730," in Plumstead, *Wall,* p. 199.

Chapter 3. The Great Awakening of Fear

1. Solomon Stoddard, *A Guide to Christ* (Boston, 1714), p. 3.

2. Cotton Mather, quoted in Perry Miller, *The New England Mind: From Colony to Province* (Boston, 1961), p. 105; Robert Pope, *The Halfway Covenant* (Princeton, N.J., 1969), pp. 134–36.

3. Paul Boyer and Stephen Nissenbaum, *Salem Possessed* (Cambridge, Mass., 1974), pp. 103, 106.

4. Solomon Stoddard, *The Presence of Christ with the Ministers of the Gospel* (Boston, 1718), pp. 26–27; Stoddard, *The Nature of Saving Conversions* (Boston, 1719), p. 96.

5. Stoddard, *A Guide,* p. 3, 5, 79.

6. Stoddard, *A Treatise Concerning Conversion* (Boston, 1719), p. 5; Stoddard, *The Efficacy of the Fear of Hell* (Boston, 1713), p. 27.

7. Stoddard, *A Treatise,* p. 86.

8. Quoted in Miller, *Colony to Province,* p. 245; Edward Taylor, "Meditation 63, second series," *The Poems of Edward Taylor* (New Haven, Conn., 1960), p. 194.

9. Jonathan Edwards, "Unpublished Letter of May 30, 1735," in *The Great Awakening: The Works of Jonathan Edwards* (New Haven, Conn., 1972), 4:109.

10. The social nature of the awakening, in Boston as well as in the countryside, is examined in Edwin Gausted, *The Great Awakening in New England* (New York, 1957).

11. Richard Bushman, "Jonathan Edwards as Great Man: Identity, Conversion, and Leadership in the Great Awakening," *Soundings* 52 (Spring 1969). Bushman's *From Puritan to Yankee: Character and Social Order in Connecticut, 1690–1765* (New York, 1970) goes into

the same analysis in depth for the Connecticut awakening. See Erik Erikson, *Young Man Luther: A Study in Psychoanalysis and History* (New York, 1958). In *New England Dissent* (Cambridge, 1971), 1 : chap. 18, William McLoughlin argues that the Great Awakening was "America's first Identity Crisis."

12. David Hall, "The World of Print and Collective Mentality in Seventeenth Century New England," in *New Directions*, ed. Higham and Conkins, pp. 174–77; Erik Erikson, *Youth, Identity, and Crisis* (New York, 1968), p. 22; Erikson, *Life History and the Historical Moment* (New York, 1975), pp. 19–20.

13. Robert Bellah, *The Broken Covenant: American Civil Religion in Time of Trial* (New York, 1975), p. ix; Jonathan Edwards, "Men Naturally God's Enemies," *The Works of President Edwards in Four Volumes* (New York, 1857), 4 : 42–43. Unless otherwise cited, this will be the edition referred to as Edwards' *Works*.

14. Bushman, "Jonathan Edwards," pp. 40–41.

15. Ralph Waldo Emerson, "Self-Reliance," in *Selections from Ralph Waldo Emerson*, ed. Stephen Whicher (Boston, 1957), p. 147; Jonathan Edwards, "Some Thoughts on the Revival of Religion in New England," *Great Awakening*, p. 345; Edwards, "The Distinguishing Marks of a Work of Conversion," *Great Awakening*, p. 238.

16. Edwards, "Some Thoughts," *Great Awakening*, pp. 504, 505.

Edwards was by no means the only participant to be struck by the youthful makeup of the Awakening. Charles Chauncy, who hated the Awakening, said of Whitefield, "I freely acknowledge, wherever he went he generally moved the passions, especially of the younger people, and the Females among them;" Gilbert Tennent wrote to Whitefield that "multitudes were awakened, and several had received great consolation, especially among the young people, children and Negroes." and Benjamin Colman noted that in Boston, many of the converts were "among the Rich and Polite of our Sons and Daughters." Gaustad, *The Great Awakening*, pp. 31, 35, 52.

17. Boyer and Nissenbaum, *Salem*, p. 30.

18. Peter Gay, in John Opie, ed. *Jonathan Edwards and The Enlightenment* (Lexington, Ky., 1969), p. 105; Edward Griffin, *Jonathan Edwards* (Minneapolis, Minn., 1971), p. 37; The principal work on Edwards' aesthetics is Roland Delattre, *Beauty and Sensibility in the Thought of Jonathan Edwards* (New Haven, Conn., 1968); John Opie, *Edwards and the Enlightenment*, p. vii.

19. Perry Miller, *Jonathan Edwards* (Toronto, 1949), pp. 178, 57.

20. George Bancroft, "Jonathan Edwards," in *New American Cyclopedia* (New York, 1858), 7 : 20.

21. Edwards, "Future Punishment of the Wicked Unavoidable and Intolerable," in *Jonathan Edwards, Representative Selections*, ed. Faust and Johnson (New York, 1962), pp. 146–47; For a more detailed expansion of this section, see the author's "Horses, Pigeons, and the Therapy of Conversion," *Harvard Theological Review* (October 1981).

22. Edwards, "Future Punishment," p. 147.

23. C. G. Jung, *Modern Man in Search of a Soul* (New York, 1933), p. 240.

24. Jonathan Edwards, *The Works of President Edwards in Eight Volumes* (Worcester, Mass., 1808), 8 : 9.

25. See chap. 1, n.22.

26. *The Harvard Guide to Modern Psychiatry*, ed. Armand Nicholi (Cambridge, 1978), pp. 220–21; American Psychiatric Association's *Diagnostical and Statistical Manual of Mental Disorders* (3d ed.), (Washington, 1980), pp. 187–89; Jeff Coulter, *Approaches to Insanity* (New York, 1973), p. 5. See also J. S. Kasanin, ed., *Language and Thought in Schizophrenia* (New York, 1944); Thomas Szasz, *The Myth of Psychotherapy* (New York, 1978), p. xxiv.

Among its catalogue of schizophrenic systems, the APA states: "The sense of self that gives the normal person a sense of individuality, uniqueness, and self-direction is frequently disturbed. This is . . . frequently manifested by extreme perplexity about one's own identity and the meaning of existence." DSM, p. 183.

The language used by the clinical handbooks to describe schizophrenic behavior borrows heavily (if unconsciously) from the religious. The *Harvard Guide* (p. 211) says, "Periods of fright may be followed by a sense of revelation, of suddenly understanding the true meaning of one's life." Schizophrenic language, the handbook notes, (p. 212) "tends to be excessively concrete yet privately symbolic." The authors of *DSM* are quick to point out (p. 188) that the beliefs "or experiences of members of religious or other subcultural groups may be difficult to distinguish from delusions or hallucinations. When such experiences are shaped and accepted by a subcultural group they should not be considered evidence of psychosis." Apparently, there is safety in numbers.

27. The resemblance of Edwardsian determinism to modern behaviorism has been, if not systematically analyzed, at least frequently noted. In 1932, Joseph Haroutounian recognized that a "modern rendering of this analysis is the study of human behavior in terms of 'stimulus and response,'" (*Piety versus Moralism* [New York, 1932], pp. 225–26). Perry Miller noted that Edwards dealt with the "primary intellectual achievements of modernism . . . that man is conditioned and that the universe is uniform law," insights "so profound that only from the perspective of today can they be fully appreciated" (*Jonathan Edwards*, pp. 72–73). Paul Ramsey has called Edwards' analysis "as good as anything by the latest analysts of the determinist school" ("Introduction," *Freedom of the Will* [New Haven, Conn., 1957], p. 11). And parallels between the lives of Skinner and Edwards have appeared in *The Virginia Quarterly Review* and the *Christian Century* (Daniel Shea, "The Puritan Within," *VQR* [Summer 1974]; James Woelfel, "Listening to B. F. Skinner," *The Christian Century* [30 November 1977].

28. Shea, "The Puritan Within," p. 420. However, in a letter to me dated 29 September, 1982, Skinner writes: "I did not read Jonathan Edwards in college, even though my professor of philosophy edited a journal on Edwards. I have, however, acknowledged my indebtedness to my earlier religious training in the last volume of my autobiography."

29. Herman Melville, "Hawthorne and His Mosses," in *The Works of Herman Melville* (New York, 1963), p. 129.

30. Jonathan Edwards, *Freedom of the Will: The Works of Jonathan Edwards*, ed. Paul Ramsey (New Haven, Conn., 1957), vol. 1; Edwards, "A Faithful Narrative," in *Great Awakening*, p. 168.

31. Edwards, "Revival of Religion in New England," in *Works*, 3:280; Edwards, "Religious Affections," in *Works*, 3:3.

32. Edwards, "Remarks," appended to *Freedom of the Will*, in *Works*, 2:183.

33. Edwards, "Freedom of the Will," in *Works*, 2:4, 7. Edwards discusses the problem of the origins of the "strongest motive" in pt.1, sec.2, of *Freedom of the Will*.

34. Edwards, "Of the Prejudices of the Imagination," in *Scientific and Philosophical Writings: The Works of Jonathan Edwards*, ed. Wallace Anderson (New Haven, Conn., 1980), 6:196; Edwards, "The Nature of True Virtue," in *Works*, 2:292, 283.

35. B. F. Skinner, *About Behaviorism* (New York, 1976), p. 60. This latest summary of Skinner's position is the principal work on Skinnerian Behaviorism used for this book. Although Skinner has several books to his credit, this one work adequately sums up his basic position.

Edwards, "The Mind," in *Scientific Writings*, pp. 373–74.

36. Edwards, "The Mind," in *Scientific Writings*, p. 345.

37. Skinner, *About Behaviorism*, p. 231. It is for this reason that Skinner often gives the impression of believing that ideas have no part in determining human behavior, as if people were simply mechanical devices reacting without thought. He prefers to speak only

of stimulus and response and to avoid the mental connection between them. To speak, as Edwards did, of ideas and inclinations would to Skinner be to flirt with the fallacy of "mentalism." He is skeptical about the possibility of actually observing what happens in the nervous system. Still, some form of "mentalist" theory is needed to fill the gap between perception and reaction even in Skinner's system.

38. Edwards, "The Mind," in *Scientific Writings*, pp. 344, 353.

39. Edwards, "Men Naturally God's Enemies," in *Works*, 4:42–43.

40. Edwards, "True Virtue," in *Works*, 2:300; Edwards, "Freedom of the Will," in *Works*, 2:129.

41. Rudolph Otto, *The Idea of the Holy* (New York, 1957). See also Thomas Haskell, "Deterministic Implications of Intellectual History," in *New Directions*, ed. Higham and Conkins, p. 140: "Intellectual history has repeatedly taught that the deepest layers of assumption in human belief systems are so tenacious that they shape experience far more often than they are shaped by it. The lesson is not new, but never before has it been taught so forcefully."

42. For a modern comparison, see Paul Tillich, *The Courage to Be* (New Haven, Conn., 1959), p. 39: "The human mind is not only, as Calvin said, a factory of idols, it is also a permanent factory of fears—the first in order to escape God, the second in order to escape anxiety. . . . For facing the God who is really God means facing also the absolute threat of non-being. . . . The basic anxiety, the anxiety of a finite being about the threat of non-being cannot be eliminated. It belongs to existence itself."

43. Edwards, "Religious Affections," in *Works*, 3:38, 139–40.

44. Edwards, "Revival of Religion in New England," in *Works*, 3:337–38.

45. Edwards, "Religious Affections," in *Works*, 3:39; Edwards, "Extracts From his Diary," in *Works*, 1:9; Edwards, "Diary," in *Works in Ten Volumes* (New York, 1829), 1:92.

46. Edwards, "Religious Affections," in *Works*, 3:188.

47. Edwards, *Works in Eight Volumes*, 7:30; Edwards, "Religious Affections," *Works*, III, pp. 227, 71.

48. Edwards, "The Divine and Supernatural Light of God," in *Selections*, p. 109; Edwards, "Covenant of Redemption," in *Selections*, p. 373; see n.7.

49. Edwards, "Some Thoughts," in *Great Awakening*, p. 310.

50. Gal. 5.1; Edwards, "A Faithful Narrative," in *Great Awakening*, p. 183; Karl Barth, *Church Dogmatics*, II–2 (Edinburgh, 1957), p. 735.

51. Edwards, *Works in Eight Volumes*, 7:58.

52. Edwards, "Some Thoughts," in *Great Awakening*, p. 346.

Chapter 4. Revival and Revolution

1. Alan Heimert, *Religion and the American Mind* (Cambridge, Mass., 1965) remains the major statement tracing the influence of the Great Awakening to the Revolution.

2. Jonathan Edwards, "Some Thoughts Concerning the Revival," in *Works* (New Haven, Conn., 1972), 4:353, 356.

3. Jonathan Edwards, Letter "To the Rev. Thomas Prince," in *Works*, 4:550, 564. Unless otherwise cited, *Works* in this chapter refers to the Yale edition.

4. Jonathan Edwards, "Religious Affections," in *Works*, vol. 2.

5. Perry Miller, "Jonathan Edwards and the Sociology of the Great Awakening," *New England Quarterly* 21 (1948): 55.

6. Joseph Bellamy, "True Religion Delineated," in *Works* (originally published in 1750), 1:49; "Vindictive Justice an Amiable Perfection in the Deity; A Beauty in the Divine Character," in *Works* (originally published in 1758), 2:472.

7. Harriet Beecher Stowe, *Old Town Folks* (Boston, 1869), p. 374; Israel Holly, *God Brings about His holy and wise Purpose* (Hartford, 1774), pp. 16–17.

8. Samuel Quincey, quoted in Alan Heimert and Perry Miller, eds. *The Great Awakening* (New York, 1967), p. 488.

9. See chap. 1, n.51; chap. 2, n.20.

10. Jonathan Edwards, "Men Naturally God's Enemies," in *Works* (New York, 1847), 4:42–43.

11. C. G. Jung, *Collected Works,* 11:50.

12. Erik Erikson, *Young Man Luther,* p. 262; Rollo May, *Existence: A New Dimension in Psychiatry and Psychology* (New York, 1967), p. 50.

13. Sidney Mead, *History and Identity,* A.A.R. Studies in Religion 19 (A.A.R., 1979), p. 11.

14. Hadley Cantril, *The Psychology of Social Movements* (New York, 1941); Erik Erikson, "Autobiographical Notes on the Identity Crisis," *Daedalus* 99 (Fall 1970): 733.

15. Jonathan Edwards, *The Nature of True Virtue* (Ann Arbor, 1960), pp. 77–79.

16. Mason Lowance, *The Language of Canaan* (Cambridge, Mass., 1980), p. 295); Joseph Bellamy, *Works* (New York, 1811), 1:211.

17. Gordon Wood, "A Pluralistic Conception," in *The Ambiguity of the American Revolution* ed. Jack Greene (New York, 1968), p. 175. Originally "Rhetoric and Reality in the American Revolution," Wood, *William and Mary Quarterly* 23 (1966).

18. Wood, "Pluralistic Conception," p. 171.

19. John Adams, *The Works of John Adams* (Boston, 1856), 10:288.

20. Quoted in Edmund Morgan, *The Stamp Act Crisis* (Chapel Hill, N.C., 1953), p. 234.

21. I am indebted to Jon Alexander O.P., whose "Stand Fast in Liberty: Preaching on Galatians 5:1 on the Eve of the American Revolution," an unpublished paper, was read at the A.A.R. Convention in 1978.

22. Bernard Bailyn, *The Ideological Origins of the American Revolution* (Cambridge, Mass., 1967), pp. vi, x.

23. Robert Middlekauf, *The Glorious Cause* (New York, 1982), p. 48.

24. Tom Paine, *Common Sense,* in *Colonies to Nation 1763–1789* ed. Jack Greene (New York, 1975), p. 281. The significance of Paine's evangelical style has been argued in Harry Stout, "Religion, Communications, and the Ideological Origins of the American Revolution," *William and Mary Quarterly* 34 (1977): 519–41; Rhys Isaac, "Preachers and Patriots: Popular Culture and the Revolution in Virginia," in *The American Revolution* ed. Alfred Young (DeKalb, Ill. 1976), p. 153. See also Michael Greenberg, "Revival, Reform, Revolution: Samuel Davies and the Great Awakening in Virginia," *Marxist Perspectives* 3 (1980).

25. Michael J. Crawford, ed., "The Spiritual Travels of Nathan Cole," *William and Mary Quarterly* 33 (1976): 89–126.

26. Cole, pp. 95, 98, 99.

27. Ibid., p. 10.

28. Ibid., pp. 102, 103.

29. Ibid., p. 104.

30. Ibid., p. 103.

31. Ibid., p. 109, 112.

32. Ibid., pp. 120, 121.

33. Ibid., p. 123.

34. Ibid., pp. 125–26.

35. Jonathan Edwards, "To the Rev. Thomas Prince," in *Great Awakening,* p. 564.

36. Edward Countrymen, "Out of the Bounds of the Law," in *The American Revolution,* ed. Alfred F. Young (DeKalb, Ill., 1976), pp. 51, 52.

37. John Adams, quoted in Sacvan Bercovitch, *The American Jeremiad* (Madison, Wis.,

1978), pp. 130–31; *Records of the colony of the Massachusetts Bay in New England,* vol. 4, pt. 2, p. 133; see references to the Salem witch trials in chap. 3, p. 86.

38. Joel T. Headley, *The Chaplains and Clergy of the Revolution* (New York, 1864), p. 14.

39. Peter Oliver, *The Origin and Progress of the American Revolution* (Stanford, Calif., 1967), pp. 24, 41, 104; quoted in Henry May, *The Enlightenment in America* (New York, 1976), p. 14; Perry Miller, "The Garden of Eden and the Deacon's Meadow," *American Heritage* 7 (December 1955): 58.

40. Margaret Willard, ed., *Letters on the American Revolution, 1774–1776* (Boston, 1925), pp. 12, 120, 67, 16.

41. Willard, *Letters,* pp. 213, 308.

42. Quoted in Stewart Beach, *Samuel Adams: The Fateful Years* (New York, 1965), p. 147; William G. McLoughlin, "Enthusiasm for Liberty; The Great Awakening as the Key to the Revolution," in *Preachers and Politicians* (Worcester, Mass., 1977), p. 50; Headly, *Chaplains,* pp. 319–20; Willard, *Letters,* p. 9.

43. Ebenezer Baldwin, "A Settled Fix'd Plan for Inslaving the Colonies," in *Colonies to Nation,* ed. Greene, pp. 213–18.

44. Holly, *God Brings about his holy and wise Purpose,* pp. 21–22.

45. Carl Bridenbaugh, *Mitre and Sceptre* (New York, 1962); see n. 19 above.

46. Richard Brown, *Revolutionary Politics in Massachusetts* (Cambridge, Mass., 1970), pp. 115, 116.

47. Brown, *Revolutionary Politics,* pp. 117, 115, 120, 215.

48. John H. Hazelton, *The Declaration of Independence: Its History* (New York, 1906), p. 47. Note also Adams letter to Joseph Hawley, 15 April 1776, in *The Writings of Samuel Adams, vol. 3, John C. Miller, Sam Adams; Pioneer in propaganda* (Stanford, Calif., 1936). On p. 85, Miller writes, "The glimpse Adams caught of 'Puritanism' in 1740 had profound influence upon his later career. It became one of his strongest desires to restore Puritan manners and morals to New England; in his eyes the chief purpose of the American Revolution was to separate New England from the 'decadent' mother country in order that Puritanism might again flourish as it had in the early seventeenth century." See also William A. Williams, "Samuel Adams: Calvinist, Mercantilist, Revolutionary," *Studies on the Left* 1 (Winter 1980): 47–57.

49. E. Francis Brown, *Joseph Hawley: Colonial Radical* (New York, 1931), pp. 158, 169.

50. C. H. Butterfield, ed., *The Adams Papers,* ser. 2, vol. 1 (Cambridge, Mass., 1963), Abigail to John, 7 May 1775, p. 194.

51. Butterfield, *Adams,* John to Abigail, pp. 215, 410.

52. Joseph Montgomery, *A Sermon Preached at Christiana Bridge and Newcastle the 20th of July, 1775* (Philadelphia, 1775), p. 7; William Bailey, *Records of Patriotism and Love of Country* (Washington, D.C., 1826), p. 25. See David Williams, ed., *Revolutionary War Sermons* (Delmar, N.Y., 1985).

53. *"A Warm and Zealous Spirit:" John J. Zubly and the American Revolution; A Selection of His Writings,* ed. Randall Miller (Macon, Ga., 1982), p. 13; Rhys Isaac, *The Transformation of Virginia* (Durham, N.C., 1982), p. 301.

54. Bernard Bailyn, *Pamphlets of the American Revolution* (Cambridge, Mass., 1965), pp. 591, 593, 596, 585–86.

55. Stephen Johnson, *Some Important Observations Occasioned by, and Adapted to, the Publick Feast ordered by Authority, December 18th, A.D., 1765* (Newport, R.I., 1766), pp. 1, 19, 56.

For an example of the way the word "Liberty" was used both for political and religious purposes, and both inextricably together, see John Allen, *An Oration on the Beauties of Liberty* (Boston, 1773), especially pp. 64–65.

56. Headley, *Chaplains,* p. 93.

57. John Seelye, *Prophetic Waters: The River in Early American Life and Literature* (New York, 1977), p. xix.

58. Jonas Clarke, *The Fate of Blood-Thirsty Oppressors* (Boston, 1776), p. 5.

59. Samuel Sherwood, *The Churches Flight into the Wilderness* (New York, 1776), p. 9.

60. Ibid., p. 23.

61. Ibid., p. 29.

62. Ibid., p. 30.

63. Ibid., pp. 38–39, 42.

64. Nicholas Street, *The American States Acting Over the Part of Israel in the Wilderness, And Thereby Impeding Their Entrance into Canaan's Rest; Or, The Human Heart Discovering Itself Under Trials* (New Haven, Conn., 1777). One place this sermon can be found is in Conrad Cherry's excellent anthology, *God's New Israel: Religious Interpretations of American Destiny* (Englewood Cliffs, N.J., 1971).

65. Street, pp. 7–8, 9, 10.

66. Ibid., p. 13.

67. Ibid., pp. 21, 23.

68. Ibid., p. 31.

69. Sherwood, *The Churches Flight*, p. 39.

70. John Adams to William Tucker, 18 September 1818, in *Works*, 10:359.

71. The term, "Civil Religion," has been used, most recently by Catherine Albanese, *Sons of the Fathers* (Philadelphia, 1976), to identify that national belief system that supposedly grew out of the Revolution. However, this system owes more to the prevailing religious identity of the period and is not as original in the Revolutionary era as these critics imply.

72. Orville Dewey, *Letters of an English Traveller to His Friend in England on the "Revivals of Religion" in America* (Boston, 1828), p. 83.

Chapter 5. The Transcendental Growth

1. See, for example, Joel Porte, "In the Hands of an Angry God: Religious Terror in Gothic Fiction," in *The Gothic Imagination: Essays in Dark Romanticism*, ed. G. R. Thompson (Washington State University, 1974).

2. Stephen Whicher, ed., *Selections from Ralph Waldo Emerson* (Boston, 1957), p. xvii; Perry Miller, "New England's Transcendentalism: Native or Imported?" in *Literary Views*, ed. Camden Carroll (Chicago, 1964), p. 121; Perry Miller, ed., *The Transcendentalists* (Cambridge, Mass., 1950), p. 10.

3. Solomon Stoddard, *A Treatise Concerning Conversion* (Boston, 1719), p. 86; Jonathan Edwards, "The Excellency of Christ," in *Jonathan Edwards: Representative Selections* ed. Clarence Faust and Thomas Johnson (New York, 1962), p. 373; Octavius B. Frothingham, *Transcendentalism in New England* (Philadelphia, 1972), p. 108.

4. "From Edwards to Emerson" can be found in Perry Miller, *Errand into the Wilderness* (Cambridge, Mass., 1956), pp. 184–203; Harriet Beecher Stowe, *Old Town Folks* (Cambridge, Mass., 1966), p. 260; Henry B. Parkes, *The Pragmatic Test* (San Francisco, 1941), p. 34. In Joel Porte's *Emerson: Prospect and Retrospect* (Cambridge, Mass., 1982), Phyllis Cole discusses Mary Moody Emerson's "intellectual position between Jonathan Edwards and Ralph Waldo Emerson."

5. Emerson did read Edwards. In his *Journal*, 1823, he wrote: "Oct. 5. Milord W. from Andover let me into his mystery about Edwards on the will & told me withal that the object of the piece was to prove that President E. has not advanced human knowledge one step . . . the subject which, though so intricate before as to have ever been debateable ground, is made so plain by the able & skillful statements of Edwards, that we are made to see the

truth, & wonder that it ever was disputed. Waldo E. will please consult upon this topic. . . ." In addition, Emerson had a copy of Edwards' *Religious Affections* in his library.

6. Parkes, *The Pragmatic Test*, p. 34.

7. Considering the amount of published literature devoted to Emerson and the Transcendentalists, it is surprising how little has been written about Mary Moody Emerson. There are no biographies of her and her enormously influential letters are only now being prepared for publication. Emerson's own recollections, "Mary Moody Emerson," in his *Complete Writings*, vol. 2 (New York, 1929), remains the major source. MME is dealt with in passing in most of the critical and biographical works on Emerson, but rarely do the critics go beyond Emerson's own anecdotes. The list of scholarly articles on MME is quite short: George Tolman, "Mary Moody Emerson," a paper read before the Concord Antiquarian Society and printed privately in 1902, later published in Cambridge in 1929; Van Wyck Brooks, "The Cassandra of New England," *Scribner's* 81 (1927); Rosalie Feltenstein, "Mary Moody Emerson: Gadfly of Concord," *American Quarterly* (Fall 1953); Nancy Barcus, "Emerson, Calvinism, and Aunt Mary Moody: An Irrepressible Defender of New England Orthodoxy," *The Christian Scholar's Review* 7 (1977). See also the biographical sketch in *Notable American Women*. Two recent additions are Phyllis Cole, "The Advantage of Loneliness: Mary Moody Emerson's Almanacks, 1802–1855," in *Emerson: Prospect and Retrospect*, ed. Joel Porte (Cambridge, Mass., 1982), and Evelyn Barish, "Emerson and the Angel of Midnight," in *Mothering the Mind*. ed. Ruth Perry and Martina Brownley (New York, 1983).

8. Emerson, "Mary Moody Emerson," p. 1065; Brooks, "Cassandra," p. 125.

9. Ralph L. Rusk, *The Life of Ralph Waldo Emerson* (New York, 1949), p. 29.

10. Whicher, *Selections*, p. 4.

11. Brooks, "Cassandra," p. 125; Emerson, "Mary Moody Emerson," pp. 1064, 1065; Emerson *Journals and Miscellaneous Notebooks* [hereafter *JMN*] (Cambridge, Mass., 1965), 5:323–24; *JMN*, 7:445. In his journal, Emerson used the anagram "Tnamurya," sometimes shortened to "Tnam," to identify his aunt.

12. Emerson, "Mary Moody Emerson," p. 1073; Mary Moody Emerson, notebook 4, p. 232. In the Houghton Library Emerson Collection are four notebooks into which Emerson apparently copied portions of his aunt's letters and journal entires. MME's "Almanack" has only recently been found, and according to Phyllis Cole it is now in the Houghton Library. Mary Moody Emerson's letters and journals are quoted here by permission of the Houghton Library.

13. Emerson, "Mary Moody Emerson," p. 1069; MME, notebook 3, p. 3; MME, notebook 2, p. 27.

14. Emerson, "Mary Moody Emerson," p. 1068; MME, notebook 2, p. 4.

15. MME, notebook 3, pp. 70–71; notebook 4, p. 129.

16. Emerson, "Mary Moody Emerson," p. 1072; Jonathan Edwards, "Vindictive Justice a Beauty in the Divine Character," in *Works*, vol. 4 (New York, 1854); Emerson, "Mary Moody Emerson," p. 1072; Letter, MME-CCE, notebook 1, p. 15.

17. MME, notebook 3, p. 44; notebook 2, p. 205.

18. Ralph L. Rusk, *The Letters of Ralph Waldo Emerson* (New York, 1939), 1:116 n.22; Joel Porte, *Emerson and Thoreau: Transcendentalists in Conflict* (Middletown, Conn., 1965), pp. 69–70.

19. MME, notebook 4, p. 30.

20. Letter, MME–CCE, notebook 1, p. 15; MME, Notebook 2, pp. 39, 49.

21. Emerson, *JMN*, 1:49; MME, notebook 2, pp. 29–30.

22. MME–RWE, 1821, *JMN*, 1:336; MME–RWE, 1821, *JMN*, 1:333.

23. MME–RWE, 1822, notebook 1, p. 14; MME–RWE, 1821, *JMN*, 1:196.

24. MME–RWE, 1822, *JMN*, 2:373–74.

25. MME–RWE, 1822, *JMN*, 2:375.

26. MME–RWE, 1824, *JMN*, 2:383.

27. RWE-MME, 1924, *JMN*, 1:357; Emerson, *The Journals of Ralph Waldo Emerson* (Boston, 1909), 1:324, 375.

28. MME–RWE, 1824, *JMN*, 2:384; MME–RWE, 1824, *Journals*, 2:32–33.

29. MME–RWE, 1824, *JMN*, 2:382, 385.

30. MME–RWE, 1825, notebook 1, p. 61; MME–RWE, Letter of 21 Feb. 1826 (Houghton Library); MME–RWE, 1826, Notebook 1, p. 130.

31. RWE–MME, 1827, *Journals*, 2:180, 221–22, 212, 222–23; Emerson, *Journals*, 17 Dec. 1827, p. 223.

32. RWE–MME, 1822, Rusk, *Letters*, 1:115; ibid., 1823, p. 133.

33. MME–RWE, 1824, Notebook 1, pp. 138–39; MME, notebook 2, pp. 16–17; MME–RWE, 1827, *JMN*, 2:393; MME–RWE, 1829, Notebook 1, p. 153; Emerson, *Journals*, 1831, 2:437.

34. RWE–MME, 1831, *Journals*, 2:440; in George Tolman, "Mary Moody Emerson," p. 23; Emerson, *JMN*, 1835, 7:64; Tolman, "Mary Moody Emerson," p. 24; MME–CCE, 1832, notebook 1, p. 23; MME, notebook 2, p. 7.

35. Emerson, "New England Reformers," in *Complete Writings*, 1:321; Emerson, "Resources," *Writings*, 2:770.

36. Stephen Whicher, *Freedom and Fate* (Philadelphia, 1971), p. 9.

37. Oliver Wendell Holmes, "Mechanism in Thought and Morals," in *Pages From an Old Volume of Life* (Boston, 1884), p. 282; RWE–William Emerson, 1863, Rusk, *Letters*, 5:326.

38. Emerson, *Journals*, 1823, p. 295; Whicher, *Selections*, p. 11.

39. Emerson, *Writings*, 2 933; Whicher, *Selections*, p. 405.

40. Herman Melville to Evert Duyckinck, in *The Portable Melville*, ed. Jay Leyda, (New York, 1952), pp. 378–80; Whicher, *Selections*, p. 208; RWE–MME, 1826, Rusk, *Letters*, 1:171; Whicher, *Selections*, pp. 132, 135.

41. Whicher, *Selections*, pp. 24, 56, 223, 234, 233, 81. Emerson's inability to come up with a specific procedure for getting in touch with the Oversoul left a void later to be filled by the spiritualists and mind-cure proponents who followed him. In time, as Donald Meyer has argued, Norman Vincent Peale inherited the question and supplied an answer.

42. Emerson, "The Young American" in *Writings*, 1:113; Emerson, *JMN*, 2:380; Whicher, *Selections*, p. 31.

43. Whicher, *Selections*, pp. 283, 255.

44. Emerson, "Mary Moody Emerson," in *Writings*, 2:1071; Emerson, "American Civilization," *Writings*, 2:1211; MME–RWE, 1824, *JMN*, 2:380–81; MME–RWE, above, nn.22, 33.

45. Bradford Torrey, ed., *The Writings of Henry David Thoreau* (Boston, 1906), vol. 9, journal 3, p. 113. Hereafter this edition will be referred to as *W*.

46. F. B. Sanborn, *The Life of Henry David Thoreau* (Boston, 1917), pp. 137, 139.

47. Sanborn, *Life*, pp. 142, 144, 146, 148.

48. Joel Porte, *Emerson and Thoreau: Transcendentalists in Conflict* (Middletown, Conn., 1965); Sherman Paul, *The Shores of America: Thoreau's Inward Exploration* (Urbana, Ill., 1972), p. 34; *W*, vol. 8, journal 2, pp. 150–51.

49. Perry Miller, *Consciousness in Concord* (Boston, 1958), p. 76; *W*, "The Maine Woods," 3:173; *W*, "Walking," 5:224–25.

50. Miller, *Consciousness*, p. 119. Miller also tells the story of the burning of Concord woods in some detail.

51. Rudolph Otto, *The Idea of The Holy* (London, 1973); *W*, "A Week on the Concord and Merrimac Rivers," 1:141.

52. William D. Drake, "The Depth of Walden: Thoreau's Symbolism of the Divine in Nature" (Ph.D. diss., University of Arizona, 1967), pp. 46, 4–5, 128.

53. Henry David Thoreau, *Cape Cod* (New York, 1961).

54. William Drake, "A Week on the Concord and Merrimac Rivers," in *Thoreau: A Collection of Critical Essays,* ed. Sherman Paul, (Englewood Cliffs, N.J., 1962), p. 63.

55. Thoreau, *Cape Cod,* p. 1. The meaning in scripture of the images of ocean and desert wilderness are discussed in chapter one, above.

56. Ibid., pp. 6, 12, 14.

57. Ibid., pp. 48, 40.

58. Ibid., pp. 53, 56. Porcupines, of course, cannot shoot their quills. Thoreau the naturalist should have known this.

59. Ibid., pp. 58, 64.

60. Ibid., pp. 71–72, 219, 76, 80.

61. Ibid., pp. 72–73, 85, 88–89.

62. Ibid., p. 90.

63. Ibid., pp. 141–42, 188–89.

64. *W,* vol. 8, journal 1, p. 296.

65. Drake, "Depth," p. 61; *W,* vol. 15, journal 9, p. 200; Porte, *Emerson and Thoreau,* p. 129.

Chapter 6. Hawthorne, Very, and Dickinson

1. Julia Ward Howe, *Reminiscences, 1819–1899* (Boston, 1899), pp. 274–75.

2. Nathaniel Hawthorne, *The English Notebooks,* ed. Randall Stewart (New York, 1941), p. 433.

3. Hyatt Waggoner, *The Presence of Hawthorne* (Baton Rouge, La., 1979), p. 55; Herman Melville, "Hawthorne and His Mosses," in *The Portable Melville,* ed. Jay Leyda (New York, 1966), p. 406.

4. Claudia Johnson, "Regenerative Descent in the Works of Nathaniel Hawthorne" (Ph.D., diss., University of Illinois, Urbana-Champaign, 1973); Barton L. St. Armand, "Hawthorne's Haunted Mind: A Subterranean Drama of the Self," *Criticism* 13 (1971): 9, 15.

5. Nathaniel Hawthorne, "The Haunted Mind," in *Selected Tales and Sketches,* ed. Hyatt Waggoner, pp. 410–14; St. Armand, "Hawthorne's Haunted Mind," pp. 25, 18.

6. Hawthorne, "Night Sketches," in *Selected Tales,* pp. 430, 432, 433. At Enfield Edwards preached, "Sinners in the Hands of an Angry God."

7. Hawthorne, "Night Sketches," pp. 434–35; Waggoner, *Presence,* p. 54.

8. Hawthorne, "Young Goodman Brown," in *Selected Tales,* pp. 150, 157, 160; Robert Morsberger, "The Woe that is Madness: Goodman Brown and the Face of Fire," *Nathaniel Hawthorne Journal* (1973): 178. See also Gene Bluestein, "The Brotherhood of Sinners: Literary Calvinism," *New England Quarterly* 50 (June 1977): 195–213.

9. Hawthorne, "Young Goodman Brown," pp. 162, 163.

10. Waggoner, *Presence,* discusses two authors who believe Hawthorne to have been "anti-Christian;" Solomon Stoddard, chap. 3, n. 4.

11. Hawthorne, "Young Goodman Brown," p. 156.

12. Edwin Gittleman, *Jones Very: The Effective Years* (New York, 1967), p. 190. The only other full account of Very's career is William Bartlett, *Jones Very: Emerson's Brave Saint* (Durham, N.C., 1942), p. 119.

13. Jones Very, Letter to Henry Bellows, 29 December 1838, in which Very describes what happened to him while he was "under the spirit." Massachusetts Historical Society Library.

14. Gittleman, pp. 250, 55.

15. Samuel Gray Ward's Account of a Visit from Jones Very, "Come with Me to the Feast; or Transcendentalism in Action," *Massachusetts Historical Society Miscellany 6* (Boston, 1960), p. 4.

16. Charles Brooks, letter published in *The Life and Services to Literature of Jones Very: A Memorial Meeting, Tuesday, Dec. 14, 1880*, Bulletin of the Essex Institute 5, 13 (Salem, Mass., 1881), pp. 29–30; Gittleman, pp. 265–66.

17. Bartlett, *Jones Very*, p. 119.

18. Ralph Waldo Emerson, "Self-Reliance," in *Selections from Ralph Waldo Emerson*, ed. Stephen Whicher (Boston, 1957), p. 149; Ralph Waldo Emerson, *Journals* (Boston, 1909), 5:220; *Selections*, p. 94.

19. Jones Very, *Poems and Essays* (Boston, 1886), p. 73.

20. Gittleman, p. 337; James Freeman Clarke, "Biographical Notice of Jones Very," in *Poems and Essays*, p. xxv.

21. Letter, Nathaniel Hawthorne to Sophia Peabody, in Julian Hawthorne, *Nathaniel Hawthorne and His Wife* (Boston 1884), 1:221; Letter, Sophia Peabody to Elizabeth Peabody, in Robert Cantwell, *Nathaniel Hawthorne: The American Years* (New York, 1967), p. 290.

22. Gittleman, p. 282.

23. Hawthorne, "Egotism, or, The Bosom Serpent," in *Selected Tales*, pp. 258, 262. See Robert D. Arner, "Hawthorne and Jones Very: Two Dimensions of Satire in 'Egotism; or, The Bosom Serpent,'" *New England Quarterly* 42 (June 1969): 267–75.

24. Hawthorne, *The Blithedale Romance* (New York, 1958), pp. 79, 149.

25. William P. Andrews, "Introductory Memoir," in *Poems by Jones Very* (Boston, 1883), pp. 10–11. Hawthorne also wrote to Elizabeth Peabody that he found Very "always vain in his eye—though it was an innocent vanity" (Gittleman, p. 284); Emerson, quoted in Bartlett, p. 111.

26. See Stephen Oates, *To Purge This Land with Blood: A Biography of John Brown* (New York, 1970), pp. 22–24; Ralph L. Rusk, *The Life of Ralph Waldo Emerson* (New York, 1949), p. 402.

27. Gittleman, pp. 282–83; Hawthorne, "A Virtuoso's Collection," in *Selected Tales*, p. 449.

28. Nathaniel Hawthorne, "The American Notebooks," 1 August 1837, in *The Centenary Edition of the Works of Nathaniel Hawthorne* (Columbus, Ohio, 1972), 8:64.

29. Karl Barth, *The Epistle to the Romans* (Oxford, 1972), pp. 253, 267.

30. Whicher, *Selections*, p. 95.

31. L–99; Jonathan Edwards, "The Future Punishment of the Wicked Unavoidable and Intolerable," *Representative Selections*, ed. Clarence Faust and Thomas Johnson (New York, 1962), p. 147; J–1323; J–281.

Hereafter, poems will be cited in the text according to the numbers of *The Complete Poems of Emily Dickinson*, ed. Thomas H. Johnson (Boston, 1960). Letters will be cited in footnotes according to the numbers of *The Letters of Emily Dickinson*, ed. Thomas H. Johnson (Cambridge, Mass., 1958). The similarity between ED and MME was first noted in Barton L. St. Armand, "Paradise Deferred: The Image of Heaven in the Work of Emily Dickinson and Elizabeth Stuart Phelps," *American Quarterly* 29 (1977).

32. One noteworthy exception to this is William Sherwood, *Circumference and Circumstance: Stages in the Mind and Art of Emily Dickinson* (New York, 1968). Ronald Lanyi, "'My Faith that Dark Adores': Calvinist Theology in the Poetry of Emily Dickinson," *Arizona Quarterly* 32 (1976): 264–78, finds evidence of ED's belief in the five points of the Synod of Dort. Such literal dogmatic readings of ED's Calvinism, while not wrong, tend to obscure the spiritual aspect of her poetry and do not add to our appreciation of ED as an artist.

33. John Cody, *After Great Pain: The Inner Life of Emily Dickinson* (Cambridge, Mass., 1971), p. 24.

34. Thomas H. Johnson, *Emily Dickinson: An Interpretive Biography* (Cambridge, Mass., 1955), p. 4.

35. Richard B. Sewall, *The Life of Emily Dickinson* (New York, 1974), pp. 19–20; Karl Keller, *The Only Kangaroo Among the Beauty: Emily Dickinson and America* (Baltimore, 1979), p. 72; Albert J. Gelpi, *Emily Dickinson: The Mind of the Poet* (New York, 1965), pp. 60, 72.

36. Clara Newman Turner, quoted in *The Years and Hours of Emily Dickinson*, ed. Jay Leyda (New Haven, Conn., 1960), p. 136; See chap. 2, nn. 51, 54.

37. L–10.

38. L–35.

39. L–39.

40. L–261.

41. Sherwood, *Circumference*, p. 138. Although recognizing that ED's trauma was essentially a "conversion" as the Calvinists understood it, Sherwood was unable to reconcile his religious interpretation with ED's mental instability, arguing that her experience was not "a crack-up . . . , but a conversion. . . . (p. 138) Unfortunately, too many critics, fearing the negative implications of psychological terminology, have resisted the obvious. John Cody's words bear consideration: "If one can be induced to stare unflinchingly for a moment into the psychic hell that for a time overwhelmed her, one sees that the psychotic are not necessarily mindless and absurd—in fact they are far more frequently preternaturally aware of their deeper psychic processes, hypersensitive, and gentle. And . . . their mental and emotional perturbations may become the vehicle through which genius is kindled" (p. 11).

42. L–11; Jones Very, "The New Birth," see above n.19; L–154; L–182; L–185.

43. L–209; L–216; for an example of one of the first "disordered" letters, see L–195, written 6 November 1858.

44. Cody, pp. 313–14.

45. L–261.

46. L–517.

47. Gelpi, p. 92.

48. Jonathan Edwards, "The Excellency of Christ," *Selections*, p. 373: "When we behold the fragrant rose and lily, we see His love and purity. So the green trees, and fields, and singing of birds are the emanations of His infinite joy and benignity"; Joseph Bellamy, "True Religion Delineated," in *Works* (New York, 1811), 1:98.

49. Octavious B. Frothingham, see chap. 5, n.3.

50. L–387.

51. L–946.

52. L–389.

53. Gelpi, p. 36; also L–916.

54. L–560; L–562; Taylor, "Preparatory Meditations, Second Series," 1, *Poems*, p. 83; Jonathan Edwards, "The Christian Pilgrim," *Selections*, p. 131.

55. L–248. Other "Master" letters are L–187 and L–233.

56. Jonathan Edwards, "A Faithful Narrative," in *Works* (New Haven, Conn., 1972), 4:178; L–874; L–522.

57. John Welles, chap. 1, n.48; Edwards, above n.1.

58. L–260.

59. L–330.

Chapter 7. Herman Melville

1. Maurice Friedman, "Bartleby and the Modern Exile," in *Bartleby the Scrivener*, ed. Howard P. Vincent (Kent, 1966), p. 64; T. Walter Herbert, Jr., *Moby-Dick and Calvinism: A*

World Dismantled (New Brunswick, N.J., 1977), p. 9; Edward F. Edinger, *Melville's Moby-Dick: A Jungian Commentary* (New York, 1975), p. 5; Henry A. Murray, "Introduction," to *Pierre* (New York, 1949), p. xxxvi; Richard Chase, "Introduction," to *Herman Melville: Critical Essays* (Englewood Cliffs, N.J., 1962), p. 7.

2. Thomas Werge, "Moby-Dick and the Calvinist Tradition," *Studies in the Novel* 1 (Winter 1969): 484–93.

3. Herman Melville, "Hawthorne and His Mosses," in *The Works of Herman Melville* (New York, 1963), 13:129; Melville to Hawthorne, letter, in Eleanor Melville Metcalf, *Herman Melville: Cycle and Epicyle* (Cambridge, Massachusetts, 1953), pp. 110–11.

4. Melville, "Moby-Dick," in *Works,* 7:1; Herbert, *Moby-Dick,* p. 6. It is Herbert's thesis that the split between a liberal father (who died in a fit of madness when Herman was thirteen) and a Calvinist mother prevented Herman from developing a consistent world-view and thus accounted for the psychological distress evident in his novels.

5. The creation of the Sabbath School Union in the Melvilles' church, if not the product of Horace Bushnell's *Christian Nurture* (New York, 1847), does reveal that Bushnell's emphasis on education instead of conversion had become a part of that congregation's practice.

For a description of American Protestantism in the Northeast in Melville's time, see Ernest Tuveson, *Redeemer Nation* (Chicago, 1968); George Marsden, *The Evangelical Mind and the New School Presbyterian Experience* (New Haven, Conn., 1970); Sidney Mead, "When 'wise men hoped': An Examination of the mind and spirit of the National Period," *The Lively Experiment: The Shaping of Christianity in America* (New York, 1963).

6. H. Richard Niebuhr, *The Kingdom of God in America* (New York, 1959), p. 193.

7. See William G. McLoughlin, *Modern Revivalism* (New York, 1959), chaps. 1 and 2. For a description of the Melville family religion, see Herbert, *Moby-Dick and Calvinism,* especially chap. 1 and the letters provided in Metcalf, *Herman Melville,* the opening chapter. A brief description is also provided in William Braswell, *Melville's Religious Thought* (Durham, N.C., 1963).

8. Herbert, *Moby-Dick,* p. 90.

9. Melville, "White Jacket," in *Works,* 6:189; Melville, "Israel Potter," in *Works,* 11:203, 209, 221, 224.

10. Werge, *"Moby-Dick,"* p. 484.

11. Metcalf, *Cycle,* p. 110.

12. Ibid., p. 60.

13. Ibid., p. 161.

14. Melville, "Typee," in *Works,* 1:12, 262, 168–69, 165.

15. Ibid., pp. 30, 320.

16. Melville, "Mardi," in *Works,* 3:9, 11.

17. Jonathan Edwards, "The Great Awakening," in *Works* (New Haven, Conn., 1972), 4:27.

18. Melville, "Mardi," in *Works,* 3:106.

19. Melville, "Mardi," pp. 368–69.

20. Melville, "Mardi," in *Works,* 4:20–21, 400.

21. Metcalf, *Cycle,* p. 108.

22. Melville, "Moby-Dick," in *Works,* 7:144, 107.

23. Melville, "Moby-Dick," in *Works,* 8:298; Calvin, see chap. 1, n.23; Joseph Bellamy, "True Religion Delineated," in *Works* (New York, 1811), p. 57.

24. Melville, "Moby-Dick," in *Works,* 7:1, 8, 129.

25. Ibid., pp. 132–33.

26. Ibid., pp. 50, 56, 57.

27. Ibid., p. 58.

28. Ibid., p. 198.
29. Ibid., p. 204; in *Works*, 8:123.
30. Ibid., 7:229, 243–44.
31. Jonathan Edwards, see chap. 3, n.38.
32. John Welles, see chap. 1, n.48.
33. Melville, "Moby-Dick," in *Works*, 7:243–44.
34. Melville, "Moby-Dick," in *Works*, 8:180.
35. Ibid., p. 169.
36. Ibid., pp. 275, 327, 365, 366.
37. Ibid., p. 169.
38. Melville, "Pierre," in *Works*, vol. 9; Henry Murray, "Introduction."
39. Melville, "Pierre," p. 16.
40. Ibid., pp. 66, 231.
41. Ibid., p. 253.
42. Ibid., pp. 425, 426.
43. Ibid., pp. 471–72; Metcalf, *Cycle*, p. 161; Braswell, *Melville's Religious Thought*, p. 106.
44. Melville, "The Piazza," in *Works*, 10:17–18.
45. Melville, "Benito Cereno," in *Works*, 10:120, 139, 164, 143.
46. See chap. 3, n.42; Melville, "Benito Cereno," in *Works*, 10:167.
47. Emory Elliot, *Puritan Influences in American Literature* (Chicago, 1979), p. xix.
48. Melville, "Billy Budd," in *Works*, 13:100.
49. John 3.16; Melville, "Billy Budd," pp. 102–3.
50. Jonathan Edwards, *The Nature of True Virtue* (Ann Arbor, Mich., 1960).
51. Melville, "Billy Budd," p. 93 n.

Chapter 8. Wilderness Lost

1. Oliver Wendell Holmes, "Autocrat of the Breakfast Table," *The Atlantic Monthly*, September 1858, 496. The entire series was first published in book form the following year as *The Autocrat of the BreakFast Table* (Boston, 1859); unsigned review of Holmes in *Scribner's Monthly Magazine* 18 (May 1879): 117–27; Eleanor Tilton, *Amiable Autocrat: A Biography of Dr. Oliver Wendell Holmes* (New York, 1947), p. 420 n.23.

2. James O. Murray, D.D., "What a Preacher May Learn From the Writings of Dr. Oliver Wendell Holmes," *Homiletic Review* (September 1895): 205.

3. Barrett Wendell, *A Literary History of America* (New York, 1900), pp. 20, 422. A partial list of critics agreeing with Wendell includes: V. L. Parrington, *The Romantic Revolution in America* (New York, 1930), p. 454; V. W. Brooks, *The Flowering of New England* (New York, 1936), p. 488; Perry Miller, *The New England Mind: The Seventeenth Century* (New York, 1939), p. 115; "The reign of logic in the New England mentality . . . continued unbroken until . . . Dr. Holmes wrote its epitaph in the supremely logical construction of a One-Hoss Shay."

4. S. I. Hayakawa and Howard Mumford Jones, eds. *Oliver Wendell Holmes: Representative Selections* (New York, 1939), p. 455.

5. Tilton, *Amiable*, pp. 420 n.23, 244.

6. George Arms, *The Fields were Green* (Stanford, Calif., 1953), pp. 112, 113, 36; See OWH's "American Academy Centennial Celebration."

7. Miriam Rossiter Small, *Oliver Wendell Holmes* (New York, 1962), p. 99.

8. Howard Webb, "Item 17," *The Explicator* 24 (October, 1965).

9. Hyatt H. Waggoner, *American Poets* (New York, 1968), pp. 56, 13.

10. J. Stanley Mattson, "Oliver Wendell Holmes and 'The Deacon's Masterpiece:' A Logical Story?" *New England Quarterly* 41 (March 1968): 106, 113.

11. Mattson, "Oliver," p. 114.

12. *American Heritage* 24 (December 1972): 68–69.

13. Jill Perkins, "Oliver Wendell Holmes's Rhymed Problem," *American Transcendental Quarterly* 22 (1974): 105, 106.

14. Oliver Wendell Holmes, "Jonathan Edwards," *Pages From an Old Volume of Life* (Boston, 1884), p. 401. Holmes's contemporaries recognized that the shay was an object of pride and not ridicule. A number of carriage manufacturers used the "One-Hoss Shay" as a symbol of their own products without Holmes's objections. One company passed out elegant reprints of the poem, and, as an afterword, added this contribution to literature:

> Now we build our work to 'beat the taown'
> 'N' the Kounty 'n' all the Kentry raoun'
> 'N' they're all so built that they can't break daown:
> 'Fur,' as the deacon says, 'its mighty plain
> That the weakes' place mus' stand the strain'
> And like the deacon, we, too, maintain,—
> That the way to fix it, without doubt,
> Is to always leave the weak spot out.
>
> So we built our work as the Deacon planned:
> —Our fame is known throughout the land.—
> If you want the best, and you surely do,
> Then the deacon's plan is the plan for you.
>   Columbus Buggy Company, Columbus, Ohio
>   (John Hay Library, Harris Collection, Brown University)

15. Waggoner, *American Poets*, p. 56.

16. Holmes, "The Pulpit and the Pew," *Pages*, pp. 424, 426; Holmes, "Jonathan Edwards," *Pages*, p. 376.

17. Harry Clark, "Dr. Holmes: A Reinterpretation," *New England Quarterly* (March 1939): 33 n. For examples of Holmes's life-long battle with determinism, see *Elsie Venner* (Boston, 1861): *The Guardian Angel* (Boston, 1867); *A Moral Antipathy* (Boston, 1885); and *Pages from an Old Volume of Life* (Boston, 1884).

18. Holmes, "Mechanism in Thought and Morals," *Pages*, pp. 282, 289, 286. See also V. W. Brooks, "Dr. Holmes: Forerunner of the Moderns," *Saturday Review of Literature* 14 (June 1936) in which he calls "Mechanism in Thought and Morals" a "brilliant anticipation of Dr. Freud." Claren Oberndorf, M.D., *The Psychiatric Novels of Dr. Oliver Wendell Holmes* (New York, 1943), is also relevant.

19. Holmes, *The Professor at the Breakfast Table* (Boston, 1891), p. 16.

20. See chap. 6, n.1.

21. George M. Frederickson, *The Inner Civil War: Northern Intellectuals and the Crisis of the Union* (New York, 1965), p. 70. An even better example than the "Army Hymn" is Holmes's war poem, "To Canaan"; Letter to the Editor, "A New Professor in an old theology," signed "Cecil," in *The Autocrat's Miscellanies* ed. Albert Mordell (New York, 1959), p. 354.

22. Clark, "Dr. Holmes," p. 19 (see also p. 28).

23. Letter, OWH to HBS, in John T. Morse, Jr., *Oliver Wendell Holmes: Life and Letters* (Boston, 1896), 2:246.

24. William G. McLoughlin, *The Meaning of Henry Ward Beecher* (New York, 1970), p. 39.

25. Above, n.16; chap. 7, n. 19.

26. See chap. 6, n.3.

27. See chap. 5, n.35.

Chapter 9. Conclusion

1. See chap. 3, n. 39.

2. Victor Turner, *Dramas, Fields, and Metaphors: Symbolic Action in Human Society* (Ithaca, N.Y., 1974), pp. 64, 36.

3. Miller, "Marrow," in *Errand,* p. 51.

4. See chap. 1, n.27.

5. "The Conversion of Ron Reagan," *The Boston Sunday Globe,* 11 January 1981, p. 52.

6. Lloyd Dendinger, "The Irrational Appeal of Frost's Dark Deep Woods," *The Southern Review* 2 (October 1966): 822. Robert Frost, "Desert Places," in *The Complete Poems of Robert Frost* (New York, 1964), p. 386.

7. See Introduction, n.7.

Bibliography

Primary Texts

Adams, John. *The Works of John Adams.* Charles F. Adams, ed. Boston: Little, Brown, 1856.

Adams, Samuel. *The Writings of Samuel Adams.* New York: Putnam's, 1908.

Allen, John. *An Oration on the Beauties of Liberty.* Boston: E. Russell, 1773.

American Psychiatric Association. *Diagnostical and Statistical Manual of Mental Disorders.* 3d ed. Washington: 1980.

Ames, William. *Cases of Conscience.* Book 2, London: J. Rothwell, 1643.

———. *The Marrow of Sacred Divinity.* London: J. Rothwell, 1643.

Augustine, Saint. *On Christian Doctine.* New York: Liberal Arts Press, 1958.

Bailyn, Bernard, ed. *Pamphlets of the American Revolution.* Cambridge: Belknap Press, 1965.

Baldwin, Ebenezer. "A SETTLED FIX'D PLAN FOR INSLAVING THE COLONIES." In *Colonies to Nations 1763–1789.* Jack Greene, ed., New York: Norton, 1975.

Barth, Karl, *Church Dogmatics.* Edinburgh: T & T Clarke, 1958.

———. *The Epistle to the Romans.* New York: Oxford University Press, 1972.

Baxter, Richard. *Miscellaneous Works.* Springfield, Mass.: T. Dickman, 1814 (originally published 1657).

Bellamy, Joseph. *The Works of the Rev. Joseph Bellamy.* New York: S. Dodge, 1811.

Bulkeley, Peter. *The Gospel Covenant.* London: Matthew Simmons, 1651.

Butterfield, L. H., ed. *The Adams Papers.* Cambridge: Belknap Press, 1963.

Calder, Isabel, ed., *The Letters of John Davenport.* New Haven: Yale University Press, 1937.

Calvin, Jean. *Commentaries on the four last Books of Moses, arranged in the form of a Harmony.* Vol. 1. Edinburgh: Calvin Translation Society, 1852.

———. *Institutes of the Christian Religion.* John McNeill, ed., Ford Battles, trans., Philadelphia: Westminster Press, 1960.

Clarke, Jonas. *The Fate of Blood-Thirsty Oppressors.* Boston: Powars & Willis, 1776.

Cole, Nathan. "The Spiritual Travels of Nathan Cole." Michael J. Crawford, ed. *William and Mary Quarterly* 33 (1976): 89–126.

Cotton, John. *A Brief Exposition on the Whole Book of Canticles.* London: Philip Nevil, 1642.

———. *The Covenant of Grace.* London: John Allen, 1655.

———. *God's Promise to His Plantations.* Old South Leaflets, no. 53. Boston: Directors of the Old South, 1896.

———. *The Way of Life.* London: L. Fawne, 1641.

Danforth, Samuel. "A Brief Exposition on New England's Errand into the Wilderness." In A. W. Plumstead, ed., *The Wall and the Garden.* Minneapolis: University of Minnesota Press, 1968.

Dewey, Orville. *Letters of an English Traveler to His Friend in England on the "Revivals of Religion" in America.* Boston, 1828.

Dickinson, Emily. *The Complete Poems of Emily Dickinson.* Thomas Johnson, ed. Boston: Little, Brown, 1960.

———. *The Letters of Emily Dickinson.* Thomas Johnson, ed. Cambridge: Harvard University Press, 1958.

———. *The Years and Hours of Emily Dickinson.* Jay Leyda, ed. New Haven: Yale University Press, 1960.

Drake, William D. "The Depth of Walden: Thoreau's Symbolism of the Divine in Nature." Ph.D. diss., University of Arizona, 1967.

Edwards, Jonathan. *The Nature of True Virtue.* Ann Arbor: University of Michigan Press, 1960.

———. *Jonathan Edwards: Representative Selections.* Clarence Faust and Thomas Johnson, eds. New York: Hill & Wang, 1962.

———. *Freedom of the Will: The Works of Jonathan Edwards.* Vol. 1. Paul Ramsey, ed. New Haven: Yale University Press, 1957.

———. *The Great Awakening: The Works of Jonathan Edwards.* Vol. 4. C. C. Goen, ed. New Haven: Yale University Press, 1972.

———. *Scientific and Philosophical Writings: The Works of Jonathan Edwards.* Vol. 6. Wallace Anderson, ed. New Haven: Yale University Press, 1980.

———. *The Works of President Edwards in Eight Volumes.* Worcester, Mass.: Isaiah Thomas, 1808.

———. *The Works of President Edwards in Four Volumes.* New York: Leavitt and Allen, 1857.

———. *The Works of President Edwards in Ten Volumes.* Vol. 1. "Diary," Sereno Dwight, ed. New York: S. Converse, 1829.

Eliot, John. "The Learned Conjectures of Mr. John Eliot Touching the Americans," in Thomas Thorowgood. *Jewes in America.* London: Henry Brome, 1660.

Emerson, Mary Moody. Letters in the Emerson Collection. Houghton Library, Harvard University.

———. Notebooks 1, 2, 3, 4. These four notebooks also in the Emerson Collection contain excerpts copied from MME's Journal by R. W. Emerson. For permission to use these notebooks and the letters of MME, I am grateful to the Houghton Library and the Ralph Waldo Emerson Memorial Association.

Emerson, Ralph Waldo. *The Complete Writings of Ralph Waldo Emerson.* New York: William Wise, 1929.

———. *The Journals of Ralph Waldo Emerson.* Boston: Houghton, Mifflin, 1909.

———. *Journals and Miscellaneous Notebooks.* Cambridge: Harvard University Press, 1965.

———. *Selections From Ralph Waldo Emerson.* Stephen Whicher, ed. Boston: Houghton, Mifflin, 1957.

Hawthorne, Nathaniel. "The American Notebooks." Vol. 8 in *The Centenary Edition of the Works of Nathaniel Hawthorne.* Columbus: Ohio State University Press, 1972.

———. *The Blithedale Romance.* New York: Norton, 1958.

———. *The English Notebooks.* Randall Stewart, ed. New York: M.L.A., 1941.

———. *Selected Tales and Sketches.* Hyatt Waggoner, ed. New York: Rinehart, 1970.

Holmes, Oliver Wendell. *The Autocrat of the Breakfast Table.* Boston: Phillips, Sampson, 1859.

———. *Pages From an Old Volume of Life.* Boston: Houghton, Mifflin, 1884.

———. *The Professor at the Breakfast Table.* Boston: Ticknor and Fields, 1891.

Hooker, Thomas. *The Poor Doubting Christian Drawn to Christ.* Boston: D. Henchman, 1743.

———. *Redemption: Three Sermons.* Gainesville, Fla.: Scholars facsimiles and reprints, 1956.

———. *The Soules Humiliation.* London: A. Crooke, 1637.

———. *The Soules Preparation for Christ, or, A Treatise of Contrition.* London: Robert Dawlman, 1632.

———. *Thomas Hooker: Writings in England and Holland, 1626–1633.* George Williams, et al., eds. Cambridge: Harvard University Press, 1975.

Howe, Julia Ward. *Reminisences,1819–1899*. Boston: Houghton, Mifflin, 1899.

Johnson, Edward. *The Wonder-Working Providence of Sion's Savior in New England*. New York: Barnes and Noble, 1910.

Johnson, Stephen. *Some Important Observations Occasioned by, and Adapted to, the Publick Feast Ordered by Authority, December 18, A.D., 1765*. Newport, R.I.: S. Hall, 1766.

Jung, Carl G. *Modern Man in Search of a Soul*. New York: Harcourt, 1933.

Keach, Benjamin. *Tropologia: A Key to Open Scripture Metaphors*. London: n.p., 1681.

Mather, Cotton. *The Angel of Bethesda*. New London: T. Green, 1722.

———. *Magnalia Christi Americana*. Hartford, Conn.: S. Andrus & Sons, 1853.

Mather, Increase. *The Day of Trouble is Near*. Cambridge, Mass.: M. Johnson, 1674.

———. "Preface" to Samuel Torrey, *An Exhortation Unto Reformation*. Cambridge, Mass.: M. Johnson, 1674.

Mather, Samuel. *The Figures or Types of the Old Testament*. Dublin: Holmes, 1683.

Melville, Herman. *Herman Melville: Cycle and Epicycle*. Eleanor Melville Metcalf, ed. Cambridge: Harvard University Press: 1953.

———. *The Portable Melville*. Jay Leyda, ed. New York: Viking Press, 1952.

———. *The Works of Herman Melville*. New York: Russell & Russell, 1963.

Montgomery, Joseph. *A Sermon Preached at Christiana Bridge and Newcastle of 20th of July, 1775*. Philadelphia: Humphreys, 1775.

Morse, John, T. *Oliver Wendell Holmes: Life and Letters*. Boston: Houghton, Mifflin, 1896.

Nicholi, Armond, ed. *The Harvard Guide to Modern Psychiatry*. Cambridge: Harvard University Press, 1978.

Norton, John. *Abel Being Dead Yet Speaketh*. London: L. Lloyd, 1658.

Oakes, Urian. *New England Pleaded With*. Cambridge: S. Green, 1673.

Oliver, Peter. *The Origin and Progress of the American Revolution*. Stanford, Calif.: Stanford University Press, 1967.

Otto, Rudolph. *The Idea of the Holy*. New York: Oxford University Press, 1957.

Perkins, William. *A Cloud of Faithful Witnesses Leading to the Heavenly Canaan*. London: W. Stansby, 1622.

———. *The Works of that Famous and Worthie Minister of Christ*. Cambridge: J. Legat, 1608.

Preston, John. *A Liveless Life*. London: A. Crooke, 1633.

Prince, Thomas. "Election Sermon of 1730." In A. W. Plumstead, ed., *The Wall and the Garden*. Minneapolis: University of Minnesota Press, 1968.

Rowlandson, Mary. *Narrative of the Captivity of Mrs. Mary Rowlandson*. In *Narratives of the Indian Wars, 1675–1699*. Charles Lincoln, ed., New York: Scribners, 1913.

Shepard, Thomas. *Eye-Salve*. Cambridge: S. Green, 1673.

———. *God's Plot: The Paradoxes of Piety: Being the Autobiography and Journal of Thomas Shepard*. Michael McGiffert, ed., Amherst: University of Massachusetts Press, 1972.

———. *Works*. New York: AMS Press, 1967.

Sherwood, Samuel. *The Churches Flight into the Wilderness*. New York: S. Loudon, 1776.

Skinner, B. F. *About Behaviorism*. New York: Random House, 1976.

Stoddard, Solomon. *The Efficiency of the Fear of Hell*. Boston: B. Green?, 1713.

———. *A Guide to Christ*. Boston: N. Boone, 1714.

———. *The Presence of Christ with the Ministers of the Gospel*. Boston: B. Green, 1718.

———. *A Treatise Concerning the Nature of Saving Conversions*. Boston: D. Henchman, 1719.

Street, Nicholas. *The American States Acting Over the Part of Israel in the Wilderness, And Thereby Impeding Their Entrance Into Canaan's Rest; or, The Human Heart Discovering Itself Under Trials*. New Haven, Conn.: Thomas and Samuel Green, 1777.

Taylor, Edward. *The Poems of Edward Taylor*. New Haven: Yale University Press, 1960.

Thoreau, Henry David. *Cape Cod*. New York: Thomas Crowell, 1961.

———. *The Writings of Henry David Thoreau*. Bradford Torrey, ed. Boston: Houghton, Mifflin, 1906.

Tillich, Paul. *The Courage to Be*. New Haven: Yale University Press, 1959.

Unsigned. *The Life and Services to Literature of Jones Very: A Memorial Meeting, Tuesday, Dec. 14, 1880*. Bulletin of the Essex Institute, 5, 13. Salem, Mass.: 1881.

Very, Jones. Letters, Massachusetts Historical Society.

Very, Jones. *Poems and Essays*. Boston: Riverside Press, 1886.

Ward, Samuel, Gray. "Come With Me to the Feast; or, Transcendentalism in Action." Samuel Gray Ward's Account of a Visit from Jones Very. *Massachusetts Historical Society Miscellany 6*. Boston: Massachusetts Historical Society, 1960.

Welles, John. *The Soules progresse to the celestiall Canaan*. London: H. Shepard, 1639.

Wheelwright, John. "A Fast Day Sermon." In *The Antinomian Crisis.* David Hall, ed., Middletown, Conn.: Wesleyan University Press, 1968.

White, John, et al. *The Planter's Plea.* London: 1630. Facsimile; Rockport, Mass.: Sandy Bay Historical Society, 1930.

Wigglesworth, Michael. *The Diary of Michael Wigglesworth.* Edmund Morgan, ed. New York: Harper and Row, 1946.

Willard, Margaret, ed. *Letters on the American Revolution, 1774–1776.* Boston: Houghton, Mifflin, 1925.

Williams, Roger. *Experiments of Spiritual Life and Health.* London: S. Rider, 1652.

———. *Key Into the Language of America.* John Teunissen and Evelyn Hinz, eds., Detroit: Wayne State University Press, 1973.

———. "Letters." *Complete Writings.* Vol. 6. New York: Russell & Russell, 1963.

Winthrop, John. "A Short Story of the Rise, Reign, and Ruin of the Antinomians." In *The Antinomian Controversy.* David Hall, ed., Middletown, Conn.: Wesleyan University Press, 1968.

———. *Winthrop Papers.* V. II, Boston: Massachusetts Historical Society, 1931.

Secondary Texts

Albanese, Catherine. *Sons of the Fathers.* Philadelphia: Temple University Press, 1976.

Andrews, William, P. "Introductory Memoir." *Poems by Jones Very.* Boston: Houghton Mifflin, 1883.

Arms, George. *The Fields were Green.* Stanford, Calif.: Stanford University Press, 1953.

Arner, Robert D. "Hawthorne and Jones Very: Two Dimensions of Satire in 'Egotism; or, The Bosom Serpent.'" *New England Quarterly* 42 (June 1969): 267–75.

Bailey, William. *Records of Patriotism and Love of Country.* Washington: n.p., 1826.

Bancroft, George. "Jonathan Edwards." In *New American Cyclopedia.* Vol. 7. New York: 1858.

Barcus, Nancy. "Emerson, Calvinism, and Aunt Mary Moody: An Irrepressible Defender of New England Orthodoxy." *The Christian Scholar's Review* 7 (1977): 146–52.

Bartlett, William. *Jones Very: Emerson's Brave Saint.* Durham, N.C.: Duke University Press, 1942.

Beach, Stewart. *Samuel Adams: The Fateful Years.* New York: Dodd, Mead, 1965.

Bellah, Robert. *The Broken Covenant: American Civil Religion in Time of Trial*. New York: Seabury Press, 1975.

Bercovitch, Sacvan. *The American Jeremiad*. Madison: University of Wisconsin Press, 1978.

————. *The Puritan Origins of the American Self*. New Haven: Yale University Press, 1975.

————, ed. *Typology and Early American Literature*. Boston: University of Massachusetts Press, 1972.

————. "Typology in Puritan New England: The Williams-Cotton Controversy Reassessed." *American Quarterly* 19 (Summer 1967): 166–91.

Bluestein, Gene. "The Brotherhood of Sinners: Literary Calvinism." *New England Quarterly* 50 (June 1977): 195–213.

Boyer, Paul, and Stephen Nissenbaum. *Salem Possessed: The Social Origins of Witchcraft*. Cambridge: Harvard University Press, 1974.

Braswell, William. *Melville's Religious Thought*. Durham, N.C.: Duke University Press, 1963.

Bridenbaugh, Carl. *Mitre and Sceptre: Transatlantic faiths, ideas, personalities, and politics, 1689–1775*. New York: Oxford University Press, 1962.

————. *Vexed and Troubled Englishmen: 1590–1642*. New York: Oxford University Press, 1967.

Brooks, Van Wyck. "The Cassandra of New England." *Scribners* 81 (February 1927): 125–29.

Brown, E. Francis. *Joseph Hawley: Colonial Radical*. New York: Columbia University Press, 1931.

Brown, Richard. *Revolutionary Politics in Massachusetts*. Cambridge: Harvard University Press, 1970.

Brumm, Ursula. *American Literature and Religious Typology*. New Brunswick, N.J.: Rutgers University Press, 1970.

Bushman, Richard. *From Puritan to Yankee*. New York: Norton, 1970.

————. "Jonathan Edwards as Great Man: Identity, Conversion, and Leadership in the Great Awakening." *Soundings* 3 (Spring 1969).

Caldwell, Patricia. *The Puritan Conversion Narrative*. New York: Cambridge University Press, 1983.

Cantril, Hadley. *The Psychology of Social Movements*. New York: Wiley, 1941.

Cantwell, Robert. *Nathaniel Hawthorne: The American Years*. New York: Rinehart, 1967.

Carroll, Peter. *Puritanism and the Wilderness: The Intellectual Significance of the New England Frontier, 1629–1700*. New York: Columbia University Press, 1969.

Chase, Richard, ed. *Herman Melville: A Collection of Critical Essays.* Englewood Cliffs, N.J.: Prentice-Hall, 1962.

Clark, Harry. "Dr. Holmes: A Reinterpretation." *New England Quarterly* 12 (March 1939): 19–34.

Cody, John. *After Great Pain: The Inner Life of Emily Dickinson.* Cambridge: Belknap Press, 1971.

Coulter, Jeff. *Approaches to Insanity: A Philosophical and Sociological Study.* New York: Wiley, 1973.

Cowing, Cedric. *The Great Awakening and the American Revolution.* Chicago: Rand, McNally, 1971.

Delattre, Roland. *Beauty and Sensibility in the Thought of Jonathan Edwards.* New Haven: Yale University Press, 1968.

Edinger, Edward, F. *Melville's Moby-Dick: A Jungian Commentary.* New York: New Directions, 1978.

Elliot, Emory. *Power and the Pulpit in Puritan New England.* Princeton: Princeton University Press, 1975.

———. *Puritan Influences in American Literature.* Chicago: University of Illinois Press, 1979.

Erikson, Erik. "Autobiographical Notes on the Identity Crisis." *Daedalus* 99 (Fall 1970).

———. *Identity, Youth, and Crisis.* New York: Norton, 1968.

———. *Life History and the Historical Moment.* New York: Norton, 1975.

———. *Young Man Luther: A Study in Psychoanalysis and History.* New York: Norton, 1958.

Feidelson, Charles. *Symbolism and American Literature.* Chicago: University of Chicago Press, 1953.

Feltenstein, Rosalie. "Mary Moody Emerson: Gadfly of Concord." *American Quarterly* 5 (Fall 1953): 231–46.

Fredrickson, George, M. *The Inner Civil War: Northern Intellectuals and the Crisis of the Union.* New York: Harper and Row, 1965.

Friedman, Maurice. "Bartleby and the Modern Exile." *Bartleby the Scrivener.* Howard P. Vincent, ed. Kent, 1966.

Frothingham, Octavious Brooks. *Transcendentalism in New England.* Philadelphia: University of Pennsylvania Press, 1972.

Frye, Northrop. *The Great Code: The Bible and Literature.* New York: Harcourt, Brace, Jovanovich, 1982.

Galdon, Joseph A. *Typology and Seventeenth Century Literature.* The Hague, Paris: Mouton, 1975.

Gaustad, Edwin. *The Great Awakening in New England.* New York: Harper, 1957.

Gelpi, Albert J. *Emily Dickinson: The Mind of the Poet.* New York: Norton, 1965.

Gittleman, Edwin. *Jones Very: The Effective Years.* New York: Columbia University Press, 1967.

Greene, Jack, ed. *The Ambiguity of the American Revolution.* New York: Harper & Row, 1968.

Griffin, Edward. *Jonathan Edwards.* Minneapolis: University of Minnesota Press, 1971.

Hall, David. *The Faithful Shepherd.* Chapel Hill: University of North Carolina Press, 1972.

Haroutounian, Joseph. *Piety Versus Moralism: The Passing of the New England Theology.* New York: Holt, 1932.

Hawthorne, Julian. *Nathaniel Hawthorne and His Wife.* Boston: Houghton, Mifflin, 1884.

Hayakawa, S. I., and Howard Mumford Jones. *Oliver Wendell Holmes: Representative Selections.* New York: American Book, 1939.

Hazelton, John H. *The Declaration of Independence: Its History.* New York: Dodd, Mead, 1906.

Headley, Joel T. *The Chaplains and Clergy of the Revolution.* New York: Scribners, 1864.

Heimert, Alan. "Puritanism, the Wilderness, and the Frontier." *New England Quarterly* 26 (September 1953): 361–82.

——. *Religion and the American Mind: From the Great Awakening.* New York: Bobbs-Merrill, 1967.

Heimert, Alan, and Perry Miller, eds. *The Great Awakening.* New York: Bobbs-Merrill, 1967.

Herbert, T. Walter. *Moby-Dick and Calvinism: A World Dismantled.* New Brunswick, N.J.: Rutgers University Press, 1977.

Higham, John, and Paul Conkins, eds. *New Directions in American Intellectual History.* Baltimore: Johns Hopkins, 1979.

Holly, Israel. *God Brings about his holy and wise Purpose.* Hartford, Conn., 1774.

Isaac, Rhys. *The Transformation of Virginia.* Chapel Hill: University of North Carolina Press, 1982.

Johnson, Claudia. "Regenerative Descent in the Works of Nathaniel Hawthorne." Ph.D. diss., University of Illinois, Urbana-Champaign, 1973.

Johnson, Thomas H. *Emily Dickinson: An Interpretive Biography.* Cambridge: Harvard University Press, 1955.

Jung, Carl G. "Psychology and Religion." In *Collected Works.* Vol. 11. Princeton: Princeton University Press, 1976.

————. "The Symbolic Life." In *Collected Works*. Vol. 18. Princeton: Princeton University Press, 1976.

Keller, Karl. *The Only Kangaroo Among the Beauty: Emily Dickinson and America*. Baltimore: Johns Hopkins University Press, 1979.

King, John. *The Iron of Melancholy*. Middletown, Conn.: Wesleyan University Press, 1983.

Kocher, Paul. *Science and Religion in Elizabethan England*. San Marino, Calif.: Huntington Library, 1953.

Lanyi, Ronald. "'My Faith that Dark Adores': Calvinist Theology in the Poetry of Emily Dickinson." *Arizona Quarterly*. 32, 3, 1976, pp. 264–278.

Levin, Harry. *The Power of Blackness*. New York: Knopf, 1958.

Lowance, Mason. *The Language of Canaan*. Cambridge: Harvard University Press, 1980.

McLoughlin, William G. "Enthusiasm For Liberty: The Great Awakening as the Key to the Revolution." In *Preachers and Politicians*. Worcester, Mass.: American Antiquarian Society, 1977.

————. *The Meaning of Henry Ward Beecher*. New York: Knopf, 1970.

————. *New England Dissent*. Cambridge: Harvard University Press, 1971.

Matthiessen, F. O. *American Renaissance*. New York: Oxford University Press, 1941.

Mattson, J. Stanley. "Oliver Wendell Holmes and 'The Deacon's Masterpiece': A Logical Story?" *New England Quarterly* 41 (March 1968): 104–14.

Mauser, Ulrich. *Christ in the Wilderness*. Naperville, Ill.: Allenson, 1963.

May, Henry. *The Enlightenment in America*. New York: Oxford University Press, 1976.

May, Rollo. *Existence: A New Dimension in Psychiatry and Psychology*. New York: Simon and Schuster, 1967.

————. *Symbolism in Religion and Literature*. New York: G. Braziller, 1960.

Mead, Sidney. *History and Identity*. A.A.R. Studies in Religion, 19. Missoula, Mont.: Scholars Press, 1979.

Miller, John C. *Sam Adams: Pioneer in Propaganda*. Stanford, Calif.: Stanford University Press, 1936.

Miller, Perry. *Consciousness in Concord*. Boston: Houghton, Mifflin, 1958.

————. *Errand into the Wilderness*. Cambridge: Belknap Press, 1956.

————. "The Garden of Eden and the Deacon's Meadow." *American Heritage* (December 1955).

————. *Jonathan Edwards*. New York: William Sloane, 1949.

————. "Jonathan Edwards and the Sociology of the Great Awakening." *New England Quarterly* 21 (March 1948): 50–77.

————. *The New England Mind: From Colony to Province.* Cambridge: Harvard University Press, 1953.

————. *The New England Mind: The Seventeenth Century.* Boston: Beacon Press, 1961.

————. "New England's Transcendentalism: Native or Imported?" In *Literary Views.* C. Carrol Camden, ed. Chicago: University of Chicago Press, 1964.

————. *Roger Williams: His Contribution to the American Tradition.* New York: Atheneum, 1962.

————. *The Transcendentalists.* Cambridge: Harvard University Press, 1950.

Miller, Perry, and Thomas Johnson. *The Puritans: A Sourcebook of Their Writings.* New York: Harper & Row, 1963.

Miner, Earl. ed., *Literary Uses of Typology From the Late Middle Ages to the Present.* Princeton: Princeton University Press, 1977.

Mordell, Albert, ed. *The Autocrat's Miscellanies.* New York: Twayne, 1959.

Morgan, Edmund. *The Puritan Family.* New York: Harper and Row, 1966.

————. *Roger Williams: The Church and the State.* New York: Harcourt, 1967.

————. *The Stamp Act Crisis.* Chapel Hill: University of North Carolina Press, 1953.

Morsberger, Robert. "The Woe that is Madness: Goodman Brown and the Face of Fire." *Nathaniel Hawthorne Journal,* 1973, pp. 177–82. Englewood, Colo.: Microcard Books, 1973.

Murray, Henry A. "Introduction." *Pierre.* New York: Hendricks House, 1949.

Murray, James O. "What A Preacher May Learn From the Writings of Dr. Oliver Wendell Holmes." *Homiletic Review* 30 (September 1895).

Nash, Roderick. *Wilderness and the American Mind.* New Haven: Yale University Press, 1973.

Niebuhr, H. Richard. *The Kingdom of God in America.* New York: Harper, 1959.

Oates, Stephen. *To Purge This Land with Blood: A Biography of John Brown.* New York: Harper and Row, 1970.

Oberndorf, Clarence. *The Psychiatric Novels of Dr. Oliver Wendell Holmes.* New York: Columbia University Press, 1943.

Opie, John, ed. *Jonathan Edwards and the Enlightenment.* Lexington, Ky.: D. C. Heath, 1969.

Parkes, Henry B. *The Pragmatic Test.* San Francisco: The Colt Press, 1941.

Sherman, Paul. *The Shores of America: Thoreau's Inward Exploration.* Urbana: University of Illinois Press, 1972.

————. ed. *Thoreau: A Collection of Critical Esays.* Englewood Cliffs, N.J.: Prentice-Hall, 1962.

Perkins, Jill. "Oliver Wendell Holmes's Rhymed Problem." *American Transcendental Quarterly* 22 (1974): 105–8.

Pope, Robert. *The Half-way Covenant.* Princeton: Princeton University Press, 1969.

Porte, Joel. *Emerson and Thoreau: Transcendentalists in Conflict.* Middletown, Conn.: Wesleyan University Press, 1965.

————. "In the Hands of an Angry God: Religious Terror in Gothic Fiction." In *The Gothic Imagination: Essays in Dark Romanticism.* G. R. Thompson, ed. Washington State University, 1964.

————, ed. *Emerson: Prospect and Retrospect.* Cambridge: Harvard University Press, 1982.

Rusk, Ralph L., ed. *The Letters of Ralph Waldo Emerson.* New York: Columbia University Press, 1939.

————. *The Life of Ralph Waldo Emerson.* New York: Scribners, 1949.

St. Armand, Barton L. "Hawthorne's Haunted Mind: A Subterranean Drama of the Self." *Criticism* 13 (Winter 1971): 1–25.

Sanborn, F. B. *The Life of Henry David Thoreau.* Boston: Houghton, Mifflin, 1917.

Seelye, John. *Prophetic Waters: The River in Early American Life and Literature.* New York: Oxford University Press, 1977.

Sewall, Richard B. *The Life of Emily Dickinson.* New York: Farrar, Straus, 1974.

Shea, Daniel. "The Puritan Within," *Virginia Quarterly Review* 50 (Summer 1974): 416–37.

Sherwood, William. *Circumference and Circumstance: Stages in the Mind and Art of Emily Dickinson.* New York: Columbia University Press, 1968.

Shurr, William. *Rappaccini's Children: American Writers in a Calvinist World.* University Press of Kentucky, 1981.

Slotkin, Richard. *Regeneration Through Violence.* Middletown, Conn.: Wesleyan University Press, 1973.

Small, Miriam Rossiter. *Oliver Wendell Holmes.* New York: Twayne, 1962.

Stout, Harry. "Religion, Communications, and the Ideological Origins of the American Revolution." *William and Mary Quarterly* 34 (1977): 519–41.

Stowe, Harriet Beecher. *Old Towne Folks.* Boston: Fields, Osgood, 1869.

Szasz, Thomas. *The Myth of Psychotherapy: Mental Healing as Religion, Rhetoric, and Repression.* New York: Doubleday, 1978.

Thomas, Lewis. "Debating the Unknowable." *The Atlantic Monthly,* July 1981.

Thompson, Lawrence. *Melville's Quarrel with God.* Princeton: Princeton University Press, 1952.

Tilton, Eleanor. *Amiable Autocrat: A Biography of Dr. Oliver Wendell Holmes.* New York: H. Schuman, 1947.

Tolman, George. "Mary Moody Emerson." Concord (Mass.) Antiquarian Society, 1902.

Turner, Victor. *Dramas, Fields, and Metaphors: Symbolic Action in Human Society.* Ithaca, N.Y.: Cornell University Press, 1974.

Unsigned article. *American Heritage* 24 (December 1972): 68–69.

Unsigned review. *Scribner's Monthly Magazine* 18 (May 1879): 117–27.

Van Dusen, Albert. *Puritans Against the Wilderness: Connecticut History to 1763.* Chester, Conn.: Pequot Press, 1975.

Waggoner, Hyatt. *American Poets.* New York: Houghton, Mifflin, 1968.

———. *The Presence of Hawthorne.* Baton Rouge: Louisiana State University Press, 1979.

Webb, Howard. "Item 17." *The Explicator* 24 (October 1965).

Wendell, Barrett. *A Literary History of America.* New York: Scribners, 1900.

Werge, Thomas. "Moby-Dick and the Calvinist Tradition." *Studies in the Novel* 1 (Winter 1969): 484–93.

Whicher, George. *This was a poet.* Ann Arbor: University of Michigan Press, 1965.

Whicher, Stephen. *Freedom and Fate.* Philadelphia: University of Pennsylvania Press, 1971.

Williams, George H. *Wilderness and Paradise in Christian Thought.* New York: Harper & Bros., 1962.

Winters, Yvor. *Maule's Curse: Seven Studies in the History of American Obscurantism.* Binghamton, N.Y.: New Directions, 1938.

Woelfel, James. "Listening to B. F. Skinner." *The Christian Century,* 30 November 1977.

Young, Alfred, ed. *The American Revolution: Explorations in American Radicalism.* DeKalb: Northern Illinois University Press, 1976.

Zuckerman, Michael. "The Fabrication of Identity in Early America." *William and Mary Quarterly* 34 (April 1977): 183–214.

Index